A Theology of Love

A Theology of Love

The Dynamic of Wesleyanism

by

MILDRED BANGS WYNKOOP

BEACON HILL PRESS OF KANSAS CITY
Kansas City, Missouri

Copyright 1972
By Beacon Hill Press of Kansas City

Printed in the
United States of America

ISBN: 083-412-0003

10 9 8 7

Contents

6 / *Contents*

Preface

A "four-letter word," LOVE, is the contemporary "in" word. It is a catchword, protected from the sacrilege of criticism by a mystical and emotional ambiguity which defies the intrusion of rational inquiry. It is a magic cliché pulling for the attention of all of us caught in a technological world which has all but shut itself off from compassion. In a programmed society manned by programmed automatons the idea of love is especially appealing because people cannot, at least until genetic engineering has done its work, be totally programmed. But love is linked with ideas which react back on its traditional meaning—ideas not essential to it but which are confused with it. Its sacrosanct ambiguity makes any critical exploration into its "complex" tantamount to a rejection of love itself and its critic an apparent "enemy of the people."

There is a companion word which vies with *love* for attention, namely, *meaning*, and, strangely, the "meaning of meaning." Meaning has escaped us and slipped away, leaving a distressing void. Perhaps, we think, love can bring back meaning. Without them, life has gone dull, and frustration has turned to virtual cynicism. So we grab for what passes for love and hope that meaning may be found hiding within it.

But *love* is a weasel word, and *meaning* is a will-o'-the-wisp. *Love* may mean anything—or nothing. It has lost its moorings and stands for "what I want"—a most deceptive concept and despotic tyrant. The Greek language has a number of words for social relationships which English in its poverty translates into one word, (generally) *love*. And the kind of meaning which the human heart seeks is not found at the end of every one of "love's" beckoning rainbows.

This book is about love. Being a religion book about love, the concept of love will include its religious meaning but not limit it to the religious. It will explore the many meanings which in English are subsummed under that one word. The awareness of the contemporary cynicism regarding the religious dimension of love will be in constant attention. Love is a "hollow word," drained of its promise of fulfillment by those who have betrayed it by unfulfilled promises. The Church has not demonstrated, says the world, the kind of love it professes. Perhaps so. But this is no new problem, unfortunately.

Eighteenth-century England was a vest-pocket edition of to-day's cynical world. It helped to imprison love in "low" forms unredeemed by love's "higher" relationships. It glorified a cruel, vulgar, sodden life-style reaching from the palace down to the lowest level of society. In it, human life had little value and no meaning. It is significant that in that age of unrestrained permissiveness—called love—John Wesley, the modern "Apostle of Love," should have appeared. He proclaimed holiness, the highest possible spiritual value, in terms of love, in the face of love's lowest possible connotation.

Wesley equated holiness with love. But the antidote of holy love, in counteracting its diseased namesake, displayed a morally healing power which wooed us to the Source of Wesley's concepts, the Bible. Is there a way of conceiving of love which will rescue it from its moral exile and make it a useful guide in recovering "holiness" from its ivory-tower irrelevance? Strangely, this is the thing that the New Testament writers did with the one word which has been made to bear the meaning of holiness. It is the word *agape*, which is not in the common category of social love at all but has been tailored to express a concept which includes the ultimate in meaning and which "sanctifies" all love without downgrading it or rejecting it. *Agape* has suffered almost irreparable damage by translating it "love," without the catharsis of careful scholarship.

We are indebted to two modern expositions of love. Both are definitive in the field though standing at opposite poles from each other "presuppositionally." Anders Nygren, in *Agape and Eros,* makes the clear and proper distinction between *agape* and human social love, which he equates with *eros* (not, incidentally, a biblical, and hence not quite a proper biblical antithesis). Nygren's profound insight, however, makes it impossible to fail in serious scholarship to take the contrast between agape and eros into consideration. Whether or not "love" is used to refer to agape, the qualitative difference must always be made a point of clarity.

The more recent work, *The Spirit and Forms of Love,* by

Daniel Day Williams, contributes what I believe to be a more biblical approach to agape. Nygren, in Williams' mind, has set agape and eros in irreconcilable opposition. Never the twain meet. From a very different metaphysical presupposition Williams finds it possible and more biblical to relate agape and eros, or to unite them, without losing the specific character of either. "Process Theology" makes a much needed correction to the dualisms of a former day. It is my considered opinion that, though the metaphysical foundation of process thought is not the only solution to theological problems, its insights are inescapable in a biblical theology. The *dynamic* emphasis in relation to God, man, love, grace, nature, and salvation and interpersonal relations is crucial to the Christian faith.

John Wesley's understanding of love can be supported only by an underlying "metaphysic" which is dynamic in nature. His theological position was not, however, derived from a philosophical point of view. Rather, his religious and biblical insights lead to a metaphysic which, it is believed, commends itself to modern man's new understanding of nature and furnishes a ground for the Christian meaning of life which all men seek, whether or not they know what it is they seek.

This study is undertaken with the above considerations in mind. The attempted "creative" approach is rooted deeply in more experience of contact with scholarly minds than can be itemized here. The immediate "inspiration" is John Wesley, and the consuming interest is in a biblical theology. Wesley always leads to the Bible. Wesley's 14-volume *Works* furnishes the sources of his ideas. The most simple documentation possible has been utilized. The biblical studies are *preliminary* to a proper scholarship rather than scholarship itself. The provincialisms of an older Biblicism have obscured the most obvious meanings of the biblical passages. It is this obscurantism that we have tried to correct.

Of the many to whom credit is due I must gladly acknowledge the support and encouragement of my husband, who has often and consistently urged my continued work in the years of study and intellectual and spiritual anguish necessary to bring this work to birth. Without that backing no achievement could possibly have been forthcoming.

—M. B. W.

CONCERNING REFERENCES TO WESLEY'S WRITINGS

Because of the large number of quotations from John Wesley's own writings throughout this volume, a code system has been devised to identify each in lieu of otherwise voluminous footnoting. There are four major sources of these quotations, which are listed below along with the code designation:

The Works of the Rev. John Wesley (Kansas City, Mo.: Nazarene Publishing House, n.d.; and Grand Rapids, Mich.: Zondervan Publishing House, 1958, concurrent editions), 14 vols. Code: *Works.*

Wesley's Standard Sermons, edited by Edward H. Sugden (London: The Epworth Press, 1921), 2 vols. Code: *Sermons.*

The Letters of the Rev. John Wesley, edited by John Telford (London: The Epworth Press, 1931), 8 vols. Code: *Letters.*

Explanatory Notes upon the New Testament (New York: Eaton and Mains, n.d.). Code: *Notes.*

o   o   o   o   o

LOVE takes the Harshness out of Holiness.
Love takes the Incredibility out of Perfection.
Love takes the Antinomianism out of Faith.
Love takes the Moralism out of Obedience.
Love takes the Gnosticism out of Cleansing.
Love takes the Abstraction out of Truth.

Love puts the Personal into Truth.
Love puts the Ethical into Holiness.
Love puts Process into Life.
Love puts Urgency into Crisis.
Love puts Seriousness into Sin.
Love puts Fellowship into Perfection.

—M. B. W.

Love is the end of every commandment of God. It is the *Point* aimed at by the whole and every part of the Christian institution. The foundation is faith, purifying the heart, the end Love, preserving the conscience (*Works*, XI, 416).

On January 1, 1733, I preached . . . on "the Circumcision of the Heart," an account of which I gave in these words: "It is that habitual disposition of soul which, in sacred writings, is termed holiness, and which directly implies, the being cleansed from sin, . . . the being so "renewed in the image of the mind", as to be "perfect as our Father in heaven is perfect." (See *Works*, V, 203.)

In the same sermon I observed, "Love is the fulfilling of the law, the end of the commandment." It is not only "the first and great commandment," but all the commandments in one. . . . The royal law of heaven and earth is this, "Thou shalt love the Lord thy God with all thy heart, and with all thy soul, and mind and strength." . . .

I concluded in these words: "Here is the sum of the perfect law, the circumcision of the heart." . . .

It may be observed, this sermon was composed the first of all my writings which have been published. This was the view of religion I had then, which even then I scrupled not to term *perfection*. This is the view I have of it now, without any material addition or diminution" (*Works*, XI, 367-68).

This Religion we long to see established in the world, a religion of love, and joy, and peace, having its seat in the inmost soul, but ever showing itself by its fruits, continually springing forth, not only in all innocence (for love worketh no ill to his neighbor), but likewise in every beneficence, spreading virtue and happiness all around it (John Wesley, *An Earnest Appeal to Men of Reason and Religion*, London: Wesleyan Conference Office, n.d., 14th edition, p. 4.).

CHAPTER I

The Clue

The question which occasions the writing of this book is, simply, Is there a principle of interpretation—a hermeneutic—which can explain Christian doctrine and Christian life in the same system without either one undercutting the integrity of the other? I.e., Can theology and real human existence meet meaningfully? Of course, this is not a simple question. It breaks out into an explosion of questions even as one looks at it. And this is good.

The study of this matter started with the plethora of intellectual questions and problems raised by the apparent ambiguity between theory and life in my own mind and in the minds of others. The painfully slow process of honestly tracking down every problem to its source has been exciting and rewarding.

Many problems are self-created; i.e., questions are posed which arise either from a faulty concept of the nature of reality or by attempting to impose a rigid concept of reality upon the very dynamic thing human personality really is. Categorizing such questions is not as difficult as correcting their matrix of thought because the unsuspected roots of the questions are often carefully protected by emotional and irrational fears.

A never-to-be-forgotten philosophy course in the university introduced me to the "never-never land" of hidden and undreamed-of, but discoverable, basic presuppositions which account for the way we think and the conclusions we are willing to entertain as truth. The greater surprise to me was the assertion that not everyone built his thinking on the same "self-evident" truths. I was the last one to suspect the presence of such important biases, and certainly the most naive about what they might be, once I began to search for them. It was a profitable, if shocking, enterprise. A search for and the discovery of the controlling theory of criticism of any area of human thought and difference of opinion and position opens the way to a deeper understanding than I ever dreamed was possible. It became to me one of the keys to the unlocking of problems heretofore resisting every attempt at solution.

This book is the result of trying to determine why our theological and religious problems are problems. There are ways of thinking which underlie many questions which are impossible to answer the way they are asked because they are born in categorical errors and/or uncriticized presuppositions antithetical to rationality and the Christian faith. These need exposure if not correction.

It is this author's considered opinion that John Wesley has contributed a sound and usable approach to theology which is worthy of consideration in the solutions of the problems relating to the theology/life syndrome. His "hermeneutic" was "love to God and man." This theme runs throughout his works. At least, when each doctrine of the Christian faith is identified and defined by him, the basic meaning invariably comes out "love." Wesley's thought is like a great rotunda with archway entrances all around it. No matter which one is entered, it always leads to the central Hall of Love, where, looking upward toward the dome one gazes into the endless, inviting sky. There is no ceiling to love. The return flow of love back through each doctrine in preaching and life serves to link every doctrine together into one dynamic architectonic and to show the theological stature and integrity of John Wesley.

This "Rotunda Theology," circular in form rather than the "Stairstep" approach, creates a problem for the theological analysis of Wesley. Theology should have a systematic form. Each element should be clearly distinguished from every other element or doctrine. Each should follow logically from the one before it and lead comfortably into the one ahead. But in Wesley such neatness is impossible to capture because it is not there. Wesley's doctrines cannot be so sharply separated from each other and from the whole thing that love is. They are not "abstract." This "problem" will become obvious in this study, where an inevitable duplication of theme and quotation will often become apparent. In almost every Wesley passage long enough to complete the point being made (and it is unfair to do less) almost every major doctrine is implicated. The theological terms are interlinked so tightly that to touch any one is to touch them all. Almost any significant passage could illustrate almost any central doctrine.

Let it not be imagined, however, that Wesley's emphasis on love cancels out definition. No Christian doctrine is neutralized by love, nor its sharp line of identity feathered off by it. Any concept of love which tended to erode away rational integrity had short shrift in Wesley's hand. Christian doctrines *did* "come alive" in human experience, but that is a far cry from the dissolution of doctrine in a mystical fog.

Nor did love, for Wesley, cancel out controversy, or drain off creative tensions in human social relations, whether religious, home, church, or any other. Love was not a soft, permissive cover-up of human personality, as explosive as it might be. Love, or holiness as he interpreted it, was not the end of wholesome, even intense, human reactions but rather the disciplining of them. Christian love creates an atmosphere in which all the creative conflicts may not only exist but be matured and fully utilized without tearing apart the fabric of Christian unity.

Wesley's "love" would belong to the same kind of thing that God's love is, because that is where Wesley got the idea. It creates freedom and achievement. It "takes on" anything that would destroy it. It has poise in, and thrives on, the wholesome give-and-take of persons in relationship. The theological solution which our study seeks, therefore, will not be the solution which is designed to end all thinking and difference of opinion and debate but to encourage a lively "dialogue" which will serve to strengthen us where we may be weak and to lead the way out of some of the confusions that inhibit effective Christian service.

John Wesley, specifically, has been chosen as the "catalyst" for a study of the foundations of Christian doctrine for the following reasons. First, Wesley's concept of love is a more complete catalyst than any other that I know of; i.e., when both theology and life are considered together, love, as Wesley conceived it, solves more theological and religious problems than other concepts seem able to do. The second reason follows the first in that love as the central truth makes better sense out of the gospel than do some other aspects of theology. Love *is* the gospel message. Christian love, revealed by God in Christ, is the correction of man's limited, selfish, selective, perverted love. It stands against any human concept of love projected into a theory of God's nature and His way with man.

It is precisely this unlimited, impartial, indestructible love that needed to be "revealed" because the best in human love has been limited. The very nature of sin is love's perversion which makes the self the object of its own dedication. Could the dogma of particular election as understood by some theological traditions be the projection of faulty human love into the very nature of God? The gospel was not born in human philosophy but in God's heart revealed in Christ. This Wesley declared.

A third reason is the emphasis on the profoundly moral and personal and spiritual relationship between God and man which the concept of love supports. This is in contrast to any merely legal, mechanical, automatic, or mathematical "thing-manipulation" which so easily becomes a substitute for the personal and spiritual realities of the gospel.

A fourth reason is Wesley's wholesome freedom from provincialism in theology. Not all of his followers have been so discreet. A narrow exclusivism in the Church is Gnostic in spirit and derives from very ancient roots. Theological and religious provincialism must always be suspect. James Stewart said in an article in the *Scottish Journal of Theology*, "The trouble with heresy [re the Colossian problem], as Paul saw it, was its dreadful provincialism" ("A First Century Heresy," Nov., 1970. Love as it is revealed in Christ stands at the opposite pole from the age-old sin—*The Sin*—the self against God and anyone who might threaten the autonomy

of the self or invade its "rights." Wesley was not provincial in his
concept of the gospel or his understanding of it. Love, to him,
was the divine solution to the problem of divisiveness.

Wesley was a "man of one Book," as he characterizes himself,
and he rested his faith on it. What could not be clearly spelled out
in the Word of God was not binding on him. As this is so, Wesleyanism is, or should be, a biblical theology. In keeping with this
ideal there will be found in this study several rather lengthy biblical
studies. The choice of which of the several doctrines surveyed in
this book was to be studied biblically was made on the basis of the
nature of the control question. Wherever the greatest problems
are raised in the tension between doctrine and life the deepest
probe was made.

In these cases all even remotely relevant references to the
specific words under examination are recorded in order to avoid
the suspicion that any arbitrary selection of passages was made in
order to make a point. Conclusions must be made in the light of
the whole picture. Biblical theology is rooted in the Bible as a
whole, not in selected portions of it. These studies are not heavy,
scholarly studies but obvious contextual observations often missed
in casual proof-text compilations. Without this foundation biblical
theology cannot even begin. True and careful scholarship, it is
believed, will not prove to be antithetical to what is concluded in
these studies.

John Wesley was a theologian, as we hope to show. He worked
out from a "system" which in his mind was not materially different from traditional Christian doctrine. He added a spiritual
dimension which put theology into a new framework—personal
relationship and experience. This "addition" threw the balance of
doctrines into a different configuration but did not actually alter
the system. His entire ministry was an explication of the altered
configuration. Love, the essence of the new perspective, served
as a unifying factor in theology and a humanizing application to
life. The structure of theology was, under Wesley's hand, made to
fit human possibilities. This does not destroy theology but it does
ask penetrating questions of it.

At the heart of Wesley's contribution was the reinstatement of
sanctification into theology as a viable element, clearly distinguished from justification but integral to it. Luther corrected the

Catholic confusion of the two as it put sanctification prior to justification (which was then to be achieved by works), by declaring
that justification was by faith, not works. But Luther lost the meaning of sanctification in this correction by confusing *it* with works.
The faith by which justification became a reality was limited by
his concern to keep faith from any suspicion of human merit.

Wesley saw that justification and sanctification were two
aspects of one truth, not separated by time or experience but in
relationships. Everything he saw sanctification to be by way of
dynamic vitality was rooted in the work of Christ—the atonement
—which justified—reconciled—all men potentially to God. The
appropriation of God's grace of forgiveness by each individual—by
faith—was the beginning of sanctification. He presupposed justification in every subsequent "stage in the way."

Justification, then, is prevenient grace guarded from univer-
salism, not by God's selective decree (which was to Wesley a
travesty of God's universal love), but "by faith," which grace
makes *possible* to all men, but *not inevitable*.

It would be a mistake to suppose that Wesley considered justification and sanctification as merely mathematical values distinct only in quantitative measure—first one is justified and later
he may add sanctification. By declaring that sanctification, as well
as justification, is by faith, a concept of faith is proposed that goes
beyond Luther. One does not believe *for justification* and then,
later, believe *for sanctification,* but he begins to trust *in Christ*
(a personal relationship), by which he appropriates God's grace
and begins the life of holiness. His new relationship to God rests
in justification and issues in the newness of life which faith initiates. In this new life there are crucial crisis points integral to moral
experience. Only a clear and full and adequate concept of justification can support a biblical concept of sanctification. This book begins at this point and proceeds on the basis of this assertion.

Toward a Theology of Love

The thesis of this book is that love is the dynamic of Wesleyanism. After any substantial research into John Wesley's writing one becomes aware of the high importance of love to his theology and preaching concerns. No matter which door one enters into his thinking—holiness, sanctification, perfection, cleansing, faith, man, God, salvation, or any other—not only does each of these begin to flow together and intertwine with the others, but the whole is channeled inevitably into love. Rather than Wesley representing a theology of holiness it would be more faithful to his major emphasis to call it a theology of love. It is suggested here as a thesis to be explored, researched, and defended, that Wesleyanism (that segment of the Church taking its cue from Wesley) in its most authentic moments interprets Christian theology in terms of love. It is not "authentic" when it fails to do so.

John Wesley's theological and religious contribution to the Church was not new dogma but a real, spiritual vitality infused into traditional, mainline Christianity. This vitality is love, and love is by its very nature dynamic.

Love is so central to John Wesley's total message that we cannot do better at this point than to quote one of his strongest passages on this subject.

> It were well you should be thoroughly sensible of this, "The heaven of heavens is love." There is nothing higher in religion; there is, in effect, nothing else; if you look for anything more than love, you are looking wide of the mark, you are getting out of the royal way, and when you are asking others, "Have you received this or that blessing?" if you mean anything but more love, you mean wrong; you are leading them out of the way, and putting them upon a false scent. Settle it then in your heart, that from the moment God has saved you from all sin, you are to aim at nothing more, but more of that love described in the thirteenth of the Corinthians. You can go no higher than this, till you are carried into Abraham's bosom" (*Works*, XI, "Plain Account," p. 430).

A few preliminary words need to be said in explanation of the thesis that love is the theological key to Wesley's thinking. When it is said that love is the dynamic of Wesleyanism, something is said by implication about holiness which is the specific emphasis for which Wesleyanism stands. It says that holiness is dynamic and that the character of holiness is love. The problem encountered is as least twofold. (1) Is love a strong enough concept to do justice to holiness? Does not the priority of love rob holiness of its unique character and power? And (2) is it proper to *relate* the terms *holiness* and *love* so closely as to appear to equate them if not actually to do so?

The answer is also twofold. Whatever one may feel to be the proper theological relationship between holiness and love, in a study of Wesley it is only right to ask him what he taught. It is an obvious fact that Wesley did, indeed, not merely *relate* these two words (and the concepts they represent) but *equated* them. They are not, to him, two concomitant aspects of grace but one blazing unity of truth. In the second place, something of the relationship of these two terms begins to come clear when it is seen that the concept "dynamic" when applied to these terms puts them into a framework of thought where living relevance is. That framework is "personal relationship." The juxtaposition of the terms *holiness* and *love,* together with "personal relationship," puts a meaning to each term, as well as uniting them. This transforms them from mere abstract terms into dynamically biblical concepts.

There are now four key concepts, *holiness, personal relationship, dynamic,* and *love.* It is at the point where these concepts intersect and interrelate, semantically, that a principle of interpretation can begin to be developed.

AN EXISTENTIAL GLOSSARY

1. "Holiness," as used in this study, reflects the ambiguity commonly encountered where the term is used. Three levels of meaning must be distinguished before the term can be employed accurately.

a. Holiness as a noun, an abstract word, cannot be equated with any other word whether it be love, perfection, consecration, cleansing, or any other. It has a stable meaning secured by hundreds of years of history. As such it is inviolate.

b. When *holiness* is put into a theological context, it takes on the color of whatever *system* of theology it is in. It must interrelate with every other term in the system and in harmony with the system. Catholic *holiness* is quite different from Calvinistic *holiness.* But it is still an abstract term in the sense of being in an idea framework.

c. A third category must be distinguished. When *holiness* becomes a *religious* term with an existential involvement, then it must yield its autonomy to the whole complex of living relationships. It is not violated by *love* and *perfection* but rather each enhances the other and the sharp semantic barriers protecting each term dissolve, leaving a spiritual reality that no theology book or dictionary can cope with.

For failure to distinguish these three categories in the use of the word, the purist (philosopher) can call the realist (the Wesleyan) either a theological ignoramus ("anyone knows no human person can conform to a holiness standard") or dishonest ("he changes the meaning of holiness to suit his convenience"). *Holiness,* it must be said again, is a religious word.

In this preliminary statement one further question needs attention at this point. Are *love* and *holiness* equated in Wesley? Or should they or should they not be equated in theology?

This is not a simple question and something of its complexity ought to be discussed. The reason for diagnosing the question before Wesley is given a chance to explain his concept of love and holiness is that he apparently did not have this specific question in mind. If we should force an answer to a question he had no thought of answering, we may misinterpret him. If our question is clear, however, we may be able to interpret what Wesley says in a way which will point to the answer we seek.

Holiness and *love* are two different words for two different things. In the realm of formal definition each is distinct. They cannot be interchangeably used in any one context. But this is in the realm of words as words. In the realm of existential meaning something of their relatedness begins to come through. But it would be inaccurate to say they are "related." To say holiness and love are not identical but related would imply that they were *associated* in experience but not *vitally and essentially* connected in life. It would say that each has an autonomy apart from the other. Somewhat in the sense that a house and a home, a person and a lawyer, an institution and a school can be equated, holiness and love can also be. But it becomes obvious that the second elements of these pairs stand in a different category of thought from the first. They point to a sort of character, or use, or activity of the first. We could call it the "dynamic" of the first elements.

When holiness and love are put together, the analogy of the two sides of a coin would be closer to the truth. Neither side can be both sides at the same time. Sides are not to be equated, but the obverse side is as essential to its existence as the face. Love is the essential inner character of holiness, and holiness does not exist apart from love. That is how close they are, and in a certain sense they can be said to be the same thing. At least Wesley consistently defined holiness, as well as perfection, as love.

2. In this analogy an important emphasis is implicit. If love is the character, the outflowing, the communication of holiness and that which gives existence to it, and love is a quality of a person, never a "thing," something is said about holiness that Wesley never missed, namely, that holiness has to do with *persons in relationship.*

3. A realistic approach is "personal relationship." It is within the personal dimension of reality that revelation as God's self-exposure is given and received, that communication has meaning, that rationality and morality are encountered, that individual and society are significant, that holiness and sin have definition. In-animate nature is a tool of revelation, but only persons can manipulate the tool to make it reveal, or bear, communicated meaning. God communicates himself to kindred personal beings, and only persons are the object of His redemptive love.

4. Dynamic, then, characterizes the relation of persons. The very moral freedom essential to the idea of person, in contrast to men as mere entities to be manipulated, speaks of the dynamic quality of "personness."

The dynamic of personal relationship is love. Love is a quality of response between persons. *Love can exist only in freedom.* It cannot be coerced. Freedom is the most fundamental ingredient of love. When love is spoken of, freedom is presupposed and persons are involved. *Love* describes the kind of response that exists between persons. Love may link the persons into a fellowship or it may short-circuit about itself and reject other persons. In either case it is the relation between persons that is at issue.

Love, then, positively or negatively defines holiness or sin. Love, being dynamic, and free, includes or excludes others in its search for fulfillment. When the object of love, that about which the total self centers, is God, holiness is described. When, in this process, love centers in the self, God is excluded and sin is de-scribed. Holiness and sin are quality evaluations having to do with the kind of relationship the self sustains to God. They have meaning in the locus of personal relationship, not otherwise.

The Dynamic of Love

Keeping these distinctions in mind, it is now possible to dis-cuss the centrality of love in Wesley, and in authentic holiness doctrine. *Love characterizes holiness as presented to us by New Testament writers.* The complex of thinking which suggests a statement like that goes something like this:

1. "*God so loved the world,* that he gave his only begotten Son."

2. *Jesus' purpose* in His coming, life, and death was to "sanctify the people" (Heb. 13:12); "*Christ also loved the church,* and gave himself for it; that he might sanctify and cleanse it" (Eph. 5:25-26); et al.

3. The fulfilling of everything God demands of men, Jesus said, was *total love to God and love to neighbor* in the measure that one loves himself (Mark 12:28, et al.).

4. Paul, in outlining the ethical structure of the Christian life, peaks his argument with the same command. He said the commandments "are all summed up in the one rule, 'Love your neighbour as yourself.' Love cannot wrong a neighbour; therefore *the whole law is summed up in love*" (Rom. 13:9-10, NEB).

5. *The test of our right relationship with God is love.* "This is his command: to give our allegiance to his Son Jesus Christ and love one another as he commanded. When we keep his commands we dwell in him and he dwells in us. And this is how we can make sure that he dwells within us: we know it from the Spirit he has given us" (I John 3:23-24, NEB).

As has been noted, it does not take long, in reading Wesley, to discover that love is the theme of his entire ministry, thinking, interpretation of theology, actions in respect of humanity, and everything he said or did. It is his hermeneutic. Were one to collate all Wesley's discussions about or references to love, this book would be almost as big as all his works combined. It could be summed up by the sentiment so frequently found, "Religion is nothing more, or less, than pure love to God and man." Why then write the 14 volumes of standard works and scores of volumes of miscellany? All this is a commentary, an elaboration, an exegesis of love, because love is a "many-splendored thing" and touches every possible aspect of life and human relations.

If one is committed to a Wesleyan theology, he must realize that his commitment is to a theology of love. It was to this concept of Christianity—the centrality of love—that Wesley was committed. He believed that it was scriptural, and devoted himself to "holiness" because he believed it biblical, and that the Bible characterized it as love. Only this link between Wesley and ourselves would be a legitimate ground for a "biblical" theology to be called Wesleyan. Wesley is accepted as a safe mentor only because he grasped the central gospel truth so well and worked out its implications in theology and life so satisfactorily.

It would be irresponsible to pick and choose from among Wesley's teachings only those that are needed to defend some doctrinal "distinctive," then call it Wesleyan, without making the choice on the basis of some principle which would do justice to Wesley's own intention. It is a mistake to call one's theology Wesleyan, and by that mean a theology of holiness which limits the meaning to some lesser concept of holiness than love as Wesley conceived it. Love is more definitive of Wesley's theology than any methodology of the experience dimension presumed to be Wesley's. This is what this book is all about.

IMPLICATIONS OF A THEOLOGY OF LOVE

When Wesleyanism is encountered and understood as a theology of love, some significant things begin to appear.

1. *Love is deeper than the popular concept of it.* Love, in the biblical sense, and in Wesley's understanding of it, is a profound correction of the popular, modern concept of love. It must be distinguished sharply from these romantic, soft, erotic, paternalistic, permissive, emotional connotations. Love includes every aspect of human relationship but it also structures these relationships in a different way than is done in modern thought.

2. *Love implicates us in ethics.* As holiness is characterized by love, it is then ethically structured. This is much different from "moralism" and must not be confused with that kind of superficiality. "Holiness theology" has tended to revert to that superficiality which is a denial of the original biblical, true ethical meaning of holiness. Love preserves holiness from moralism. Holiness is ethically relevant and love lies at its heart. There are ethical consequences to biblical religion.

3. *Love is a uniquely personal thing.* The full measure of its meaning is limited to "persons," and in a large measure defines "person." Love demands the concept of the dynamic in personhood. It is its inner drive, its outreach, its atmosphere, its social cohesion. It is fellowship, relationship, sociality. It is the unrestrained intercommunion of spirits which, alone among all satisfactions, is the ultimate satisfaction and fulfillment. When St. John said, "God is love," something was said about the nature of God and the nature of man that begins to make sense out of the word "personal."

4. *Love is "happiness"* (in Wesley's sense of the word). Happiness is not an emotional titillation but a harmony of the whole of the self. Holiness is not a glorified maladjustment, a neurosis, as its critics like to say. It is health, vitality, wholeness; the end of disharmony, edginess, and out-of-jointness. Love goes straight to the heart of personal relationships and demands a right ground for fellowship. It mercilessly, but healingly, sorts out the motives and directs the realignment of attitudes and relationships. It stands in judgment against any attitude or act which, in its name, and claiming its authority wrongly, destroys fellowship. It is not soft, but highly discriminating. It is not blind, but keenly alert to anything which ruptures fellowship. It is not amorphous, unrelated to law, but the very inner structure of moral law, the conservator of moral integrity.

5. Love is never superficial. It always deals with key issues. It sorts out the central from peripheral matters in its zeal to create and preserve the true relationship. It stands guard over self-esteem lest it inadvertently slip into selfishness. It protects personal integrity from an over-concern about personal rights.

6. *Love "sturdies" the soul.* Friedrich Nietzsche thought that love was the "slave morality"—that weak, worthless people justified and glorified their weakness by calling it love. In spite of Nietzsche's most revolting teaching—a teaching that ultimately plunged the world into a ghastly war—a quiet reading of his works reveals a tragic, deep misunderstanding in his mind of the Christian ethic of love. Where did he learn such? It is mentioned here because the popular concept of love when read back into the Christian faith perpetuates the same devastating reaction. Christian love is

not weak, spineless, without character. It is precisely the courage and stability of "The Terrible Meek." Alfred Lord Tennyson had noble Sir Galahad say, "My strength is as the strength of ten, because my heart is pure."

7. *Love is creative.* Creation in the midst of the tensions and conflicts of life is the essence of the kind of love Wesley, and the Bible, talk about. Love that needs peace to grow in is not biblical love. Love that exists in the interaction between persons must be of the calibre that not only endures the conflict between free and self-conscious persons but which thrives in such interchange. Love does not obliterate that kind of creative encounter but discovers the deeper dimensions of personal reality in it. Wesley seemed to understand this and his advice given in the voluminous correspondence available bears this out. Wholesome discoveries of the depths of reality occur where persons are in conflict.

Love does not reduce life to dull, monotonous placidity. It, rather, drives one into the unknown, the dangerous, the tumultuous human experiences all around us. A home with no differences of opinion is either dominated by one person or is a nonentity—a tomb, not a real home. The most vibrant and happy homes are those in which each member is a free, creative, exuberant, irrepressible personality—but respecting everyone else though ideas are worlds apart. The Christian community that witnesses to God's love does not level off the sharp edge of individuality but demonstrates the fathomless goodwill that defines Christian love.

8. *Love is outreach.* It destroys indifference, isolationism, the pride that cuts off fellowship, partiality, aloofness, exclusiveness. It must be confessed that there is a tendency among Christians to interpret holiness as withdrawal from society, civic concerns, "bad" people, and everything secular. It is true that there is in holiness this apartness; but on the other side of holiness, and saturating it to its core, is love. Holiness is self-identity; love is losing oneself in others. Holiness is wholeness; love is sharing that wholeness. Neither holiness nor love is Christian without the other. They are logically distinct but only one thing in life. It is the division of one from the other in life that distorts both. Love without holiness disintegrates into sentimentality. Personal integrity is lost. But holi-

ness without love is not holiness at all. In spite of its label, it displays harshness, judgmentalism, a critical spirit, and all its capacity for discrimination ends in nit-picking and divisiveness.

9. *Love is psychologically oriented.* That is, when love is spoken of, it is the action and reaction of the conscious life of people that is meant. It must be viewed through the human drives, thinking, prejudices, customs, culture, intelligence, mental characteristics, heritage, disposition, health, personality, human stresses and adjustments, and in reactions to others. It is in joy, sorrow, tension, pain, power, frustration, moods, modes of behavior —these and everything else having to do with that complex which is life—that love must be viewed. It is at this practical and inescapable point that theology must speak meaningfully or not at all. Here men live and experience, or reject, God's grace. These may be controversial points, but take note that Wesley did not retreat from that kind of controversy.

In a particularly beautiful and extended letter, Wesley answers the question, "Who is a Christian?" What is real, genuine Christianity and how does one know it is of God? Among the several evidences he lingers longest on love, a part of which follows.

> Above all, remembering that God is love, he [the Christian man] is conformed to the same likeness. He is full of love to his neighbour, of universal love, not confined to one sect or party, not restrained to those who agree with him in opinions or in outward modes of worship, or to those who are allied to him by blood or recommended by nearness of place. Neither does he love those only that love him or that are endeared to him by intimacy of acquaintance. But his love resembles that of Him whose mercy is over all His works. It soars above all these scanty bounds, embracing neighbours and strangers, friends and enemies—yea, not only the good and gentle, but also the froward, the evil, and unthankful. . . .
>
> His love, as to these, so to all mankind, is in itself generous and disinterested; springing from no view of advantage to himself, from no regard to profit or praise—no, nor even the pleasure of loving. This is the daughter, not the parent, of his affection. By experience he knows that social love, if it mean the love of our neighbour, is absolutely different from self-love, even of the most allowable kind—just as different as the objects at which they point. And yet it is sure that, if they are under due regulations, each will give additional force to the other till they mix together never to be divided.

And this universal, disinterested love is productive of all right affections. It is fruitful of gentleness, tenderness, sweetness, of humanity, courtesy, and affability. It makes a Christian rejoice in the virtues of all, and bear a part in their happiness, at the same time that he sympathizes with their pains and compassionates their infirmities. It creates modesty, condescension, prudence, together with calmness and evenness of temper. It is the parent of generosity, openness, and frankness, void of jealousy and suspicion. It begets candour, and willingness to believe and hope whatever is kind and friendly of every man, and invincible patience, never overcome of evil, but overcoming evil with good. . . .

This is the plain, naked portraiture of a Christian. But be not prejudiced against him for his name. Forgive his particularities of opinion and (what you think) superstitious modes of worship. These are circumstances but of small concern, and do not enter a veil of love, and look at the substance—his tempers, his holiness, his happiness.

Can calm reason conceive either a more amiable or a more desirable character? (*Letters*, II, 376-80).

Love is so central to Christian faith that to touch it is to find oneself entangled with every element of Christian doctrine and life. As will be seen, Wesley's discussions of any segment of Christian truth led him quickly into love. "God is love." Every aspect of the atonement is an expression of love; holiness is love; the meaning of "religion" is love. Christian perfection is perfection of love. Every step of God toward man, and man's response, step by step, is some aspect of love. Faith works by love. Ethics is the outflowing of love. To say that Christian holiness is our *raison d'être* (reason to be) is to say we are committed to everything love is, and that is a large order indeed. It is impossible to extract a doctrine of holiness out of Wesley and suppose that love may be discarded with impunity. Christian perfection, cut off from the aorta of all that love is, becomes sterile, cold, dead, incredible. (A further elaboration is made of Wesley's position regarding love in the chapter dealing with "the image of God.")

LOVE AND FELLOWSHIP

There is one more dimension of the problem of love and holiness in their religious sense. The evidence of love/holiness is said to be fellowship, and that fellowship is the evidence of being in

Christian grace and the evidence to the world that Christian religion is true. This is easy to say but not so easy to live—unless the meaning of fellowship is properly understood. *Love* is the key word. Because *love* is used in so many different ways, it is wise to try to remove the ambiguities and attempt to apply the proper meaning to each situation.

The Greek language is not limited to one word to express the various relationships of life as is the English, which must lump together nearly all the experiences identified as some aspect of love under the one word. There are at least four Greek terms, *eros, storge, philia,* and *agape,* which are translated by "love." All but *eros* are found at least in some derivative form in the New Testament. But in a study of love, *eros* cannot be omitted, for it contributes to an understanding of the rich significance of love. Though not found as a word in the New Testament, its meaning is well represented.

Eros, William Barclay says in *More New Testament Words,* is love on the physical level or on the more elementary plane. It is used to refer to sexual attraction as well as such things as intense and fanatical patriotism. It is the most instinctive and "natural" type of attraction and feeling. It is not to be regarded as sinful but quite a normal response to life.

Storge refers to family affection. It is used a few times in the New Testament. The strong personal loyalty and mutual devotion to those in a family-type social structure is characterized by this word. "Brotherly affection" or "kindly affectioned" (KJV) is often the translation of it.

Philia is warm personal friendship, deep affection between two—or sometimes more—persons. Examples of its use in the New Testament include the Father's love for the Son (John 5:20), the devotion of friendship to Jesus (I Cor. 16:22), Jesus' love for Lazarus (John 11), and the mutual friendship between Jesus and "the beloved disciple" (John 20:2). It should be noted that Jesus did not require that a Christian's love for an enemy should be on the basis of this relationship. It was this close personal devotion that Peter violated when he denied knowing Jesus. In the questioning later about his love for Jesus, this was the kind of dedication—warm, true, personal—that was at issue.

All these are "natural" to humanity. They describe an emotional or deep heart response to another. It requires little or no effort to love in these ways. These are social cohesive forces without which mankind could not exist as a society. They define mental, psychological, spiritual wholeness.

Agape, however, is a completely different dimension of love. It is a quality of a person rather than a different kind of love. It is a principle by which one orders life—or by which life is ordered. Out of it all the relationships of life derive their character. It is not a new, infused ability but a personal orientation reaching first to God and then, by necessity, to all other persons and things in life. It is called Christian love—and indeed it is unique in its fullness in Christ. It is not first of all an emotion but a deliberate policy whereby the relations sustained with other persons are kept in balance by one's deliberate orientation to God and his own self-respect—in the right sense, self-love.

Our first introduction to this kind of love in the New Testament is in the troublesome passage in Matt. 5:48, "Be . . . perfect, even as your Father . . . in heaven is perfect." The tendency is to assume this kind of perfection must belong to another life because, as we say, "Who can be as perfect as God?" But a more careful reading of the context shows that it is in God's "Fatherness" that *agape* love is revealed, not in the absolute perfection of God. The old law protected justice by the "eye for an eye" principle of retribution. This was a vast advance over the "tooth and claw" philosophy. The moral law said one should love his neighbor. This the Jews well knew. Now Jesus raises the "law" to its zenith—love for one's enemy. Failure to keep the distinctions in love in mind has caused many sincere people to draw back from that impossible standard. But Jesus did not leave us with an empty idealism. The pattern of that love is the way the Heavenly Father sends all the advantages of rain and sun and all other needful things on all men, good and not good, thankful and unthankful, obedient and disobedient. And this is the best definition of *agape* to be found—impartial goodwill.

The love which we call Christian love, then, is not a substitute for the other loves, nor is it an addition to those loves, but it is a quality of the entire person as it is centered in Christ. The distorting self-orientation, which flaws all other relationships because it uses them to personal advantage (often in most subtle and devious ways), is brought into wholeness by the abiding presence of the Holy Spirit. In this relationship all other relationships of life are enhanced and beautified and made holy.

Because *agape* is a matrix for all relationships, the task of bringing a Christian character into *eros* and *storge* and *philia* becomes possible, albeit difficult. It is possible because it is in the realm of moral orientation and integrity. It is difficult because it *is* in this moral realm where character is achieved by dint of diligent effort. If *agape* love were automatic in the Christian life, there would have been no need for the biblical exhortations about increasing in love and growing in it.

So we are not left with an abstract term. *Agape* cannot be defined but it can be demonstrated. It is this demonstration that God gives to us in Christ. Paul says in Romans 5 that, "while we were yet sinners, Christ died for us." The initiative is God's and that initiative is the crux of the matter relative to love. "God was in Christ, reconciling the world unto himself" (II Cor. 5:19). This is not selective love but the inclusion of all men, else it is not love (John 3:16). We know about selective, cliquish love which has no place for the one outside. This is *philia*. When we arbitrarily project our *philia* love back onto the meaning of God's love in Christ and say that He limits His love for whatever reason to select persons, excluding all others, we are engaging in the most crude and dangerous anthropomorphism.

It is precisely this kind of exclusion that Christ came to deny. God is *not* partial. This is the righteousness of God which Paul defends in Romans and which men are bereft of, and which is an evidence of their sin. *Agape* love is God's dimension of love which He wants to restore to all men. This is holiness. And when holiness becomes a part of man's experience, he too must open his heart to all men. The concept of "particular predestination" impugns the holiness of God.

God in Christ tells us what this love is; it is forgiveness. Forgiveness is taking all the *hurt* given by an "enemy" (even in the form of our friends) without demanding reparations. The cost is all on the one who offers the forgiveness. It is accepting the one who has delivered the blow, or the injustice, as if he had never transgressed against us. Reconciliation costs the reconciler more than it can ever cost the one to whom reconciliation is offered. It is an aggressive confronting of a situation in which mutual barriers alienate persons. It is the deliberate creation of an atmosphere in which humiliation on the part of the transgressor is made impossible. It lifts the "sinner" to his feet and treats him like a person worth loving. He may draw a circle to keep me out, "but Love and I had the wit to win: we drew a circle that took him in." Jesus was enunciating a sound psychological principle when He said that our forgiveness from God is conditioned, not on God's willingness, nor on His decree, but on our own willingness to offer forgiveness to those who despitefully use us.

Because *agape* and fellowship are so closely related, a word needs to be said regarding this. Much misunderstanding about the status of fellowship has occasioned much despair. Must fellowship based on mutual attraction be the badge of the Christian community? Christian fellowship begins in our relationship to God. There must be no personal, moral barrier to His presence. In this openness is cleansing (I John 1:7). But this same openness to others, whether it is returned or not, is the fellowship of the household of God. The barriers deep within our own beings are the barriers to Christian fellowship. The fellowship of goodwill and freedom from vindictiveness and underhanded intrigue in a community of persons whose temperaments, ideals, goals, and cultural biases are at sharp odds with each other, is the kind of thing that is amazing and winsome. And this is not an easy atmosphere to create and maintain. To keep communication open is the way to communion—and that is the foundation of Christian fellowship.

AGAPE AND SIN

But another word needs to be said about love before entering into the matter more deeply in a later chapter (Sin and Holiness).

While *agape* is the term used to characterize divine love and the Christian's proper relationship to God and self and others, a disturbing truth begins to threaten this whole structure of thought. Passages are encountered in the New Testament in which *agape* is used in a most pejorative sense. "Demas hath forsaken me, having loved [*agapēsas*] this present world" (II Tim. 4:10). St. John sets an unequivocal absolute, "Love not the world . . . If any man love *[agapá]* the world, the love *[agápe]* of the Father is not in him" (I John 2:15). This does not say that there is anything wrong with the world but is an indication that when something other than God is substituted for Him, or He is shut out of His rightful place, *"The Sin"* has been committed. That which belongs to God alone has been given to another. And *agape* is the word used to say it.

There are some interesting corollaries arising from all that has been said about *agape* as it runs into these highly derogatory usages. Is it possible that we have here the absolute core of the distinction between holiness and the fundamental thing that sin is? To make a god of anything other than the true God is the ultimate moral disintegration. That dedication, that centering, that total self-giving which, when "aimed at" God (Wesley's term), brings holiness and wholeness and fellowship with God can be prostituted. The resulting dedication to the self and the world becomes the real meaning of "anti-Christ." It is *the Sin* in sin's deepest meaning. "Thou shalt have no other gods before me [or ahead of me]," defines the irreconcilable distinction between what it is that makes for holiness or sin. Jesus' summary of the Decalogue, "Love *[agapéseis]* God with the whole of the heart, mind, soul, and strength," expresses in a positive way exactly what the Decalogue says negatively. These are the most stringent and serious warnings against idolatry ever to be uttered, simple yet powerful. Idolatry is, first of all, of the heart, and idolatry is the ultimate sin because the religious function of the whole man is set against God, man's only true end, and set on a false god. It is exchanging *The Truth* for *The Lie* (Rom. 1:25).

Man, to be a human person, must have a master. He is made this way. And being a responsible creature, *he must choose his master.* In this is his freedom. No one can coerce another's mind without destroying that mind. Even a man in chains "enjoys" freedom to determine his own thoughts and loyalties. Man is a servant. This is his glory. He *finds* himself in service. This is the paradox of rational existence. But the problem with men arises when they reject the only One who is big enough to furnish adequate credibility and fulfillment, big enough to be a worthy Master —God, in Christ. It is not that man simply chooses not to serve God but that he cuts himself off from the possibility of finding what only God can provide. He must serve something, so he *creates* a master to serve. He enthrones himself—substitutes his own ego for God. He exchanges his own weak, limited, fallible, imperfect self for the power and strength and glory of the limitless God. He forfeits fulfillment for the fantasy of freedom.

It should also be observed that, in the New Testament, *agape* is not to be a substitute for other forms of love. Nothing of human relatedness and social cohesion—whether *eros, storge, philia,* or any other—is evil. Nor is *agape* said to be superior to other loves. Love for God does not conflict with the varied human relationships termed love. The strong indication is that when *agape* is set right, all other relationships are enhanced and find the fulfillment intended by each of them. *Agape* set on God brings all life's involvements into harmony and creativity. But *agape* set on the self throws all human relationships into chaos and distortion. Is not this the thrust of Paul's magnificent passage in the thirteenth chapter of Corinthians?

The meaning of sanctification, as understood by Wesley and those who follow him, could well be explained by the reorientation of man's *agape* in which the antagonistic and feuding sectional gods tearing the human heart apart by contrary loves are cleansed by the presence of the Holy Spirit. This happens as Christ is made the absolute Lord of all the heart, mind, soul, and strength.

Would it not be better to say that social loves and this more fundamental life "set" should be clearly distinguished? *Eros, storge,* and *philia* can be directed in only a very limited way. But *agape* is a deep set of the soul that, when it is exposed for what it is under the ministry and illumination of the Holy Spirit, must be deliberately set straight—*on God*—or forfeit the grace of God. Transactions on this deep level of the personality are ultimately crucial.

In defense of this presentation is the observation that in all serious discussions about Christian love in theological literature *agape* love is always said to be a different kind of love. The difference is itemized much as it has been done in this study. But by using the same word—*love*—the difference is not explained. To translate *agape* by the simple word "love" is to rob it of a uniqueness that the association with the term *love* dissipates. Another word is needed to preserve the significance of the biblical meaning. Perhaps *agape* itself would do, never confusing one for the other.

In this book this suggestion has not been carried out, partly because the total implication of this idea has not been fully explored and partly because in the study of Wesley the old terms must be preserved. But, it must be said, Wesley's use of the term love does better justice to *agape* than to any of the popular connotations of love. Hence, in the treatment of such matters as Christian love, divine love, perfect love, and others of like nature the insights expressed in this chapter are assumed.

CHAPTER III

The Credibility Gap

Our problem is a credibility gap. Of all the credibility gaps in contemporary life, none is more real and serious than that which exists between Christian, and particularly Wesleyan, doctrine and everyday human life. The absolute of holiness theology may satisfy the mind but the imperfection of the human self seems to deny all that the perfection of Christian doctrine affirms. We seem to proceed from a different world of thought when preaching doctrine than when we preach "practical" sermons. The practical sermon "pulls the stinger" out of the doctrinal presentation. This has created a vast and disturbing dualism between idea and life, between profession and practice. Such a dualism fosters either bewildered dishonesty (in the interest of loyalty) or abject discouragement. The ultimate result is rejection of the Christian message as itself unrealistic and unbelievable if not actually false.

This is not a new problem in the history of the world. God faced it whenever He approached men. His own holiness terrified those whose sin had created an unfathomable gulf between them. God's method of bridging that gap was in the living, experienceable "Word," in the person of Jesus. "God was in Christ, reconciling the world unto himself" (II Cor. 5:19). The person of Jesus was God's answer to the greatest credibility gap. "So the Word became flesh; he came to dwell among us, and we saw his glory" (John 1:14, NEB). To John, the Incarnation was the convincing truth of the gospel.

But Jesus, too, faced a credibility gap. How could He communicate redemptively with alienated and suspicious men? Before He went away He prayed that that gap would be bridged by fallible and exceedingly faulty and limited men. He did not pray that they would be delivered from the world, or that they should retreat into a protective society congenial to their personal desire to escape exposure to evil. He prayed that they should be kept from evil in order that the world might believe that God had sent Him and that God loved *them* (John 17). In this same vein St. Paul says that to us has been given the ministry, and the word, of reconciliation (II Cor. 5:18-19). The objective atonement (i.e., "not imputing their trespasses unto them") remains a credibility gap until men hear the living word of reconciliation from, and in relation to, men like themselves, men who have been reconciled.

W. E. Sangster speaks to this interesting question, thoughtfully,

> One of the most obvious ways by which a teacher might preserve his message in the world is by writing a book. But Jesus Christ wrote no book. . . . The more I ponder the problem the more pleased I feel that Jesus wrote no book.[1]

Sangster said the book would become a fetish, lending itself to bibliolatry. Jesus did not write a creed because no form of human words could encompass all living truth. Creeds arise out of life; they do not create it. "Jesus chose the Apostles to be with him that they might see the life he lived and then live it themselves. It was the only way . . . Theirs was a way of life."[2]

Dr. Paul Culbertson, in an unpublished position paper read in a recent theological conference, speaks to the problem of this gap which is challenging our best and deepest scholarship and grace. "One of the most effective and winsome ways," he says, "of presenting the Arminian-Wesleyan view of personal sanctification is in terms of personal relationships" ("Dynamics of Personal Sanctification," Nazarene Theology Conference, Overland Park, Kans., Dec. 4-6, 1969).

This approach points two ways: (1) back to the necessary abstract and difficult theological statements which, when spoken only with the lips, create the gaps; and (2) forward to the solution which seems to be the biblical way, namely, the personal dimension. *The Word must always become flesh and dwell with men.* Thus a concern with terminology (or words) is not beside the point. The "Eternal Word" is God in Christ communicating himself with men. If man is to take up the assigned and continuing task of reconciliation, all that is involved in words, semantically and existentially, is important to him.

The Problem of Words

John Wesley was concerned about the credibility gap occasioned in part by the problem of words. Wesley's comments in the preface to his *Standard Sermons* are well worth our consideration, not only as an introduction to a study of the man, but as an expression of the point of view which underlies this entire book.

> Every serious man who peruses these [sermons], will see in the clearest manner, what these doctrines are, which I embrace and teach, as the essentials of true religion.
>
> But I am thoroughly sensible, these are not proposed as some may expect. Nothing here appears in an elaborate, elegant, or oratorical dress. If it had been my desire and design to write thus, my leisure would not permit. But, I now write, as I generally speak, *ad populum;* to the bulk of mankind, to those who neither relish or understand the art of speaking, but who, notwithstanding, are competent judges of these truths, which are necessary to present and future happiness. I mention this, that curious readers may spare themselves the labor of seeking for what they will not find.
>
> I desire plain truth for plain people: therefore, of set purpose, I abstain from all nice and philosophical speculations;

from all perplexed and intricate reasonings; and, as far as possible, from even the show of learning, unless in sometimes citing the original Scriptures. I labor to avoid all words which are not easy to be understood, all which are not used in common life; and, in particular, those kinds of technical terms that so frequently occur in bodies of divinity,—those modes of speaking, which men of reading are intimately acquainted with, but which, to common people, are an unknown tongue. Yet I am not assured, that I do not sometimes slide into them unawares: it is so extremely natural to imagine, that a word which is familiar to ourselves is so to all the world (*Sermons*, V. 1 ff.).

A WORD ABOUT WORDS

As important as the definition of words is, it is the connotation of words that makes them sparks of flaming life or tombstones. Words can reveal life, or conceal dry bones. Paul Rees has said the "pricking" word:

> If we are authentically Christian, nothing that is authentically human is beyond the pale of our concern. Say, if you wish, that "holy worldliness" without the transforming Cross of Christ is simply "worldly." But don't stop there. Be willing to say also that correct speech about the Cross of Christ which does not issue in "holy worldliness" is neither "holy" nor "worldly." *It is escapism* (italics mine).[3]

It is our conviction that in the lives of some of us our "holy words" may have become escapes from thinking and action—substitutes for the vital Christian freedom and holy aggression which belong to the Spirit-filled life and to the "holiness" message.

But this "escape" is a reaction to a real area of misunderstanding. The Hebrew connotation of "Word" as personal (in nature, action, revelation, and communication) ought in the Wesleyan tradition always to prevail over the more static and formalized and abstract concepts. The personal does not always so prevail, hence serious misunderstandings ensue. To the Hebrew, his "word" was an almost physical projection of his person. His word was personal. He was frugal with words lest by carelessness his words betray him.

Our concern with terminology is a concern about communication, about communicating the dynamic of the Christian life. We may approach our task from the standpoint of a Hellenistic presupposition, the abstract, or from the Hebraic point of view, the personal. The one is basically concerned with the important word of theology; the other, with the vital word of communication and reconciliation. The former will seek basically to preserve "the Faith" by way of the words of the creed; the latter, with the living Word of Life. The source of the credibility gap may arise in some measure in the ambiguity between terminology considered as words *about the faith*, and words as *faith incarnate* in living men. Our task is to bridge this gap, preserving both creed and meaning, word and life. This is not intended to be an indictment against theology and the Christian creeds, but rather a challenge to clothe mere words with life.

The great Christian words of our faith *can* become defenses like Moses' veil, which was a cover to hide the fading glory of his once shining face (II Corinthians 3). In an article in *Christianity Today* (Oct. 27, 1958), entitled "Hollow Words," J. Wesley Ingles reminds us that the great Christian words are no more than a mockery to our cynical age because they have often been spoken by lips while betrayed by hands and feet. They must become incarnated again in the living, daily experience of Christians profoundly involved in life by lips and hands that move in harmony. He said:

> Every abstract word is hollow until we pour life into it. Honor, glory, sacrifice, loyalty, love, joy, peace, courage and endurance, faith and faithfulness, democracy and brotherhood, justice and mercy—what are these? Words. Abstract words. Hollow words—until we fill them with deeds, with life, and hence with meaning. . . .
>
> The great words of the Christian faith—grace, forgiveness, redemption, faith, hope and love—are all hollow words until we pour our Christian experience into them.

Yes, the great words are hollow; and yet, filled full of life, they could shake the world again as they have done in the past, not as disembodied sounds, however correct, but as poured-out life penetrating to the heart of the world.

Scriptural holiness means much more than lacing theology together with the proper words—even biblical words. It means to hold together in vital, everyday life such diverse matters as life and doctrine, crisis and process, the absolute and the relative, divine and human, spiritual and natural, the individual and society, separation from the world and full involvement in it, proclamation and reconciliation (to name a few), without losing the essential vitality of either. Gerhard Ebeling well said, "Man in this world of his, is historical man, caught up with the world in constant change . . . who must be addressed and confronted as the one who is now in his world."[4]

Modern man cannot "hear" the disembodied word—mere sounds whose connotation to him has not been formed by contact with living examples of their true meaning. Holiness theology must become incarnate *in history* as Calvinistic theology need never be. The peculiarity of Wesleyan theology is its emphasis on holiness as personal experience. As this author stated in an article published in the *Preacher's Magazine* (Oct., 1958), "Holiness can never be accepted merely intellectually, as a philosophy of life. It turns gangrenous apart from the constant flow of living blood out of the deepest heart."

Wesleyanism is impaled on a problem. Its peculiar and identifying and absolutely essential character is God's grace actualized in life. It cannot back off from this and be what it purports to be. It cannot protect itself by elaborate verbal defenses. Jesus' profound dictum, "Whosoever will save his life shall lose it," applies here with compelling urgency. When this theology retreats from "history," curling back in on itself in protective isolation, it becomes no more than an empty shell whose beauty condemns it.

Wesleyanism, then, must come to terms with human weakness, immaturity, ignorances, foibles, and failures. Since Calvinism divorces the absolute of divine truth and the relativity of sinful men, it is protected from irrelevance and restatement. The human element can never flaw the perfection of that kind of theology as it can do to Wesleyanism. The relativity of humanness forces on Wesleyanism the ever lively task of reinterpretation. And interpretation demands a most thorough involvement and understanding on the part of the interpreter—in intimate knowledge of God and men. It is theology in experience. There are its potential power and perpetual risk.

> The sermon must be interpretation because the word of Holy Scripture is historical, because proclamation is a historical process, and because the man to whom proclamation is addressed is historical along with his world. . . . Whenever historicity is not

taken seriously, there is also a failure to take really seriously either the text of Scripture or the man to whom this text must be interpreted.[5]

Wesleyanism is characterized (or should be) by the personal dimension, or religious consciousness. Religion is not, in this view, mere opinion, dogmatic correctness, ritual, good works; it is love to God and man. It relies on the conscious life of the Holy Spirit's indwelling in the human person for its authenticity. Herein is the risk, not only that this theology may slip into the hazards to the right and to the left, but also that the abiding vitality of the Spirit of God may thrust men out into new and unconventional dimensions of Christian outreach and that the forms which structure the organization and language may not be flexible enough to accommodate its own life.

Wesleyanism, or a theology based in John Wesley's methodology, must accept the fact that it is fraught with risk. It may settle back into a safe dogmatism on the right side, and this is fatal to it, or it may opt for a very far left stance which will flatten out and lose itself in the marshes and mudholes of undisciplined thought and fanaticism and unguarded individualism.

Wesleyanism is not a new theology proposed by Wesley. He was most vehement about the historical soundness of his faith. It must not be a cult today, that is, a position which puts a segment of truth in the place of the whole. Wesley eschewed such provincialism. Where one follows the true Wesleyan way, a deep humility accompanies a genuinely teachable spirit There is a questing for the best grasp of truth. In this spirit, Wesley moved. Who could resist the winsomeness of the following plea?

> But some may say, I have mistaken the way myself, although I take it upon me to teach it to others. It is probable many will think this, and it is very possible that I have. But I trust, where in so ever I have mistaken, my mind is open to conviction, I sincerely desire to be better informed. I say to God and man, "What I know not, teach thou me!"
>
> Are you persuaded you see more clearly than me? It is not unlikely that you may. Then treat me as you would desire to be treated yourself upon the change of circumstances. Point me out a better way than I have yet known. Show me it is so, by plain proof of Scripture. And if I linger in the path I have been accustomed to tread, and I am therefore unwilling to leave it, labor

with me a little; take me by the hand, and lead me as I am able to bear. But be not displeased if I entreat you not to beat me down in order to quicken my pace: I can go but feebly and slowly at best; then I should not be able to go at all. May I not request of you, not to give me hard names in order to bring me into the right way. . . . For God's sake, if it be possible to avoid it, let us not provoke one another to wrath. . . . For, how far is love, even with many wrong opinions, to be preferred before truth itself without love!

We may die without the knowledge of many truths, and yet be carried into Abraham's bosom, but if we die without love, what will knowledge avail? The God of love forbid we should ever make the trial! May He prepare us for the knowledge of all truth, by filling our hearts with all his love, and with all joy and peace in believing (*Works,* V, 5-6).

In such a shadow one may stand tall. In spite of risks, perhaps because of them, this book is conceived. The danger is that, on the one hand, those who stand on the right may not understand the purpose of the study and find the theologically unconventional presentation a denial of "the faith." On the other hand, those on the left may feel this work does not really break new ground and is too traditional to be useful. It is the author's hope that the book can point the way to a bridge between the conservative center and the growing edge. We need both.

THE SEMANTIC CREDIBILITY GAP

The "credibility gap" needs to be clearly defined if the needed bridge is to find good footing on each side of the great gulf. The questions raised and expressed at this point are probably meaningful only in the circles we have termed provincial. That is, the more narrow the provincialism, the greater the problems seem to be. The justification for considering them here is that they represent a profile of general misunderstanding at deeper levels mostly expressed in other ways but actually springing from the same roots. These questions will be pursued as a springboard into the more significant problems which are discussed in this book.

THE QUESTIONS

Wesleyans speak of a second work of grace or a second crisis or blessing in the Christian life. What is the significance of *two* special moments among the many in life? Why two, not one or three or 100? How is one recognized from the other or how does one distinguish the first from the second? If a Christian loses one "blessing," which one does he lose, and what happens to the other, and how would one know when he had recovered what was lost? Does God withhold some measure of grace from the first experience that is later given in the second? Or does He solve only part of the sin problem in each "work of grace"?

Is one fully saved when he is regenerated or only partially saved? If God does not save completely, couldn't He if He would? And if He could, why does He not do so in the new birth? If one is wholly saved in the new birth, why must he have another special moment to prepare him for heaven? And, back of these, why a *crisis* experience? And why is there any mathematical designation in reference to it? What is crisis? Process? The relation between the two? What is perfection? Cleansing? Love? Faith? Sanctification?

THE SOURCE OF THE GAP

There are three related core problems which funnel down through at least three theological mistakes. These, in turn, reflect on and exaggerate the mistakes. That is, certain positions force logical problems:

1. There is a tendency to make too sharp a distinction between justification and sanctification considering them as totally discrete and unrelated. Where in Calvinism common and saving grace are said to be of different kinds, Wesleyanism tends to consider justification as one kind of grace with no essential continuity with "sanctifying grace"—a new infusion.

2. There is too much confidence put in the "crisis experiences" to solve all human problems. The means (the crises) become the end (perfection). An uncritical "hyper-supernaturalism" issues in a virtual belief in spiritual magic.

3. There is, in consequence, an almost complete neglect of an understanding of the relation of real-life problems to the experience of grace. The sharp definition of theological exposition is inadequately related to the fallibility of human existence. Prac-

tical application seems to grow on a different tree from theological affirmation.

After reviewing Wesley's general approach to theology and life and noting the elements which make up his "hermeneutic," it is difficult to see how the particular problems arise among those who, today, build theological emphases in the Wesleyan traditions. Where some of these same problems confronted Wesley in his day, he was able to resolve them by constant reference to the principles which structured his thinking. It was, actually, the fact of these confrontations and Wesley's polemic which give the clearest guidelines to the solution to the kinds of problems which "holiness theology" raises. Wesley's principles are probably not spelled out, but when they are recognized it will be seen that they explain his whole theological and religious point of view.

The problems can be traced down to at least three related ways of thinking. These lie at the heart of the "Wesleyanisms" which diverge from Wesley. The three ways are related in a logical sequence.

1. The foundation "way" is a latent tendency toward Greek rather than Hebrew concepts. The Greek language has been an indispensable tool in biblical literature and theological development. Language arises out of the experience and interpretations of a people so that meaning in language is an ineradicable element in its structure. We are profoundly indebted to the Greek culture for its contribution to Christian communication. But more has clung to the language than was intended by the New Testament writers. Not all the ontology of Greek philosophy belongs to Christian theology. We speak particularly of the pagan dualism in cosmology which, whenever it modifies Christian theology, causes problems.

To the Greek, particularly Plato, man is a combination of a divine soul and an evil body. All matter is evil, so that it fouls everything it touches. Human nature is evil. This gives rise to the soteriological misconception, so contrary to biblical thought, that salvation consists in an escape from this body and from this world. Death is a savior. Corollary errors follow: a withdrawal from life, social insensitivity, rejection of nature and its beauty and human joy and full family experience, and many other aberrations to be mentioned in the course of the development of thought in this book.

The Hebrew/Christian concept is completely different. Man is a unity, not a union of parts. Sin is something wrong with the whole man, not just his body or human nature. Salvation is the redemption of the whole man, lifting his entire being into the orbit of grace. The body is not sin-bearing but essentially good. Sin is not a substance but rebellion.

2. Deriving from this is the *substance* concept of reality and salvation in contrast to the *relational* or religious concept. Following logically from the dualism in Platonic philosophy, sin is interpreted genetically—an evil inhering in the flesh and propagated as the physical body is propagated. Great concern is given to the substance of the soul. Sin is in that substance, sub-rational, essential to humanity, real. If it be granted that sin can be removed, in the Greek way of thinking a virtual operation would be required removing, quite literally, *something*. Then the debate about the sin of mankind, and freedom from it, is conducted in a framework of thought foreign to the Bible.

This stands in direct contradiction to the Hebrew/Christian interpretation. In Hebrew thinking, sin is always a religious "malfunction." It is a wrong relation to God. It is rebellion on the part of responsible manhood. It is alienation, a moral disorder.

St. Augustine, the great Christian father of the Church, taught two theories of sin. In one theory it was considered to be concupiscence, and this has led much of the Church into the idea of sin as not only genetically propagated but includes the act of procreation as itself partaking of sin—inevitable, to be sure, but sin nonetheless. At other times, Augustine defined sin as perverted love, the concept on which Wesley builds his theology of grace.

3. The inadequacy—even danger—of the above positions lies exposed in the next logical step. It is the contrast between the magical versus moral interpretation of salvation. This means that a sub-rational, psychological mutation defines cleansing from sin. The problem here is that men come to expect a substance alteration of the soul in salvation which occurs below the level of rational

life and which, apart from personal involvement, changes the impulsive reactions of the self. Anger and pride and all other normal human emotional equipment is said to be removed, so that responsibility for discipline and proper channeling of the emotions is considered a suppression which denies what God ought to do.

The moral interpretation stresses the full participation of the self in every step in grace, strengthening rather than weakening moral integrity and taking responsibility for the ordering of all human impulse and powers around a central and controlling love. Nothing human is despised or rejected but made to serve a new master.

These three assumptions—(1) the Greek versus Hebrew concept of man, (2) the substantial versus relational concept of sin, and (3) the magical versus moral concept of salvation—create a vastly different "Wesleyanism" (if that term could any longer be used) than Wesley himself taught.

A materialistic interpretation of the self, sin, holiness, even of the Holy Spirit, robs men of a basis for an understanding of all aspects of redemption as moral relationship with God and men. When these spiritual matters are reduced to the level of substance, the entire holiness enterprise is fatally compromised. The danger is that the language of the Bible, so thoroughly and wholesomely spiritual and psychological, may be hardened by the just demands of theology into nonpersonal categories submitting to nonmoral, even magical manipulation.

Ontological trichotomy, a recent revival of Gnostic thought in some Christian circles, undermines a concept of the unity of personality so basically assumed in Hebrew thought. It raises no barriers to—in fact it actually suggests and encourages—a virtual depersonalizing of the self. If man is only the sum of so many entities, he is simply an aggregate of selves, a split personality, a double mind; not a responsible, valid, centralized self. Any pluralistic concept of personality destroys the foundation of biblical holiness which is characterized by love, and which is a wholly personal quality capable of being experienced, truly, only by a unified person.

It has always been the most profound conviction of Wesleyanism that the Bible speaks to the moral relationships of men and not about sub-rational, nonpersonal areas of the self. Sin is basically self-separation from God, not in measurable distance but in moral unlikeness and spiritual alienation. Holiness is moral to the core —love to God and man—qualities of the self in relation to the person of God and of men.

To affirm that holiness and sin are personal relationships, not things which can be counted and weighed, often sounds like a betrayal of holiness doctrine and actually heresy to some people. When the very words in Scripture that arise out of the most vital and living situations are interpreted in a way that robs them of life, a transvaluation of the gospel becomes both alarming and dangerous. That biblical exegesis should become the victim of this transvaluation is spiritual tragedy.

The tendency to depersonalize the Christian message permits an evaluation of spiritual values by quantity measurements which totally destroys the value. Qualities are lost when the attempt is made to add and subtract them. It is the characteristic of quantity that it is measured by the smaller units. We compute quantities by adding and/or subtracting and by comparing worth by mathematics, weight and time units.

But it is the peculiarity of quality value that it is measured against the highest perfection. Impersonal things are counted; personal excellences are compared with the best conceivable. A perfect marriage is not the sum total of the number of gifts and kisses but the measure of perfect love and loyalty and devotion. To judge personal religious experience by the wrong measuring standard is to distort the meaning of religion. When spiritual progress is calculated in mathematical terms, the ultimate tension and frustration and ambiguity are encountered between theology, Scripture, and psychology. Certainly no such tension and ambiguity are to be found in Scripture. A preoccupation with the finding of certain numbers of works of grace in Scripture will blind the researcher to the moral imperative which alone can make "works of grace" meaningful.

The assumptions underlying this study, then, are the second of each pair of concepts, namely, the Hebrew concept of man, the relational concept of sin and holiness, and the moral concept of salvation. It is believed that this foundation stood under Wesley's teaching. And these assumptions dissolve many of the logical problems arising in the tension between theology and life.

To anticipate Wesley's point of view regarding all of these we should say, here, that he believed that it is only by the power of Christ resting every moment upon us that "we are enabled to continue in spiritual life, and without which, notwithstanding all our present holiness, we should be devils the next moment" (*Standard Sermons*, ed. Sugden, II, 393).

To Mrs. Pawson, Wesley wrote from London, November 16, 1789, regarding Christian perfection:

> You do well strongly to insist that those who do already enjoy it cannot possibly stand still. Unless they continue to watch and pray and aspire after higher degrees of holiness, I cannot conceive not only how they can go forward but how they can keep what they have already received (*Letters*, VIII, 184).

CONCLUSION

If holiness is wholehearted love to God and men, it must be morally structured and be as dynamic as life and as relevant to our ever changing personalities and situations as the constantly renewed blood in our physical bloodstream. Holiness is wholesome life in God poured out, of moral necessity, into the lives of those around us, measured by our proper self-concern. Wesley said he knew of no holiness that was not social holiness—nor do we.

CHAPTER IV

What Is Wesleyanism?

To name a theology after any specific man narrows the relevance of that particular way of thinking to a limited segment of people. Any such name, or definitive title, creates and perpetuates a provincialism: Wesleyanism, Lutheranism, Calvinism, even Catholicism (in spite of the universal implications of the word), and most particularly, Roman Catholicism. These are labels designed to distinguish one's theology from others and to defend that distinction. They are fences to guard the sheep rather than open up pastureland in which to feed them.

With full appreciation of the handicap involved and not at all supposing that it is finally possible to completely transcend historical conditioning, it is our intention to do a "self-study" of the theological tradition in which we find our greatest satisfaction. Is

there in Wesleyanism a biblical perspective broad enough to qualify it as a biblical or Christian theology that can make positive affirmations so wisely that it does not back itself into a corner by its
faulty foundation and logic?

Theology, of course, by the very nature of its task, defines,
organizes, relegates, and affirms. To be a Christian theology limits
it most decisively. This is understood. But the real question is
whether it is possible to sort out the most essentially Christian affirmations from those, however treasured by various traditions,
which merely divide without also inviting.

John Wesley would have been the last to permit his name to
define any theology. Without doubt, Luther and Calvin and others
of like calibre would stand with Wesley at this point. In using the
designation "Wesleyanism," therefore, we are making concessions
only to the need for identifying a certain way of thinking in the
interest of brevity and common understanding.

Our personal interest in Wesley's "Wesleyanism" is enhanced
by his "catholic spirit"—his tolerance with those who belonged to
other communions and who had other emphases. This was not a
theological compromise on his part but a rare ability to segregate
the essential from nonessential elements in the Christian faith.

> Every man necessarily believes that every particular opinion
> which he holds is true; (for to believe any opinion is not true, is
> the same thing as not to hold it;) yet can no man be assured that
> all his own opinions, taken together, are true. Nay, every thinking
> man is assured they are not . . . "To be ignorant of many things,
> and to mistake in some, is the necessary condition of humanity."
> This, therefore, he is sensible, is his own case. He knows in the
> general, that he himself is mistaken; although in what particular
> he mistakes, he does not, perhaps he cannot, know. . . .
>
> Every wise man, therefore, will allow others the same liberty
> of thinking which he desires they should allow him; and will no
> more insist on their embracing his. He bears with those who differ
> from him, and only asks him whom he desires to unite in love
> that single question, "Is thy heart right, as my heart is with thy
> heart?" . . .
>
> But what is properly implied in the question? . . . The first
> thing implied is this: Is thy heart right with God? . . . Does the
> love of God constrain thee to serve Him with fear? . . . Is thy heart
> right toward thy neighbor? . . . Do you show your love by your
> works? . . . Then, "thy heart is right, as my heart is with thy heart."

"If it be, give me thy hand." I do not mean, "Be of my opinion." You need not: I do not expect or desire it. Neither do I mean, "I will be of your opinion." I cannot: It does not depend on my choice; I can no more think, than I can see or hear, as I will. Keep you your opinion, I mine; and that as steadily as ever. You need not even endeavour to come over to me, or bring me over to you. I do not desire you to dispute these points, or to hear or speak one word concerning them. Let all opinions alone on one side and the other: Only "give me thine hand."

I do not mean, "Embrace my modes of worship;" or, "I will embrace yours." This also is a thing which does not depend either on your choice or mine. We must both act as each is fully persuaded in his own mind. Hold you fast that which you believe is most acceptable government to be Scriptural and Apostolic. If you think the Presbyterians or Independents are better, think so still, and act accordingly. I believe infants ought to be baptized; and that this may be done either by dipping or sprinkling. If you are otherwise persuaded, be so still, and follow your own persuasion. It appears to me, that the forms of prayer are of excellent use, particularly in the great congregation. If you judge extemporary prayer to be of more use, act suitably to your own judgment. My sentiment is, that I ought not to forbid water, wherein persons may be baptized; and that I ought to eat bread and drink wine, as a memorial of my dying Master; however, if you are not convinced of this, act according to the light you have. I have not desire to dispute with you one moment upon any of the preceding heads. Let all these smaller points stand aside. Let them never come into light. If thine heart is as my heart, if thou lovest God and all mankind, I ask no more: "Give me thine hand" (*Works*, V, 494-99).

WESLEY'S APPROACH

It is the thesis of this study that Christian theology arose out of personal involvement in God's saving grace and that its dynamic is perpetuated by a recovery of the personal relationship which gave it its initial life and form. Theology apart from this personal dynamic atrophies into static brittleness and is incapable of maintaining its ability to contain the vital truths it is designed to preserve, much less to commend them.

In particular, "holiness theology" (which is, or ought to be, an *emphasis*, not a different kind of Christian thinking) is more obligated to recognize this personal dimension of Christian experience than would be the case in other emphases. It is precisely the personal dimension that distinguishes holiness from the abstract in theology. It keeps theology viable.

John Wesley's major contribution to Christian thinking was the concept and experience of the personal involvement in grace that Reformation theology seemed to have lost. He would have also rejected our contemporary proposition that men are saved in principle but not in fact. It was the "fact," with all the needed recognition of and explanation for the fallibility of man, that concerned him. The neatness of theological and philosophical absolutes was surrendered to the never finished task of relating God's grace to man's imperfections without losing the absolute of grace or the moral structure of humanity. His task was to close the gap between theology in its philosophical form and religion as a practical experience.

In a letter to Mr. Law dated January 6, 1756, Wesley expresses something of his attitude, though the letter dealt with other matters primarily.

> At a time when I was in great danger of not valuing the "law and the testimony" enough, you made that important observation; "I see where your mistake lies. You would have a philosophical religion; but there can be no such thing. Religion is the most plain, simple thing in the world. It is only, 'We love him because he first loved us'. So far as you add philosophy to religion, just so far you spoil it." This remark I have never forgotten since; and I trust in God I never shall (*Works*, IX, 466).

Not all Wesleyanism has been so circumspect nor caught the specific thing that Wesley espoused—religion as a personal involvement in God's grace.

Approaching Wesley

Many excellent, definitive studies have been made of Wesley's theological position. It would seem presumptuous to add anything to this. There are devotional literatures of various types well laced with Wesley's comments on the spiritual life. The influence of Wesley on social and political concerns is well documented. Methodism acknowledges its debt to Wesley in many ways, by organization, creed, institutions, societies, literature, publishing, to mention but a few of the ways Wesley has left his mark on the religious world. Wesley's emphasis on sanctification has given rise to several religious movements each using his name as a specific theological identification. Some of these movements understand Wesley's emphasis on "Christian perfection" to be the focal point of theology as a whole. Others tend to isolate Wesley's teaching on "full sanctification" or "second blessing" from the rest of his theology, thereby tending to develop various provincialisms. All this is preserved in a large and growing literature.

The specific task of this chapter is to locate a deeper point of view from Wesley's teachings which can serve to interpret his entire approach and by which a legitimate judgment may become possible relative to his use of terms dealing with soteriology. Without this, Wesley, as with St. Paul, Augustine, Luther, Arminius, and any thinker to whom truth is greater than logic, can be made to contradict himself. We seek to understand Wesley in the light of his intention, as he exhorts us to do when reading St. Paul: "We must not so interpret the apostle's words as to make him contradict himself" (*Works*, V, 151). Such courtesy is demanded of any honest reader.

Wesley would have fully appreciated a fellow countryman of modern times, C. S. Lewis, who said wryly, in an essay, "On Criticism,"

> A great many people start by thinking they know what you will say, and honestly believe they have read what they expected to read. But for whatever reason . . . you will find yourself repeatedly blamed and praised for saying what you never said and for not saying what you have said.[1]

In the letter to Countess Huntingdon dated June 19, 1771, Wesley expressed his concern along this line (though the subject under discussion was his position on faith and holiness):

> I have continued to declare this for above thirty years, and God has continued to confirm the word of his grace. But during this time well-nigh all the religious world hath set themselves in array against me and among the rest many of my own children, following the example of one of my eldest sons, Mr. Whitefield. Their general cry has been, "He is unsound in the faith; he preaches another gospel!" I answer, Whether it be the same which they preach or not, it is the same which I have preached for above thirty years. This may easily appear from what I have published during that whole time, I instance only in three sermons: that on

Salvation by Faith, printed in the year 1738; that on the Lord, Our Righteousness, printed a few years ago, and that on Mr. Whitefield's funeral, printed only some months ago [*Works*, V, 7-16, 234-36; VI, 167-82]. But it is said, "Oh, but you printed ten lines in August last which contradict all your other writings!" Be not so sure of this. It is probable, at least, that I understand my own meaning as well as you do! and that meaning I have yet again declared in the sermon last referred to. By *that* interpret those ten lines, and you will understand them better; although I should think that anyone might see even without this help that the lines in question do not refer to the condition of obtaining, but of continuing in the favor of God. But whether the sentiment contained in those lines be right or wrong . . . the Gospel which I now preach God does still confirm by new witnesses in every place; perhaps never so much in this kingdom as within these last three months. Now, I argue from glowing, undeniable fact: God cannot bear witness to a lie (*Letters*, V., 259).

There are a number of observations that can and ought to be made relative to John Wesley that could help us to interpret him fairly and not merely read into his thought prejudicial opinions which would lead us astray. Some exhortation along this line comes from Wesley himself. He was painfully conscious of unfair criticism and unwarranted charges against him. Seeking, as we do, as true a "Wesleyanism" as possible, we will try to outline his main emphases, idiosyncrasies, character, and insights.

Three groupings of Wesley's characteristic ways of thinking will follow, ranging from the most obvious to those not always taken into consideration.

A. *Wesley, a Man Among Men*

1. *Wesley's Semantics—Plain Words*

At the risk of laboring the point it seems wise to point out what we believe has been one of the reasons for the distortion of Wesley's thought. It is an inadequate exposure to the wide scope of Wesley's works coupled with the selective choice of his works to defend a position. This plagued Wesley in his day and continues to cause misinterpretation of him today.

John Wesley met an important need in his societies by compiling a hymnbook. In his preface to the enlarged edition two interesting and instructive comments are made, one having to do with the language of the hymns and the other concerning the theological content of them. Both are helpful to our understanding of Wesley.

1. In these hymns there is no doggerel; no botcher; nothing put in to patch up the rhyme; no feeble expletives. Here is nothing turgid or bombast, on the one hand, or low and creeping on the other. Here are no cant expressions; no words without meaning. Those who impute this to us, know not what they say. We talk common sense, whether they understand it or not, both in verse and prose, and use no word but in a fixt and determinate sense. Here are, allow me to say, both the purity and strength, and the elegance of the English language; and, at the same time, the utmost simplicity and plainness, suited to every capacity.

2. Such a Hymn-Book you have now before you. It is not so large as to be either cumbersome, or expensive; and it is large enough to contain such a variety of Hymns, as will not soon be worn threadbare. It is large enough to contain all the important truths of our most holy Religion, whether speculative or practical; yea, to illustrate them all, and to prove them both by Scripture and Reason. And this is done in a regular order. The Hymns are not carelessly jumbled together, but carefully ranged under proper heads, according to the experience of real Christians. So that this book is, in effect, a little body of experimental and practical divinity.[2]

It will be necessary then to take Wesley at face value; that is, he will say simply and directly just what he means. This simplicity and directness, however, is by no means shallowness or "simplistic" thinking. It has been erroneously supposed that Wesley's thought is as simple as his language, and the conclusion made that he cannot challenge scholarly minds. Actually, what Wesley demands is not only an understanding of his meaning but to keep this meaning constantly in mind so that the reader's own interpretations do not intrude upon his intentions. He goes on in the preface to say:

Many gentlemen have done my brother and me (though without naming us) the honor to reprint many of our hymns. Now, they are perfectly welcome so to do, provided they print them just as they are. But I desire they would not attempt to mend them; for they really are not able. None of them are able to mend either the sense or the verse. Therefore I beg of them one of these two favors: either to let them stand as they are, to take them for better or for worse; or to add the true reading in the margin, or at the bottom of the page; that we may no longer be accountable either for the nonsense or for the doggerel of other men.[3]

Something of his conscientiousness at this point is revealed in the preface to his *Notes on the New Testament*.

> But my own conscience acquits me of having designedly mis-represented any single passage of Scripture, or of having written one line with a purpose of inflaming the hearts of Christians against each other. God forbid that I should make the words of the most gentle and benevolent Jesus a vehicle to convey such poison. Would to God that all the party names, and unscriptural phrases and forms, which have divided the Christian world, were forgot; and that we might agree to sit down together, as humble, loving disciples, at the feet of our common Master, to hear his word, to imbibe his Spirit, and to transcribe his life in our own! (*Notes*, par. 9, p. 5).

To arrive at Wesley's intention, it is of prime importance to give him full value for what he says. He never knowingly obscures meaning *behind* words. He intends to be taken at face value. He intends that double meaning not be imposed on what he says. His language is the unadorned gateway into concepts worthy of the best in contemporary discussions and actually anticipates it. The truth is that he probably could stand with the most erudite today and hold his ground.

2. *Wesley's Searching Spirit*

Not only does the key to Wesley's thought include his forth-right use of words, the need to properly evaluate his polemic, and an appreciation for the cultural relativity which directed his "plain" speech, but also *the ever increasing richness of his thought and word* by his constant exploration into the world around him. He was well informed in the classics in Greek and Hebrew as well as the contemporary philosophy, literature, history, science, politics, travel, social problems, and medicine. He had an interest in psy-chology before its formal birth in modern times because of what his observant and sensitive spirit saw as he attempted to nurture his converts in the religious life. In an age of virile human awaken-ing, Wesley was at home, often pioneering into areas of human and social need ahead of others. Wesley's foray into medicine is a real door into his thinking and point of view theologically and should be kept in mind as his doctrine is examined.

Wesley Hill, in *John Wesley Among the Physicians,* says:

> He opened dispensaries in London, Bristol and New Castle, where he met patients for diagnosis and treatment. . . . Of his medical writings well-known and widely used *Primitive Physick* is by itself a worthy reason for his right to the title of Physician. . . . The book contains such a set of rules for good health as might usefully be studied and practiced in any age; and indeed *Primitive Physick* is listed as a book of reference in an article on Balneology in the *Proceedings of the Royal Society of Medicine,* Vol. 13, 1920. . . .
>
> The particular reason why he took on himself the duties of a physician was as a result of his preaching, the lives of thousands were so changed that, along with a spiritual renaissance, there was a desire for higher mental and physical standards.[4]

Wesley put his hand in many matters not always considered quite proper for a clergyman. Cyril J. Squire complied a list of some of Wesley's achievements and included them on a *Lythograph of Wesley* now sold in the New Room, new Chapel in Bristol, England. Among them the following are of interest here.

> He rode more than 250,000 miles and preached over 45,000 sermons.
>
> In 1748, he founded a school for boys at Kingswood, Bristol, and wrote textbooks.
>
> He published 233 original works on a variety of subjects.
>
> He compiled a Christian library.
>
> He wrote a four-volume *History of England.*
>
> He wrote a book of *Birds, Beasts and Insects.*
>
> He wrote a medical book.
>
> He set up a free medical dispensary.
>
> He adapted an electrical machine for healing, and cured more than a thousand people.
>
> He set up spinning and knitting shops for the poor.
>
> He received 40,000 pounds from his books but gave it all away.
>
> Historians write that John Wesley saved England morally and spiritually.

Such a man deserved to be heard in the eighteenth century and deserves to get the attention of twentieth-century man.

3. *Wesley's Social Concerns*

Wesley explained his reasons for spending time out of his already overcrowded days in practicing medicine to Vincent Perronet, in 1748, in a long letter outlining his concept, and history, of Methodism.

> We have ever since had great reason to praise God for His continued blessing on this undertaking. Many lives have been saved, many sicknesses healed, much pain and want prevented or removed. Many heavy hearts have been made glad, and the visitors have found from Him whom they serve a present reward for all their labour (*Letters,* II, 306).

Wesley's decision to help relieve men's physical problems becomes an important commentary on the concept he had of the relation of the spiritual to the physical and his responsibility to this.

> But I was still in pain for many of the poor that were sick; there was so great expense, and so little profit. And first I resolved to try whether they might not receive more benefit in the hospitals. Upon the trial, we found there was indeed less expense, but no more good done than before. I then asked the advice of several physicians for them; but still it profited not. I saw the poor people pining away, and several families ruined, and that without remedy.
>
> At length I thought of a kind of desperate expedient. "I will prepare and give them physic myself." For six- or seven-and-twenty years I had made anatomy and physic the diversion of my leisure hours; though I never properly studied them, unless for a few months when I was going to America, where I imagined I might be of some service to those who had no regular physician among them. I applied to it again. I took into my assistance an apothecary and an experienced surgeon; resolving at the same time not to go out of my depth, but to leave all difficult and comlicated cases to such physicians as the patients should choose.
>
> I gave notice of this to the Society; telling them that all who were ill of chronical distempers (for I did not care to venture upon acute) might, if they pleased, come to me at such a time, and I would give them the best advice I could and the best medicines I had (*Letters,* II, 308-10).

In this same letter Wesley explains the provisions he made for "feeble, aged widows" by bringing them together in one house, "providing them with things needful for the body; toward the expense of which I set aside first the weekly contributions of the bands, and then all that was collected at the Lord's Supper." He was concerned also about the "abundance of children" who because parents could not afford to put them in school were like "wild ass's colts," and learned "all kinds of vice," on the streets. These he brought into his own house to learn the basics of education. Lack of money to carry on business because of excessive interest rates in England stirred Wesley to go "from one end of the town to the other," exhorting "those who had this world's goods to assist their needy brethren." As a result, a very reasonable lending service was expended and "two hundred and fifty were assisted within the space of one year" (*Letters,* II, 310).

> In five months medicines were occasionally given to above five hundred persons. Several of these I never saw before; for I did not regard whether they were of the Society or not. In that time seventy-one of these, regularly taking their medicines and following the regimen prescribed (which three in four would not do), were entirely cured of distempers long thought to be incurable. The whole expense of medicine during this time was nearly forty pounds. We continued this ever since, and by the blessing of God with more and more success (*Letters,* II, 306-8).

With such a dynamic personality and unconventional (or at least teachable) mind, honed to an ever higher degree of sharpness and efficiency, it would be a great mistake to categorize Wesley by some conventional label. No more would it be right for some "Wesleyanism" to try to compress Wesley's concept of sanctification into a narrow provincialism (particularly American). Wesley may have been a *homo unius libri,* in one sense, but that Book was the focal point of all the wide creation of God and the key to understanding man in his humanness. The Book did not restrict him; it released him from restrictions. Wesley's doctrine of salvation is not an exception to his catholic interests.

4. *Wesley, a Man of His Time*

Wesley was a man of his day, speaking the language of his day, caught in the cultural milieu of his nation and generation and captivated by the significance of his church with its history, ritual, and religion. He was an Anglican through and through. It was his "parent" and his mentor. He was marked by the prejudices, beliefs, and biases of eighteenth-century Britain. Though he transcended England's moral "ideals," the essential historical conditioning of the man must be fully taken into consideration as we attempt to interpret what he said.

He believed in ghosts. He thought that earthquakes were

direct divine judgments against sin, and that public repentance could prevent them (*Works,* VII, 386).

He had no sympathy whatsoever with the American colonists who desired independence and insisted on running the Methodist missions in the "States" from his English "office." He appointed Francis Asbury to the bishopric in America, which position Asbury declined until by vote of the American church the will of the people was declared.

He was opinionated and sometimes testy, but was usually big enough to finally accept defeat in argument and policy with more or less grace. One of the more winsome examples of his graciousness is found in a letter to the Countess Huntingdon. He wrote, "When I was much younger than I am now, I thought myself almost infallible; but bless God I know myself better now" (*Letters,* V, 259).

B. *Wesley as a Scholar*

1. *Wesley in Controversy*

Controversy was the atmosphere in which Wesley moved, created by the kind of message he had. He did not create the controversy but what he said raised questions in the established church world in which he moved. He did not speak and write in a vacuum. In the give-and-take of attack and counterattack, one tends to overstate a position. Not always does a controversialist guard his arguments from the rear from all possible misunderstandings, assuming usually that the full situation is known by those who hear or read. Wesley was not an exception to this rule and, in interpreting him, the specific point at issue must be given due consideration.

The pressure of controversy has characterized much, if not most, of theological literature in Christian history. It was in controversy that the issues became clear and theological affirmations were worked out. This fact should alert us to a pair of truths in Wesley's case: (1) He could transcend his environment. His convictions set him apart as a leader. He had convictions significant enough to challenge men and raise worthy controversy. (2) But much of what Wesley said was largely polemic in nature. We ordinarily hear but one side of the conversation and tend sometimes to make judgments of him on the basis of these one-sided dialogs as if that were his well-rounded and considered opinion. It takes some patience and care to get around the full circle of theological debate and eventually find the true center of his thought. But it is worth the doing.

2. Wesley's "Open-ended" Thinking

Stemming from the above observations is the uncomfortable discovery (which we may conclude is a weakness) that *Wesley changes his mind.* He does not always "stay put." This can be somewhat disturbing until a little deeper observation reveals interesting things. Wesley was not afraid to alter his position when circumstances demanded it. He even *reversed* his stand; for example, from the conviction that one who has found "perfection" could never lose it, to the reluctant concession that it could be lost—and regained—but *need not* be lost, or *may not* be regained. He altered his opinion about the relative importance, and the timing, of crisis over process, at times stressing the growth and at other times the crisis aspect of sanctification.

But when one sorts out the subjects about which he allows himself the luxury of change (in the face of the unchangeable), it becomes obvious that he is discovering the difference between the "substance" of doctrine and the "circumstance" of it, a category of analysis which he considers of real importance. In other words, some truths are firm, and biblical study and experience continue to prove them firm. They are the "fundamentals," such as the truth that men may be saved from all sin in this life. The method, time, adaptation to imperfect humanity, and a host of other questions having no direct scriptural word, yield their truth to us only in experience. As important as these truths may be, they are not revealed truths, but historical and in that sense peripheral. Wesley did not consider any question relative to faith beneath his dignity or unworthy of his concern. But he did not fall into the trap of confusing the circumstance with the substance of truth. Though he spent some time discussing the peripheral issues, he did not permit them to become central and divisive or distracting. How wise would his professed followers be were they to emulate this rare quality!

We who would aspire to a more authentic Wesleyanism should explore again and again those areas in holiness theology and practice which are biblically central and unchanging and skirt those areas which are tentative and subject to constant openness of mind. Wesley declared:

> I have again and again, with all the plainness I could, declared what our constant doctrines are; whereby we are distinguished only from heathens, or nominal Christians; not from any that worship God in spirit and truth. Our main doctrines, which include all the rest, are three,—that of repentance, of faith, and of holiness. The first of these we account, as it were, the porch of religion; the next, the door; the third, religion itself (*Works*, VIII, 472).

Perhaps the greatest "weakness" in Wesley was his greatest strength. We seek principles of interpretation derived from Wesley himself, by which to understand him today. Could it not begin by noting the very flexibility of his mind and heart, rooted in a sound sense of history?

We could well observe that Wesley's was not a closed thought system, unchangeable and static. A clue to his approach to life and religion which gives direction to his theological pilgrimage can be found in the fact of his searching spirit. His lifelong search for perfection constitutes the secret of Wesley's temper. This is not to be interpreted as a fruitless, failing quest of an ever receding "will-o'-the-wisp." Nothing could be farther from the truth. But he was a "file leader" in religion because he never rested in the achievement of the moment. The very nature of the Christian life is progress. Perfection is not a static "having" but a dynamic "going." Love is not "perfect" in the sense of having reached its zenith, but in its quality as a dynamic relationship subject to infinite increase.

3. *Wesley's Critical Approach*

Wesley's most sticky problems came from the "tentative" areas. He handled such questions with great care, aware of the risk in speaking about them. He knew the "loaded question" when one came. In every case he would take the question apart, lay out the parts, clarify ambiguities, state the objections, and finally answer forthrightly.

An example of Wesley's insistence on clear thinking is found in his *Farther Appeal to Men of Reason and Religion*. A question was put to him with a number of parts having to do with the possibility of instantaneous change in the new birth. He answers each part; but when the third part comes in for attention, he quotes the question and gives a new kind of answer.

> Q. 3. Whether this improvement is not a better foundation of comfort, and of an assurance of a Gospel new-birth, than that which is founded on the doctrine of a sudden and instantaneous change.
>
> A. A better foundation than that. *That*. What? To what substance does this refer? According to the rules of grammar . . . you must mean a better foundation than that foundation which is founded on this doctrine. As soon as I understand the question, I will endeavor to answer it (*Works*, VIII, 66).

It may be possible that the divisions in Wesleyan circles are the result of failure to be as circumspect—and whimsical. The tendency is to give every sermon, letter, treatise, from the earliest to the latest, from theology to practice, equal value. Wooden interpretation of anything rational, whether Wesley or Scripture or any other work from the humanities to science, results in grotesqueness rather than sense.

4. *Wesley's "Foresight"*

Another factor, an unexpected one, in Wesley's makeup, is significant for this study. In a man as fundamentally conservative as he, it is refreshing to find *a most independent spirit*. In many ways he was traditional, ritualistic, dogmatic, aristocratic, in complete control of himself and others (if they stayed in his good graces). It is said that Wesley never lost control of his emotions. He was cold and wholly unsentimental. Only the most compelling circumstances and arguments on the part of George Whitefield induced him to preach in an unconsecrated place—the open field. But it is this one "weakness" (if such it was) which proved in the end to be his strength—the openness, however reluctant, to adapt unconventional means to the needed end.

It could have been called casuistry—this ability to find a good reason to violate the most sacred conventions. The classic example, after years of temporizing to meet contingencies, was his "illegal" act in consecrating Francis Asbury as a bishop with an authority not his in any traditional sense.

We are not interested in the rightness or wrongness of what he did but only in the fact that he was able to introduce novelty into stable situations which became barriers to his vision. These breaks with "law and order" were traumatic to one whose every breath thrived on proper protocol. The charge against him, most painful to his sensitive soul, was that he drew away from "The Church" and separated his converts from it. This he denied. He knew the history of independent groups who, because they felt themselves to be superior to the old church, began to claim to be "holier than thou." Methodists, he said, are not a sect or party. They are members of the Church. "I believe one reason why God is pleased to continue my life so long [1789 at this time] is, to confirm them in their present purpose, not to separate from the church" (*Works,* VIII, 278).

To clarify his position in the face of "warm men" who insisted that he *did* separate, and "warm men" who criticized him for not doing so, he said,

> I hold all the doctrines of the Church of England. I love her liturgy. I approve her plan of discipline, and only wish it could be put into execution. I do not knowingly vary from any rule of the Church, *unless in those few instances, where I judge, there is an absolute necessity* (*Works,* VIII, 278, italics mine).

Some of the "necessities" were (1) when denied a church to preach in, he "preached abroad"; (2) where no suitable prayer existed, he "prayed extempore"; (3) he gathered needy people together for "spiritual instruction"; (4) he "fixed the stations" of the preachers for the year. The reason for all of this is interesting. He enunciates two principles: "The one, that I dare not separate from the church, that I believe it would be a sin to do so; the other that I believe it would be a sin not to vary from it in the points mentioned" (*ibid.*).

Wesley was caught between two *facts* of rational life: the absolute need for system and stability in any human society, yet the equally great need for "foresight" and action if progress is to be experienced. Perhaps Wesley would have found Alfred North Whitehead's discussion of this matter most agreeable.

> It is the beginning of wisdom to understand that social life is founded on routine. . . . Society requires stability, foresight itself presupposes stability, and stability is the product of routine. But there are limits to routine, and it is for the discernment of these limits, and for the provision of the consequent action that foresight is required.[3]

It is of more than passing importance that Wesley not only had "foresight" (as Whitehead termed the unconventional and courageous prophet), but he also was a man of action. And this quality of personality emerged after he found the assurance of God's love for him personally and his deep conviction of responsibility for sharing that experience of assurance with others. Wesley was not a rebel—ever—but he was a revolutionary under the impetus of the indwelling Spirit of God.

5. *Wesley's Teleology*

It would be impossible to correctly characterize Wesley without taking into consideration his teleological point of view. God created the world and man, not whimsically, but for a purpose. This purpose requires a history to achieve. The history/teleology complex is the very matrix of moral existence. Life is probation. History is the workshop of moral development. Man was made to glorify God but he could not realize this "end" apart from an environment in which moral choice could confirm and develop love. No holiness is automatic or impersonal. It is both a quest and a relationship, a way and a quality of life.

In the providence of God, the child becomes a man; the ignorant one, by dint of effort, becomes knowledgeable; the immature maturate; the seed dies, sprouts, grows, and bears fruit; innocence becomes holiness; holiness is perfected in love and faith; faith is "intercourse with God."

Teleology implies *change* within *continuity*. Change which simply leaps from one state to another with no essential link between is not teleological. Yet change is an essential ingredient of teleology. All this Wesley saw, and we should be prepared to see in his entire thinking a real relationship linking the "stages in the way," not only in history and nature, but in theology and Christian experience. No arbitrariness on God's part relative to man's election could square with purpose. The coming of Christ, His death on the Cross, and the gospel appeal have no place in the non-historical, even anti-historical, concept of the particular predestination theory.

If men are already destined to be saved or lost, the meaning of life is totally eliminated. (Wesley's sermon on "Free Grace," Vol. VII, pp. 373-86, is a strong argument for this point.) Wesley's theological insistence on free grace (not "free will") against absolute personal predestination was not emotional or superficial. It was a vigorous defense for holiness which he believed, along with the Calvinists, was the purpose of creation, namely to glorify God.

> This is the plain proof that the doctrine of predestination is not a doctrine of God, because it makes void the ordinances of God; and God is not divided against Himself. . . . It directly tends to destroy that holiness which is the end of all the ordinances of God. It has a manifest tendency to destroy holiness in general; for it wholly takes away those first motives to follow after it, so frequently proposed in Scripture (*Works,* VII, 376).

Absolute election destroyed the fact of continuity and relationship, and consequently for holiness, which is of the essence of relationship. Wesley's insistence on both was intellectually responsible and respectable thinking and was reflected in his doctrine of sanctification (as we shall see), and accounts for his stress on process in the Christian life and the close relation of justification and sanctification.

Every man "aims" at something. Wesley uses this term frequently. In a sermon on "The Single Eye" he contrasts those who aim at the pleasure of sense, imagination, praise of men, and riches (which plunge one into darkness), and the aiming at God. This "aiming" is the meaning of faith which either leads away from God or opens all the resources of God to men.

One may have a clear knowledge of the divine will but,

> not without the *means* but in the use of all those means which God has furnished him with. And, walking in this light, he cannot but "grow in grace, and in the knowledge of our Lord Jesus Christ." He will continually advance in all holiness, and in the whole image of God (*Works,* VII, 299).

In this passage something of the teleology implicit in Wesley is introduced. There is, in embryo, these emphases (to be developed later): (1) that God made man unfinished; (2) that man is involved in the finishing process; (3) that the finishing is a process; (4) that God has furnished the material for the task; (5) that finishing is not something implanted in man apart from his activity in respect of it; (6) that holiness is dynamic and is the way and the goal of the restoration of and development in the whole image of God.

Wesley's teleology is the basis of his dynamic concepts of man and salvation.

> The *one perfect Good shall be your one ultimate end.* One thing shall ye desire for its own sake,—the fruitation of Him that is All in All. One happiness shall ye propose to your souls, even an union with Him that made them; the having "fellowship with the Father and the Son;" the being joined to the Lord in one Spirit. *One design you are to pursue to the end of time,—the enjoyment of God in time and in eternity.* Desire other things, so far as they tend to this. Love the creature as it leads to the Creator. But in every step you take, be this the glorious point that terminates your view. Let every affection, and thought, and word, and work, be subordinate to this. *Whatever ye desire or fear, whatever ye seek or shun, whatever ye think, speak, or do, be it in order to your happiness in God, the sole End, as well as Source, of your being* (*Works*, V, 207-8).

DEPTH, THE WESLEYAN DIMENSION

As we go deeper into Wesley's significant and valuable insights, it will be noted that he anticipated today's thinking. If one word could characterize Wesley's contribution to the religious enterprise in a greater way than any other, it would be "depth" in the sense this word is used today. Depth recognizes the dimension of life that lies in the area of meaning. The word could substitute for "spiritual" in contrast to the world of sense. It points to quality as over against mere substance. Its significance comes to a focus in "personness" rather than "thingness." Martin Buber reaches for something of its dimension in his "*I and Thou*" concept. A word of great richness and relevance to give positive direction of thought is *love*—Wesley's own word.

When we speak of depth we are leaving behind the whole world of secondary values—the impersonal—and pushing back to the area of primary values—the personal—where the secondary "worth" derives meaning. The church which has made religious judgments mainly on the level of the secondary is what has been called in a pejorative sense "religion." Such religion has given the Church as a whole a false image. When we hear such people as Dietrich Bonhoeffer advocate "religionless Christianity," it is not a denial of religion or Christianity, but an emphasis upon the need for true Christological interpretation.

Wesley would have agreed with Bonhoeffer. Where *anything* has become a barrier to the vital, inner, personal relationship to God—or a substitute for it—that thing must be exposed for what it is and put into right perspective or removed. In a discussion of this matter in a sermon, "The Unity of the Divine Being," Wesley speaks of the "idols" which may lead our minds away from God. Of the last one of which he speaks, he says, "There is still one more dangerous idol than all the rest; that is religion." He continues:

> It will easily be conceived, I mean false religion; that is, any religion which does not imply the giving the heart to God. Such is First, *a religion of opinions; or what is called orthodoxy.* Into this snare fall thousands of those who by faith, mean only a system of Arminian or Calvinian opinions. Such is, Secondly, a *religion of forms;* of barely outward worship, how constantly soever performed; yea, though we attend the Church Service every day, and the Lord's Supper every Sunday. Such is, Thirdly, a *religion of works;* of seeking the favour of God by doing good to men. Such is, Lastly, a *religion of Atheism;* that is, every religion whereof God is not laid for the foundation; In a word, a religion wherein "God in Christ, reconciling the world unto himself," is not the Alpha and Omega, the beginning and the end, the first and the last Point (*Works*, VII, 269).

There is reason to believe that Wesley and Bonhoeffer would have had many vital things in common.

It may seem strange to say that a man who spoke in such plain, common, "simple" language would be a thinker in depth but one misses precisely Wesley's point when the depth dimension is not recognized. It was the "blind streets" of religion which identified the superficial in his experience. Moralism, with all its "holy" facade, had left him empty though he had dedicated himself to it as few men ever do. The broken promise of the emotionalism of mysticism violated his deepest sense of rational integrity. The excessive "devotional" life (as understood by the "Holy Club") tended to develop a morbid introspection and separation from society. It finally gave way to the "social holiness" he gradually came to understand as the real meaning of religion.

It was the insensitivity of the Church to the true calling to serve men's spiritual and life needs that induced him to take liberties with its forms and ritual, however much he loved the Church. And it was the antinomianism of the Reformed interpretation of

Christian faith of that day which drove him to the exploration of "Biblical Holiness," an interpretation of religion that saw that Christ saves from all sin rather than saving men in their sins.

To Wesley, sanctification was an ethical relationship, never a moralism, never an emotion or a deliverance from emotions, never a magical elimination of a thing ("like a sore tooth") or the addition of something, even the "addition" of the Holy Spirit (in the superficial sense so often associated with irrational and "enthusiastic" experiences said to be religious). The direction of one's attention and "aim" was not toward an examination of one's emotional states, or the quantity of one's religious acts and obeyed rules. Religion to Wesley was in the quality and object of one's love. It was not even the attempt to measure one's religion abstractly, but to direct it concretely.

> True religion is right tempers towards God and man. It is, in two words, gratitude and benevolence; gratitude to our Creator and supreme Benefactor, and benevolence to our fellow-creatures. In other words, it is the loving God with all our heart, and our neighbour as ourselves.
>
> It is in consequence of our knowing God loves us that we love him, and love our neighbour as ourselves. Gratitude towards our Creator cannot but produce benevolence to our fellow-creatures. The love of Christ constrains us, not only to be harmless, to do no ill to our neighbour, but to be useful, to be "zealous of good works;" "as we have time, to do good unto all men;" and to be patterns to all of true, genuine morality; of justice, mercy, truth. This is religion, and this is happiness; the happiness for which we were made (*Works,* VII, 269).

We are again faced with Wesley's "magnificent obsession" —love. Every door into his thought leads into love. Love is the true depth of God's way with men, and nothing less than love can truly characterize a real Christian. The urgency of this love is expressed in his sermon "Scriptural Christianity."

> He [any Christian of the Early Church] that thus *loved* God, could not but love his brother also; and "not in word only, but in deed and in truth." "If God," said he, "so loved us, we ought also to love one another;" (I John iv. 11) yea, every soul of man, as "the mercy of God is over all his works." (Psalm cxlv. 9) Agreeable hereto, the affection of this lover of God embraced all mankind for his sake; not excepting those whom he had never seen in the flesh, or those of whom he knew nothing more than that

they were "the offspring of God," for whose souls his Son had died; not excepting the "evil" and "unthankful," and least of all his enemies, those who hated, or persecuted, or despitefully used him for his Master's sake. These had a peculiar place, both in his heart and in his prayers. He loved them "even as Christ loved us" (Works, V, 40).

Without busying ourselves, then, in curious, needless inquiries, touching those extraordinary gifts of the Spirit, let us take a nearer view of these his ordinary fruits, which we are assured will remain throughout all ages;—of that great work of God among the children of men, which we are used to express by one word, *Christianity; not as it implies a set of opinions, a system of doctrine, but as it refers to men's hearts and lives*" (Works, V, 38).

Depth, in religion, as in any part of life, has to do with the personal, and the personal with relationships—personal relationships. Depth is not a casual acquaintance with abstract ideas but a saturation of oneself in the fiery furnace of dynamic thinking as thinking partakes of life involvement. Depth in religion must issue in action. "Subliminal" learning does not build character nor become holiness. Emotional excitations whether induced by the reading of a novel, by watching a television drama, or by any kind of emotional appeal or worship device which does not issue in some kind of appropriate action are psychologically damaging.

Emotions are designed to initiate action, not to be expended on the person who is moved by them. They are not to enjoy for themselves but to drive the wheels of life. The energy built up by emotion when short-circuited and fed back into the psyche without outlet burns out physical, mental, and moral health. Great emotions aroused by great challenges which are not translated into action finally lose their ability to create a challenge. Instead, a moral dualism develops in which ideal and action are divorced. The personality unified in depth becomes less and less possible. A moral schizophrenia, as devastating as mental abberations, results.

Emotions which can no longer spark action finally destroy moral integrity. Congregations which have been exposed to great preaching and high religious challenge and feeling but which do not gear that feeling into the work of the Christian ministry in the lives of people about it become indifferent, cold, isolated, withdrawn. To fail to engage latent spiritual power into service creates a "split personality" that usually substitutes for missions and service and wholesomeness, a sense of superior "spirituality" which judges others to be defective in grace.

Whatever criticism is legitimate of Wesley's approach to religion, it cannot be justly charged against him that he countenanced anything that prevented the transformation of the human heart from destructive "brokenness" and dualism toward wholeness and holiness. Holiness was to him what we are meaning by depth.

By emphasizing depth—the personal, moral, and spiritual in religion—against the abstract, mechanical, magical, ultra-supernatural, Wesley was not making religion less radical and thoroughgoing but more so. In recognizing this quality in Wesley as a proper interpretation of the Christian faith, we are not "clipping the wings" of holiness theology but attempting to restore the wingspread of theology and Christian experience so that the infinite ceiling of spiritual sky may once again be explored.

The man John Wesley needs to be seen among his own people in his own generation and culture. He, in many ways, towered above them, as evidenced by his searching spirit, his keen social sensitivity, the valuable controversies in which he was engaged, his critical concern for clear thinking, and his dynamic concept of religion. But what were his deeper assumptions which gave rise to the particular theological and religious points of emphasis which makes him remembered, and by which his whole contribution may be interpreted? This question will structure the next chapter.

CHAPTER V

A Hermeneutical Approach to Wesley

The Methodological Problem

John Wesley's theological and religious contribution to the Church has been honored by numerous interpretations, all called Wesleyan, but differing in more or less important ways from Wesley's total thought and/or from other "Wesleyanisms." Just as there are several Calvinisms and Lutheranisms, Augustinianisms, Liberalisms, and Conservatisms, so there are several Wesleyanisms.

The problem lies in the realm of methodology. Almost any system of theology can be derived from Wesley as from Luther or Augustine. But each is built on a selection of passages from his works congenial to the basic philosophic assumptions of the author, who often is not aware of his own bias. The choice and organization of ideas, then, may be consciously or unconsciously selected on the basis of a prior point of view which is seldom questioned. The result can be an Aristotelian Wesley, a Platonic Wesley, a Schleiermachian Wesley, a Whiteheadian Wesley, a Social-Gospel Wesley, a Second-Blessing Wesley, or any number of other kinds of theology termed Wesleyanism, depending on the personal orientation of the author. None of this is necessarily wrong. It may even be good. But right or wrong, good or bad, it must at least be recognized and acknowledged.

The present author, convinced that Wesley can become contemporary, will not be unaware of the problem involved in interpretation. Wesley was a man of his day. He spoke out of the thought forms of his day and to the peculiar problems of men in that day. If he is to speak to us in our day, some method of interpretation will be needed to bridge over the historical changes that separate us.

The theology which is presented in this book is hopefully and frankly a Wesleyan theology; but which Wesleyanism? The theology is not Wesleyan in the sense that it is assumed that Wesley is an authority—or even that his interpretation of the Bible is considered authoritative for it. Wesley was orthodox in the traditional sense, yet he called himself a man of one Book—the Bible. Here are creed and Scripture, two authorities for Christian faith, neither yielding its autonomy to the other. Systematic theology and biblical theology have not yet merged. There is a dilemma here which Wesley never solved nor did he attempt to do so. It was an "openness to the future" which urged him on into creative insights and which urges us on into further discoveries in the same spirit. Only in Wesley's openness to the depths of truth do we consider this to be Wesleyan, though we share in the dynamic insights which we understand were his.

WESLEY'S CONTRIBUTION

Wesley's concern was the relating of God's grace to human experience, theology to religion, logic to life, the Church to society. Nothing can define sanctification in practical terms any better than that which is involved in such relations. Belief in salvation, "in principle but not in fact," was to him the major weakness of the Church of his day. Most particularly did he object to the interpretation of the Calvinism of his day which condoned a concept of freedom from the consequences of sin which did not grant freedom from sin itself.

Wesley's profound and dynamic religious insight and emphasis was the power of the Holy Spirit in the life of the Christian. This power was a real, spiritual energy linking the divine reality to human experience. It was the "personness" of God touching the "personness" of men. It was an actual moral transformation of human life. It engaged all that the human person is in grace. It put the individual believer into the Church—the corporate fellowship. It put the Church into the midst of society with a task to do in transforming the world in which men find themselves.

The lure of Wesley is not primarily his theology; that was traditional enough. He was not an innovator. The contribution of Wesley is in his ability to put theology into flesh and blood. The goal was theology incarnated in mere man. And herein lies the power—and the problem—of Wesleyanism. The *power* of the Spirit-filled life is not limited to the Wesleyan segment of Christianity. One does not have to believe in any "Wesleyan" position to experience that. The problem lies in that attempt to rationalize the perfection of theological absolutes to the imperfections of human nature, and yet to be able to honestly witness to a Christian experience of total love to God and man.

"Wesleyanism," as already introduced, needs more precise description. Whatever a Wesleyan theology may be, it cannot honestly be limited to any one aspect of Wesley's own many-faceted teachings and life emphasis. To abstract from the complex of truths is to distort his truth and caricature his teachings. When "holiness" is presumed to be his central message (which is the presumption of this study), it must be the totality of what he conceived to be holiness and not some particular aspect of it which neglects or is blind to the full-orbed scope of holiness. There are numbers of excellent studies about Wesley and his views on theological points such as perfection, social sensitivity and outreach, Christology, the sacraments, and many others. The present approach of this study will be an attempt to push back into some of John Wesley's presuppositions and apply these concepts to a related number of doctrines necessary to holiness theology and life. In the present Wesleyan framework, this is the area in which serious problems most often arise.

The key to Wesley's theological emphasis was his concept of God (which is, incidentally, true of any approach to theology or Christian thought). One of the clearest and most helpful treatises of his concept is to be found in his "Thoughts upon God's Sovereignty," in which ideas of both God as Creator and God as Governor—two sides of the personal God—are carefully distinguished.

He refused to speculate about God. What God has revealed is what we need to know. What we need to know about Him has to do with man's salvation. Therefore, knowledge of God will be in respect of those who need salvation, namely, mankind. In this way, Wesley avoids the pitfalls of a philosophic approach to God which results in ideas about Him very far from that revealed in Scripture and which reacts back on soteriology. Since God has revealed himself in Christ, through the Holy Spirit's ministry, it is in the relationship of man to God at the point of revelation and response that his major theological emphasis is to be found.

Without losing anything of the biblical concept of the sovereignty of God, Wesley could come to terms with the idea of man in relation to God which does full justice to his true dignity as man, and his sin as the truly serious and deadly thing that it is. Wesley was fully aware of the theological implications of his own insights and consequently ran into logical difficulties with his church peers (as they were not slow to point out). As rational as Wesley was, he was less embarrassed by such contradictions than he was about a possible surrender of the insight which he believed to the biblical. And it was because the more he knew about human nature, the more practical the Bible seemed to him to be, that he was willing to be a man of one Book rather than to be merely logical for the sake of theological consistency.

MAN

These insights are the concerns that we want to lift up for review and then apply to the doctrines which sanctification includes. They have to do with man as (1) historical, (2) personal, (3) dynamic, and (4) social. Whether or not Wesley would itemize these particular features or not, or list them in this order, is essentially irrelevant. The fact is that his major affirmations make sense when understood in the light of these insights and do not make sense otherwise.

1. *Historical*

Wesley had a sound sense of history. Man participates in history. He has roots in the past, profound involvement in the present, and on this "pad" he launches himself into the future. He is not an observer out there but a part of the happening here and now. He is, in a real sense, a product of his environment, shares in its ideals and prejudices, understands and communicates in its idiom, is limited to its structure, thinks in its terms. He is not set apart from human life but lives as a vital and participating element in it. But he is not, by the grace of God, imprisoned by this environment, unable to make contrary choices and embark on creative enterprises; but his choices, understandings, progress, and prejudices must take his relationship to history into account.

History, too, meant personal participation in God's grace. We may use the term "experience" if we understand by this, not an emotion, but a real, living involvement in grace that makes a difference in actual life situations. In fact, it was Wesley's insistence that holiness be experienced that contributed a wholly new dimension to the word as used then. When he said that holiness is love, the whole concept of holiness did a radical retake, and could and did create problems in theology not settled to this day. Holiness that could fit a man who is in history without taking him out of history seemed like a denial of the absolutisms of holiness; and it is a denial of any abstraction in the name of holiness. Love is not and cannot be abstract. It bears the biblical responsibility for "historicizing" holiness or putting holiness into history, or into life.

2. *Personal*

Whatever else may be said of man, it is his personal relationships with which Wesley was concerned because he felt that this was what the Bible predicated about man. "Personal" means anything, and everything, about man having a bearing on his moral, intellectual, spiritual, responsible self. It is opposed to man considered as an "it." It cannot include any merely physical, as distinguished from human, aspect of man—nothing below the rational. Man is responsible down to the core of his being and in this responsibility relates himself, rightly or wrongly, to God and man. "Personness" excludes the notion of sin as a thing, as a "bad tooth," which is to be pulled out. Holiness is not a thing, a new mechanism, which is implanted into the sum total of personality after the subtraction of sin has been accomplished. Less than this concept would make room for an amoral, even antinomian idea of man, destroying the high and holy thing sanctification is all about.

Holiness and sin are religious terms. Holiness as love to God and man, not a state (a term Wesley was reluctant to employ because of its mechanical implications), emphasized the personal aspects of all steps in soteriology and, when consistently applied as an interpretive principle of Wesleyan theology, clarifies most of its difficult features. Man is both in history and is a personal being sustaining religious relationships to God and man. Legal, mechanical, and numerical figures of speech are just that—figures by which a spiritual, and dynamically personal, religious truth is symbolically portrayed.

3. *Dynamic*

If a man is a historical being, and a person, then *dynamic* is a proper word by which to characterize him. Man is not a lump of clay upon which are written the events of his life. He is, rather, a rational being reaching out, searching, reacting to, desiring, loving, changing, selecting and rejecting, reorganizing, maturing, making choices between alternatives—in short, a thoroughly dynamic entity. He has in some way a continuity of identity throughout the transformation, yet he is in the process of radical re-creation (at least potentially) so long as he maintains rational life. Wesley was not shackled by a static concept of man, whatever his philosophical bias might have been. Hence, terminology which would seem to refer to a static, passive being is not typical of him.

Wesley left a literature filled with ideas of man as one "in process." Yet this process was not automatic or determined but very dependent upon man's own response to life, to his fellows, and to God. He exhibited this dynamic dimension in his own life, drawing into himself and utilizing to the full the broad areas of information available in his day, for he was a relentless student and had an unlagging curiosity about God's earth. Then, in turn, he poured himself outward with all his vigor and genius into the lives of people all around him. He expected others to do the same.

> When you have attained a measure of perfect love, when God has circumcised your hearts, and enabled you to love him with all your heart and with all your soul, think not of resting there. That is impossible. You cannot stand still; you must either rise or fall; rise higher or fall lower. Therefore the voice of God to the children of Israel, to the children of God, is, "Go forward" (*Works*, VII, 202).

Whatever Wesley conceived to be the nature of man made in God's image, he was a realist, and he found St. Paul a source of help to him in this respect. He found no reason for downgrading the "earthen vessel." He felt that man must not undervalue himself.

> They who are truly meek, can clearly discern what is evil; and they can also suffer it. They are sensible of everything of this kind, but still meekness holds the reins. They are exceedingly "zealous for the Lord of hosts;" but their zeal is always guided by knowledge, and tempered, in every thought, and word, and work, with the love of man, as well as the love of God. *They do not desire to extinguish any of the passions which God has for wise ends implanted in their nature* [emphasis mine]; but they have the mastery of all: They hold them all in subjection, and employ them only in subservience to those ends. And thus *even the harsher and more unpleasing passions are applicable to the noblest purposes;* even *hatred, and anger, and fear,* when engaged against sin and *regulated by faith and love,* are as walls and bulwarks to the soul, so that the wicked one cannot approach to hurt it *(Works,* V, 263).

Neither Paul nor Wesley was insensitive to the weaknesses of human flesh—even sanctified human flesh. But neither did they give ground to those who, capitalizing on human weakness, overstated what God would do and what man could assume God would do. They tried to push Wesley to say that God does all for man without any responsibility on man's part to work with God in his salvation.

> This I dare not say: for I cannot prove it by Scripture; nay, it is flatly contrary thereto, for the Scripture is express, that (having received power from God) we are to "work out our own salvation," and that (after the work of God is begun in our souls) we are "workers together with Him" (*Works*, X, 230-31).

Speaking again of the relationship of God's grace to man's nature and responsibility, he warns against supposing that the mild-sounding virtues (such as meekness) are alterations in the basic structure of the human personality, so that no vigorous emotions remain.

> [Christian meekness] keeps clear of every extreme, whether in excess or defect. It does not destroy but balance the affections, which the God of nature never designed should be rooted out by grace, but only brought and kept under due regulations. It poises the mind aright. It holds an even scale, with regard to anger, and sorrow and fear; preserving the mean in every circumstance of life, and not "declining either to the right hand or the left" (*Works*, V, 263).

In reference to Paul's assertion in II Cor. 4:7 that "we have this treasure in earthen vessels," Wesley says in his *Notes on the New Testament,*

> We have this treasure—of Divine light, love, glory, in earthen vessels—in frail, feeble, perishing bodies. Paul proceeds to show that afflictions, yea, death itself, are so far from hindering the ministrations of the Spirit, that they even farther it, sharpen the ministers and increase the fruit, that the excellency of the power which works these in us, may undeniably appear to be of God (p. 455).

So aware was Wesley of the human problem that his extant letters are filled with most sage and remarkably contemporary advice to people, young and old, plagued with the ills so well known today. Rather than to cast doubt in the mind of the sufferer regarding his standing before God, as some less understanding spiritual counselors often do, Wesley lifted the hands which hung down and made straight paths for lame feet. In this he points to a sound attitude toward human failings which he did not call sin. Rather than human frailty being a hindrance to holiness, Wesley found it an occasion for the display of God's power to redeem broken humanity. Wesley's deep understanding of the interaction of the physical body and nerves on the total personality is revealed in a letter written to a Mrs. Bennis, dated October 28, 1771.

> As thinking is an act of an embodied spirit, playing upon a set of material keys, it is not strange that the soul can make but ill music when her instrument is out of tune. This is frequently the case with you; and the trouble and anxiety you then feel are

a natural effect of the disordered machine, which proportionately disorders the mind. But this is not all; as long as you have to wrestle, not only with flesh and blood, but with principalities and powers, wise as well as powerful, will they not serve themselves of every bodily weakness to increase the distress of the soul? But let them do as they may; let our frail bodies concur with subtle and malicious spirits; yet see that you cast not away your confidence, which hath great recompense of reward . . . where unto you have attained, hold fast; and when you feel the roughest and strongest assault, when the enemy comes in like a flood, do not (in one sense) fight with him; but sink down in the presence of your Lord, and simply look up, telling Him, "Lord, I cannot help myself; I have neither wisdom or strength for this war; but I am Thine, I am all Thine; undertake for me; let none pluck me out of Thine hands. Keep that safe which is committed to Thee, and preserve it unto that day" (*Letters*, V, 284-85).

The strange beauty of this letter is seen against Mrs. Bennis' problem, which apparently was not so much a physical ailment as it was an interpersonal tension occasioned by someone in the church who displeased her for just or imagined errors.

There is little room for doubt that Wesley would have found himself at home among those who are attempting to understand and bring solutions to the problems of modern man. At least, as we have seen, he put his hand and heart deep into the human problems of his day.

Among the contemporary problems are those that apparently rise from causes other than one's own sins: the interaction of the self with deep-seated cultural inequities; the mechanizations of society to the point of depersonalizing men, or at least cutting off the possibility of satisfying the human search for identity; the awful loneliness of men tightly packed together in overpopulated areas; the accelerated breakdown of emotional poise and wholeness under the impact of problems too great to face; the dangerous retreat into a drug culture; ecological disintegration threatening the continued existence of life on earth; the general loss of faith in a God who, to human eyes, seems not to be able or willing to do anything about war, poverty, sickness, death, and, maybe worse, the impotence of the Church to speak the prophetic and redeeming word.

Wesley was not silent in his day about the problems which fathered our own distress today. He was an evangelist *all the way*, but his evangelism had longer arms than ours and stronger hands, but more tender fingers. He knew more ways than preaching to reach the world's heart, and he reached that heart. He knew that the crisis experience, as vital as that is, was only one aspect of the process of salvaging life for God. He kept spiritual priorities in order.

In the crush of contemporary anguish, the over-simple answer is likely to prevail. The easiest to reach is what has been called the "paranoid projection," that is, projecting our own faults outward until we no longer associate them with ourselves. They then can be handled as some external power. They may be called society, "they," an unhappy childhood, the government, the Establishment, the Church, any movement or group we can pin our own fears to (Communism, Fascism, Maoism, etc.) or, to get closer to the subject of this book, "carnality." The solutions may take equally varied forms. We can excuse ourselves, and either destroy society or put another party into power. We can excise carnality and end all our troubles, or "hole up" and wait out history until the Kingdom comes down out of the sky—anything to avoid coming to grips with real issues.

Wesley's concept of the image of God did not permit him to resort to simplistic answers to human problems. The fundamental problem is sin—and no one could describe it in deeper-dyed hues —but it is the *person* who sins, not sin in the abstract. The consequences of sin go deep into human life, into society, into the fabric of the social structure, and even into physical and mental life. God's saving grace "strikes at the root" of sin, but the restructuring of broken men, broken bodies and minds, distorted society is a task God and man do together.

Terms which used to describe holiness and the victorious Christian life (and which Wesleyans borrow) may sound too idealistic for the fallible, ignorant, weak, prejudiced, temptable thing men know themselves to be. Racial effects of sin haunt the best of saints; prejudice limits the usefulness of the most dedicated Christian. Possibly no one is really free from some sort of handicapping neurosis or personality quirk. Some men are naturally buoyant, optimistic, and extrovertive (not necessarily good men). Others are subject to depression and moodiness bordering on the erratic (not necessarily all bad men).

The impulse to express love is not always strong or wisely exhibited. It is not always clear just what love is or ought to do in a given situation. Self-concern often seems to overshadow love for others—even God. Wesley himself, he tells us, suffered debilitating depressions in which he doubted he had ever been a Christian. He was wise enough to know that all of this is not inconsistent with the kind of perfection of love he tried to describe as the fulfilling of the whole law. Holiness, in Wesley's mind, was not the "possession" of any man, but was only the continued, total humble reliance of each Christian on the merits of Christ.

Nor, on the other hand, are we to live in fear and torment lest in the midst of our weakness, temptation, and depression God should leave us. Somehow the superb, unchangeable, and unchanging love of God, crowding us with its sufficiency and support, supplies the grace needed when the level of human fallibility sinks to impossibily low reserves. In fact, it is precisely a character of true holiness that it is ever more sensitive both to deviation from God's perfect law and to failure in one's own life. Holiness is the moment-by-moment impartation of the life of Christ to the human heart. In Him, not in us, is holiness.

This treasure is in earthen vessels—"pots of clay." In this, Wesley concurred. The humanness of men is not the real handicap, nor a matter for apology. Certainly it is not something to be discarded, either in this life or in the next. It is the human which is the basis for fellowship, the means for communication, the arena for displaying the reflection of the glory of God. Jesus was man, God incarnate, the *ideal* man, not idealized man. In His own person He brought God and man together and showed us what man ought to be and can be by the grace of God.

4. *Social*

The historical, personal, dynamic, human entity outlined above culminates in the fact that he is a social being. This is the most fundamental thing that can be said about man because it includes all the rest. In emphasizing the need to be in right relationship to God as an element of holiness, it is all too easy to forget the equally imperative matter of being in right relationship to men. Wesley never forgot this, at least after his "heart warming" experience, and no Wesleyanism is authentic which loses this truth.

Holiness, to Wesley, could not ignore or become insensitive to or withdraw from one's fellows. Here again the nature of love as the meaning of holiness prevailed over any ascetic or less worthy concept. The evidence for holiness, to Wesley, was the recognizable social fruits of love. And Wesley's life demonstrated his faith. He knew no holiness but social holiness, he said.

> Directly opposite to this [mysticism] is the Gospel of Christ. Solitary religion is not to be found there. "Holy Solitaries" is a phrase no more consistent with the Gospel than holy adulterers. The Gospel of Christ knows of no religion, but social; no holiness, but social holiness. Faith working by love is the length and breadth and depth and height of Christian perfection.[1]

Religion as Personal Relationship

In this light, it is our desire to illuminate another aspect of Wesley's teaching which is very easy to demonstrate but is often overlooked in applying his insights to "holiness" doctrine. This is the observation that at every point the relation between God and man is a fully personal one. By this is meant that salvation does not occur in any of its phases on sub-rational, nonmoral, substance (either corporeal or non-corporeal) levels of human existence. A key (perhaps "the" key) to this fact is, again, in the word *love*.

Love is the most personal word in human language, certainly the most personal aspect of human relations. This love is not the romantic, biological-physiological reaction of sexual response, though this is certainly not excluded in the total meaning of love. In the biblical and Hebraic sense it is the deepest motivational focus of personality. It is that centering, organizing principle which gives direction to life. It is everything the person is and *does* to find personal fulfillment. It is the dynamic of the personality. It is perhaps the only truly free thing about man. It cannot be coerced. It is no longer love, in the sense spoken of, when it is violated by external manipulation.

It is not surprising, then, that Wesley stresses love as God's relation to man, and man's relation to God and to his fellowmen. This, to him, is the key to the nature of God and to the meaning of holiness. Love touches the *quick* of rational existence. The gospel appeal, then, is grounded in this kind of divine-human interaction.

If man be in some measure free; if, by that light which "lighteneth every man that comes into the world" there be "set before him life and death, good and evil", then how gloriously does the manifold wisdom of God appear in the whole economy of man's salvation. Being willing that all men should be saved, yet not willing to force them thereto; willing that men should be saved, yet not as trees or stones, but as men, as reasonable creatures, endued with understanding to discern what is good, and liberty either to accept or refuse it; how does he suit the whole scheme of his dispensations to this his plan, "the counsel of his will"? (*Works*, X, 232).

Notice that from the very first awakening of man to his need of God the appeal is to him as a responsible person. God seems to be calling on men to leave their irresponsible childishness and to stand up in the dignity of their beings to address themselves to Him. The crucial importance of this will be seen as we progress in Wesleyan thought.

How is every part of it suited to this end! to save man, as man; to set life and death before him, and then persuade (not force) him to choose life. According to this grand purpose of God, a perfect rule is first set before him, to serve as a "lantern to his feet, and a light in all his paths." This is offered to him in a form of a law, enforced with the strongest sanctions, the most glorious rewards for them that obey, the severest penalties on them that break it. To reclaim these, God uses all manner of ways; he tries every avenue of their souls. He applies sometimes to their understanding, showing them the folly of their sins; sometimes to their affections, tenderly expostulating with them for their ingratitude, and even condescending to ask, "What could I have done for you" (consistent with my eternal purpose, not to force you) which I have not done?" He intermixes sometimes threats, —"Except ye repent, ye shall all likewise perish;" sometimes promises,—"Your sins and your iniquities will I remember no more." Now, what wisdom is seen in all this, if any man may indeed choose life or death! But if every man be unalterably consigned to heaven or hell before he comes from his mother's womb, where is the wisdom of this; of dealing with him, in every respect, as if he were free, when it is no such thing? What avails, what can this whole dispensation of God avail a reprobate?

What are promises or threats, expostulations or reproofs to thee, thou firebrand of hell? What indeed, (O my brethren, suffer me to speak, for I am full of matter) but empty farce, but mere grimace, sounding words, that mean just nothing? O where (to wave all other considerations now) is the wisdom of this proceeding? To what end does all this apparatus serve? If you say, "To insure his damnation;" alas, what needeth that, seeing this was insured before the foundation of the world. Let all mankind then judge, which of these accounts is more for the glory of God's wisdom.

Now, if man be capable of choosing good or evil, then he is a proper object of the justice of God, acquitting or condemning, rewarding or punishing. But otherwise he is not. A mere machine is not capable of being either acquitted or condemned. Justice cannot punish a stone for falling to the ground; nor, on your scheme, a man for falling into sin (*Works*, X, 233-34).

In putting all theology in the framework of the personal, Wesley anticipated the contemporary insights in hermeneutics, dialogue, and revelation. In fact, the interpersonal events in which religion, faith, meaning, knowledge, and love take place, all come out of a concept of person, and lead back to an ever enriched definition of the personal. And when this observation is made and illustrated, if not explained, the most important thing has been said about Wesley that is significant for this study.

It is the event in which a mutual interchange—Wesley calls it "intercourse"—occurs that interests Wesley.

Q. 12. *"Can faith be lost, but through disobedience?"*
A. *"It cannot.* A believer *first inwardly disobeys,* inclines to sin with his heart: *Then his intercourse with God is cut off;* that is, his faith is lost: And *after this, he may fall into outward sin* being now weak like another man" (*Works*, VII, 283).

One need only pick up and read at random any of Wesley's works to become aware of the thoroughly personal relationship which he presupposes between God and man. This is quite different from theologies which stress first the absolute sovereignty of God to the loss of the possibility of true dialogue. With Wesley, God is seeking man, creating situations to get his attention, appealing to him, cajoling him, wanting his love, and expecting his freely given fellowship.

Certainly, nothing of God's "otherness" and transcendence and sovereignty is forfeited by this relationship, and no one would defend God with greater urgency and understanding of the problems involved than Wesley would. But in the providence of God, the full measure of man's created potential is taken seriously. Man must approach the rendezvous with God with the totality of his being. He must *contribute* something to the interchange. He cannot know without giving himself. This is the meaning of intercourse. It mirrors the Old Testament expression "to know" someone. In this "knowing" the most real kind of "dialogue" is experienced. Two people, at least two, have surrendered something of their own worlds of being to the other and received in return a vital contribution which changes each essentially.

In this interpretation of Wesley a mere rejuggling of words is not the purpose. There is an attempt to say again in words and idiom of today's thought what Wesley meant—his intention—in the eighteenth century. This is what is meant, here, by "hermeneutics." Obviously, this kind of communication—dialogue—was Wesley's purpose in all he said. This mutual, interpersonal openness and receptivity and self-givingness of the parties concerned was also necessary and possible in man's knowledge of God and all that religion means in its truest sense.

This also defines *personal*. To know God, to "be saved," is to love Him—and love is the most personal thing in the world. In fact it could be said that what one loves is what one is. Love is self-giving and receiving. It is the totality of the self finding itself in the totality of another. It is not a state but a movement, a relationship; it is not a quantity but a quality; it is not a law but a life. In his *Notes*, Wesley said, "We love him because he first loved us —[I John 4:19]. This is the sum of all religion, the genuine model of Christianity. None can say more. Why should anyone say less? or less intelligibly?"

On every page of Wesley's works, dialogue "is writ large." God speaks; man responds. But also, man speaks and God listens and answers. This is not a mystical "beyond history" sort of thing but something that occurs in experience, *in* history. In the confluence of the "personness" of God and man the relationship deepens. God makes himself known and man is enabled to focalize more of his complex and growing self into the relationship. Man may begin this exciting adventure a shrivelled, pinched, prejudiced, distorted self, but in the encounter of dialogue he cannot remain small. As he opens himself to God, he opens himself to men also, and expansion and depth and transformation take place. There is no place in Wesley's thought for any God-man relationship which in its arbitrariness and "itness" (Martin Buber) violates the moral/

personal reality of mankind. It is impossible for salvation to take place—or to come into the sphere of salvation—without this beginning and ongoing self-contribution to the event.

WESLEY'S INTERPRETATION OF CHRISTIAN GRACE

Wesley's point of view clashes sharply with any approach to theology that understands God's sovereignty to negate in any way man's moral responsibility. This does not mean that man has any natural goodness or ability. Such Pelagianism was anathema to Wesley. No Calvinist could express more radically than he the depth of human sin and devilishness. But to leave the matter there would seem to contradict the gospel, which speaks to all men as if all men could hear it and take a position concerning it. If this were not the case, salvation would make man less than truly man and God's will would substitute for man's will and hence destroy it. In this view grace weakens rather than strengthens Christian manhood.

Though the title to Wesley's treatise, "Predestination Calmly Considered," sounds "cool" enough, he manages to infuse a lot of warmth into it—if not fire.

> You [Calvinists] say, The reprobates cannot but do evil: and that the elect, from the day of God's power, cannot but continue in well-doing:
> You suppose all this is unchangeably decreed; in consequence whereof, God acts irresistibly on the one, and Satan on the other. Then it is impossible for either one or the other to help acting as they do; or rather, to help being acted upon, in the manner wherein they are. For if we speak properly, neither the one nor the other can be said to act at all. Can a stone be said to act, when it is thrown out of a sling? . . . No more can a man be said to act, if he be only moved by a force he cannot resist. But if the case be thus, you leave no room either for reward or punishment. Shall the stone be rewarded for rising from the sling or punished for falling down? Shall the cannon ball be rewarded for flying towards the sun, or punished for receding from it? As incapable of either punishment or reward is the man who is supposed to be impelled by a force he cannot resist. Justice can have no place in rewarding or punishing mere machines, driven to and fro by external force. So that your supposition of God's ordaining from eternity whatsoever should be done to the end of the world; as well as that of God's acting irresistibly in the reprobates; utterly

overthrows the Scripture doctrine of rewards and punishments, as well as of a judgment to come (*Works*, X, 224).

The very character of God is involved in one's view of grace and man's responsibility as a person. Any concept of man which in any sense whatsoever robs him of "personness" is a denial of God's love as revealed in Scripture.

> So ill do election and reprobation agree with the truth and sincerity of God. But do they not agree least of all with the scriptural account of his love and goodness, that attribute which God peculiarly claims?
>
> Wherein he glories above all the rest. It is not written, "God is justice," or "God is truth"; (although he is just and true in all his ways:) But it is written, "God is love," love in the abstract, without bounds: and "there is no end of his goodness". His love extends even to those who neither love nor fear him. He is good, even to the evil and the unthankful; yea, without any exception or limitation, to all the children of men. For "the Lord is loving" (or good) "to every man, and his mercy is over all his works."
>
> But how is God good or loving to a reprobate, or one that is not elected? (You may choose either terms: for if none but the unconditionally elect are saved, it comes precisely to the same thing.) (*Works*, X, 227).

So fervently did the Wesleys believe in God's everlasting love as essential to the character of God and the reality of salvation that this belief was cast into poetic form and the theology of it burned into the fabric of every Christian as he sang theology. The following sections from *Wesley's Hymns on God's Everlasting Love* illustrate this.

I. *The Wesleyan Position*

A. *Hymn I (verses 1, 2, and 4)*

> *Father, whose everlasting love*
> *Thy only Son for sinners gave,*
> *Whose grace to all did freely move*
> *And sent Him down a world to save,*
>
> *Help us Thy mercy to extol,*
> *Immense, unfathom'd, unconfined;*
> *To praise the Lamb who died for all*
> *The general Saviour of mankind.*

> *Jesus hath said, we shall hope;*
> *Preventing grace for all is free.*
> *"And I, if I be lifted up,*
> *Will draw all men unto Me."*

B. *Hymn XVI—"Free Grace"*

> *Come let us join our friends above,*
> *The God of our salvation praise,*
> *The God of everlasting love,*
> *The God of universal grace.*
>
> *'Tis not by works that we have done;*
> *'Twas grace alone His heart inclined.*
> *'Twas grace that gave His only Son*
> *To taste of death for all mankind.*
>
> *For every man He tasted death;*
> *And hence we in His sight appear,*
> *Not lifting up our eyes beneath,*
> *But publishing His mercy here.*
>
> *By grace we draw our every breath;*
> *By grace we live, and move, and are;*
> *By grace we 'scape the second death;*
> *By grace we now Thy grace declare.*
>
> *From the first feeble thought of good*
> *To when the perfect grace is given,*
> *'Tis all of grace; by grace renew'd*
> *From hell we pass through earth to heaven.*
>
> *We need no reprobates to prove*
> *That grace, free grace, is truly free;*
> *Who cannot see that God is love,*
> *Open your eyes and look on me;*
>
> *On us, whom Jesus hath call'd forth*
> *To assert that all His grace may have,*
> *To vindicate His passion's worth*
> *Enough ten thousand worlds to save.*

John Wesley said in his *Notes*, regarding I John 4:8, "God is love":

> This little sentence brought John more sweetness than the whole world can bring. God is often styled holy, righteous, wise,

but not holiness, righteousness, or wisdom in the abstract as he is said to be love: intimating that this is . . . his reigning attribute; the attribute that sheds an amiable glory on all his other perfections.

But listen to the contrast—

II. *The Calvinistic Position*—"Horrible Decree"

A. *Hymn III*

> Surely I once believed,
>   And felt my sins forgiven;
> Thy faithful record I received,
>   That Thou hast purchased heaven
> For me and all mankind
>   Who from their sins would part;
> The peace of God I once could find,
>   The witness in my heart.
>
> But soon the subtle fiend
>   Beguiled my simple mind.
> Darkness with light he knew to blend;
>   Falsehood and truth he join'd.
> Pride (he remember'd well)
>   Had cast him from the skies;
> By pride the first transgressor fell,
>   And lost his paradise.
>
> Arm'd with this fiery dart,
>   The enemy drew nigh,
> And preach'd to my unsettled heart
>   His bold, presumptuous lie.
> "You are secure of heaven,"
>   The tempter softly says,
> "You are elect, and once forgiven,
>   Can never fall from grace.
>
> "You never can receive
>   The grace of God in vain;
> The gift, be sure, He did not give,
>   To take it back again;
> He cannot take it back,
>   Whether you use or no

His grace; you cannot shipwreck make
    Of faith, or let it go.

"God is unchangeable,
    And therefore so are you;
And therefore they can never fail
    Who once His goodness knew.
In part perhaps you may,
    You cannot wholly fall,
Cannot become a castaway
    Like non-elected Paul.

"Though you continue not,
    Yet God remains the same;
Out of His book He cannot blot
    Your everlasting name.
Cut off you shall not be;
    You never shall remove,
Secure from all eternity
    In His electing love.

"And did they fright the child,
    And tell it it might fall,
Might be of its reward beguiled,
    And sin, and forfeit all;
Might to its vomit turn,
    And wallow in the mire,
And perish in its sins, and burn
    In everlasting fire?

"Ah, poor, misguided soul!
    And did they make it weep!
Come, let me in my bosom lull
    Thy sorrows all to sleep.
Thine eyes in safety close,
    Secure from all alarms,
And take thine undisturb'd repose
    And rest within my arms.

"They shall not vex it so,
    By bidding it take heed;
You need not as a bulrush go,

> Still bowing down your head.
>> Your griefs and fears reject;
>>> My other gospel own.
>> Only believe yourself elect,
>>> And all the work is done."

B. *Hymn IX*

> "For them, and not for all mankind,
>> The Saviour of the world was given;
> Millions of souls He cast behind,
>> And only mock'd with hopes of heaven.

> "To damn the world, and not to save,
>> The Father sent His only Son,
> That none but they might pardon have,
>> They—the whole world of them alone.

> "He willeth not that all should come
>> To faith and heaven, through saving grace;
> He reprobated from the womb
>> The most of Adam's helpless race.

> "God, ever merciful and just,
>> With newborn babes did Tophet fill;
> Down into endless torments thrust,
>> Merely to show His sovereign will."

> This is that "Horrible Decree"!
>> This is that wisdom from beneath!
> God (Oh, detest the blasphemy!)
>> Hath pleasure in the sinner's death.

C. *Hymn XVII*

> Ah! gentle, gracious Dove;
>> And art Thou grieved in me,
> That sinners should restrain Thy love,
>> And say, "It is not free;
> It is not free for all;
>> The most Thou passest by,
> And mockest with a fruitless call,
>> Whom Thou hast doom'd to die"?

Oh, Horrible Decree,
  Worthy of whence it came!
Forgive their hellish blasphemy
  Who charge it on the Lamb,
Whose pity Him inclined
  To leave His throne above,
The Friend and Saviour of mankind,
  The God of grace and love.

Sinners, abhor the fiend;
  His other gospel hear—
"The God of truth did not intend
  The thing His words declare;
He offers grace to all,
  Which most cannot embrace,
Mock'd with an ineffectual call
  And insufficient grace.

"The righteous God consign'd
  Them over to their doom,
And sent the Saviour of mankind
  To damn them from the womb;
To damn for falling short
  Of what they could not do,
Or not believing the report
  Of that which was not true.

"The God of love pass'd by
  The most of those that fell,
Ordained poor reprobates to die,
  And forced them into hell."
"He did not do the deed,"
  Some have more mildly raved.
"He did not damn them—but decreed
  They never should be saved."

They think with shrieks and cries
  To please the Lord of Hosts,
And offer Thee, in sacrifice,
  Millions of slaughter'd ghosts.

With newborn babes they fill
The dire infernal shade,
For such (they say) was Thy great will,
Before the world was made.

Arise, O God, arise;
Thy glorious truth maintain;
Hold forth the bloody Sacrifice,
For every sinner slain!
Defend Thy mercy's cause,
Thy grace divinely free.
Lift up the standard of Thy cross;
Draw all men unto Thee.

Prevenient Grace

The fact of moral responsibility and man's ability to make a genuine moral choice has been established as a Wesleyan teaching in many places by many students. In our approach in this study, not only is this position important, but the corollaries to it should be emphasized. Wesley's reliance on the Arminian conviction that what freedom man has is a benefit purchased by Christ's death for us—"prevenient grace" must never be forgotten.

> We are to observe that great and important truth which ought never to be out of our remembrance: "It is God that worketh in us both to will and to do of his good pleasure." The meaning of these words may be made more plain by a small transposition of them: It is God that of his good pleasure works in you both to will and to do. This position of the words, connecting the phrase, *of his good pleasure,* removed all imagination of merit from man, and gives God the whole glory of his work. Otherwise we might have had some room for boasting, as if it were our own desert, some goodness in us, or some good thing done by us, which first moved God to work. But his expression cuts off all such vain conceits and clearly shows his motive to work lay wholly in himself, in his own mere grace, in his unmerited grace (*Works,* VI, 508).

● ● ●

> Seeing all men are by nature not only sick, but "dead in trespasses and sins," it is not possible for them to do anything well till God raises them from the dead. . . . It is impossible for us to come out of our sins, yea, or to make the least motion toward it,

till He who hath all power in heaven and earth call our dead souls into life. . . .

Yet this is no excuse for those who continue in sin, and lay the blame upon their Maker saying, "It is only God that must quicken us; for we cannot quicken our own souls. For allowing that all the souls of men are dead in sin by *nature,* this excuses no one, seeing that there is no man that is in a state of mere nature; there is no man, unless he has quenched the Spirit, that is wholly devoid of the grace of God. No man living is entirely destitute of what is vulgarly called *Natural conscience.* But this is not natural: It is more properly called *preventing grace.* Every man has some measure of that light . . . which lightens every man that comes into the world. And every one . . . feels more or less uneasy when he acts contrary to the light of his own conscience. So that no man sins because he has not grace, but because he does not use the grace which he hath. . . .

Even St. Augustine, who is generally supposed to favour the contrary doctrine, makes that just remark, *Qui fecit nos sine nobis, non salvabit nos sine nobis;* "He that made us without ourselves, will not save us without ourselves" (*Ibid.,* pp. 511-13).

HOLINESS AS PERSONAL RELATIONSHIP

These are the insights regarding man's nature under grace which made it possible for Wesley to "preach holiness," and thereby to make the mark on the Church and in his world which has transcended his own denomination and age, and continues to challenge the Church to explore the deeper depths of the possibilities of grace. No Wesleyanism should be judged negatively or positively without recognizing this approach to an interpretation of Wesley.

It must be granted that Wesley's theology as a systematic whole lacks the logical consistency one could hope to find. This is not a reflection on his ability or intellectual integrity. Wesley was an Anglican divine, but the impact of his religious conversion introduced dynamic elements into his thinking which necessarily put new emphases on formal theology. One dare not forget the nonconformist influence of his mother, the deeply spiritual emphasis of the mystics, and his own dynamic personal experience at Aldersgate. John Deschner says it well in his *Wesley's Christology.*

Wesley did not receive on May 24, 1738 . . . a brand-new theology direct from heaven. Rather the old theology was reborn that night. The influence that led him to seek salvation for his own soul was cut off its old tree and grafted onto a new one. The old branch never lost its character, but the nourishing roots and sap and fruit were new.[2]

Wesley was sensitive at this point.

> A serious Clergyman desired to know, in what points we differed from the Church of England. I answered, "To the best of my knowledge, in none. The doctrines we preach are the doctrines of the Church of England; indeed, the fundamental doctrines of the Church, clearly laid down, both in her Prayers, Articles, and Homilies" (*Works*, I, 224-25).

Theology infused with a personal experience of God's grace— this is Wesleyanism. We cannot account for Wesley by viewing him through his theological background but we may understand his theological journey (for such it was) through his experience of grace. The new dimension of the possibility of a personal appropriation of the benefits of the atonement gradually reacted back on formal theology and, in Wesley's case, there was neither time nor desire to iron out all the details of theology into a new system. It is not our intention to derive a "theology of sanctification" from Wesley's works but rather to apply Wesley's dynamic spiritual insights to Christian theology and interpret it accordingly. Wesley's "heart warming" was not the fruit of a theological concept of sanctification, but sanctification received a new meaning as the warmed heart partook of the reality of which theology spoke.

The warmed heart provided that new dimension to theology which we are calling the personal dimension, and the several aspects described above form a unit—a principle of interpretation which should help in defining Wesleyanism.

These insights and points of view lie as a foundation of thought under the Wesleyan presentation of the gospel. They are a unit of interpretation, a theory of criticism. Wesley's fundamental point of view, the characteristic which made it identifiable from other points of view, is the conviction that man's relationship to God and God's relation to man is a personal relationship and that all facets of theology and life partake of this personal nature and must be interpreted in this light. He felt that this way of thinking was biblical and did justice to what he knew about human nature and total personal experience—his own and others.

"Holiness doctrine" which claims to be truly Wesleyan (as well as any social concern which is said to derive from this), must rest its case on and interpret its viewpoint from the total Wesleyan intention. This is in keeping with Wesley's own principles. Intention, to him, was of primary importance, not only in a faithful interpretation of what other men said and what Scripture teaches, but in respect also of the motive underlying human action which characterizes it as right or wrong.

The question, now, is this: Why Wesley? Was he right? Is he a theological authority? The answer must be that it is only as Wesley, in recovering the dynamic of theological sanctification (as Luther recovered the dynamic of justification), leads us to the proper source of truth and illuminates that truth that he is a reliable leader.

With this background as an underlying principle of interpretation it is now possible to apply this principle to the Wesleyan doctrine to determine its validity and to reinterpret, if necessary, any faulty concepts which may have slipped into the understanding of it. In every case we shall be concerned to appeal to the Authority which Wesley recognized as the final appeal—the Scriptures.

A total systematic theology is not the goal of this study. Such is not the immediate need, nor is it within the competence of this author. The need, as we see it, is to apply the basic Wesleyan concepts to several of the doctrines particularly emphasized by Wesleyans, to discover any inconsistencies, and to bring harmony and strength and winsomeness to the faith we declare.

John Wesley's Dynamic—Love

The summarizing word—Wesley's ultimate hermeneutic— is *love*. Every strand of his thought, the warm heart of every doctrine, the passion of every sermon, the test of every claim to Christian grace, was love. So central is love that to be "Wesleyan" is to be committed to a theology of love.

CHAPTER VI

Man, Made in the Image of God

What Is Man?

What man thinks of man determines in a large measure how he relates himself to his earth and to his fellows. Religious and social systems, governments and institutions, as well as technological manipulation and "fabrication" of human genetics (see Paul Ramsey's *Fabricated Man,* Yale University Press, 1970, and William Kuhn's *Environmental Man,* Harper and Row, 1969) fall into the mold of man's self-understanding, for better or for worse.

As the mysteries of the earth and the entire universe are pushed back and man becomes more and more the master of his domain, it is said by some that he has less and less need for religion and prayer and God. The claim is that religion is a carry-over from the childhood of the race, prayer is no longer the way to get the things that we have now learned to get for ourselves, and, anyway, God is dead. But the consequences of this philosophy are already "backfiring." Man has set in motion forces he did not foresee and cannot control. Orphaned and frightened, he is looking out toward the occult, and into the depths of his own psyche, for direction. He is attempting to "expand" his mind by drugs, to communicate with his fellows by breaking down the walls of privacy and self-identity—trying desperately to break his way out of his self-built prison into the meaning he lost when he dismissed God.

The more man becomes the master of nature, the less he knows about himself—the less he is his own master. Today, the one great mystery is man himself. What is this creature on earth which is most restless and curious and discontented and disenchanted as he becomes more and more mature and intelligent and educated? *Things* do not satisfy him. His capacity for creativity and his un-shackled spiritual hunger drive him out of the comfortable nest he laboriously builds around himself and his family. He is too big for what he is able to build. He shrugs off the achievements of his hand and brain. He chafes against his own affluence. At his best, he lifts his face to the great unknown and burns out his energies reaching for new heights of discovery that never satisfy him. He must always disdain what he can conquer. He will always plant impatient feet on the accomplishments of the past and leap reck-lessly toward the mysteries beyond.

Man seems to be structured in a way that compels him to reach out beyond himself for fulfillment with relentless imperative. He dies in moral rottenness when this impulse is turned inward or earthward only. He does not possess fulfillment. He can never possess it. Fulfillment is always something just beyond him and which in its pursuit enlarges and fills and intrigues and calls and excites him. Fulfillment is not in achievement but in the process of achieving. He grows as he looks outward and there seems to be no limit to this growth.

What kind of creature is this? What is man?

In this study we seek to understand more fully the biblical concepts regarding the nature of man. Only as we understand something of him can we understand God.

When we seek to elaborate a Christian doctrine of man, we become aware that the Scriptures say very much *to* man but so little directly *about* him. In deducing something "Christian" about man, it will be necessary to catch "on the fly" those things said to him, and interpret as well as we can what kind of creature it would be that could make sense out of the things said to him. Sydney Cave has expressed it well, "There is no Christian doctrine of man, and yet there is a Christian estimate of man"[1] It is that estimate that we seek, for in its light we should be better able to read the Bible meaningfully and find any answer it may have to the most acute and universal problems of mankind.

There are some things we do know about ourselves—about "man." It may be well to begin there.

He is, first of all, a creature who uses language to convey ideas. By means of a rational language he can and does communicate with other creatures. The very fact of written records silently but powerfully says something tremendously profound about man. We have called it intelligence. The Bible is directed to man as a medium of communication on the rational plane.

That man is capable of entering into meaningful "dialogue" with God where self-disclosure is mutually exchanged points to a quality in man which is religious, not merely superstitious. The Bible is a conversation between God and man. It is possible and desirable to enter that conversation and become a participant in it.

The fact of sin as a voluntary act, a moral defection, is an eloquent commentary on the biblical estimate of man. The fundamental fact is the moral nature and freedom which is the heritage of mankind. We are not driven by blind impulse. We are not bound to the narrow limits of physical survival and the shallow search for comfort and approval. We are not Christian or non-Christian because of some supernatural decree about which we have no choice. We have the inestimable privilege of guiding our affections and deliberating our loyalties, of sharing our love or withholding it. Though sin is not necessary to moral freedom, as Nels Ferré says, "Rebellion against God is necessary at some point in our lives if we are to become free sons, glorifying him out of love and gratitude."[2] There is a profound truth lying at the heart of Ferré's insight, namely, that it is only in the fact of a *possibility of rebellion* that true moral integrity can exist.

In a word, man made in God's image seems to refer to whatever there is about man that makes it possible to experience any communication with another intelligent being, and particularly to establish a rapport with God—or to reject that fellowship.

"CHRISTIAN" MAN

There have been two main theories about man and God's image in Christian history, the substantial and the relational.

The substance theory is based on the idea that something *in* man can be identified as the image of God. The "image of God *in* man" is the typical expression. Then, either a corporeal substance, or some function of the human person (such as reason, a divine spark, creative ability), or being in possession of a spirit as well as a soul and a body, distinguishes man from nonhuman beings. The loss of the *Imago Dei,* in this view, does not change the "manners" of man but does constitute a loss of whatever it is that relates man to God. If the image is restored, it would have to constitute a replacement of whatever is conceived to be lost, whether corporeal or non-corporeal.

Logical development in this theology leads to the very nonspiritual and nonmoral interpretations of soteriology which Wesley opposed. In projecting this theory into the practical approach to the Christian life, as today's holiness theology often does, the source of some of the "credibility gaps" became very obvious. The most serious problem is that some sincere Christians expect a real numerical addition to personality, either a new "spirit," or the Holy Spirit. Out of this a nest of problems arises relative to when this occurs, how one knows it has occurred, the relation of sinful humanity to the new addition, and the status of the person before God. Is a man more perfect with this addition or is he actually a part of Deity now that the Spirit of God indwells him? And could such a person sin?

The *relational view* stresses a completely different approach to the subject. There is no need to find some entity, feature, or function in man which identifies him as man. This is not always convincing in any case. It is *man before God* and the communication between them, the mutual response, the relation of one to the other, the mirroring of one in the other that points to the meaning.

Wesley said, "Man is capable of God" (*Works*, VI, 244). It is a "posture," an inner attitude toward God, a fundamental position one takes toward God and His will. Man made "in the image of God" (the biblical wording) distinguishes this view from "the image of God in man," which is typical of the substance concept.

WESLEY'S UNDERSTANDING OF MAN

Wesley did not speculate about the "image." He was content to see man in terms of religion. His statements relative to the image usually were in reference to some factor in the saving procedure. We probably never find Wesley speaking of what man might be ontologically. That which is involved, then, in any discussion of the *Imago Dei* in Wesley will be found to be a spiritual quality. The "image" is a religious matter, not a substance matter.

What is conceived to be the meaning of the image of God and man's relation to it sets the direction of soteriology. Wesley's theology cannot be properly evaluated without at least an introduction to his approach to this concept.

WESLEY'S CONCEPT OF MAN
AS DISTINGUISHED FROM NATURE

Now, "man was made in the image of God." But "God is a Spirit;" So therefore was man. (Only that spirit, being designed to dwell on earth, was lodged in an earthly tabernacle.) As such, he had an innate principle of self-motion. And so, it seems, has every spirit in the universe; this being the proper distinguishing difference between spirit and matter, which is totally, essentially passive and inactive, as appears from a thousand experiments. He was, after the likeness of his creator, endued with understanding; a capacity of apprehending whatever objects were brought before it, and of judging concerning them. He was endued with a will, exerting itself in various affections and passions: And, lastly, with liberty, or freedom of choice; without which all the rest would have been in vain, and he would have been no more capable of serving his Creator than a piece of earth, or marble; he would have been as incapable of vice or virtue, as any part of the inanimate creation. . . .

His understanding was perfect in its kind; capable of apprehending all things clearly, and judging concerning them according to truth, without any mixture of error. His will had no wrong bias of any sort; but all his passions and affections were regular, being steadily and uniformly guided by the dictates of his unerring understanding; embracing nothing but good, and every good in proportion to its degree of intrinsic goodness. His liberty likewise was wholly guided by his understanding: He chose, or refused, according to its direction. Above all, (which was his highest excellence, far more valuable than all the rest put together,) he was a creature capable of God; capable of knowing, loving, and obeying his Creator. And, in fact, he did know God, did unfeignedly love and uniformly obey him. This was the supreme perfection of man; (as it is of all intelligent beings;) the continually seeing, and loving, and obeying the Father of the spirits of all flesh (*Works*, VI, 242-43).

WESLEY'S CONCEPT OF MAN
AS A RELIGIOUS CREATURE

In the image of God was man made, holy as he that created him is holy; merciful as the Author of all is merciful; perfect as his Father in heaven is perfect. As God is love, so man, dwelling in love, dwelt in God, and God in him. God made him to be an "image of his own eternity," an incorruptible picture of the God of glory. He was accordingly pure, as God is pure, from every spot of sin. He knew not evil in any kind or degree, but was inwardly and outwardly sinless and undefiled. He "loved the Lord his God with all his heart, and with all his mind, and soul, and strength."

To man thus upright and perfect, God gave a perfect law, to which he required full and perfect obedience. He required full obedience in every point, and this to be performed without any intermission, from the moment man became a living soul, till the time of his trial should be ended. No allowance was made for any falling short: As, indeed, there was no need of any; man being altogether equal to the task assigned, and thoroughly furnished for every good word and work.

To the entire law of love which was written in his heart, (against which, perhaps, he could not sin directly,) it seemed good to the sovereign wisdom of God to superadd one positive law: "Thou shalt not eat of the fruit of the tree that groweth in the midst of the garden;" annexing that penalty thereto, "In the day that thou eatest thereof, thou shalt surely die" (*Works*, V, 54).

WESLEY'S CONCEPT OF THE "LOST IMAGE"

Accordingly, in that day he did die: He died to God,—the most dreadful of all deaths. He lost the life of God: He was separated from Him, in union with whom his spiritual life consisted. The body dies when it is separated from the soul; the soul, when it is separated from God. But this separation from

God, Adam sustained in the day, the hour, he ate of the forbidden fruit. And of this he gave immediate proof; presently showing by his behavior, that the love of God was extinguished in his soul, which was now "alienated from the life of God." Instead of this, he was now under the power of servile fear, so that he fled from the presence of the Lord. Yea, so little did he retain even of the knowledge of Him who filleth heaven and earth, that he endeavoured to "hide himself from the Lord God among the trees of the garden:" (Gen. iii. 8:). So had he lost both the knowledge and the love of God, without which the image of God could not subsist. Of this, therefore, he was deprived at the same time, and became unholy as well as unhappy. In the room of this, he had sunk into pride and self-will, the very image of the devil; and into sensual appetites and desires, the image of the beasts that perish (*Works*, VI, 67-68).

WESLEY'S CONCEPT OF THE IMAGE OF GOD AS LOVE AND RIGHTEOUSNESS

Righteousness, as was observed before, is the image of God, the mind which was in Christ Jesus. It is every holy and heavenly temper in one; springing from, as well as terminating in, the love of God, as our Father and Redeemer, and the love of all men for his sake (*Works*, V, 267).

The most eloquent and revealing commentary on Wesley's concept emerges out of what he considered to be necessary for salvation, the condition of man and what grace did for him.

While a man is in a mere natural state, before he is born of God, he has, in a spiritual sense, eyes but sees not; a thick impenetrable veil lies upon them; he has ears, but hears not; he is utterly deaf to what he is most of all concerned to hear. His other spiritual senses are all locked up: He is in the same condition as if he had them not. Hence he has no knowledge of God . . . either of spiritual or eternal things; therefore, though he is a living man, he is a dead Christian. But as soon as he is born of God, there is a total change in all these particulars. . . .

Wherefore, to what end, is it necessary that we should be born again? It is very easily discerned, that this is necessary. First, in order to holiness. For what is holiness according to the oracles of God? Not a bare external religion, a round of outward duties, how many soever they be, and how exactly soever performed. No: Gospel holiness is no less than the image of God stamped upon the heart; it is no other than the whole mind which was in Christ Jesus; it consists of all heavenly affections and tempers mingled together in one. It implies such a continual, thankful love to Him who hath not withheld from us his Son, his only Son, as makes it natural, and in a manner necessary to us, to love every child of man; as fills us "with bowels of mercies, kindness, gentleness, long-suffering:" It is such a love of God as teaches us to be blameless in all manner of conversation; as all we have, all our thoughts, words and actions a continual sacrifice to God, acceptable through Christ Jesus. Now, this holiness can have no existence till we are renewed in the image of our mind. It cannot commence in the soul till that change be wrought; till, by the power of the Highest overshadowing us, we are "brought from darkness to light, from the power of Satan unto God;" That is, till we are born again; which, therefore, is absolutely necessary in order to holiness (*Works*, VI, 70-72).

WESLEY'S CONCEPT OF THE IMAGE OF GOD AND SANCTIFICATION

"What is it to be sanctified?" was the subject of discussion on June 26, 1744. His answer, "To be renewed in the image of God, in righteousness and true holiness" (*Works*, VIII, 279). The next question and answer shed some light on this.

Q. "Is faith the condition, or the instrument, of sanctification?"
A. "It is both the condition and instrument of it. When we begin to believe, then sanctification begins. And as faith increases, holiness increases, till we are created anew (*Ibid.*).

In this passage the process aspect of sanctification is clearly indicated.

With the historic concepts undoubtedly in his mind, Wesley carefully divided "image" into its possible categories. He distinguished *natural image* (the spiritual nature), *political image* (his governing commission), and his *moral image* (holy love). It was this third aspect of man that engaged his attention and must be understood as his use of the term "image" is encountered.

THE IMAGE OF GOD AS LOVE

In this image of God was man made. "God is love:" Accordingly, man at his creation was full of love; which was the sole principle of all his tempers, thoughts, words, and actions. God is full of justice, mercy, and truth; so was man as he came from the hands of his Creator. God is spotless purity; and so man was in the beginning pure from every sinful blot (*Works*, VI, 66).

This will highlight the following quotation in which the meaning of salvation is set over against the meaning of the image of God.

> By salvation I mean, not barely, according to the vulgar notion, deliverance from hell, or going to heaven; but a present deliverance from sin, a restoration of the soul to its primitive health, its original purity; a recovery of the divine nature; the renewal of our souls after the image of God, in righteousness and true holiness, in justice, mercy, and truth. This implies all holy and heavenly tempers, and, by consequence, all holiness of conversation.
>
> Now, if by salvation we mean a present salvation from sin, we cannot say, holiness is the condition of it; for it is the thing itself. Salvation, in this sense, and holiness, are synonymous terms. We must therefore say, "We are saved by faith." Faith is the sole condition of this salvation. For without faith we cannot be thus saved. But whosoever believeth is saved already.
>
> Without faith we cannot be thus saved; for we cannot rightly serve God unless we love him. And we cannot love him unless we know him; neither can we know God unless by faith. Therefore, salvation by faith is only, in other words, the love of God by the knowledge of God, or, the recovery of the image of God, by a true, spiritual acquaintance with him (*Works*, VII, 47-48).

John Wesley's concept of the image of God as love puts both man and love in a dynamic framework and bears significantly on his position regarding sanctification and Christian perfection. The passages cited already indicate a very different emphasis than some "Wesleyanisms" project. In a word, holiness was to Wesley the recovery of the image of God. That image was love characterized by Christlikeness. His concern was that men should begin to orient their total experience as responsible Christians about Christ as Lord. The dynamic aspect of redemption, without at all neglecting the crisis points, was Wesley's constant emphasis. This contrasts rather radically with some contemporary "holiness" teaching and preaching that majors in concern about the crisis aspects almost entirely.

It will be our task now to search diligently in Scripture for the approach to man and his redemption which ought to characterize any theology claiming to be biblical, as Wesleyanism does claim. The following biblical studies may seem to be tedious and unnecessarily detailed for the kind of book this is. But any *selectivity* of biblical passages could be interpreted as "proof-texting." When every word or thought regarding any point under discussion is explored, the whole picture is drawn in and a more objective conclusion made feasible.

We will first look into the Old Testament for instructive hints. In the Genesis accounts more is included than usually meets the eye. A survey will be made of the meaning in the Hebrew and Greek of the terms "image" and "likeness." This leads to important theological conclusions.

MAN OF DUST, MADE IN THE IMAGE OF GOD

The Genesis account of the advent of mankind (Adam-man) is far more eloquent and significant than a casual reading of the passage in English might suggest. In this majestic "Poem of the Dawn" or "Hymn of Creation" (cf. H. Orton Wiley, *Christian Theology*, Vol. I, Nazarene Publishing House, Kansas City, Mo., pp. 450 ff.), the metaphorical use of the terms "dust," "image," "likeness," "create," "made," "breath of life," and others, contributes much to biblical understanding of man, sin, redemption, holiness, and all the implications of "grace" in relation to man.

The writer of the Genesis story chose his words carefully. In 1:26 he tells us that God said, "Let us *make* man in our image after our likeness," and (1:27) then, "God *created* man in his own image . . . male and female created he them." Strangely, the second account (Genesis 2) introduces a most mundane and earthy note to the almost too idealistic and incredible first description. "The Lord God *formed* man of dust from the ground, and breathed into his nostrils the breath of life ['lives,' Hebrew plural, here]; and man became a living being" (Gen. 2:7; RSV). Note the progress; *formed, breathed into,* and then the process of *becoming.* There will be no attempt made here to formulate any theory of man's appearance on earth. These terms are noted to suggest that the wording gives room for more than one interpretation.

However, no attempt to interpret these passages from the standpoint of modern science should be permitted to obscure the main ideas proposed in Genesis 1—2. This is not a scientific account nor was it in any sense intended to be. The role of science is to unpack all the facts possible which are built into man and his history and world. But the *meaning* of man and his universe must be derived from another source. And it is this meaning that the biblical story seeks to impart. This starkly beautiful, unembroidered introduction to man as made in his Creator's image establishes the fundamental religious meaning of man as he stands in relationship to God and to nature. This noble concept must precede and throw light upon all that the Hebraic-Christian teaching will assume about man—a sinful creature as of now, yet created in the *Imago Dei.*

But this is only half the story. Left here, there would be no understanding of man as he is. Surely experience proves that man is not God—and his most despicable moments occur when he mistakes his role in life and attempts to be God. Man, made in God's image but "formed of dust," puts the two paradoxical truths together and in this creative tension man can begin to understand himself and live not only toward the fullness of his potential but also within most definite limitations. Only by keeping these two foci in perspective can a biblical understanding of man, his freedom and his bondage, his holiness and his sin, his unimaginable and largely untapped potential and his weakness and defeats, be approximated and an intelligible assessment be made of that most mysterious and complex creature, man.

Gen. 1:27 and 2:7 need not be considered contradictory. Each account contributes an insight about humanity that would be impossible for any single symbol to suggest about the majestic, corruptible, redeemable, ignorant, fallible, creative, sinful being that man is.

The term "dust" is highly significant. The Old Testament use of the word comes about as close to a philosophical concept as can be found in Hebrew thought. Dust, with its characteristic of formlessness and tenuous particles, stood for disintegration, dissociation, mourning, death—the "many" in absolute distinction from "the One," the Divine Unity.[3] "Dust is the very figure of death, the final outcome of decay, an object of disgust and abomination."[4]

A Jew's response to personal, family, or national bereavement, disaster, or disgrace was to clothe himself in sackcloth and throw dust and ashes over his head. In no more eloquent way could he say, "God has forsaken me. Life is falling apart. Woe is me!"

God cursed the offending "serpent" for his part in man's defection, by condemning it to crawling in the dust, and eating dust (Gen. 3:14). Nothing could be more significant of the ultimate degradation, decadence, rejection implicit in sin.

Man himself, made in God's image, would ever be reminded of his sin and constant need of God's mercy by the mournful divine "sentence" delivered against him. "You will return to the ground, for out of it you were taken; you are dust," precisely because it separated him from the unifying power of life and the solidarity of his social nexus. To him death was not necessarily extinction but disintegration, separation, loneliness, darkness. Death did not liberate him from the sorry prison of his body, for he knew nothing of an existence of his spirit denuded of flesh. Death was something that happened to *him* as a whole man.

But final redemption is to be in connection with this "man of dust," who shall be taken up into eternal life, where death has no sting nor the grave victory (see I Cor. 15:49). This completes the story begun at man's genesis. Made of dust, he will experience the full dynamic of eternal life in the Son through the resurrection of the body.

Dust stands in absolute contrast to the unity of personality which the Old Testament everywhere assumes. Life, divine life, takes up dust to transform it into a living thing. This is Hebrew "materialism." Hebrew man did not despise himself, his work, his world, because God's breath was in all created things. When God's breath, or Spirit, withdrew, then what was left was death, and dust. But he understood that "dust is not the cause of death, it is death which fathers dust."[5]

Sin is the source of disintegration and death and dust. A moral meaning lay at the heart of reality.

Dust is not a preexistent entity. It is not a power. It is not "antimatter," discreativity, a principle of being or non-being. God only is the Principle of being. He is Life and Power. Death simply is to be outside His hand. To be made of dust, then, was not a metaphysical affirmation about man's "substance," but a religious faith about God, who formed him of that which had no power in itself to produce life.

Man "made from the dust" but "in God's image" emphasizes two important concepts of man which will be instructive throughout our biblical study of man. He is a creature of the earth with a "natural history." His body is shared with the natural order. He is *in history*, a part of it. This must never be forgotten.

But he is also a "living being" of a different order from the animate life below him. His life transcends the life of animals in a way that is simply described, not explained.

Genesis 2 tells us in its most unique and symbolic way some important things about man. In Genesis 1, man is the highest order of creation and the final creature to appear. This is a "natural history" of the earth, the order of which is confirmed by most modern scientific theory. Genesis 2 is basically an interpretation of the *meaning* of man, and the entire order of creation is reversed in order to focalize attention on man himself and on his moral and spiritual relationship to the earth. In this chapter we follow man's awakening to his world. We watch the dawn of self-consciousness, conscience, and social awareness. Buried in the strange imagery of the account is a profound psychological history and analysis. If one does not over-literalize the highly significant and sophisticated symbolism, and thereby lose in "woodenness" a sensitive and eloquent revealing, a picture of human wholeness and health—physical, moral, and spiritual—emerges. It is the history of what it means to be a spiritual being.

1. First of all, man is a body. Though formed of dust, it is "the *sine qua non* condition of all human thought."[6]

One cannot think without a body, and language and communication (the unique powers of the human person) depend upon thinking. By means of this body-thought-language complex, and only by this means, is the essential avenue established by which communication is possible between God and man. And only in this way is understanding possible.

2. Understanding, in the second place, depends upon man as a dynamic being. His most elementary sensations are active, not passive. Consciousness is "intentional," a breaking out toward the world.[7]

Man grasps the "given" through his senses. He selects, examines, masters his environment. "The act of understanding is not actualized, *does not* exist, without movement."[8]

Man is a dynamic being, and in the light of this fact, Adam "discovered" his world as if it were a new creation. It was pleasant, beautiful, fruitful, satisfying. In it were life (the "tree of life") and knowledge ("tree of the knowledge of good and evil"). To work in it and keep it was not drudgery but his delight.

3. The next dimension of human consciousness was a personal perspective beyond himself. Man could commune with God. In this communication came a moral dimension which must always accompany the intelligible relationship of rational creatures. Fellowship must always respect the uniqueness and identity of the other—a guard against the loss of fellowship and the suffering of alienation. Spirituality matures in a right relationship to God. The moral law guarded that basic fact of man's existence. It did not violate his freedom. Law was protective, not restrictive.

4. The fourth level of human self-understanding is presented as man's need for human fellowship—another dimension of spirituality. Man is a social being. Although the individual in the Old Testament could be as truly an individualist as any twentieth-century personality, the very conception of "individuality" was foreign to his thought. To be alone, to be separated from one's kind, and to live without contact with other men, that was the ultimate fear of Old Testament man.[9] Adam and Eve complemented each other, something no animal could do for man. Together they would take dominion of the earth. Together they would multiply their own bodies to populate the earth. Together they would meet temptation and finally yield to it. This social cohesion was so strong that whole families took on the identity of the "head," a pyramid as solid as a mountain. If that "head" sinned, all were considered guilty of the sin of the one (see story of Achan), and suffered a common punishment. "Pure individualism is a modern phenomenon,"[10] Western at that, a fact that often distorts our biblical interpretation when it is not well understood and guarded from extremes. The "corporate personality" concept is important to biblical thought.

It would be quite foolish to be offended by the rich symbolism of the biblical creation story. How better could so much be said so simply and be so universally understood?

To summarize in a bit different way, it could be said that Genesis 2 tells us in its symbolic way (1) that man was superior to the animals in intelligence, insight, self-understanding, purpose, and spirituality; (2) that he is essentially a social being, a society (male and female); and (3) that his world, the earth, is his home, his domain, his palace; but (4) that he himself is the very shrine of God (in this is his distinction from all other orders of creation, his glory, and then the bitterness of his shame); (5) that in mankind there is the constant poignant reminder of his fallibility. "He knows our frame; he remembers that we are dust" (Ps. 103:14, RSV). But being dust does not itself constitute him sinful. It is not dust that predominates, but the breath of God, by virtue of which dust is lifted to dignity and man then stands in a relation to his Master so akin to Him as to make him a companion to God—a relation both treasured and terrible.

In the light of these considerations the significance of "man created in God's image" can better be grasped and more surely be "rescued" from Pelagian humanism, and the fallibility of man "made of dust" be "rescued" from an extreme Augustinian pessimism regarding man as totally depraved. It should also be possible to see the importance of the incarnation of Christ to mankind, and to history, in a more profound light than is often the case. Eternal life, not as a temporal dimension, but as a quality of "personness," as integration in contrast to death, can be put into a meaningful context if our interpretation of these Genesis symbolisms is reasonably correct.

IMAGE AND LIKENESS

We must now ask questions about the meaning of man made in God's image if a useful understanding of biblical psychology and a relevant theology are to be obtained. The question arises whether *image* and *likeness* are to be regarded as a simple, meaningless Hebrew parallelism or whether some helpful distinction is indicated which could be valuable in understanding man and his development, his sin and recovery from the Fall. Catholic theology has traditionally taken the position that *image* and *likeness* are distinctly different. The *image*, interpreted as sanctifying grace, a supernatural gift, though lost, can be restored in baptism. The apparent substance concept of this "gift," unessential to man as a true human person, has made Protestantism wary of this view. It is possible, however, to interpret both *image* and *likeness* in other ways, more truly biblical.

A. *Hebrew Word Study*

1. *Image*

"God said, 'Let us make man in our image, after our likeness . . . So God created man in his own image, in the image of God he created him; male and female he created them" (Gen. 1:26-27, RSV). It would be possible to conclude that the words *image* and *likeness* simply follow the well-known Hebrew pattern of parallelism in poetic literature were it not for the very specific distinctions in the use of these terms in the Old Testament. The Septuagint carefully preserves these distinctions and the New Testament writers maintain them. To deny or affirm the distinction on theological grounds would not be permissible in a soundly biblical study; but if a distinction is warranted, a theological consequence might follow. Or, at least, some light might be shed on certain theological affirmations.

According to Gesenius,[11] the word translated "image" *(çelem)* is a cognate of the verb *(çālam)*, "to be shady or dark." From this concept of *shade*, the idea of *shadow* developed. A shadow then, being the dark portion cast in the outline of the original object, was an image. Gesenius referred to the Greek word *skía* as a proper synomyn, which Thayer said was "an image cast by an object and representing the form of that object."[12]

After the reference to man as being made in the "image of God" in Gen. 9:6, in no other place in the Old Testament does *image* refer to man again. In every other case it is used as a representation of persons or things in some concrete form, as idols, hewn or molten. There were images of things (I Sam. 6:5, 11), of men (Ezek. 16:17; 23:14), and of gods (Num. 33:52; II Kings 11:18; Ezek. 7:20).

Only in the creation account in Genesis 1 and the recapitulation of it in Genesis 5 (with the added statement regarding Seth's relationship to Adam, and an exhortation against taking human life, Gen. 9:6) is the term used of man in relation to his Maker. *Image* everywhere in Old Testament usage, carries the idea of a concrete substance representing some idea or prototype. It is definite conformity to a pattern or mold.

2. *Likeness*

Likeness stands in contrast to this idea, having in it more the thought of comparison, imitation, or becoming. A. B. Davidson said it meant "to be or become like (in the Niphil), to resemble (in the Piel), to compare with or become like."[13] To liken in one's mind, to imagine, to think (Ps. 50:21; Isa. 10:7), to purpose (Isa. 14:24), to remember (Ps. 48:10) are some of the Old Testament uses of the term. *Likeness* in most other cases in the Old Testament is used to introduce a figure of speech, not intended to equate the pair but to show points of comparison. For example, "like unto . . . beryl" (Ezek. 1:16), "like the poison of a serpent" (Ps. 58:4), "like . . . a lion" (Ps. 17:12), "like a roe" (Song of Sol. 2:9, 17).

Other usages follow as obviously: "What likeness will ye compare unto [God]?" (Isa. 40:18); "Out of the midst . . . came the likeness of . . . creatures (Ezek. 1:5). As with the word *image*, so with *likeness* in that no reference relates it to the Genesis account of creation. Once only (Isa. 14:14) the "son of the morning" was said to have declared he would be "like the most High," but the context makes it quite clear that his aspiration was not to become God, but was a challenge to His position as the Sovereign of the universe. He wished to usurp the authority of God and become a substitute for God. Perhaps this passage best leads our thinking into the heart of the matter.

Even the prepositions serve to distinguish between *image* and *likeness*. The *be* (in) in *beçalmēnū* (Gen. 1:26) primarily denotes the being and remaining in a place. The original form is here conceived of as the rule or standard within which a copy is kept.[14] The *ke* (as, like, as if) in *kedemūthēnū* denotes resemblance—"like a flock of sheep" (Job 21:11).[15]

B. *Septuagint Word Study*

Continuing the investigation through the Septuagint translation of the Hebrew scriptures into Greek, the discovery was made that for *çelem* the ancient Greek scholars had put *eikōn* and for *demūth*, *homoíosis* (*Vetus Testamentum Graece*, Lipsiae Sumtipus Ernesti Bredtii, 1868). These translations and distinctions are consistently held throughout the entire Old Testament (according to Gesenius and Thayer and others).

C. Greek Word Study

1. Image

The word *eikón* (image) in classical Greek usage came up through an interesting history. On the Rosetta stone it is used to designate a statue *(eikóna)* of Ptolemy which was being built.[16] In other early records it was used for the description of individuals in official documents. Thieme has well pointed out how the ancient practice of erecting images *(eikónes)* of their gods would give significance to such New Testament passages as Col. 3:10 and II Cor. 4:4. Of the occurrences of the word, outside the Book of Revelation (where the language is clearly symbolic), one refers to *law*. The law is not the real thing but a shadow (Heb. 10:1). One refers to idols made in the form of men or animals, birds, or reptiles (Rom. 1:23). One (in each of the Synoptics) describes Caesar's picture on a coin (Matt. 22:20; Mark 12:16; Luke 20:24). One is applied to man made in God's image (I Cor. 11:7). One points to a heavenly image after the analogy of the earthly image which men bear here (I Cor. 15:49). All of these usages suggest quite definite, concrete, objective entities, either the mold or that which is molded. In five occasions, it refers to Christ himself as the Image of God bearing various relationships to man (Rom. 8:29; II Cor. 3:18; II Cor. 4:4; Col. 1:15; 3:10).

The concreteness of the idea of image as revealed in a fairly careful attention to these passages should be noted. Also, it should be pointed out that the passages that speak of a change in man toward likeness to the image of Christ are expressed in the progressive present tense, *metamórphouste* (transformed), *anakainoumenon* (renovation, renewal, Col. 3:10), and *sommorphous*, (conformed, Rom. 8:29).

The same distinction between *likeness* and *image* was noticed in Greek usage as in the Hebrew. *Homoíosen* and its cognates, according to Thayer, means "Like, similar, resembling, correspondence to, to be or become like, to compare one thing with another or to make like."[17] Moulton and Milligan said, in part, "of like nature"; "same rank or station" (classical Greek); "in the same way" (Heb. 4:15; 7:15).[18] As distinguished from *eikón*, which implies an archetype, the "likeness" or "form" in *homoíoma* may be "accidental," "as one egg is shaped like another."

"In examining the New Testament passages using this term, it was observed that in 34 occasions of the word they introduce comparisons in parabolic form (Matt. 7:24; Mark 4:30; Luke 7:31; etc.). Eight are comparisons of someone to physical, moral, or spiritual qualities of another, such as, "tempted like as we are" (Heb. 4:15), like Melchizedek (Heb. 7:15), "in the likeness of [sinful] men" (Phil. 2:7), "Elias was a man subject to like passions as we are" (Jas. 5:17). Six or seven occurrences have moral and spiritual likeness to God, or of Christ to His brethren, as a subject. For example, "We shall be like him; for we shall see him as he is" (I John 3:2).

The distinction which needs to be made can be most clearly pointed up by noting the following passages. Melchizedek was *like* the Son of God in specific ways, not as to identity as a person (Heb. 7:3).

In Phil. 2:6-8 there is found an interesting conjunction of terms. Christ, who was "in the form *[morphe]* of God" "took . . . the form of a servant" (contrasting a relationship, not an ontology). As a Servant, He then was born in the likeness of men; and as such He died on the Cross, "in the likeness of sinful flesh," Paul says in Rom. 8:3. Christ's flesh resembled sinlessly the flesh of the race stained by sin.

There seems to be a significant semantic difference between *image* and *likeness,* a difference not lost on the early Church fathers in their defense of the Christian faith.

Eikón always assumes a prototype from which it has been derived and drawn; while *homoiótes, homoíosis,* and words of this family express a similarity or resemblance which implies no ontological kinship. Only the term *image* could be applied to Christ in His relationship to God, never merely a *likeness.* The first is a family tie, a solid filial relationship; the second is a comparison of some detail, an approximation. It may be important to observe that Christ is never said to be like God in the sense that He was said to be like man.

The great Alexandrian theologians taught that the *image* was something common to all men, continuing even after the Fall. They said that the *likeness* was something toward which man was created, that he might strive after it and ultimately attain it.

In summary, it may be said that both *image* and *likeness* are analogies, not descriptions of an ontological structure of being. As stated earlier, the biblical writers seem not to speculate about what man is in himself but are concerned about his relationships and moral responsibility. *Image* seems to refer to the experience of "standing before God" in responsible personhood. Likeness makes sense when it is a way of saying what man ought to do and what he does do about that experience of moral freedom.

BIBLICAL WORDS FOR MAN

That the Bible does not assume or teach a monotypic man is one of the significant insights which is derived from a study of the terms referring to man and the way these terms are used. There seems to be no ontological curiosity about him. Rather, the rich vocabulary of the Old and New Testaments relating to man has to do primarily with what he thinks and does, and impulses of his heart, his attitudes and character.

While man is a well-defined entity sharing many essential qualities with every other man, he is also a real individual in a different sense than animals are within any species. Roger J. Williams, in *You Are Extraordinary*,[19] emphasizes this remarkable truth. Men are unique in a significant sense, varying from the "normal" in mood, intelligence, insight, disposition, reaction, and in innumerable ways important to the business of being human. Philosophy and theology, especially in the rationalistic periods of history, have sought for "universal laws of human behavior under the aegis of a rationalist dogma of fixed human nature, always and everywhere the same,"[20] but have always failed.

But the more that is understood about man, the less real reliance can be placed on any universal absolute proposed about him. Even I.Q. tests merely indicate the relation of an individual to that which is considered average. It gives a high priority to normalcy. As Sydney Harris perceptively writes: "So-called 'normal' types may be reliable for second-echelon jobs, but first-rate men (in any field) do not conform to standards."[21] In other words the very fact of difference and unpredictability gives man his value as man.

This dynamic quality of mankind which is recognized and about which the Bible is concerned is one of the things that makes

Bible study exciting and worthwhile. The Book presents a ka-leidoscopic perspective of man and we rob it of its most important impact and power for moral and spiritual renewal when we attempt to impose an artificial, inflexible, too simple, black-and-white classification of human nature onto its own estimate of man. No such neat examples of the normal, good or bad, appear in everyday life. No stereotype appears in Scripture.

Though the New Testament borrows the terms provided by the Greek language, such as mind, body, soul, and spirit, no case can be made for the familiar dualistic view of man which was de-rived from Platonism and carried somehow into Christian theology —to its hurt.

The Old Testament writers could express their dynamic view of man only by characterizing his many moods, manifestations, and "soul" by what various parts of the body suggested to him.

The soul of man as a totality finds its expression in many ways in the central organs of the body, such as the heart, the liver, the kidneys, and the bowels; but also in peripheral organs like the tongue, the ear, and the eye. Any one of these may at a given mo-ment express the "soul" in one of its various manifestations. [22]

These characterizations are not static. Feet, for instance, are quoted by Paul twice (Rom. 3:15 and 10:15) from Isaiah (52:7 and 59:7-8) as saying, they are "swift to shed blood," or are "beautiful" as they bear "good tidings." The problem, in other words, was not with the feet, nor were the feet a constituent part of man—an entity. The use one made of his feet pointed to the kind of man he was.

Non-biblical Concepts

By using Greek terms, the New Testament writers were able to refine and make more accurate the teaching regarding man. But the Greek terms do not carry along with them the pagan connota-tions into New Testament usage. The unity of personality is every-where assumed. Heart, mind, soul, spirit, conscience, flesh, body are not distinguishable parts of man put together as something that man has. These, with various grammatical variants important to the subject, are what a man is.

Speculative trichotomy—body, soul, and spirit—cannot sur-vive the encounter with the *heart* and *mind* of the New Testament.

How *conscience* can be added to this complex baffles the one who has settled for Platonic concepts. It is possible that Hellenism made an attempt to introduce some measure of "movement" or dynamism into the idea of man by means of its trinitarian (or trichotomous) concept.

The Hebrew man found his dynamism, not in static beingness, but in his social relatedness. His "living" self, his totality, stood in relation to a larger unity, the social entity. We, in the West, need to sense this profound communal consciousness typical of both Hebrew and Oriental peoples if we are to understand the Bible. Hebrew man was in an essential way *one* with "his fathers" and his family, his tribe and his nation. This was not a crude metaphysical or genetic unity (by which interpretation Paul is misunderstood in Romans 5), but a spiritual interconnectedness that penetrates to the core of what mankind is. (To be in Abraham's loins [Heb. 7:10] or to sin personally with Adam must not be philosophized into some theory of genetic transmission of goodness or guilt. Even here we must restrain our speculative tendency and think as Hebrew men thought. The ontological question is not raised or answered in Scripture.)

Only in this way can man be understood in relation to a God who communicates himself to him, and with whom fellowship is possible.

A great deal of extra-biblical liberty has been taken to explain the meaning of the image of God in relation to man. The Catholic asserts that "reason" is the image of God in man. Aside from the fault of positing anything *in* man as itself "the image," the further error is in supposing that the Hebrew man thought in terms of reason as that which related him to God. There is no word in Hebrew which carries the Greek connotation of *reason*. Reason was not an intellectual activity separable from the total man. It was the man himself in responsible, rational relation to life.

Protestant writers have looked for "the image" in man. Calvin said it was the state of innocence before the Fall. He said it is "the uncorrupted excellence of human nature, which shone in Adam before his defection, but was afterwards so corrupted, and almost obliterated, that nothing remains from the ruin but what is confused, mutilated and defiled" (*Institutes*, XIV, 4). But this idea is inconsistent with Gen. 9:6, which says of man after the fall that, because man was made in God's image, to shed his blood (murder) would be compensated for, or punished, by the blood of the murderer himself. Fallen man was still made in God's image.

CHRIST AS THE IMAGE OF GOD

A study of the biblical meaning of the *Imago Dei* would not be complete without reference to Christ himself. In II Cor. 4:4, Paul says that *Christ . . . is the image of God*. Again in Col. 1:15 he declares that the Son is the *image of the invisible God*. The Jewish scholar who (undoubtedly) wrote Hebrews gives us the most vivid expression of this concept. God's Son is the *apaugasma* (a Greek word meaning "radiance, the daybreak, to shine or give forth light, to discern") of His glory, and the *charakter* (the Greek word which indicates the exact thing as distinguished from any substitute or "stand-in") of God's person. It is the word from which the English *character* stems and means the inherent identity by which a specific thing is recognized. In this case, the author is saying that Christ displayed the precise attributes of God because He was God. He was the personification, not merely the representative, of God.

A more relevant dimension is disclosed in the few passages which relate man to God through Christ. Men are predestined "to be conformed to the image of his [God's] Son (Rom. 8:29), in order "that *he* might be the firstborn among many brethren." The Col. 1:15 passage also links His being the "first-born of all creation" (RSV) to the image metaphor. The dynamic of this relationship is emphasized in II Cor. 3:18: "Beholding the glory of the Lord, [we] are being changed into his likeness from one degree of glory to another" (RSV); and Col. 3:9-10, "Do not lie to one another [or, rather, 'Put away the lie'], seeing that you have put off the old nature with its practices and have put on the new nature, which is *being* renewed in *knowledge after the image of its creator*" (RSV, italics mine).

CHAPTER VII

New Testament Man

Jesus' concept of man is important to a biblical estimate of man. In considering a Christian view, our Lord's attitude toward those He labored for and with ought to be significant to our study. Paul is also an important source. He seemed to have an understanding of human nature and the inner drives of mankind that in some ways anticipated the age of psychology such as we know it. But both Jesus and Paul limit their discussions of man to his religious nature, not otherwise.

JESUS' ESTIMATE OF HUMAN NATURE

Jesus said a great deal about man, for it was to him He came and for him He died. "His persistent use of the title, 'Son of Man,' for himself, marked His identification with humanity, and suggested the truth that the final understanding of human nature must result from a knowledge of himself."[1] His teaching regarding human nature falls into two categories, both of which are pertinent to this study: First, "those which reveal man ideally, or essentially, that is, according to a divine purpose; and secondly, those revealing man actually or experimentally, that is, as Jesus found him."[2]

Man, ideally, is revealed in the Man as *He* lived. Remembering the statement in the letter to the Hebrews to the effect that He "was in all points tempted like as we are, yet without sin" (4:15), we may, no doubt, presume that the author had in mind, among other events, the wilderness temptation, which can become a commentary upon the nature of man.

In that temptation, physical life was recognized. "Command that these stones be made bread" (Matt. 4:3). In it, also, the reality of personal relationship to God and the possibility of moral choice were recognized. "Cast thyself down: for it is written, He shall give his angels charge concerning thee" (Matt. 4:6). But beyond this, man's vocation, or the purpose of God in the world, is implied. "All these things [the kingdoms of the world] will I give thee, if thou wilt fall down and worship me" (Matt. 4:9). Here was the temptation to sell honor in exchange for the dominion which only honor can actually achieve.

Jesus' answer to all these is His estimate of the worth of man and his place in the economy of God's creation. The true sustenance of human life is the Word of God; the true object of human life is the worship of God. The true unity of man's being is stated in the words of Jesus: "The light of the body is the eye: if therefore thine eye be single, thy whole body shall be full of light. But if thine eye be evil, thy whole body shall be full of darkness. If therefore the light that is in thee be darkness, how great is that darkness!" (Matt. 6:22-23) In other words, only a single-hearted man, or one with a single motive, can realize the purpose for which he was made. James's exhortation to men who are "unstable," because "double-minded" (1:8; 4:8), points up the force of this passage.

The primacy of the spiritual perspective in man is the teaching of Jesus in the following passages:

> *Fear not them which kill the body, but are not able to kill the soul: but rather fear him which is able to destroy both soul and body in hell* (Matt. 10:28).

> *What is a man profited, if he shall gain the whole world, and lose his own soul? or what shall a man give in exchange for his soul?* (Matt. 16:26)
>
> *A man's life consisteth not in the abundance of the things which he possesseth* (Luke 12:15).

The full implications of the probationary life of man have nowhere been more clearly stated than in the answer of Jesus to the questioner who wanted to know what constituted the greatest commandment (Matt. 22:37-40). All the demands of the moral law, He said, would be satisfied in the voluntary and deliberate choice of a complete and thoroughgoing dedication to God and to one's neighbor. "The love of God is the master-law of life."[3] Equally as important to probation, in its recognition of self-consciousness as the ground of responsible choice, is the command to love others as oneself. This, too, is on the basis of principle—not emotion—and equates the personal estimate of self with the estimate in which one holds others. Only in this careful balance and direction of goodwill and concern can the full dignity of man be realized.

Over against this "ideal" view of man stood actual man as Jesus saw him. Men, who possessed an active capacity for the highest as expressed in a love for their children, were "evil" and hurtful and murderous in other relationships. "If ye then, being evil, know how to give good gifts unto your children . . ." (Matt. 7:11), was a recognition of the dual condition of human beings: (1) the capacity for good, (2) immorally occupied in dispensing an evil influence. This thought is even more vividly declared in another place where the idea of a responsible person (as evidence by the standard of judgment, namely, his "words") is joined with the idea of an evil heart. "O generation of vipers, how can ye, being evil, speak good things? . . . [yet] by thy words thou shalt be condemned" (Matt. 12:34-37).

Jesus always located sin in the "heart" of man. In the same heart that should have been occupied with loving God, he discovered the fountain of evil. "From within, out of the heart of men, proceed evil thoughts, adulteries, fornications" (Mark 7:21; cf. Matt. 15:17-20). The proof of man's defilement is the array of evil things which proceed from him.

The unregenerate, spiritually dead condition of men is revealed in the conversation with Nicodemus, "That which is born

of the flesh is flesh; and that which is born of the Spirit is spirit.
. . . ye must be born again" (John 3:5-7). The natural appetite of
the unregenerate is described as follows: "Men loved darkness
rather than light, because their deeds were evil. For every one that
doeth evil hateth the light" (John 3:19-20).

The prodigal dissipation of the one faculty which links man to
God, namely, his faith, will according to Jesus be the final basis of
judgment. "He that believeth not is condemned already, because
he hath not believed in the name of the only begotten Son of God"
(John 3:18). On the contrary, "He that heareth my word, and believeth on him that sent me, hath everlasting life, and shall not
come into condemnation; but is passed from death unto life" (John
5:24).

In all Jesus' contacts with people never did He show a condescending attitude or think of man as "mere man." To Him they
all seemed savable. His deep respect for each person no matter
who he might be, how evil he might be, what his response was to
Jesus, did not show a hint of a "superiority complex." The very
anger He displayed toward some, the whip He wielded in the Temple, all said in effect, "You are My equal. My anger shows My
respect for you. Now, be the man you can be and ought to be." He
never forced himself on anyone. He did not call any man to Him
under false pretenses—promising an easier yoke than would be the
case. He called men to die with Him. He tried to push back all
self-deception and faced men with what they were in themselves.
He made people think for themselves—and think honestly. All
this is Jesus' estimate of man.

Paul's Concept of Human Nature

Paul's teaching about human nature does not conflict with
Jesus' view so much as it comes to the subject from another direction. Holiness is seen against the background of man's sinfulness.
The nature of this sinfulness, however, lays a foundation for
holiness.

Paul's thorough understanding of human nature furnished a
background through which a profound revelation could be made
of the nature of sin in man. Among his figures of speech are these:
"old man" (Rom. 6:6; Eph. 4:22; Col. 3:9); "body of sin" (Rom.
6:6); "law of sin" (Rom. 7:23); "body of death" (Rom. 7:24);

"carnal mind" (Rom. 8:7); "bondage of corruption" (Rom. 8:21). Other descriptions included: "dead in trespasses and sins" (Eph. 2:1); "alienated from the life of God" (Eph. 4:18); "spirit of the world" (I Cor. 2:12); "the sin which dwelleth in me" (Rom. 7:20); "a reprobate mind" (Rom. 1:28); "sin" *(hamartías),* in many places; the "law of sin and death" (Rom. 8:2); and "natural man" *(psyche)* (I Cor. 2:14). It is in his more extended discussions, however, that a complete picture of the nature of man and his sin (two things that must be kept together) is best seen.

A. ROM. 1:18

The story of the degradation of man through the perversion of the human intelligence is well told here. The just wrath of God is revealed against those who "hinder truth in unrighteousness," or, who "by their wickedness suppress the truth" (RSV). Sin began in man, not by overt disobedience, but by entertaining a question about the character of God. "God knows," goes the temptation, "that you will not die when you eat the fruit. He knows that you will become as wise as He if you do, and He does not want you to become equal with Him."

Here is not mere honest questioning about God or as to what is right or true (which is ever the proper and necessary concern of rational beings) but a rejection of truth as it is embodied in the being of God. It is transfer of the concept of truth, from God to the expediency of man's desire. It is attributing to God evil and malicious motives. It is the core of the destruction of fellowship, which is suspicion, greed, selfishness, and eventually murder. It closes the door to communication and communion between rational beings—between man and God—and inevitably between man and man. It is interpreting as evil the Source of Good. It is the substitution of evil for good. It is in the end the choice of evil in place of good and the belief that evil is good and good evil. Jesus spoke of this when men said of Him that He cast out demons by demonic power (Mark 3:22-30). This sin cannot be forgiven because it destroys the power to recognize truth, and only a rational, morally structured person can entertain such a doubt and make such a decision.

The charge is made against man, capable of knowing truth, that he is hindering or holding down or restraining *(katechónton)* truth, and that moral issues are involved in doing so. The measure of truth he may know is sufficient to incite him to the worship of God. Even natural man may know enough about the eternal power and "God-ness" (Rom. 1:20) of God—(1) by *natural revelation*, (that which may be seen), and (2) by *intuition* ("the invisible things . . . are clearly seen")—to render his darkness inexcusable.

The charge is also made against man that, as one responsible for his volitional powers, and "knowing God," he refused to glorify Him as God. This parallels Adam's sin in challenging the goodness and worthiness of God and willingly setting about, in disobedience, to obtain wisdom which was, in his estimate, maliciously withheld from him by God. The power granted to man to worship God was prostituted to the degrading worship of objects formed by his own hands as imitations of real things. And that which man bows down to worship is first an image resembling himself, then images resembling beasts, and finally images of reptiles.

The third charge Paul makes is that man dethroned the Creator and set up other gods in His place. This substitution could be tolerated only by those who had exchanged "the lie" for the truth. (Here the Greek article is used with "lie," one of only four places in the New Testament. It seems in each case to point up the specific thing which sin is, namely, that man can be his own god.) The result was an open door to unspeakable sensual depravity. The course of sin was from a refusal to acknowledge the sovereignty of God (Rom. 1:28), down to positive relish of sins known to be worthy of death (Rom. 1:32), and life lived with "the lie" as the ideal and goal.

A thoughtful analysis of this passage reveals (1) that Paul considered men fully responsible for their defection from righteousness, (2) that rejection of God's authority was deliberate and on an intelligent basis, and (3) that perversion in every part of his being was the consequence of this deliberate rejection.

B. Eph. 4:17-19

Another graphic Pauline description of the source of sin and the course of depravity is found in the Book of Ephesians (Eph. 4:17-19). Paul, in this passage, in exhorting the Ephesians to holiness, warns them against returning to the "vanity of . . . mind" characteristic of the heathen mind. Vanity *(mataíotes)*, according to Thayer, is a purely biblical word meaning "devoid of truth," a perversion, and depravation.[4] This condition characterized the blinded heathen mind *(nous)*. Resulting from this perversion of mind is a "darkened" "understanding" *(diánoia)*. It is the "ignorance" *(hágoian)* occasioned by blindness of heart, a moral condition, that has "alienated" *(apellotrioméne)* them "from the life of God." Thayer translates *alienate* as "those who have estranged themselves from God."[5]

This estrangement, it may be assumed on the strength of the passive voice used in the Greek text, was volitional. It was a deliberate choice. They, having cast off from themselves all feeling, "gave up" to uncleanness, and complete moral apostasy resulted. The depth is reached in the last phrase, "with craving." That faculty given for the purpose of loving God with holy abandonment, by a deliberate series of immoral choices, now is used to love debauchery with the same abandonment. This is the progression: (1) a mind devoid of truth, (2) blind-hearted ignorance, and (3) moral insanity.

Some further light upon the nature of this depraved condition can be gained from the parallel passage immediately following in which a series of contrasts is presented (Eph. 4:25-32). "Ye have not so learned Christ" (Eph. 4:20). The first contrast is in relation to truth. Instead of a mind devoid of truth, by moral choice, there is a mind filled with truth "as . . . [it] is in Jesus" (Eph. 4:21). The second contrast is between *darkened understanding* (Eph. 4:18), occasioned by a hardening of the heart, and a *renewed spirit* of the *mind* (Eph. 4:23). This thought is amplified by the terms *old* and *new man*. The third contrast is between moral insensibility with its evil works (Eph. 4:19) and a high degree of moral sensitivity with good works (Eph. 4:25, 32). Those contrasts serve to sharpen the concept Paul had in mind, of what sin is and does.

C. Colossians

A third passage illuminates the Pauline conception of the result of sin in man. In Colossians, it is another contrast that provokes a deeper understanding of this truth. An alienated mind (*diánoia*) is at the opposite pole from one "holy and unblameable and unreproveable in his sight" (Col. 1:22). The deep inwardness of the perversion is strongly emphasized in all of these passages. A cast of mind underlies the kind of life men live. And behind the cast of mind is an attitude toward truth and God as absolute Lord. And for it all men are held accountable and responsible. At no time is leniency in conduct ever justified because of perversion in intellectual or moral faculties.

WORD STUDY OF TERMS RELATIVE TO MAN

It will be noticed that in most cases, especially in Pauline theology, *nous*, or some cognate, is associated with this source of perversion. There are numbers of related words and derivations of this word, but the following seem to be related more particularly to the subject at hand: *diánoia, phrónema*, and *nóema*.

1. *Nous*, first, is translated simply *mind*, but with a meaning going far deeper than the Greek "mind," which was the intellective faculty untouched by any moral concern. Paul's use is more penetrating and discriminating, as is always the case with Hebrew backgrounds of thought.

Thayer says it contains the idea of perceiving, understanding, feeling, judging, and determining. It is an intellective faculty, but also a capacity for spiritual truth, of perceiving divine things, of recognizing goodness and of hating evil.[6] A review of its uses in the New Testament book by book was helpful in ascertaining the peculiar inflections of meaning. God gave the heathen over to a *reprobate mind* (Rom. 1:28). A different law warred against the law of Paul's *mind* (Rom. 7:23). With the *mind* Paul served "the law of God; but with the flesh the law of sin" (Rom. 7:25). In a burst of spiritual insight Paul cried, "O the depth of the riches both of the wisdom and knowledge of God! . . . For who hath known the *mind* of the Lord?" (Rom. 11:33-34) Paul exhorts the Romans to "be . . . transformed" by the renewal of the spirit of the *mind* regarding the days to be esteemed in honoring the Lord (Rom. 12: 2; 14:5).

In the Corinthian letter the word is used three times. Believers are to be perfected together "in the same *mind* and . . . judgment" (I Cor. 1:10). "Who hath known the *mind* of the Lord?"

(I Cor. 2:16) Those (who are spiritual) "have the *mind* of Christ" (*loc. cit.*).

Elsewhere are the following: "vanity of mind" is to be avoided by those in Christ (Eph. 4:17); rather a Christian should "be renewed in the spirit of your mind" (Eph. 4:23). In making judgment regarding ritual values of food and drink and about "holy" days and the value of visions, some persons rely on reason, "puffed up" by a "fleshly mind" (Col. 2:18). Paul exhorted the Thessalonians to be not "shaken in *mind*" (II Thess. 2:2). Crass materialism (supposing godliness a way of gain) characterizes the "corrupt" mind which is *destitute of . . . truth* (I Tim. 6:5), and men of corrupted *mind* withstand truth and become *reprobate concerning . . . faith* (II Tim. 3:8). To Titus he said, "Even their mind and conscience is defiled" (Titus 1:15).

From these passages it becomes clear that the *nous* is a faculty which relates itself morally to truth. It judges between good and evil and chooses between them. When wrongly related to truth it becomes reprobate and corrupt, leading to immoral decisions. It needs renewal and transformation and when rightly related to truth approximates even the mind of Christ. Of the total of 17 references, eight describe a depraved condition, two deal with renewal, and three with the condition of the mind of the regenerate. Four are miscellaneous references in the same vein.

2. *Diánoia,* another cognate of *nous,* means, according to Thayer, "the mind as the faculty of understanding, feeling, desiring . . . mind, i.e. spirit, way of thinking and feeling."[7]

It is found seven times in the New Testament. It is the word found in the Synoptics to express the comprehensiveness of love to God, "Thou shalt love . . . God with all . . . thy mind" (Matt. 22:37; Mark 12:30; Luke 10:27). The Old Testament promise of law written within the *mind* is twice mentioned in Hebrews (8:10; 10:16). The believer's *mind* is twice mentioned by Peter: "Gird up the loins of your *mind*" (I Pet. 1:13); and, "I stir up your pure *minds* by way of remembrance" (II Pet. 3:1). Twice reference is made to the unregenerate *mind:* "desires of the flesh and of the *mind*" (Eph. 2:3), and "enemies in your *mind*" (Col. 1:21). From this the deduction is made that this faculty of *diánoia* has to do with the *bent* of the mind, the direction of affection. It is not blind feeling but a moral persuasion. It is, in natural man, an enemy of God. It may be called to give account of itself by its possessor. It is in need of radical correction. The mind which was at enmity against God must love God—a total reversal.

3. *Nóema* is used four times. The ending "*ma*" denotes a result. So the term means "that which thinks," of the thinking and purposing faculty. Three times in the Corinthian letter Paul uses it in connection with the binding of this thinking, purposing faculty. The inability to understand the Old Testament was the veil by which "their *minds* were blinded" (II Cor. 3:14); "the God of this world hath blinded the *minds*" of the unbelieving (II Cor. 4:4). This is the faculty through which Eve was betrayed; "I fear, lest . . . as the serpent beguiled Eve . . . your *minds* [purposing faculty] should be corrupted" (II Cor. 11:3). Remembering this, Paul's benediction in Philippians is of special moment. "The peace of God . . . shall guard your . . . thoughts *[noémata]*" (see Phil. 4:7). One of the most direct clues to the seat of sin is here revealed. This thinking, purposing faculty is the area where evil is introduced. Unbelief is the sin of this faculty. Unbelief blinded the minds of the Jews to the revelation of Christ. Unbelief permits the "god of this world" entrance into the sanctuary of the moral life of man. It was this way that Eve was tempted and fell. It is here that corruption resides. It is in this area that the peace of God can guard the thinking of a man.

4. The fourth Greek word translated *mind* in the English that is significant to this investigation is *phrónema*. The verb *phronéo* will be considered first.

Thayer says it means "to direct one's mind to a thing . . . to be intent within yourselves" to a purpose, to pursue.[8] Moulton and Milligan elaborate on this idea: "It seems always to keep in view the direction which thought takes." They give an example from classical Greek: "Soueris changed her *mind,* left the mill and departed."[9] The phrase *noún kai phronón*, "being sane and in my right mind," is common. It is found about a dozen times in the New Testament (Rom. 8:12; 12:16; II Cor. 13:11; Gal. 5:10; Phil. 2:5; 3:15, 16, 19; 4:2; etc.). Several times it refers to believers having "the same *mind*" about things (II Cor. 13:11; Rom. 12:16; Phil. 2:2; 2:5; 3:16 and 4:2; Titus 2:6). Twice the exhortation is given to have the *mind* of Christ, and twice the reference is to preoccupation with things of the flesh and earthly things (Rom. 8:5-6). With this review, the significance begins to develop.

A cognate of *phronéo* is the noun *phrónema,* which with the suffix *"ma"* also indicates the result of that which the verb has done. It, then, is an inclination or set of mind. Moulton and Milligan give the content of *phronein* as "the general bent of thought and motive," pointing out that its most significant use is in Rom. 8:7: "The *mind* of the flesh is enmity against God; for it is not subject to the law of God, neither indeed can it be *(oudé dúnatai).*"[10]

There are three other occasions where this word is used and all of them are in this same chapter. The Spirit knows the *mind* of the Lord—obviously the deep desire, passion, of God's heart (Rom. 8:27). The other two are most revealing in their use. The *mind* of the flesh "is death" (Rom. 8:6). This unquestionably refers back to the first commandment in the garden, "If you eat, you shall die." This death then is the result of sin, and this sin is the one which results in death.

The *mind* of the spirit "is life and peace" (Rom. 8:6); this is not only a poignant contrast but a promise of hope for the complete reversal, in this life, of that age-long curse.

Life and Death

There is one more striking analogy that no review of the sin problem can evade. That analogy is death. It does not seem to be vital to this investigation to question the entire scope of man's being which may be included under the curse of death. It may or may not include physical death. W. Robertson Nicoll says:

> Paul, no doubt, uses death to convey various shades of meaning in different places, but he does not explicitly distinguish different senses of the word; and it is probably misleading rather than helpful to say that in one sentence "physical" death is meant and another "spiritual" death. . . . All that "death" conveys to the mind entered into the world through sin.[11]

But it is almost universally agreed that spiritual death is most certainly the most significant fact of the condition of fallen man. It is a striking fact, also, that so many of Paul's descriptions of the sin nature include some reference to death.

God decreed death as the penalty for breaking law. Whatever else may be included in the condition of fallen man, death is most particularly the major one. As has been shown, death is associated with the function of *phrónema*, which is the deepest disposition or inclination of the soul. All other faculties of fallen man are affected as a result of what decision has been made. Perversion has resulted from a deliberate choice against God and truth. But here we find, apparently, the heart of sin, so far as man is concerned, for it is here he experiences death as the curse of sin in its primary sense. Whatever this death means, Paul says that death passed from father to son, from Adam on to every human soul (Rom. 5:12). This death is coextensive and concomitant with sin (Rom. 5:21). Eight times in Romans alone, sin and death are considered as inseparable companions. The "body of . . . death" made true righteousness impossible (Rom. 7:24). All are under the sentence of death. "Christ died for the ungodly" (Rom. 5:6). We can know "we have passed [as a consequence] from death unto life" (I John 13:14).

It is not possible to present an extended analysis of the term *death* here, but the general argument would be less convincing than otherwise if some suggestion of its meaning were not included. Since there are so many theories regarding the meaning of death as Paul uses the term, a philosophy of death seems more in order than a more detailed statement. In this vein, Albert Barnes suggests the following:

> The passage before us [Romans 5] shows in what sense he intended here to use the word. In his argument it stands opposed to "the grace of God, and the gift by grace" (ver. 15); to "justification" by the forgiveness of "many offences" (ver. 16); to the reign of the redeemed in eternal life (ver. 17); and to "justification of life" (ver. 18). To all these, the words "death" (ver. 12, 17) and "judgment" (ver. 16, 18) stand opposed. . . . The evident meaning is, that the word "death", as here used by the apostle, refers to *the train of evils* which have been introduced by sin. . . . In contrasting with this the results of the work of Christ, he describes not the resurrection merely, nor deliverance from temporal death, but eternal life in heaven.[12]

This same idea of contrast is recognized by G. Campbell Morgan. He saw a threefold contrast in the fifth chapter of Romans.

> The first contrast is between the trespass and the free gift.

. . . the death sentence upon sin, and grace abounding. The disparity is indicated by the phrase "much more." . . .

The second contrast is between the issue of the trespass and the free gift, and therefore between judgment and justification. . . . The disparity is again indicated by the phrase "much more"; and the superabounding victory of justification is remarkably indicated by the fact that judgment means the reign of death over men, while justification means the ability of men to reign in life. . . .

The final contrast is between the reign of death and the reign of grace . . . the reign of sin in death and the reign of grace through righteousness unto life. Again the disparity is marked by the phrase "more exceedingly," revealing the fact that in grace overwhelming provision is made for victory over sin.[13]

The Hebrews "did not regard death as non-existence; death —'being gathered to one's fathers'—meant joining the departed souls in . . . Sheol, a dreary, meaningless existence where one was cut off from 'the land of the living.'"[14]

Death was feared, not because it ended life, primarily, but because it cut one off from the fellowship of one's family and nation. It was loneliness, an end to personal fulfillment, utter frustration and anguish of spirit. To an Oriental, whose personal existence intertwined so vitally with the family and social units, isolation from the very nexus of life could not help but be torture. It has been noted that Jean-Paul Sartre's short play, *No Exit*, touches on the anguish of spirit in "hell," where exposure to one another is absolute, but where communication is stymied in that merciless exposure and from which there is not, nor ever can be, an escape.

The New Testament writer's use of "death" to signify separation from God was well understood by the Jews, as was "life" by contrast. Death seemed to depict the finality of the hopelessness which is man's lot alienated from God. It does not, however, mean loss of any human faculty. Rather it describes the separation which exists between God and man. All the powers of personality remain alert and active but totally disoriented. The only adequate organizing center, God, is unavailable. Love, the most active faculty of the human personality, when centered in God, is termed *agape* in the New Testament and is said to satisfy all the demands of the law of God and man (Matt. 22:37-40; Rom. 13:10). But when that same faculty attempts to expend its energy upon itself, the very faculty itself loses its high quality and its expression is reduced to the category of the antithesis of love, namely, lust.

Paralleling this observation, and related to it, is that regarding life and death. In the spiritual nexus there is spiritual life and derived holiness, which is sinlessness. In H. Orton Wiley's unpublished lecture notes on "The Psychology of Holiness" he says:

> This new nature is "the new man, which after God is created in righteousness and true holiness"; and it is this new man which forms the spiritual nexus of the body of Christ. It is the channel way of blessing—the sole medium of the Spirit's indwelling presence.

To this point of view, Wesley gives argument. In speaking of the death which sin occasions he says:

> He lost the life of God: he was separated from him, in union with whom his spiritual life consisted. The body dies when it is separated from the soul; the soul when it is separated from God. . . . [Of this death] he gave immediate proof: presently showing by his behaviour, that the love of God was extinguished in his soul, which was now "alienated from the life of God" (*Works*, VI, 67).

John Fletcher was unusually lucid at this point:

> The word *dead*, etc. is frequently used in the Scripture to denote a particular degree of helplessness and inactivity, very short of the total helplessness of a corpse. We read of the *deadness* of Sarah's womb, and of Abraham's body being *dead*; he must be a strong Calvinist, indeed, who, from such expressions, peremptorily asserts, that Sarah's *dead* womb was as unfit for conception, and Abraham's *dead* body for generation, as if they both had been "dead corpses."[15]

His discussion of the body of death in Romans 7 is equally pointed and helpful. "Dead as he [Paul] was, could he not complain like the dry bones, and ask, 'Who shall deliver me from this body of death?'"[16]

A final but strong argument is that in Paul's letter to the Ephesians. Standing in contrast to the three-sided personality of men, as they are in proper relationship to Christ, is the picture of men "dead in trespasses and sins" (Eph. 2:1). The picture is not of death, as stulted senses or annihilation, but of very active faculties in varying relationships. The "Spirit of Christ" which is a test of men's relationship to Christ (Rom. 8:9) is contrasted with the "spirit that now worketh in the children of disobedience" (Eph. 2:2). The "mind of Christ" (I Cor. 2:16), which the "spiritual" have, stands against the "desires of the flesh and of the mind" (Eph. 2:3). The "love of Christ" which "constraineth" a Christian (II Cor. 5:14) has become, in fallen man, "the lusts of our flesh" (Eph. 2:3). Death, then, must be the separation of the race from the immediate presence and power of the Holy Spirit, with the consequent loss of righteousness. The work of Christ in bringing life *(zóe)* in place of death is in harmony with this concept and will be developed in a later chapter. Spiritual death and life are synonymous with sin and holiness, and are properly understood as basically in relationship to God.

There are still more word pictures in the New Testament regarding the nature of sin and the damage it occasioned, but perhaps this establishes without serious question the heart of the matter. There are several pertinent observations to be made. The mind, or personality, as representing the intellective, volitional, and affectional natures in man, is the seat of moral perversion. This threefold mind, in relating itself to truth, determines the moral quality of man. When this mind rejects truth, willfully, perversion and corruption result. Knowledge, as an implicit intuition of things divine, is lost by moral default. In no case in the Bible is the mind considered as merely a thinking machine, a morally compounding tower of pure reason. Its exercise is always enmeshed with moral matters. It is the whole man responding to the truth of God in fullest personal responsibility.

So thoroughly did Wesley understand the human propensity for failure that it reacted back on his theology and he was able to write to Miss March regarding scriptural perfection as follows:

> This much is certain: they that love God with all their heart and all men as themselves are scripturally perfect. And surely such there are; otherwise the promise of God would be a mere mockery of human weakness. Hold fast this. But then remember, on the other hand, you have this treasure in an earthen vessel; you dwell in a poor, shattered house of clay, which presses down the immortal spirit. Hence all your thoughts, words, and actions are so imperfect, so far from coming up to the standard (that law of love which, but for the corruptible body, your soul would answer in all instances), that you may well say:

> *Every moment, Lord, I need*
> *The merit of Thy death* (*Works*, IV, 208).

The most eloquent and revealing commentary on Wesley's concept emerges out of what he considered to be necessary for salvation—the condition of man and what grace did for him.

> While a man is in a mere natural state, before he is born of God, he has, in a spiritual sense, eyes but sees not; a thick impenetrable veil lies upon them. He has ears, but hears not; he is utterly deaf to what he is most of all concerned to hear. His other spiritual senses are all locked up: He is in the same condition as if he had them not. Hence he has no knowledge of God; no intercourse with him; he is not at all acquainted with him. He has no true knowledge of the things of God, either of spiritual or eternal things; therefore, though he is a living man, he is a dead Christian. But as soon as he is born of God, there is a total change in all these particulars. . . .
>
> Wherefore, to what end, is it necessary that we should be born again? It is very easily discerned, that this is necessary. First, in order to holiness. For what is holiness according to the oracles of God? Not a bare external religion, a round of outward duties, how many soever they be, and how exactly soever performed. No. Gospel holiness is no other than the whole mind which was in Christ Jesus; it consists of all heavenly affections and tempers mingled together in one. It implies such a continual, thankful love to Him who hath not withheld from us his Son, His only Son, as makes it natural, and in a manner necessary to us, to love every child of man: as fills us "with bowels of mercies, kindness, gentleness, long-suffering:" It is such a love of God as teaches us to be blameless in all manner of conversation; as enables us to present our souls and bodies, all we are and sacrifice to God, acceptable through Christ Jesus. Now, this holiness can have no existence till we are renewed in the image of our mind. It cannot commence in the soul till the change be wrought; till, but the power of the Highest evershadowing us, we are "brought from darkness to light, from the power of Satan unto God;" That is, till we are born again; which, therefore, is absolutely necessary in order to holiness (*Works*, VI, 70-72).

LOVE AND THE SELF

Wesley believed that man is not primarily an object upon which are written the events of life, the repository of "the given," a passive substance (spiritual or material), a receiver only. Man is a dynamic being reacting and responding to life, searching, reaching out, needing fulfillment. He is a hemisphere looking for his other half.

It has been observed that man is basically a communication center. Every nerve, organ, function, thought, act, tissue is a transmitter and receiver. He is only whole when another *person* is listening, understanding, responding to him. Everyone needs an audience, and *is* an audience. A person cracks up when no one listens—when aloneness closes in around him.

The power source of the communication center could be called love. Man is made for that union of spirit which we call fellowship, love. In fellowship, the deepest longings find fulfillment. *Fulfillment* is a proper word for a proper concept. It may be used in improper destructive ways but it is not the impulse that is wrong but the way one seeks, and the object of his seeking—that which becomes his god or center.

In some religious circles, great emphasis is put on a "death of self," and self-love is rejected as being the essence of sin. This is a misunderstanding of Jesus' great word, "If anyone wishes to be a follower of mine, he must leave self behind; he must take up his cross and come with me" (Matt. 16:24, NEB). The problem is in imposing a faulty concept of "self" onto this statement, supposing that the self is a sort of detachable segment of the person which is itself evil, and by its deletion or subjugation evil is destroyed or suppressed and holiness is produced in the person.

Jesus' very careful statement that the satisfying of the whole law is in loving God with the whole heart, and one's neighbor *as oneself*, should correct this misapprehension. Self-love is as necessary to wholeness as love for others; but love for others, even for God, requires a measure of self-acceptance and self-esteem which holds the "ego" in self-conscious identity and respect.

In Wesley's *Notes* on Eph. 5:28, he points out that the measure of a man's love for his wife is his love for himself. "Self-love," Wesley says, "is not a sin, but an indisputable duty." The sin is *selfishness*, which is a distortion of love, not its essence. It has usurped the place of centrality and compels everything to come to terms with it.

The stronger the sense of need for fulfillment in fellowship, the stronger is the self. Such a self may be extremely aggressive. It can also love deeply because of its aggressive strength.

A self, seeking and needing fellowship, reveals a dimension of human life that is important to understand. Mankind is a society, and only in society can fulfillment take place. Ironically, the more men are crowded together, the lonelier they become, creating invisible walls of space around them as a self-defense to prevent an unwanted "other" from intruding into his private world. This reluctance to be touched becomes a barrier to proper fulfillment and the result is a morbid elevation of the self as its own center. And as impossible as it may seem, some *object* may usurp that sacred right.

Alienation—self-created—is the description of sin, and it is a good description. The basic drive of the self for fulfillment, designed by God to open the self to God and His world, when turned inward closes out everything man was made to need. He strangles himself with his own intensity and isolates himself from the fellowship he seeks. Love does not end in a self cut off from God and others. The tragedy is that love does not end. Hell could eventually burn out without ending the passionate desire of men for fellowship. But hell, whatever else it may be, is perpetuated and stoked by a yearning that cannot be satisfied. Sinful love is turned to lust, and lust destroys its object—self—without annihilating it. The terrible demand of human love cannot be satisfied with a self no bigger than itself. Men turn against themselves, loathe themselves, destroy themselves in the end.

To this self comes the call from God, winsomely, urgently, constantly in some measure, to share His heart, His fellowship, His love. The gospel call does not drive men to an unwanted relationship. It does not violate the fundamental yearning of the human heart. But the alienated one misinterprets God, becomes more cynical the longer God is held off. The self, in its darkness, thinks God wants to force it into slavery, to deprive it of freedom, to crush its spirit. It says, "If I love God with my whole being, I am denied the love of my wife and friends and life. I'll take life."

Francis Thompson expressed his lifelong fear of God in "The Hound of Heaven." Francis, a drug addict, dragging himself through life and sinking deeper and deeper into self-destruction, finally found—or was found by—God. His strange, heart-gripping poem tells of his fear of the "pounding feet" of the Holy Spirit pursuing him from hiding place to hiding place. He was afraid that God would rob him of all the things he wanted so passionately and had sought in vain.

> *I fled Him, down the nights and down the days;*
> *I fled Him, down the arches of the years;*
> *I fled Him, down the labyrinthine ways*
> *Of my own mind; and in the midst of tears*
> *I hid from Him, and under running laughter.*
>
> *Up vistaed hopes, I sped;*
> *And shot, precipitated,*
> *Adown Titanic glooms of chasmed fears,*
> *From those Feet that followed, followed after.*
>
> *But with unhurrying chase,*
> *And unperturbed pace,*
> *Deliberate speed, majestic instancy,*
> *They bear—and a voice beat*
> *More instant than the Feet—*
>
> *"All things betray thee, who betrayest Me."*
> . . . .
> *Halts by me that footfall:*
> *Is my gloom, after all,*
> *Shade of His Hand, outstretched caressingly?*

Something of Francis Thompson's common fear and misunderstanding of God's "demanding" love must have prompted the question to which Wesley gave answer in "A Farther Appeal to Men of Reason and Religion."

> Cannot the love both of God and our neighbor be practiced, without breaking in upon the common duties of life? Nay, can any of the common duties of life be rightly practiced without them? I apprehend not. I apprehend I am then laying the true, the only foundation for all those duties, when I preach, "Thou shalt love the Lord thy God with all thy heart, and thy neighbor as thyself" (*Works,* VIII, 59).

Man fears that God will smother out his individuality, his identity, his selfness. But God made man to find himself, in his love for Him. That love is not restrictive, a narrowing down, an annihilation of all man desires, but an openness to everything that he really wants. Love is the end of bondage and fear. It is a life directive, a guard against that which destroys, a prod to that which explores and discovers and finds the source of all fulfillment in God.

Every step in creation, in existence, in sin (as a violation of love), in the recovery from sin, in Christ's work of redemption; every step required of man toward, and in, holiness, is to be viewed through God's eyes of love. This is intensely personal in that love seeks the inner response of the one loved. No induced, or forced, or imposed, response satisfies love. Each of the persons involved must elect from the core of the self to open itself to and reach out for the other.

What God in Christ has done *for* us is to remove the barriers between man and God. Every man is born into a world of love—God's love. God has anticipated every situation. No man need beg God to forgive him. This God has done. This God offers to all men through Christ.

No one needs to cry and plead for the Holy Spirit. He is pleading for us and crowding us and wooing us. We need to recognize this call and open the door to Him. The change of attitude needs to come from our side. We do not earn God's favor by our crying and working.

The image of God has to do with love, and love is dynamic. Love to God sets the soul in the right direction—the satisfying direction. As love grows stronger, integration begins; healing takes place; the provincial, prejudiced mind is forced to expand; the heart is stretched out to a world needing God.

> We see, on every side, either men of no religion at all, or men of a lifeless, formal religion. We are grieved at the sight; and should greatly rejoice, if by any means we might convince some that there is a better religion to be attained,—a religion worthy of God that gave it. And this we conceive to be no other than love; the love of God and of all mankind; the loving God with all our heart, and soul, and strength, as having first loved us, as the fountain of all the good we have received and of all we ever hope to enjoy; and the loving every soul which God hath made, every man on earth, as our own soul.
>
> This love we believe to be the medicine of life, the never-failing remedy for all the evils of a disordered world, for all the miseries and vices of men. Wherever this is, there are virtue and happiness going hand in hand. There is humbleness of mind, gentleness, long-suffering, the whole image of God; and at the

same time a peace that passeth all understanding, and joy un-speakable and full of glory (*Works*, VIII, 3).

O let your heart be whole with God! Seek your happiness in him and him alone. Beware that you cleave not to the dust! "This earth is not your place." See that you use this world as not abusing it; *use* the world, and *enjoy* God. Sit as loose to all things here below, as if you were a poor beggar. Be a good stew-ard of the manifold gifts of God; that when you are called to give an account of your stewardship, he may say, "Well done, good and faithful servant, enter thou into the joy of thy Lord!" (*Works*, VII, 222).

Summary Observations

Nowhere is it said in Scripture that the image of God is (or was) *in* man. Any attempt to locate some *thing* in man which is God's image must lead to failure and/or to mere speculation and consequently to disappointment. Wesley was not always careful to make this distinction and because of this some logical problems arose in his preaching that otherwise would not have arisen.

The Genesis account says that man was created *in the image of God*—a very different thing. Only Christ is said to *be* the Image of God.

From a biblical standpoint it seems legitimate to distinguish between *image* and *likeness* in reference to man's relationship to God. The Hebrew terms are distinct and probably never confused in usage throughout the entire Old Testament. The Septuagint consistently translates *eikón* for *çelem* and *homoíosis* for *demūth* The New Testament usage of *image* and *likeness* is even more exact and significant than the Hebrew use of the terms and carries out the same emphasis in each corresponding word.

But it must be said clearly that to distinguish *image* and *likeness* does not mean that Hebrew man held to any idea of a dual-ism. Quite the contrary. He knew nothing of an Aristotelian bifur-cation between matter and form, essence and substance, numina and phenomena. Hebrew man was a materialist in the best sense. He lived in a real world, a good world. He profoundly respected himself because he believed God had made him. He was not con-cerned with metaphysics but with personal relationships. What he experienced was the real, not a shadow. Man was a real man;

never a static, neutral, invisible something that could be distinguished from what he did and said and thought.

If there is any significance to the distinction we have pointed out, it would seem to indicate a dynamic, in contrast to a static or passive, concept of man. Three things characterize the Hebrew understanding of man: (1) He comes from God's hand and is in some ways akin to God; (2) He is made out of dust and held in integrity by the very breath of God; (3) He is a living being, moral and responsible, fallible and ignorant, but capable of great achievement and character, or tragic self-destruction and disintegration.

Image includes all that is essential to human beings as such, in a very concrete way, including moral qualities. God was said to have found man "very good" (Gen. 1:31). Whatever it means to be made in God's image, it is certain that so long as man is man he retains a quality of personality which, as St. Bernard well said, "could not be burned out even in hell." Whatever God is, man is His outlined shadow, not after the analogy of the illusiveness of shadows, but the "shadowing forth" of the essential features of the prototype. Conversely, without falling into gross anthropomorphisms, something definite may be known about God by a proper study of man since God said, in effect, that man was a finite picture of what He is infinitely. In this assertion there is no thought of any pantheistic identification of God and man, only that there could be rational and moral commerce between them.

Likeness, throughout the Hebrew and Greek languages, suggests a comparison of qualities of personality, a potential in moral and spiritual matters that hangs in the balance of human probation. The reality of *likeness* resides in the imagination, the purpose, and the inclination of the heart.

We do not find any biblical reference to the loss of the image of God. Hence, as would be expected, there is no word regarding the "restoration" of that image. For failure to observe this, theology has sounded many conflicting voices regarding the possibility and nature and time of salvation. If men have *lost* the image of God, practical redemption in this life is clearly impossible without a structural, miraculous alteration in human nature beyond which further sin would be impossible. This does not square with life as we know it, so the theory is rejected.

To avoid this untenable position, theologians have divided "the image" into two aspects, a natural and a moral image, the first sustaining a "hurt" in the Fall, the second being lost. But the problem is not solved by this device; it is only pushed back a step. The Catholics hold to an unimpaired natural image, and a superadded supernatural image or grace to maintain control of the natural man. In baptism, supernatural or sanctifying grace is restored, so that two levels of existence (one natural, the other supernatural) are fused together.

In Protestantism, the theory is plagued by the problem of the eternal permanency of the union and somehow does not square with Scripture or experience. The supernatural infusion of the image is too vague, abstract, intangible. In holiness theology, the idea of a "restored image" may account for the impersonal (thingness) concept of holiness and sin which raises so many and such serious problems in understanding.

If the image is lost so that man is totally depraved, then redemption must be in principle only, not in experience. Perhaps at death the image is restored, but then what is life all about on this earth? It was *here* man was made in God's image and here, on earth, where such a thing had meaning. What contribution could the image have in the next life to the one we live here?

If the moral image, the "lost" one, is restored in this life, when is it restored? And how? Some say it is restored in conversion, or at sanctification. In any case, *what* is restored and how does one know it is restored? Is there any basic difference, structurally, between a Christian and a non-Christian? Does grace add or subtract any from man? Is there a psychological mutation associated with any stage of becoming a Christian? These are some of the questions which do not have answers as they stand. The question needs correcting.

A final observation has to do with the relationship of *image* and *likeness* to a biblical estimate of man. Our conclusion that these two terms are significant in their differences does not rest in a verbal-inspiration theory. It does seem likely that the use of these two terms could indicate a verbal device attempting to express in Hebrew words a dynamic concept of human nature which could otherwise, conceivably, be interpreted in a Hellenistic way.

Man made in God's image and likeness is not primarily a metaphysical assertion, if it is in any sense. It does not tell us anything about what man *is*, only something of what he is capable of being and becoming. In the light of the use of these terms throughout the Hebrew and Greek Scriptures, it seems not unreasonable to suppose that the biblical concept of man is dynamic, rather than passive or static.

CHAPTER VIII

Sin and Holiness

In exploring the general subject of love and holiness, it is necessary to ask penetrating questions about sin, the absolute anti-thesis of holiness, which is in itself love. Holiness and sin must be considered in the light of each other. They are absolute contrasts and throw light, semantically, on each other by contrast. *Sin* cannot be biblically or theologically discussed in the abstract any more than *holiness* or *love* or *faith* or *grace* or any of the great theological words can be. It is a *relational* term and derives its meaning from its relation to the whole.

It needs to be noted that both of these terms, related as they are to *love,* are qualities or characteristics of persons, not of imper-sonal things. If holiness and sin are personal (and rooted in love), then the quality of each lies in relationships between persons because love in its proper sense exists only between rational beings —beings capable of like and mutual response and responsibility. Real love cannot be diverted from the person-to-person level of encounter. To attempt to "love" something other, and less, than personality is to destroy the basic and proper meaning of love.

As personal, it is the self with which we have to do. The self is a non-reducible reality lying within the framework of rationality. The nonrational or impersonal area in which the self functions is not the "dwelling" of holiness or sin. It is at the point where the rational self engages itself with other rational beings that moral qualities are awakened and exercised. Love, as holiness or sin, is not quite love so long as something—anything—intrudes itself between the persons concerned. An intervening law, or gift, or ritual, or methodology, prevents the thing called love from happening.

The biblical contrasts between holiness and sin emphasize the dynamic, reacting character of the self as over against any passive, merely receptive concept which could harbor a nonrational and passive idea of holiness and sin.

Sin must be interpreted in keeping with the "existential" terminology of Scripture. The terms are all very personal. In order to make the proper distinction between the two dimensions of sin, commonly termed *original* sin and *actual* sin (or some such designation), it would be well to avoid any Platonic abstraction which is totally foreign to the Bible. The distinction in the Bible is an active spirit of "yielding," or dedication, to any center outside of God. Neutrality is impossible. Everyone *is* committed. Out of this commitment arise the kinds of actions which take their character from the source. The source is not impersonal but is the moral "bent" for which every man is personally responsible because of the provision for all men made by Christ's offering and death. We do not need to serve sin; original sin is not "deeper down and farther back" than our moral responsibility. It is not a thing, but a commitment of the self to a controlling center, always itself personal.

The foregoing assertions "fence in" the convictions about sin which must be examined in this brief chapter. We will let Wesley present his case. Then the implications for a doctrine of holiness will follow.

"Sin" in Wesley's Teaching

Wesley's concept of sin must be understood in order to appreciate his teaching about holiness. In a discussion about man made in God's image, he said:

Having prepared all things for him, He created man in his own image, after his likeness. And what was the end of his creation? It was one, and no other,—that he might know, and love, and enjoy, and serve his great Creator to all eternity. . . .

[Man] wilfully and openly rebelled against God, and cast off his allegiance to the Magesty of heaven. Hereby he instantly lost both the favor of God, and the image of God wherein he was created. As he was then incapable of obtaining happiness by the old, God established a new covenant with man; the terms of which were no longer, "Do this and live," but, "Believe, and thou shalt be saved" (*Works*, VII, 229-30).

In the concept of the effect of this "original" sin on mankind we begin to see Wesley's particular approach.

Do you mean [by original sin], the sin which Adam committed in Paradise? That this is imputed to all men, I allow; yea, that by reason thereof "the whole creation groaneth and travaileth in pain together until now." But *that any will be damned for this alone, I allow not,* till you show me where it is written. Bring me plain proof from Scripture, and I submit; but till then I utterly deny it.

Should you not rather say, that unbelief is the damning sin? and those who are condemned in that day will be therefore condemned, "because they believed not on the name of the only-begotten Son of God?" (*Works*, X, 223).

Wesley was not concerned about speculating regarding the way the race became involved in sin.

If you ask me, how sin is propagated; how it is transmitted from father to son: I answer plainly, I cannot tell; no more than I can tell how a man is propagated, how a body is transmitted from father to son. I know both the one and the other fact; but I can account for neither (*Works*, IX, 335).

But Wesley was practically concerned with the fact and meaning of sin.

Nothing is sin, strictly speaking, but a voluntary transgression of a known law of God. Therefore every voluntary breach of the law of love is sin; and nothing else, if we speak properly. To strain the matter farther is only to make way for Calvinism. There may be ten thousand wandering thoughts and forgetful intervals without any breach of love, though not without transgressing the Adamic law. But Calvinists would fain confound these together. Let love fill your heart, and it is enough (Telford Ed., *Letters*, V, 322).

And lest there should result in anyone's mind a too great moral relaxation regarding one's own need of constant reliance on the blood of Christ, he reminds us that "all deviation from the perfect holiness is sin." It is obvious that Wesley is speaking of two kinds of relationships, but this is typical of his willingness to carefully define his terms and not to fear to do so when the danger of confusion existed. Typical also is his conviction that such apparent contradictions should be understood for what they are, category errors, and not real contradictions.

Wesley's teachings about holiness were in keeping with his concept of sin. In fact it was his concept of holiness that made possible his definition of sin. Holiness is not the antithesis of sin (in that order), but sin is the antithesis of holiness. Holiness is prior and positive. It is not "the absence of sin" in the same way that sin is the absence of holiness. Holiness is love; pure love; personal, mutual love between God and man, and between man and man in God's love. Love is the fountain of the love of God flowing outward from the self and issuing in the fruits of the Spirit.

Wesley's expressions of the meaning of sin are as radical and thoroughgoing as any to be found in literature. Read, for example, from one of the eight sermons considered by him to contain the essential gospel truths.

> First, "repent," that is, know yourselves. This is the first repentance, previous to faith; even conviction, or self-knowledge. . . .
> Know thyself to be a sinner. . . . Know the corruption of thy inmost nature, whereby thou art very far gone from original righteousness; whereby "the flesh lusteth" always "contrary to the Spirit" through that "carnal mind" which is enmity against God, "which is not subject to the law of God, neither indeed can be." Know that thou art corrupted in every power, in every faculty of the soul; that thou art totally corrupted in every one of these, all the foundations being out of course. The eyes of thine understanding are darkened, so that they cannot discern God, or the things of God. . . . Thou knowest nothing yet as thou oughtest to know, neither God, nor the world, nor thyself. Thy will is no longer the will of God, but is utterly perverse and distorted, averse from all good, from all which God loves, and prone to all evil. . . . Thy affections are alienated from God, and scattered abroad over the earth. All thy passions, both thy desires and aversions, thy joys and sorrows, thy hopes and fears, are out of frame, are either undue in their degree, or placed on undue

objects. So there is no soundness in thy soul. . . . "Only wounds
and bruises, and putrefying sores." Such is the inbred corruption
of thy heart, of thy very inmost nature (*Sermons*, VII, 81-82).

(The reader is refered to Wesley's classic sermons, "Sin in Believers" and "The Repentance of Believers," for extended and considered treatises on the subject.)

Wesley used the language of Reformation doctrine and thereby, it is true, was never quite able to disengage himself from the
implication of a substantival concept of sin, and which made
his high view of holiness seem to be a contradiction.

As astute a man as Wesley, however, should be heard on his
own terms. When one keeps in mind his whole approach, the ambiguities, if they do not go entirely away, at least will not be absurdities. Rather than weakening the Reformation concept of sin,
as has been charged, Wesley felt he deepened and strengthened
it by closer reference to biblical teaching. It did not honor God, he
thought, for Him to make a man who could become so sin-bound
that God himself could not help him in his most urgent need. When
sin is put outside the rational and responsible nature of man, the
thing sin is, is no longer the deadly moral and spiritual force that
could occasion all that Christ found it necessary to do for mankind.

CHRIST AND SIN

Whatever sin might be, salvation—to be worthy of God—
would be the destruction of the seed of sin, here and now, where it
is a reality. How else could Scripture say that Christ came to save
us from our sins? To merely redefine sin in a Christian while leaving him bound in it, and still condemn a sinner for the same thing,
was, to Wesley, inconceivable.

> Least of all does justification imply, that God is deceived
> in those whom he justifies; that he thinks them to be what, in
> fact, they are not: that he accounts them to be otherwise than
> they are. It does by no means imply, that God judges concerning
> us contrary to the real nature of things; that he esteems us better
> than we really are, or believes us righteous when we are unrigh
> teous. Surely no. The judgment of the all-wise God is always
> according to truth. Neither can it consist with his unerring wis
> dom to think that I am innocent . . . because another is so. He
> can no more . . .confound me with Christ, than with David or
> Abraham (*Works*, V, 54).

Man cannot claim Christ's righteousness in lieu of his own. Character cannot be transferred or imputed. But man may be declared righteous by faith (when faith is defined as the Bible defines it).

So far-reaching is sin, so destructive is it, so eternally serious, that Christ came to save us from it, not simply to condone it in us. A careful rereading of his mature thinking in *A Plain Account of Christian Perfection,* will clear Wesley of any taint of Pelagianism. In this he affirms that man is not able to become holy apart from grace, nor ever to become holy in the sense that he no longer needs constant reliance on the atonement of Christ. Holiness, he says, does not reside in a man, but is sustained in the relationship of men with God. Were Christ to remove His presence from the holiest of men for one moment, that man would be unholy, said Wesley.

At no point does the personal relationship motif (between God and man) become more clear and important than here. Holiness consists of this unobstructed personal communion and deep, personal fellowship with God. God seeks our love and gives His love without measure. Sin is simply the absence of this relationship because man has repudiated it. This repudiation is ethical to the core and has consequences in all areas of the rational life of man and reaches into everything man touches. This rupture is a disintegrative force, religiously, in the psyche of the person sinning, in society, in the world, in all the relationships he sustains to persons and things.

Prevenient Grace

Much has been written about Wesley's view of sin and little more need be developed regarding it here, except to point out the way it relates to soteriology. Where Reformation theology bases all of salvation on the "mere grace of God," Wesley concurs, wholeheartedly. But he finds no place in Scripture to support the view that saving grace is reserved for a select few only—and even that by specific reference to particular individuals. Grace, being nothing other than God's love, is not selective, according to Scripture. It is said to include all man: "God so loved the world" (John 3:16). Never is it said that love is limited in any way.

This poured-out love, Wesley called prevenient grace, or preventing grace. All men are preserved savable. No man can save himself. He can claim no merit or credit for *any* good he ever does. Before he exercised his ability, this prevenient grace had been given him, and the power to use it is also a gift of God. No man, then, is now in a mere state of nature but is under the privileges and responsibilities of grace. Grace is not the irresistible power of God overcoming the will of man, but it is the loving hand of a Father enabling the child to use the resources given him in the first place by that Father.

> [There] is no excuse for those who continue in sin, and lay the blame upon their master, by saying, "It is God only who must quicken us; for we cannot quicken our own souls." For allowing that all the souls of man are dead in sin by nature, this excuses none, seeing there is no man that is in a state of mere nature; there is no man, unless he has quenched the Spirit, that is wholly void of the grace of God. No man living is entirely destitute of what is vulgarly called natural conscience. But this is not natural: It is more properly termed, preventing grace. Every man has a greater or less measure of this, which waiteth not for the call of man . . . Every one has some measure of that light, some faint glimmering ray, which, sooner or later, more or less, enlightens every man that cometh into the world . . . No man sins because he has not grace but because he does not use the grace which he has (*Works*, VI, 512).

In every respect, and in spite of the effects of sin in the human race, and in the individual's personal life, the personal aspect of relationship between man and God defines and delimits the meaning of sin and the freedom from it. This spiritual freedom was what Wesley spent his life teaching and into which he led many thousands of persons. Holiness is fullness of mutual love, great or small, limited by the person's capacity at any given time but nonetheless full, clean, whole love. Perfection is integrity of love. Integration can take place only in the framework of that love. Without love, disintegration, sin, death, hell follow inevitably.

Sin, a Religious Problem

When Wesley moved in this area of thought he was consciously following one of Augustine's insights and affirmation, namely, that sin is a religious matter. Sin is perverted love, not first of all concupiscence, for this is the consequence of sin, not its cause. None of the essential factors or functions of humanness is lost in the Fall, but the whole of man's moral mature is out of joint. As a religious fact, first of all, sin is a rupture of fellowship with God. Holiness is the healing of the religious malady. Fellowship can be restored on God's terms, only. This is the beginning of the integration of all of personal life, which then reaches out to social life and to the world and finally to the earth itself.

Any theory of man and sin which made a mockery of the death of Christ drew from Wesley the finest of his scorn. To him, when sin was put so far back and so deep down that the essential, rational, responsible nature of man was said to be destroyed to the point where man could not be restored to the image of God in this life, sin was no longer sin in the evangelical sense. It has lost its religious and ethical meaning. Sin which lay behind that which is personal was not the concern of Wesley, for to him in the religious sense it had no meaning. In his sermon "A Blow at the Root, or, Christ Stabbed in the House of His Friends," using the text, "Judas, betrayest thou the Son of man with a kiss?" (Luke 22:48), Wesley makes his point abundantly clear that a wrong concept of sin destroys the very holiness that Christ's death was meant to provide. Wesley, the calm, cool, low-key man, packs such passion into this sermon that it stands in danger of overstating his opponents' case.

> "Without holiness no man shall see the Lord." . . . Nothing under heaven can be more sure than this. . . . None shall live with God, but he that now lives to God; none shall enjoy the glory of God in heaven, but he that bears the image of God on earth; none that is not saved from sin here can be saved from hell hereafter; none can see the kingdom of God above, unless the kingdom of God be in him below. . . .
> And yet as sure as this is, and as clearly as it is taught in every part of the Holy Scripture, there is scarce one among all the truths of God, which is less received by men (*Works*, X, 364).

After showing this to be the case among the "heathen," the Roman church, and some Protestants, he states the position which he feels accords with the Word of God.

> No man can have the mind which was in Christ, till he is justified by his blood, till he is forgiven and reconciled to God through the redemption that is in Jesus Christ. And none can

be justified, they are well assured, but by faith, even faith alone. . . .

What evasion now? What way could Satan take to make all this light of none effect? . . . What, indeed, but to persuade the the very man who had received it, to "turn the grace of God into lasciviousness?" To this end Simon Magus appeared again, and taught, "that Christ had done, as well as suffered, all; that his righteousness being imputed to us, we need none of our own; that seeing there was so much righteousness and holiness in Him there needs none in us; that to think we have any, or to desire or seek any, is to renounce Christ; that from the beginning to the end of salvation, all is in Christ, nothing in man." . . .

This is indeed "a blow at the root," the root of all holiness, all true religion. Hereby Christ is "stabbed in the house of his friends." . . . For wherever this doctrine is cordially received, it leaves no place for holiness. . . . It makes men afraid of personal holiness, afraid of cherishing any thought of it, or motion toward it, lest they should deny the faith, and reject Christ and his righteousness (*Works,* X, 366).

There is so much material in Wesley's works on the subject of sin one is tempted to bring more and more to the study of his position. The conclusion of it is that the real question is not, Is holiness not too high a standard for mere man to reach? but, Are we defining sin in such a way that we blind ourselves to what the Scripture is telling us about holiness? When asked in this way, the whole problem is approached from a biblical point of view.

HOLINESS AND SIN AS RELATED TO LOVE

It is Wesley's emphasis on love that becomes the key not only to the meaning of holiness but also to the meaning of sin. Sin is love, but love gone astray. Man is a creature who is not free not to love something. He is a committed person. Every conscious act reaffirms that commitment—or challenges it. Love is the most powerful drive of the human person; the deepest fact about rational man. But it is exactly in this drive where he is most free and most responsible. "Coerced" love is not love at all. At no point is the human person more responsible, therefore more "free," than the ordering of his love. He is not the slave of his love unless he surrenders his humanity to impersonal drives. He may abdicate his humanity but he is not thereby absolved from responsibility for doing so.

Men find themselves locked by their own love into an orbit about a center. Sin is love locked into a false center, the self. The falseness is always multi-faceted, excentrific, destructive. Sin is the distortion of love. It is a substitute for the real, resembling it superficially. But sin cannot deliver the real. It cannot create. It destroys the good it seeks. Sin says, "Look at the freedom I offer, with none of the restraint and labor and conformity God demands. Discard God's stultifying, restrictive rules. Begin to enjoy the fruit without tediously cultivating the vine. Have love, cheaply, freely." But no one can continue to love the false and remain whole. Sin carries the seed of its own destruction.

Holiness is love locked into the True Center, Jesus Christ our Lord. Being "true," all of the self—and progressively all of life—comes into harmony and wholeness and strength.

By placing sin in juxtaposition to love, something is said about what sin is and what freedom from it involves. It must be said again that love is a personal quality, a relationship established with or against persons. It has to do with the nature of its object. The object reacts back on and defines the quality of love. The essence of humility and true personal moral grandeur is to set one's heart on God. The epitome of pride and carnal arrogance is to raise one's own miserable self to the pretension of being a god. And here is the "watershed" between holiness and sin; integration versus destruction, life versus death. "Choose you this day whom ye will serve." "No man can serve two masters." "Ye cannot serve God and mammon."

HOLINESS—THE NEW AFFECTION

But this leaves one more vital question to be considered. Granted that the tenacity of love is perhaps the most unbreakable bond of the human spirit and manifests itself either as the powerful and indestructible moral vitality of heroic Christians, or in the unspeakable corruption of men in moral vileness and cold brutality. How is it possible to change the commitment of love from one object to another? How can any man change from one orbit to another? How can any *coup d'etat* upset the ancient dynasty of self-worship when it is the self which must act? The answer is brief and to the point: He cannot do it *in his own strength.*

This impasse could not be broken were it not for God's grace. But a too shallow concept of grace can betray truth here. In some way God must be able to make it possible for the man most firmly in the grip of the consequence of his own free choice to make the traumatic contrary choice which the new commitment demands without robbing him of the only claim he has to the freedom which makes him a man and not an automaton.

God acts, but He acts in moral magnificence. He wins His way into man's heart by a counter display of His love and fulfillment. "God was in Christ, reconciling the world unto himself." The splendor of God's reality and promise casts contrary loves into the shade. God does not force His way into the heart; He excites the jaded hopes of men until the old, cheap loves look shoddy and corrupt. God attacks the "want to" in man. There is some truth in Peter Abelard's theory of the atonement which conceived of Christ's death as a demonstration of God's love designed to win men's confidence and allegiance. It is more, surely, but it is a reconciling act of love, too.

God acts in the only area of man's true freedom and makes decision not only possible and desirable but mandatory. No man is free not to take a position relative to moral decision in the light of this very deep and profound, divine self-revelation and offer of life. God acts in the only area of man's existence where real change begins. He does not demand a cold, unmotivated, deliberate, purely intellectual decision to change the object of one's commitment from self to God. The Spirit of God comes time and time again to manifest the beauty of Christ and the excellency of His lordship, and by contrast the poverty and ugliness of one's own best achievements and possessions.

True moral and spiritual values are set in comparison and contrast. Life and death are placed before us with all the allurement of God's love contrasted with darkness and death. Only in this holy hour can any man move toward God; never apart from God's initiative. Jesus said, "If I had not come . . . they had not had sin: but now they have no cloke [excuse] for their sin" (John 15:22). He brought light and winsomeness as well as the motivation to love Him, and we can love Him only because he first loved us. There is a real measure of truth in the book title *The Expulsive Power of a New Affection.*

"Old Man" Versus "New Man"

This chapter opened with the assertion that sin can be defined properly only against holiness, and that neither sin nor holiness can be discussed meaningfully in the abstract, or apart from the whole of religion. A discussion of sin, therefore, would not be adequate were it not to give some attention to the meaning of the Pauline terms "old man" and "new man," as well as the significance of Adam and Christ in relation to these terms and in relation to each other.

It is necessary to introduce a Hebraic concept termed in theology "federal headship"; and in biblical studies, "corporate personality." Edmond Jacob, in *Theology of the Old Testament*, quotes Wheeler Robinson, who gives the "classical formulation" of this idea: "The whole group, including its past, present and future members, function as a single individual through any one of those members conceived as representative of it."[1] In the Hebrew way of thinking, the individual and the "head" of the community of which he was a part sustained a relation to each other of real, not ideal, unity. The head was an "incarnation" of every unit in the group. Every individual "incarnated in his own person the whole community," or, "the individual can be thought of *in* the community and the community in the individuals."[2]

This seems to be the sense in which Paul conceives all men to be in Adam. The substantival, biological structure of the race has often been made the ground for a materialistic theory of sin and its transmission on the basis of Paul's comments in Romans 5. A deeper analysis of this passage will show the inadmissibility of such an interpretation. Whatever Paul meant, the direct contrast by analogy between being in Adam and being in Christ puts both in a spiritual, not substance, framework of thought. Wesley expresses this idea thus:

> My reason for believing Adam to be the Federal Head or
> Representative of mankind is this: Christ was the representative
> of mankind, when God, "laid on him the iniquities of us all, and
> he was wounded for our transgressions." But Adam, was a type,
> or figure of Christ, therefore he was also, in some sense, our
> representative; in consequence of which, "all died" in him, as
> "in Christ all shall be made alive" (*Works*, IX, 332).

Even more relevant to our point is Wesley's further comment in the same discussion, quoting, with approval, a part of his opponents' own position:

> "As Adam was a public person, and acted in the stead of all mankind, so Christ, likewise, was a public person, and acted on behalf of all his people; that as Adam was the first general representative of mankind, Christ was the second and last; that what they severally did in this capacity, was not intended to terminate in themselves, but to affect as many as they severally represented." . . .
>
> [Wesley adds] This is, indeed, the truth. For "all that was lost to us by Adam's disobedience is fully recovered by Christ's obedience; however we denominate the relation in which the one and the other stands to us." In this we agree (*Ibid.*, p. 333).

It is this analogy that Paul uses to link all men with Adam (*anthropos*). As head of the race he represents all men, and what he did can be said to be what all men do. In Adam, men are born into a race which is "alienated from the life of God." The centering of devotion is not on God but, in pride, on self and the things of "the world." Everything that "in Adam" stands for is the "old man," the false and destructive orientation of the self outside of Christ. This is the "kingdom of the world," the *reign* of sin and death, the locus and dominion of sin. This situation defines sin. It is not a mere "principle" but an existential fact in the experience of the race and in each man in the race. Wesley describes it well:

> If man should be willing to find the miseries of his fall, his understanding might furnish him with reasons for constant mourning; for despising and denying himself; might point out the sad effects of turning away from God and losing his Spirit, in the shame and anguish of a nature at variance with itself; thirsting after immortality, and yet subject to death; approving righteousness, and yet taking pleasure in things inconsistent with it; feeling an immense want of something to perfect and satisfy all its faculties, and yet neither able to know what that mighty thing is, otherwise than from its present defects, nor how to attain it, otherwise than by going contrary to its present inclinations (*Works*, VII, 510).

In total contrast to this is the headship of Christ, the Second, or Last Adam, the "new man." Christ is the true Head, the First-born of all creatures, whose authority had been usurped by the "old man." At this point the profound significance of the Incarnation is revealed. Christ, as the true Corporate Person (in relation to mankind), takes on himself the whole heritage and sin of the race of mankind. No one else can do this. He is the Lord of the kingdom of God. In Him is the reversal of all that the old man has done. By His death and resurrection He established His headship and ends the alienation of the race from God. He is God with us, Emmanuel. In Christ, the true Head of the Church, men become one with the new Corporate Personality. In each believer is incarnated the total life of the new race; and Christ, the Head, incorporates into himself, as the New Man, every believer. This is the kingdom of God. This is the Life of God in each Christian. When Jesus said, "*I* am the *way*, the *truth*, and the *life*," He was contrasting His headship with the contrary, destructive, deceptive way which was the lie and death. The Adamic orientation is this false way.

This should give practical meaning to the strange wording of Paul, "*Put off* the old man with his deeds," and, "*Put on* the new man" (Col. 3:9 and Eph. 4:21-25, italics mine). This act of total renunciation of the loyalties and dedication to a life as characterized by Adam, and the total new alignment with Christ the New Man, constitute a vivid commentary on the meaning of both sin and holiness. It also puts the new responsibility for serving under the Kingdom of one's choice, squarely on the individual person who comes to Christ.

Some of the New Testament passages vividly illustrating the contrast between the two ways follow:

HOLINESS	VERSUS	SIN
Matt. 6:24. Serving God		Serving mammon
John 3:16. *(et al.)* Believing on Jesus		Unbelief (rejection)
Rom. 1:25. Truth of God exchanged for		"The Lie"
Rom. 6:13, 16. Yielding to God Eternal life		Yielding to sin Death
Rom. 6:19. Yield your members to righteousness unto sanctification		Members yielded to impurity unto death

Rom. 8:2. "The law of the Spirit of life in Christ Jesus"	"The law of sin and death"
Rom. 8:5. They that are of the Spirit mind the things of the Spirit.	They that are after the flesh mind the things of the flesh.
Rom. 8:6. The mind of the Spirit is life and peace.	The mind of the flesh is death.
I Cor. 12:3. "Jesus is . . . Lord"	Jesus is "accursed"
Gal. 5:16-24. The fruit of the Spirit (itemized)	The works of the flesh (itemized)
Eph. 4:25. Speak the truth	Speaking the lie
I Thess. 4:3, 7. The will of God, your sanctification	Uncleanness and moral impurity
I Pet. 1:14-15. Be holy in all your conduct	Conformed to the passions of your former ignorance
Gal. 6:8. He that soweth to the Spirit shall of the Spirit reap eternal life.	He that soweth to the flesh shall of the flesh reap corruption.

In summary, sin and holiness must be understood in spiritual and moral dimensions rather than in substantival and/or mathematical dimensions. These terms must be measured against the highest perfection. They can never be truly evaluated in terms of units because they are moral and personal (individual and social) through and through. And as personal they describe moral values, never mathematical additions and/or subtractions.

Something of this misunderstanding has occasioned the theological abberations to which Wesleyanism is the intended corrective. In one tradition the limitation of the extent of the atonement is the result of calculating sin in weight or number or legal terms. It affirms that Christ died for a specific and measured amount of sin, no more, no less, else all sin would be "paid for" and all men would be saved. In another tradition Christ's merit cancels "original sin" only. The baptized person subsequently makes satisfaction for all his own sins committed in daily life.

In some religious groups there is a tendency to depersonalize "original sin." The principle of sin is sharply distinguished from committed sins and is too often a reference to a "something." It is "farther back and deeper down" than the person and beyond the place where language can go or thought conceive—a virtual substance with *real* existence in some way attached to the substance of the soul but not essential to it. Its "removal" is taken out of the moral responsibility of men and divorced from a conscious response to the demands of grace. No way of thinking is less biblical nor more magical. (Any concept of acquiring what we want without recourse to the appropriate means is belief in magic. It is the attempt to bypass the causal means between dream and reality.)

Men are always trying to find some way to escape personal responsibility for being what they are, and to avoid having to confess it and do something about it. James R. Dolby puts it this way:

> You and I are basically dishonest. . . . We have betrayed ourselves. Too often we ourselves believe the lies which we are trying to get others to accept. . . .
> Personal dishonesty is an insidious disease. Once begun, it slowly destroys the person until he is no longer aware that he has betrayed himself.[3]

They (or we) are seeking an escape from inner evil in some magical way that evades the mature demand of meeting moral demands head on. "Some people in the name of Christianity use a form of theistic magic to help escape the responsibility of making a decision."[4]

Man's problem is not a substructure of some alien substance clinging to his soul but his own alienation from God. "His problem is not ignorance but disobedience, infidelity, and the obduracy of the heart."[5]

In a word, biblical psychology is personal and is concerned wholly with personal relationships, individual and social. God's relation to men is in personal, historical context, and man's response to God cannot be gauged by any unit measure. The biblical message drives back into the heart of mankind, back to where the deepest, most responsible, most personal level of life is played out. It is ethical in the most real and profound sense.

CHAPTER IX

The Meaning of "Moral"

The whole of the gospel is set within the framework of history and responsible personhood. God is personal. Men are persons. God communicates something of himself. Men respond or react in conscious, meaningful attitudes and decisions. Such words as *personal, love, decision, personal relationship,* and *moral* are important in discussing matters pertaining to the gospel. The good news is that something God did and does opens the way to Him, but the Bible deals heavily with the kind of thing man must do if he profits by God's love.

No more important message can be spoken than that personal sanctification should be expressed in terms of personal relationships. This takes precedence over methodology and understands the person-to-person reality central in all aspects of Christian experience. The importance of this concept becomes disturbing when a covert, substantival concept of human nature is slipped under the biblical and Wesleyan theological terms. In this way of thinking, the great gulf (creating the "credibility gap") between ideas, or theological absolutes, and practical life leads to the compartmentalization of life. This is fatal to genuine Christianity.

This divorce seals off the real self from the wholesome self-criticism so necessary to authentic Christian living and integrity. It creates the false sense of assurance accompanying mechanical and/or emotional experience purported to be the evidence of genuine states of grace.

A substance interpretation of the self, sin, holiness, even of the Holy Spirit, robs men of a basis for an understanding of all aspects of redemption as moral relationship with God and men. When these spiritual matters are reduced to the level of substance, the entire holiness enterprise is fatally compromised. The danger is that the language of the Bible, so thoroughly and wholesomely spiritual and psychological, may be hardened by the just demands of theology into nonpersonal categories submitting to nonmoral—even magical manipulation.

A proper understanding, then, of these terms is exceedingly important to an understanding of Wesleyanism. Wesleyan theology stresses the *personal*. God has made man a *person*. The image of God has to do with whatever a person is. *Person* and *personal* are difficult concepts to explain. They refer to a very objective and focalized reality, but can better be approached through what a person does than through what he is.

Neither Scripture nor Wesley speculates about the nature of man, ontologically. Both are deeply concerned about his "heart," or his motivation—a spot no finger can point to and say, "This is the locus of the man." We are not relegating a man to a mere "stream of consciousness," which is nothing more than a negative ontology. We simply regard man in this study as the Bible does—a person to whom God speaks and one who can answer back in a genuine conversation.

It will never be possible to understand either Wesley or Scripture if the heart, as the moral center of the person, is not kept from all consideration of substance. To call it the "agent," as some do, solves no problem. *Agent* is as undefinable as *heart* or *person*. We will be satisfied to speak of the self as the focal point of all a man is —body and mind, heart and spirit, conscience and will. At this point man "is."

Much that he *is* he derives from his heritage, from his culture, from his relatedness with the total present, but he is not locked hopelessly in this "prison." In ways which baffle philosophy and science, man can and does elect to make contrary choices and thereby becomes a "new man." Jesus spoke to whatever it is about man that takes positions about "ultimate concerns"; and man's condemnation or approval, in God's sight, depended on what man did at this point.

Jesus' comments about the "nature" of man need more profound study. He said, "What comes out of the mouth has its origins in the heart; and that is what defiles a man. Wicked thoughts, murder, adultery, fornication, theft, perjury, slander—these all proceed from the heart; and these are the things that defile a man" (Matt. 15:18-20, NEB).

But the heart, as evil as it may be, is not a location but a disposition. It may produce evils which defile the man, but it can also love God and neighbor and thereby please God. This concept of *heart* as the reigning center of personality must not be forgotten when the problem of sin is discussed—as well as the matters of holiness and perfection and cleansing and all the other facets of theology and practice. Would it be drawing more out of Jesus' word than He intended, or than could be defended, to say that it is not the man *(anthropos)* that defiles the heart, but the heart that defiles the man? Sin, then, is not in the "humanity" of man (a generic concept) but in the very center of the motivational life of individuals—that which makes a man a person. This, too, is the locus of holiness. Holiness has to do with the heart, or center of the man. It deals with that part which loves, not *primarily* with the corporeal man. As sin has consequences in life, so holiness has consequences in life.

It has always been the most profound conviction of Wesleyanism that the Bible speaks to the moral relationships of men and not about sub-rational, nonpersonal areas of the self. Sin is basically self-separation from God, not in measurable distance but in moral unlikeness and spiritual alienation. Holiness is moral to the core —love to God and man. These are qualities of the self in relation to the person of God and of men.

To affirm that holiness and sin are personal relationships, not things which can be counted and weighed, often sounds like a betrayal of holiness doctrine, and actually heresy. When the very words in Scripture that arise out of the most vital and living situations are interpreted in a way that robs them of life, a transvaluation of the gospel becomes both alarming and dangerous. That biblical exegesis should become the victim of this transvaluation is spiritual tragedy.

The tendency to depersonalize the Christian message permits an evaluation of spiritual life by quantity measurements which totally destroys the meaning of them. Qualities are lost when the attempt is made to add and subtract them. Sydney Harris in his syndicated column, "Strictly Personal," quoted Ortego Y. Gasset, the great Spanish thinker, as saying—"The minimum is the measuring unit in the realm of quantity, but in the realm of values, the highest values are the measuring unit." It is the characteristic of quantity that it is measured by the smallest units. We compute quantities by adding and/or subtracting and by comparing worth by mathematics, weight and time units.

But it is the peculiarity of quality value that it is measured against the highest perfection. Impersonal things are counted; personal excellences are compared with the best conceivable. A perfect marriage is not the sum total of the number of gifts and kisses, but the measure of perfect love and loyalty and devotion. To judge personal religious experience by the wrong measuring standard is to distort the meaning of religion. When spiritual progress is calculated in mathematical terms, the ultimate tension and frustration and ambiguity are encountered between theology, scripture, and psychology. Certainly no such tension and ambiguity are to be found in Scripture. A preoccupation with the finding of certain numbers of works of grace in Scripture will blind the researcher to the moral imperative which alone can make "works of grace" meaningful.

The study, to this point, has proceeded on the conviction that the most fruitful way to interpret Wesleyan, or holiness, theology is by way of affirming the "interface" concerning which it speaks as *a personal relationship between man and God.*

Personal relationship does not mean simply that God is personal, that He has a will, that He initiates action intelligently, that He is a rational Being. Persons can and do act purposefully toward nonpersonal reality. A carpenter hammers nails. A dentist drills teeth. A farmer drives a herd of cattle out to pasture. Persons can and do impose their wills on other persons. In human society these "impersonal" relationships can and do prevail. In a "computer society" individuals become so much the slave of technology that the rank and file of mankind takes it for granted. The "average" is the ideal and the justification for mediocrity. The consensus is the true. Custom is king. Clever advertising substitutes for thought. Commentators mold opinion. One who prefers not to bother about decision-making may live with few to make. One who prefers to think may pay a high price for being a person—martyrdom more or less bloody but very real.

To lay this into theology helps to make the picture come clear. If God acts toward man apart from his thinking and choice; if salvation is "applied" to man by a supernatural alteration of his mind, body, psyche, "deeper down" than his conscious life, where he cannot be held responsible; if man can expect a "psychological mutation" so that he no longer needs to feel the full force of temptation, then—though God is a personal Being and man is a person —"personal relationship" is a fiction, biblical salvation is a myth.

Personal relationship becomes a reality when two selves— two "I's"—open themselves to each other, respect the moral autonomy of each other, honor the personal integrity of each other, esteem each other as they esteem themselves, share themselves with each other without demanding mindless capitulation from each other, and then respond to each other in the profound awareness of mutual intercommunication. In this encounter which defines fellowship, the integrity of each is maintained and enhanced without the surrender of anything essential to selfhood. The relationship is not marred by loss of self-identity or self-respect, and yet the self-giving is total. Only a strong self can risk the demands of self-giving inherent in true fellowship. Only such a self can know love without shattering *itself* or the *one* who stands as the object of love.

God acts toward man in terms of personal relationship. If He did not, if He took advantage of His power and position by by-passing the integrity of man whom He made for love and fellowship, He would destroy man as man. Love does not—cannot— violate the integrity of another. To do so cancels out love. A "love" which forces even "good" things on another destroys that other. When St. John can say, "God is love," he has exhausted human language. He has said something about God which is a commentary on the nature and potential of man and upon the kind of thing that redemption is, and what God is. Wesley had a word here:

> You know how God wrought in your own soul, when he first enabled you to say, "The life I now live, I live by faith in the Son of God, who loved me, and gave himself for me." He did not take away your understanding; but enlightened and strengthened it. He did not destroy any of your affections; rather they were more vigorous than before. Least of all did he take away your liberty; your power of choosing good or evil: He did not force you; but, being assisted by his grace, you, like Mary, chose the better part. Just so has he assisted five in one house to make that happy choice; fifty or five hundred in one city; and many thousands in a nation;—without depriving any of them of that liberty which is essential to a moral agent.
>
> Not that I deny, that there are exempt cases, wherein the o'erwheming power of saving grace does, for a time, work as irresistibly as lightning falling from heaven. But I speak of God's general manner of working, of which I have known innumerable instances; perhaps more within fifty years last past, than any one in England or in Europe. And with regard even to these exempt cases; although God does work irresistibly for the time, yet I do not believe there is any human soul in which God works irresistibly at all times. Nay, I am fully persuaded there is not. I am persuaded, there are no men living that have not many times "resisted the Holy Ghost," and made void "the counsel of God against themselves." Yea, I am persuaded every child of God has had, at some time, "life and death set before him," eternal life and eternal death; and has in himself the casting voice. So true is that well-known saying of St. Augustine, (one of the noblest he ever uttered.) *Qui fecit nos sine nobis, non salvabit nos sine nobis:* "He that made us without ourselves, will not save us without ourselves (*Works*, VI, 280-81).

We seek to understand the "nature" of man as made in God's image more adequately. The word *moral* is used to describe the kind of being the biblical writers seem to have in mind as they speak about man's relationship to God and His will. *Moral* is not a biblical word but may fairly bear the weight of the biblical meaning with careful definition.

Moral does not mean, in this study, that everything man does is right, or that he knows, always, what right is. But it does mean that man acts in relation to right and wrong, good and bad, true and false. He is responsible for whatever decision he makes about these pairs, however he may or may not understand what is the right or wrong, good or bad, true or false. In other words a moral "nature" is capable of integrity, and *goodness* is defined as moral integrity and *badness* as absence of integrity.

It is not to be assumed that we are equating integrity with holiness, though holiness cannot be less than integrity. We are attempting, at this stage, to establish the point that the capacity for integrity is the meaning of *moral* and that "religion" cannot be defined or experienced without a full measure of integrity. Holiness theology stands or falls at this point. Theology that does not take human integrity into consideration cannot take biblical holiness seriously. Any theology, or religion, even "holiness theology," that supposes that God bypasses the deepest moral integrity of man is not biblical. Whenever moral, or personal, integrity is relaxed in order to make way for wholly supernatural operation, or merely a legal "acquittal," the most important thrust of biblical teaching has been missed.

Biblical writers do not speculate about what a person is, as has been noted, nor do they ever attribute moral qualities, good or evil, to substance. We need also to note that no man is ever given any comfort by the suggestion that since he is "in sin" and under the bondage of sin, and deceived, and his mind is darkened and his will perverted, he is absolved from responsibility regarding it. Never can it be found in Scripture that a man sins because he cannot help it, and therefore can excuse himself.

One more word of explanation needs to be said. *This position is not Pelagianism.* We are assuming with all mainline Christian doctrine that man is very far gone from righteousness and from God. But it is also assumed that salvation has to do with mankind that is made in a moral mold and under the prevenient ministry of the Holy Spirit. Man can take a position relative to what he is shown about God and, by borrowed but freely offered grace, turn to or away from God.

When this "gracious ability" is interpreted as being humanistic and Pelagian, it should be pointed out that such a judgment is made from a much more limited and less flexible point of view than one encounters in the Bible. Augustine and Pelagius argued from the same premise, each taking an opposite position. One said, "Yes"; the other said, "No." Both were rationalists. One defended God's sovereignty against any contrary will. The other defended man's integrity against any violation of it. Both defended valid and necessary truths. But these are irreconcilable truths within the philosophical frame of reference that both accepted. They are antinomies characteristic of all logical thought. In philosophy, the question is, How can we defend freedom in a deterministic world? In theology the question is, How can human freedom be genuine within the context of God's absolute sovereignty? or, How free *is* man?—not, Is man free?

The distinction, an important one, between systematic theology and biblical theology bears on the problem before us. Systematic theology solves its crucial questions by submitting the matter to the prevailing and structuring presupposition and proceeding logically to a conclusion. The scope and dogma of systematic theologies are limited and determined by the premise of each. These various and varied presuppositions account for the radical differences in theologies. Biblical theology, on the other hand, ideally at least, first seeks answers on the basis of biblical study and works back to a basic position which is always criticizable and alterable by further understanding and study. One is deductive reasoning, the other inductive.

The Wesleyan position is not strictly systematic. It attempts to be biblical before it proceeds to dogmatic conclusions. The major difference between the philosophical framework in which the Augustinian-Pelagian alternatives lie and the biblical approach to theological matters is that biblical writers moved in an entirely different world and way of thinking. Biblical thought moves in the atmosphere of practical personal relationships rather than in speculative reasoning. The unregenerate man, in effect, says, "I know myself to be a sinner because I sin." The speculative approach is, "Man is a sinner. What causes man to sin? How come sin?" Wesley spoke of "free grace" and by this meant that the capacity man had to choose was given him by God's grace. Pelagius said man was by nature morally neutral and wholly free to will his own holiness. Augustine simply denied free will as interpreted by Pelagius as an affront to God's sovereignty.

The Meaning of "Moral"

The Christian religion is a redemptive religion. It has ethical implications. This means that it makes a practical difference in life. Christianity is a practical religion in that it is the basis of ethical life. Religion and ethics are firmly bound together as cause and effect, or better, as a tree and its fruit. In the Christian way of thinking, religion without ethical consequences would be sterile and meaningless. In fact, every religion *does* have such consequences, for good or evil, fully recognized or not. Further, what one does and justifies in himself *is* his religion and is a commentary on his "god," acknowledged as a god or not.

This union of ethics and religion raises some practical problems. For example, How is it possible to have a true moral situation and consequently a sound ethic if and when religion imposes a moral code "from the outside" onto the person? Does the Christian religion with its high ethical demands negate or affirm the freedom of choice which *moral* means?

The moral person is truly free, but that freedom is not abstract and irresponsible but lies within the framework of that which is "personal" and, in fact, defines the meaning of *personal*. Morality is not an autonomous creation of the self, but a relation of the self to other selves within a society of selves. Human freedom is not absolute but genuine within the limited area of moral responsibility, but within this area it is an inescapable necessity.

Let us turn to an analysis of *moral* in relation to holiness.

1. "Moral" Is Personal.

Moral presupposes the personal in contrast to thingness. Whatever it is that distinguishes the spiritual from the natural is personal. In this contrast, *spiritual* is identified as that in self-conscious awareness that is not bound into the cause/effect matrix of the natural. It is precisely in freedom from that kind of cause/effect continuity that it escapes naturalism and becomes spiritual or personal. It is that which transcends the natural and can say, "I," meaning, "There is a difference between *I* and *you* and between *I* and *things*."

Martin Buber's discussion of "I and Thou" in a book by that name is suggestive and semantically useful here. A very free inter-

174 / A Theology of Love

pretation is given. Each *I* is a center of the universe, seeing everything from its own perspective. It is personal to the core in the sense that there is a sharp distinction from all other entities in personal self-awareness. I am not a thing. I may be dependent on other than myself for existence and maintenance but I am not free to disclaim personal responsibility because of that dependence.

The *I* is self-determining and self-conscious. The *it* is determined. No *I* is an *it*. When two self-conscious *I*'s confront each other, two individual universes vie with each other for standing room. Two self-conscious, self-determining worlds try to occupy the center, and tension is set up. There can be a clash of "rights." When one *I* treats the other *I* as an *it* and tries to dominate and control the other, an immoral situation exists. Particularly is this true when the *I* tries to control and use the *Thou*—God. Without passing judgment upon the philosophical use Buber makes of this idea, it is useful in pointing out the need to see the *personal* element in the meaning of *moral*. One of my university professors illustrated it this way. Astronomy can never be the locus of a study in ethics; that is, astronomical patterns are not criticizable, but the astronomer is. No sensible farmer worries about tomatoes appearing on wheat stalks. Nor does a rational carpenter beat a roof that leaks in the rain. But the farmer is entirely liable for the answer to the question, "Why are you a farmer?" or, "Why did you plant wheat instead of tomatoes?" and the carpenter can be penalized for beating his wife no matter what she does to displease him. It is in the personal in contrast to thingness that *moral* begins to have meaning.

2. *The Personal Is Moral.*

Moreover, to be personal is to be responsible. Men have wills, and the will is an integral part of personality. And the will is rational, not simply a mood, instinct, or passing desire. It is purposive.

The one thing which distinguishes man as a man is this capacity to make decisions which are good or bad, right or wrong, on the basis of principle, irrespective of desirable or undesirable consequences. It is precisely at the point where the cause/effect determinism of the natural body makes its demands upon the human spirit that responsibility begins. "Natural law" is impersonal; that is, it operates apart from will.

Spiritual life is simply distinguished from the natural by its personal nature—it requires a rational will to maintain its existence. In fact, persons are not free *not* to be responsible. The more that is discovered about human personality, the more certain we become that will operates even in the lowest, most primitive levels of consciousness, and we are told that even in the deepest hypnotic state moral responsibility and will are not lost nor do they cease to function. The operator cannot force the patient to violate his conscience. Rather than to say that men *have* wills, it might be more true to say, "To be human is to will responsibly."

3. *Moral Capacity Is an Awareness of "Ought."*

Not only are men personal and responsible, but also they are aware of themselves as facing the tension of ethical situations. In fact, moral awareness is precisely in the consciousness of being in oneself the locus of moral tension. Not only do we say, "I can choose," or, "I must choose," but, "In this choice I am violating or approving the right." We may not know which of several possibilities may be best, or we may not want to do the right were we to know it, but we know that there is a right and a wrong, and that we ought to do the right and ought not to do the wrong. A moral being recognizes these ethical demands in interpersonal situations. It is a recognition of the need for a right relationship and at least displays a need for self-approval and inner peace as a result of that approval. Wesley said, "A good conscience brings a man the happiness of being consistent with himself . . . which every person will find, after all, is the thing he wants" (*Works*, VII, 572).

4. *Moral Is a Multiple-Foci Relationship.*

Moral capacity and responsibility requires a relation to another person to complete its meaning—to come into true existence. Goodness is never the autonomous achievement of a person within himself. Men were made to *fellowship*—with God and with other persons. Men were made to love, and love demands a multi-personal relationship.

Men were made to fellowship, is the basic truth. Wholesome personality is contingent upon the ability to communicate with others responsibly. This fact draws the concept of *moral* into definition. It parallels, if it does not actually become equated with self-realization or the actualization of personality. But self-realization alone, though important in a number of ways, is not and cannot be the expression of the person as a moral being. And weed or animal by surrendering to the laws of its being "realizes" itself; but personality cannot be so defined because the single identifying element, the moral, is ignored. Even apart from any consideration of human sinfulness, uninhibited individual self-development is not, *per se,* moral growth. Contemporary psychology recognizes the absolute need for interpersonal communication for wholesome development. So much more so ought Christian theology to recognize this fact.

Moral quality can inhere only in persons, never in things. Personality is not a thing, and only in the relations which characterize freedom of persons can morality have meaning. The self which develops apart from responsibility to other persons is not moral and *is not truly personal.*

The relationship which determines the quality of moral is the interpersonal dependence and interaction of *I'*s, which gives significance to each unit in the organism. One of the most fundamental qualities of a person is the love urge. It may not be too much to say that this urge is so basic to selfhood that no person is free *not* to love. This "urge" can no more be denied or thwarted without serious disturbance of personality than can the herd urge or sex urge. There is a foundational need inherent in every human person to love someone and to be loved. The self is completed and integrated and wholesome only when there is rapport with others. Mental hospitals are full of people who cannot communicate with others. They distrust, dislike, hate, and finally withdraw from the world of other persons. The condition is called schizophrenia. The need for fellowship is much deeper than sentiment; it is basic to mental health and ultimately to truly human existence. It is not the totally independent person who is the epitome of strength, but precisely the person who is capable of responsible mutual interrelatedness with others while at the same time maintaining a sharp and growing self-identity.

Just as fellowship is necessary in human relations, so it is necessary in the spiritual life, which actually is the pattern of all that is involved in the personal dimension. Men seek an object of affection to complete themselves. They must love something. If the searching self settles for things, it idolizes—makes a god of—material things and the *moral* existence is thwarted and distorted. If the self fastens on other human beings, moral life is improperly developed. If one attempts to love himself in this ultimate way, the result is moral perversion—grotesque, destructive, ugly. Augustine was right when he saw that men are made for God and cannot find rest until they rest in Him. It is no idle thing to say that men were made to fellowship with God. To cut off that fellowship is to throw personality off balance, to say the least. Theologically, it is "the sin" which unseats moral integrity and ends in moral idiocy.

It is probably true to say also that human nature was never intended to exist apart from the presence of the Holy Spirit. That is, the personal fellowship, the mutual rapport and harmonious response, of God and man was the natural and intended atmosphere of fellowship and holiness. In fact, holiness could be defined by this state of affairs. In the atmosphere of fellowship with God, holiness is. Moral life has two foci, not one. Only as men trust and love God is morality valid and holiness possible. A refusal to use the moral capacity to maintain this relationship is sin. Holiness and sin are, thus, two kinds of relationship to God, one positive, the other negative, but both active because it is the person, forced to decision, choosing the right or wrong object of his love.

Wesleyan theology rejects the concept of original holiness as an impersonal goodness, in favor of a more biblical idea of holiness which stresses a right personal relationship to God. Holiness, or morality, is never a quality of impersonal substance but the way one reacts to God and to persons. To understand this is to help correct the idea that sin has substance or is a thing which can be—or cannot be—removed as a diseased part of the body.

Holiness is not metaphysically conditioned substance, but a proper relationship to God by the Holy Spirit. In this relationship to God, holiness is moral integrity, and sin is the lack of moral integrity. This is responsible consciousness at its highest and shows the proper context in which moral has meaning.

This concept is not Pelagianism, as has been noted. Lest the reader should come to this conclusion, a further word needs to be said at this point in anticipation of the later argument in this book. The discussion above attempts to give an account of moral responsibility—not to ground it theologically. The Wesleyan understands all human abilities to be of grace. Grace lies back of and is actively engaged in every rational activity of man. But, further, every man *is* a committed man. No one is neutral nor can he be. Everyone *is* centering his love somewhere. He *is* biased. The gospel call is a radical thing and presumes to create a radical revolution in personality. In the realm of moral persons only the fact that one can know he is loving immorally can give such a call credibility. Nor is neutrality a possibility (though honest consideration is). One breathes either foul air or clean air; he cannot quit breathing as long as life remains.

If this is true, a serious challenge to Christian ethics loses its force. The frequent charge against the Church that it requires the surrender of moral integrity rather than the strengthening of it is a misrepresentation of Christian teaching. If one must *obey* an imposed moral code, it is said, the very structure of integrity is violated. That is, if one "surrenders" his own will and moral judgment to the "control" of another, even God, he is no longer a moral man but a puppet. Kant, Nietzsche, Tillich, and Erich Fromm, among others, argue in this way and with telling force if their interpretation is true to fact.

The fallacy, as we see it, in this criticism of Christian morality is in supposing that the law to which one is to surrender is impersonal and arbitrary. The word surrender is used advisedly, for it is precisely in the idea of the passive, as a moral renunciation of personal responsibility, that the error lies. (And can it be said that the Church has not been guilty of teaching this concept of yieldedness to God?) However, surrender is not a biblical word and ought never to be used in relation to salvation, at least without limiting its popular meaning carefully. Obedience, in the evangelical sense, is not heteronomy, in the sense of surrendering moral integrity to an impersonal law. But neither is it an expression relative to autonomy in which the person makes *himself* the *object* of his obedience.

Christian morality is the person-to-person rapport, the relationship of harmony and love and mutual will which requires moral integrity to enter and to maintain. One wills to will God's will, which puts the self creatively within the context of true morality. This does not bypass the moral but it is a reestablishment of the personal fellowship which makes the law a normal and desirable expression of love. It is precisely this view of relationship to law that was a correction in the New Testament of the old Jewish moralism. No Christian is ever asked to surrender to the law, to the Church, to a creed, or to persons. It is precisely a rapport with God that is to be established which is the evangelical message. This is not anti-human. It does not violate the normal. It is not immoral. It does not tear down the structure of integrity. It is simply that which men actually desire by deepest created need. Moral law is not abrogated but fulfilled. *Obedience is the back side of love.* Love is structured by obedience. This is the basis of Christain ethics. Moral experience is completed and preserved by this relationship, not destroyed.

5. *Moral Is Structured by Love.*

Everything said thus far about the meaning of *moral* leads directly into the fact that the commitment which makes any person a moral person is that he has made a whole-man commitment. This commitment to constitute it a moral act is simply the whole man in responsible decision. It is more fundamental than will. For the moment, in the interest of this point of the discussion, it does not matter whether the chosen "center" is right or wrong (according to any particular standard) but that one has desired a certain thing enough to have pledged himself wholly to it. He may be moral or immoral, depending on the religious or cultural norms of the society in which he lives. The cohesion of this commitment is integrity. True integrity is possible only where truth is the good.

All of this defines that illusive word *love*. *Love* is a hard word to define because it is not an abstract word. It describes something about personality. *Love* and *moral* derive meaning from each other. Love is the moral integrity which gives commitment its stability. The essence of love is not emotion, not simply will, not sentiment, but man's full dedication to some object. A divided dedication is a divided heart and is the essence of an unstable moral life—the source of moral breakdown. To be moral is to love wholly. Certainly everything the New Testament says about *agape* answers to the personalizing of *moral* as we are using the term in this study. *Moral*, abstractly, is integrity. *Love* is the personalizing of moral integrity which relates it to a practical expression of man's relationship to God and men. "The end of the commandment is . . .

[love] out of a pure heart, and of a good conscience, and of faith unfeigned" (I Tim. 1:5).

That one cannot have real integrity in any other commitment than that wholly to God is the contention of Søren Kierkegaard, and his point is well taken. *"Purity of heart,"* he tells us by a title to one of his books, *"is to will one thing,"* and the only object which can engage the whole of man's devotion is He for whom men were made. Any other love is duplicity and confusion and hence not pure and not moral. In a word, *moral* is single-heartedness by its very definition, and single-heartedness is love.

6. *Moral Life Consists in Crisis-Decision Tensions.*

Deep in the heart of *moral* lies a vital characteristic that gives it the unique strength and character which it possesses, namely, decision. To be moral, life must proceed on the basis of crisis and choice—not simply cause and effect flowing indecisively from one moment to another. Moral integrity is maintained by decisive action, and even the loss of integrity by a series of wrong decisions is not simply an uncontested downward path. One does not slip imperceptibly up or down. The Scriptures recognize this extremely important truth and call all men to deep and far-reaching moral decision. Wherever men seek to avoid this clean-cut personal choice by hiding behind custom, religion, family, morality, philosophy, etc., the Holy Spirit tears away the deceptive device and requires responsible personal declaration. To avoid it is itself to make a responsible decision.

Moral decision, then, cannot end during the course of life. There may be crucial and formative decisions which overshadow others seemingly less important and which consciously determine the course of life, but the cruciality of the unbroken series of less spectacular crisis-decision events must never be forgotten. If one could picture the movement of responsible life, it would look something like stairs. To go up requires vision, purpose, determination, effort, conscious awareness. To go down requires the same things in reverse. One cannot slide down without meeting the painful protest of the edge of every step. Moral decision is not terminated by grace, but constitutes the lifelong probation necessary to character formation.

7. *Moral Integrity Is the Goal of Redemption.*

God deals with men as responsible persons and every step God requires of man from the first stirrings of conviction to the last responsible act in life is in the interest of moral integrity. This means that every individual must square up to God personally. The Holy Spirit seems to force man into a fully conscious, deliberate, personal, voluntary decision. At least, so far as the Bible teaches us, it is the rational man who stands responsibly before the God with whom he has to do.

The proper prayer never seems to be, "Give me an experience like someone else," but, "Lord, what wilt *Thou* have *me* to do?" Christian commitment cannot be patterned or stereotyped. Every step in grace is taken in sharp conscious awareness, and clear rational insight, and the most deliberate moral decisiveness. Consciousness is not bypassed, submerged, or violated. All the powers of the personality converge with full rational responsibility upon these moments, to which the Holy Spirit carefully and imperiously draws us. Nor is there any relaxation of this moral responsibility within the Christian life—rather an ever deepening capacity for it.

In the Bible *the lowest allowable level of obedience is the highest possible capacity for it at any given moment*. The capacity may vary but the responsibility is always equal to possibility. When one says "perfect obedience" and "perfect love," it does not mean that fully mature capacity is expected. A child can qualify in spite of his imperfect development. What is required is all one is at any time.

But more important even is this, that *all* we can contribute by way of moral responsibility is required. It is not the faith we do not have which is demanded but that which *is ours to exercise* by way of full commitment. Wesley's insight was sound when he took the weight off the *amount* of faith needed, to place it in the area of *quality*. Even a "little" faith is the whole available self open toward God. "There are degrees in faith; and weak faith may yet be true faith," says Wesley (*Works*, I, 276).

It is this understanding of *moral* that gives holiness its biblical meaning and preserves justification from abstraction and antinomianism. Holiness relates the provisions of Christ's death to practical life. Grace must be met by faith. God does not treat us as automatons or chessmen on a board, but as persons. Redemption is never impersonal, always related in the most practical way to life. *Moral* guards holiness from two opposite errors. On the one hand *holiness* defined philosophically, or abstractly, theoretically, ideally, simply robs it of any real meaning. Philosophical or abstract holiness is "perfectionism." The experiential dimension, or the moral, is absolutely necessary to its biblical definition.

On the other hand, it guards holiness from the charge of self-righteousness and an easy view of sin. Holiness is never the product of the good will alone; it is not so much *something* that happens to us as it is Someone who unites himself with us. It is the moral atmosphere, the spiritual climate, which is created in us when the Holy Spirit's ministry is allowed to bear fruit. In this atmosphere, so long as the Holy Spirit abides, cleansing takes place and is maintained, growth in grace proceeds, the love of God is shed abroad in our hearts, fellowship is deepened, character is strengthened, moral capacity is enlarged, and responsibility becomes ever more intelligent.

Holiness is *not* static. It is the *life* of God in the soul. It is love to the core of its existence. It is not sentimentality but the whole personality centered in God, drawing its spirit, actions, and purposes from a dynamic contact with God. If holiness is basically a moral concept, therefore, it is an intensely practical matter. The term holiness, and others relating to it, will not be abstract but relevant to life.

Summary Observations

If this analysis of *moral* is correct and if it answers to the biblical concept of holiness, several observations relative to it are pertinent to this study.

1. Biblical holiness is not amoralism. It is not the mere submission to the moral law. It is not passive obedience. It is not primarily "consecration," though it involves men to the very core of their beings. It is basically a new and dynamic relationship of the whole man to God in which a profound moral revolution begins to take place. The moral is a concern of God for men in this life. Whatever *moral* is, it is the ground for probationary existence; and probation is not ended by justification, *or by sanctification*, but only by earthly life, so far as we know.

2. This understanding of *moral* obligates believers to an ever deepening moral experience which is as necessary to soteriology as the grace which is given us by God through Christ. This is the genius of Wesley's contribution to theology. *Moral* is relevant in holiness. The benefits of grace are put into life. Holiness is a matter of experience. Grace has implications for human relationships.

3. The relevance of crisis and growth are established by the concept of *moral* and will be developed in a later chapter.

Perhaps the foregoing analysis will be accepted in the main by the majority of readers as true for the ordinary daily life of humanity. But to apply it to the Christian experience may not be as easy to do. But it is precisely this point for which we are contending. Christian faith is not an activity or function that is added to the total personality. This understanding of *moral* proceeds into a discussion of soteriology and becomes an integral part of all aspects of redemption and outward into every area of life, personal and social. This concept of *moral,* then, links God's grace and human life. The law of the moral runs into every factor of redemption from the creation of man, through the matters pertaining to sin, into the truth structuring the atonement and extending the whole length and breadth of justification, sanctification, and eternal salvation.

CHAPTER X

The Psychology of Holiness

The need at this point in the progress of this study is to examine the relation of God's grace to actual human existence. "Holiness theology" is meaningful only as it emphasizes the real bridge between theology and life. It does not create a higher barrier to *real* participation in grace but removes the barrier without compromising grace. In fact holiness is the bridge between abstract theory and practical human life, for holiness must always inhere in life; it cannot have meaning otherwise.

The subject, "Psychology of Holiness," may suggest that this will be a discussion of the application of grace to specific human problems. In keeping with the general purpose of the book, however, the aim here will be to present a principle of theology which will keep the practical applications in the same system as the theology. It will be an endeavor to restudy biblical concepts of grace and human nature and the relation between them. In this area Wesley's contribution and insight prove valuable because, in fact, at no point in his ministry can we get closer to his real message. Sanctification, he said in many ways, is for this life and for its problems. And human nature is no barrier to the full measure of the saving grace of God.

At the expense of some apparent overlap of subject matter, this chapter will explore the elements intrinsic to the nature of the subject. Overlap must be understood as an example of the essential interrelatedness of all aspects of dynamic love.

In discussing the *psychology* of anything, the area of discussion is indicated by the term *psyche,* meaning "life" (in the Greek). It will have to do with human responses and relationships. When *holiness* is included in the discussion, an ethical dimension is suggested that may, to some, seem totally incongruous. In this *theological* framework, the implication is made that both human and divine matters are juxtaposed in a relation that may or may not be considered proper, or possible.

Two assumptions are made in the light of the chapter title and the problems mentioned above: (1) that man is a moral psyche, and (2) that God's grace relates to holiness in respect of that moral man. It is not absurd to unite grace, holiness, and man in the same discussion.

The concept that there is a real and meaningful relation between man as a human person and holiness as an ideal finds support in: (1) man, as made in God's image; and (2) the discussion about the biblical psychology in which *heart, mind, soul, et al.,* were examined and observations made about the biblical use of these terms.

This chapter will speak of the relationship of God's grace to man. Since Wesleyanism is accused of being Pelagian and humanistic, it may be profitable to set this chapter in a Wesleyan setting. Wesley could not "get going" at all until he had established the fact that he *began* with God's grace and thereby shared the same foundation of faith with classical, even Reformation, theology.

Q. Does not the truth of the gospel lie very near both to Calvinism and Antinomianism?

A. Indeed it does; as it were, within a hair's breadth: So that it is altogether foolish and sinful, because we do not quite agree either with one or the other, to run from them as far as ever we can.

Q. Wherein may we come to the very edge of Calvinism?

A. (1) In ascribing all good to the free grace of God. (2) In denying all natural free-will, and all power antecedent to grace. (3) In excluding all merit from man; even for what he has or does by the grace of God.

Q. Wherein may we come to the edge of Antinomianism?

A. (1) In exalting the merits and love of Christ. (2) In rejoicing evermore (*Works*, VIII, 284-85).

Then this very important declaration, without which no theological judgment of Wesley should ever be made.

The grace or love of God whence cometh our salvation, is FREE IN ALL, and FREE FOR ALL. First, It is free IN ALL to whom it is given. It does not depend on any power or merit in man; no, not in any degree, neither in whole, nor in part. It does not in anywise depend either on the good works or righteousness of the receiver; not on anything he has done, or anything he is. It does not depend on his endeavours. It does not depend on his good tempers, or good desires, or good purposes and intentions; for all these flow from the free grace of God; they are the streams only, not the fountain. They are the fruits of free grace, and not the root. They are not the cause, but the effects of it. Whatsoever good is in man, God is the author and doer of it. Thus is his grace free in all; that is, no way depending on any power or merit in man, but on God alone, who freely gave us his own Son, and "with him freely giveth us all things (*Works*, VII, 373-74).

A PROBLEM OF LANGUAGE

At this point a word should be said about an important problem in language, lest misunderstandings should arise. Each realm of conversation or interest is characterized by specific images and sometimes technical words appropriate and meaningful only in that realm. An illustration taken from the discussion of holiness will clarify the problem. *Moral* is a word that has more than one connotation. It may mean that a person is good—"He is a moral man and thoroughly dependable. He will not steal or cheat on his wife." In Japan, *moral* meant that one was not disloyal to his country. In a previous chapter it was used in the more technical sense of the potential quality of humanhood. It would be a mistake to use this word with one intention and be interpreted as meaning another. *Moral* is not holiness in any sense, but *moral* in the sense described in the previous chapter is necessary to holiness.

When one is speaking scientifically, he speaks of facts as they are. When he is speaking in the value realm, he makes judgments about what he likes or what ought to be. The first deals with quantity, the second with quality. These do not run on the same track. One says, "You will find what you want in this green book." The other answers, "I don't like green; green makes me sick." A says, "Let's turn on the TV and listen to the report on civil rights." B replies, "I don't like the speaker. He wears a wig. He has nothing to say to me."

If I should say, "Monday is sinful," or, "Friday is unlucky," you would think me either extremely queer or possessed of a poor sense of humor. I recently heard of a preacher who was talking to an astronomer who did not want to get into a religious conversation. He said to the preacher, "I have a very simple theology: Love your neighbor as yourself." And the preacher answered, "I have a very simple astronomy: 'Twinkle, twinkle, little star.'"

A speaker who was highly competent in his own field once said, "I do not know anything about theology and psychology." He then proceeded to try to explain holiness, invading not only the fields of theology and psychology, but philosophy, history, devotional literature, science, and hermeneutics, mixing concepts in every sentence. When abstract technical words are wedded to psychological terminology, confusion always results.

It is my conviction that much of our problem in communicating the holiness message stems from just this error. There are at least three areas of potential confusion: theology/psychology; biblical literature/doctrinal interpretation; and theological/experiential. Holiness theology suffers from this possible ambiguity when it insists that textbook doctrine must become a part of human experience.

There is a great gulf fixed between abstract theological discussion and the "practical" human nature in which it comes to life. Perfect love, when equated with entire sanctification, creates some semantic problems, particularly when it is attributed to very imperfect men. When "perfect" is explained as relative to possibility, and that as possibility increases the level of perfection increases, then entire sanctification as a crisis, completed in a moment, becomes somewhat puzzling. The logic of it cannot be untangled if the realms of thinking are not carefully distinguished.

As it stands, intellectual integrity demands that either the absolute of theology be rejected or that the human experience of it be denied. Wesley spent most of his time unraveling confusions like this and he was a master of clear thinking. Theology is one realm and psychology is another. Without care it will sound like a denial of one or the other when one speaks of either. We seek in this study to point the way to understanding.

Similarly, biblical interpretation tends to suffer the same problem. When some observations are made about what can be actually found in Scripture (e.g., that "work of grace" or "state of grace," or a clear declaration of "two works" of grace, is not found in the Bible), the conclusion is sometimes made by the hearer, "That person is denying the biblical teaching of sanctification." Since observations like this are made in this book, it seems appropriate to point out that the judgment made by the hearer (or reader) is a logical fallacy, in that a matter of fact is confused with a theological conclusion and there is no necessary relation between them. We who claim to be biblical would do well to *be* biblical and to distinguish our theological judgments from "the Word." Much blood has been needlessly spilt in history, and the Christian witness has been needlessly clouded, simply because men have equated their opinions with the authority of the Bible itself by fallacious logic. Wesley, as we should be seeing, was particularly free from this confusion.

One more area of problem lies in an emotion-packed realm. In every age, some men have been touched by the glow of the abiding presence of God. This experience transcends denominational lines. Catholic, Protestant, Jew, pagan, Eastern, Western people, highborn, ignorant, mystic, and intellectual have found their hearts transformed by God's grace. The attempt to express it in human language is always made and the idiom of a varied background called into service to do a well-nigh impossible thing. Sometimes the language of Scripture is used, not with any attempt to use it in context. All together, this ecstatic, exuberant, extravagant language is picked up and gradually incorporated into theology, and the biblical language with its extra-biblical connotation becomes "orthodox." The glowing poetry of meaning is encapsulated into theology and its human meaning sanctified by tradition. With the fire gone, its cold ashes are enshrined in the terminology of a church, only to baffle the minds of serious students who think that the source of life is in the ash. When these "sacred" terms are examined and discarded as the *source* of truth, and the source of the fire is sought that made these ashes living coals, one touches a nerve that can kick back and usually does.

An illustration of this is the use of an expression often encountered in some holiness circles, "The altar sanctifies the gift." Nothing in the Bible supports the meaning which is given it today. In an attempt to clarify a theological concept Mrs. Phoebe Palmer, one of the most brilliant lights in early American holiness history, inadvertently created a cliché which has confused and confounded sincere seekers after God ever since. She is surely not to blame, but we are to blame for making a "biblical" (?) theology out of a phrase useful in a select situation. Again, Wesley was more than ordinarily careful about just this propensity. He used as many as 25 to 30 terms for what is now called entire sanctification. Yet with this freedom he avoided some terms now considered essential and "orthodox."

Daniel Steele said he had counted 26 terms from Wesley in signifying the experience of sanctification. . . .

> . . . but "the baptism of (or with) the Spirit," and "fullness of the Spirit," are not phrases used by him, probably because there is an emotional fullness of a temporary nature, not going down to the very roots of the moral nature. Nor did he use "receiving the Holy Spirit," because "in a sense of entire sanctification" the phrase is not scriptural and not quite proper; for they all received the Holy Ghost when they were justified. Wesley did not, probably for the same reason, use "Pentecostal blessing" though Charles Wesley did in a letter to John. . . . I think that the best way to restore this doctrine to the evangelical pulpits is to begin by preaching on the offices of the Holy Spirit in convicting of sin and in the new birth and the witness of the Spirit direct and indirect, topics on which many Christian people are in lamentable ignorance. [1]

So careful, indeed, was Wesley that he gave the following advice about speaking of this great grace:

> Be particularly careful in speaking of yourself: You may not, indeed, deny the work of God; but speak of it, when you are called thereto, in the most inoffensive manner possible. Avoid all magnificent, pompous words; *you need give it no general name*, [italics mine]; neither perfection, sanctification, the second bless-

ing, nor the having attained. Rather speak of the particulars which God has wrought in you. You may say, "At such a time I felt a change which I am not able to express; and since that time, I have not felt pride, or self-will, or anger, or unbelief; nor anything but a fulness of love to God, and to all mankind," And answer any other plain question that is asked with modesty and simplicity.

And if any of you should at any time, fall from what you are now, if you should again feel pride or unbelief, or any temper from which you are now delivered; do not deny, do not hide, do not disguise it at all, at the peril of your soul. At all events go to one in whom you can confide, and speak just what you feel. God will enable him to speak a word in season, which shall be health to your soul (*Works*, XI, 434-35).

It is perhaps dangerous to seek the deeper meanings of the theological language we take for granted, but experience has driven me to try to recover the spiritual dynamic of our fathers. Nothing of the fire is lost by blowing the ash away. Rather the fire can burn brighter by doing so.

It is, then, the *psychology* of the moral life as a necessary ingredient in holiness that is the subject of the next section.

Psychology of the Moral Life

The psychology of holiness simply means that grace is congenial to human nature as it is. In this discussion of it we will have to say some things about the constitution of human nature and personality and show how sanctification acts in living situations. Theology looks different in work clothes than it does in a book.

Some of the questions plaguing Christian people arise from a failure to distinguish between the formal theology of sanctification and the practical problems of living, human people. For instance, Wesleyans speak of a second work of grace or a second crisis or "blessing" in the Christian life. What is the significance of *two* special moments among the many of life? Why *two*, not *one* or *three* or *a hundred?* How is one recognized as distinct from the other or how does one distinguish the first from the second? Could they be reversed and make any difference? How are those two distinguished from the other crucial moments in one's spiritual life? If a Christian loses one "blessing," which one is lost, and what happens to the other, and how would one know when he had recovered what was lost? Does God withhold some measure of grace from the first experience that is later given in the second? Or does He solve only part of the sin problem in each "work of grace"?

Are there levels of religious living, proper for sinners, for believers and/or for sanctified persons? May one determine the amount of sin or the degree of victory over sin typical or permissible in the various states of grace or the kinds of sin characteristic of each? May one choose his level of spiritual life and adjust himself to it and disregard other states of grace? Is one fully saved when he is regenerated or only partially saved? If God doesn't save completely, couldn't He if He would? And if He could, why wouldn't He do it in the new birth? If one is wholly saved in the new birth, why must he have another special experience to prepare him for heaven? And, back of all these questions, Why a *crisis* experience?

The first problem is the *ordo salutis*, or order of salvation, and is the particular concern of systematic theology. Such matters as the temporal priority of regeneration, justification, faith, repentance, and other elements in redemption constitute the problem. Lacking clear biblical direction in this matter, it is necessary to organize these items according to a set of presuppositions which obviously lacks the necessary objectivity to structure dogmatic conversation about them. The major difference between Arminius and the Reformed church of his day was precisely here.

It is not in the province of this chapter to discuss the nature of regeneration, adoption, justification, and sanctification but only to note their relation to each other. We may begin by stating that the Wesleyan concept of God sees Him as acting toward us in the totality of His nature and acting upon the totality of human nature. This means that no divine attribute such as wrath, love, holiness, mercy, or justice is encountered apart from the whole person of God. And man experiences this totality as himself a whole person rather than with parts of himself such as his will, his mind, his heart, each separate from the others.

Holiness and justice, love and wrath are not antithetical and contradictory attributes but the effect of divine action in respect of a particular situation. Just as truly, it is the Godhead that acted in behalf of man's redemption. God did not "sacrifice Jesus," but "God was in Christ, reconciling the world unto himself." This unity of personality extends to man. The whole man receives the benefit of grace. His whole being, not just a part of the personality, is the recipient of divine activity if the concept of moral is to be maintained.

H. Orton Wiley says:

> Prevenient grace . . . is exercised upon man's entire being, and not upon any particular element or power of his being. Pelagianism regards grace as acting solely upon the understanding, while Augustinianism falls into the opposite error of supposing that grace determines the will through effectual calling. Arminianism holds to a truer psychology. It insists that grace does not operate merely upon the intellect, the feelings or the will, but upon the person or central being which is beneath and behind all affections and attributes. Thus it preserves a belief in the unity of personality.[2]

But how does this help in answering the question? Wiley suggests an interesting and profitable answer. He says that there are three analogies used in Scripture to describe the relationship of God and man: the home, the lawcourt, and the Temple service. Each of these analogies has a vocabulary consistent with its own realm. It requires all of these to communicate the things we need to know about redemption. When one analogy is isolated from the others to become the whole truth, theological distortion results; e.g., when birth is made the analogy for everything having to do with the Christian's relationship to God, the juridical and moral are sacrificed.

It is imperative that the terms used in connection with each be carefully distinguished. The home relationships are expressed in terms of natural life—father, son, birth, love, estrangement, and many more. The lawcourt is expressed in legal terminology—guilt, blameworthiness, imputation, judgment, and justification. The Temple service contributes the terms typical of its realm—sin, uncleanness, purity, sanctification, sacrifice, holiness, and dedication.

Wiley does not explicitly point out the implications of this through the whole of the doctrine of salvation (though he is fairly consistent in the use of terms) but this germ of an idea has proved helpful in this study. In our opinion, it can be projected profitably into the problem we face.

The issues in theology are confused needlessly when the careful biblical distinctions are overlooked between justification, regeneration, and sanctification. Each has an element of truth that must not be confused with the others. But these are not different events which may be separated in experience. They are different aspects of one event. This does not mean that one can be substituted for another but that the true nature of Christian experience cannot be encompassed by any one alone but by all of them together (and others as well). This means that there is an aspect of the home, the lawcourt, or the Temple which may, by analogy, help to explain God's redemptive activity in relation to mankind. The *new birth*, or regeneration, does not exhaust the biblical teaching about salvation. Justification or forgiveness is an essential element but incidental to the central purpose of salvation, which is freedom from sin, or holiness of heart. *Sanctification* must include all that regeneration and justification mean to save it from humanism. But in the Scripture all this *is* included, and theology must keep these truths in balance.

> We may say then that Christian righteousness and Christian sonship, involving justification, regeneration, adoption, and initial sanctification, are concomitant in personal experience, that is, they are offered as inseparable blessings and occur at the same time. . . . The terms are not, however, synonymous.[3]

The significance of this to the problem at hand is that there is in God's saving relation to us an objective and subjective aspect which catches up the whole of personality. It does not mean that men are perfected beyond the need for or possibility of development, but that the whole of God's grace meets the whole of man's need. The *order* of the "blessings" is logical, not simply chronological. This is another way of saying that the redemptive procedure is moral to the core.

The second problem has to do with the way men appropriate grace. A question sharpens the issue. Does faith precede or follow repentance? Is obedience necessary, and why? These simply open the door to many more questions like them.

In Scripture it is impossible to isolate such words as *faith* and *love* so that they could be said to stand in chronological order to each other. There is an element of repentance in faith that cannot be deleted. Faith is meaningless apart from enough awareness of sin and hatred of it to make believing decisive. Faith must always have enough self-awareness to reject one thing, enough to accept another. Biblical repentance is shot through with faith and obedience. In Scripture, faith is never divorced from the total personality. It must be supported by everything the man is. Obedience is a necessary ingredient of faith. Both describe love. Purity is a compound of all of them. Cleansing is dependent upon walking in the light, or obedience to the "law" of fellowship.

In other words, the whole personality participates in every contact with the grace of God. Faith is not intellectual assent only, nor is obedience an act of the will alone. Purity is not a mystical quality etched on the soul, nor love a sentiment which is beyond testing. In the first dim consciousness of the Holy Spirit's dealing with persons the whole complex of personality is awakened to alertness and concerted response, as either acceptance or rejection. Everything that is involved in the redemptive procedure contributes to moral integrity.

The classic requirement for justification is faith. Faith is not something the mind does concerning which the rest of the personality is either passive or in active repudiation. The call to the sinner is to repent and believe. An obedient spirit is the matrix of repentance and faith. Paul tells us in Romans 6 that the Christian's involvement in baptism requires "yielding." Christ is both Saviour and Lord, and a believer in the act of believing implicates himself in a new bondage when he is delivered from the old. The call to the Christian is not a different call but a continuation and deepening of the same call.

Wiley says again, "Regeneration is related to sanctification. The life bestowed in regeneration is a holy life. It is for this reason that Mr. Wesley spoke of it as the gateway to sanctification."[4]

Wesley talked about the repentance of believers. Paul in Rom. 12:1, calls the brethren to *present* themselves to God. The warning against grieving and quenching the Holy Spirit is so universally needed that evangelical ministers find no difficulty in the way of preaching this to the sinner, though it was spoken to Christians.

All of this seems to mean that there is one way, and one way only, *into* God's grace and one way to *continue* in it at every level of spiritual life—and that is the complete capitulation of the whole man to God. This is not salvation by merit but truly salvation by faith. But faith is not something other than obedience, and detached from the personality. It is not more efficacious and "religious" than obedience, but is itself a demonstration of obedience which unifies the personality rather than splitting it.

Purity is not some subsequent stage of the Christian life but the consequence of obedience and faith under the grace of God. That is, we are not free to segregate one aspect of God's requirement from the others and make it the whole. We are unstable teachers if we isolate one part of the personality as savable and neglect or reject the savability of the rest of man. Faith is not the law of one realm or state of grace and obedience the law of another. *Moral integrity* is the basis of interpretation and must characterize everything relating to grace. Holiness is ethical to the core. It is not a moralism.

The problem of faith versus works takes shape in this area of thinking. The strong polemic against works in certain theological circles is, in our opinion, based on two misconceptions at least. One is basic to the other. (1) Unless the "works" against which Paul preached is understood in its own context, the uncritical projection of the misunderstood teaching creates serious problems in our theology. The "works" which could not bring righteousness were not obedience to God's law and commands but a trust in superficial obedience to produce righteousness. Righteousness is never possible apart from obedience, but the obedience must be a dependence upon God and His mercy and grace and be "from the heart." (2) The Wesleyan emphasis on such obedience is not "salvation by works" but the whole man integrated about the grace of God. Men are not brains only, accepting a proposition, however sincerely. They are also persons, who in accepting a proposition must *act* in respect of it. There can be no true dualism between faith and obedience. Either one alone is an abstraction without real existence. It is never encountered in life.

It may be helpful to point up again a conclusion which has been forced upon us throughout the study, namely, that the subjective involvements into which the person is introduced by the grace of God are not impossible for human beings even in sin. Grace does not force unnatural and distorting obligations on the human personality but asks only that the powers inherent in humanness, and called into alertness by the Holy Spirit, be exercised about the lordship of Christ. New powers are not added but the old ones are put into proper perspective. Wiley, again, speaks cogently to this point:

> The self is not only essentially active, but was created for unlimited progress. Under grace this becomes an ever increasing advancement in the divine likeness—a change from *glory unto glory* (II Cor. 3:18). In sin the increase is "unto more ungodliness" and hence a descent from shame to shame. It must be remembered, however, that sin is but an accident of man's nature, and not an essential element of his original being. He retains his personality with all its powers, but these are exercised apart from God as the true center of his being, and are therefore perverted and sinful. Sin is not some new faculty . . . infused into man's being. . . . It is rather the bias of all powers.[3]

This is a soundly Wesleyan insight. In the following passage Wesley emphasizes the unity of personality so essential to an understanding of biblical holiness.

> They who are truly meek, can clearly discern what is evil; and they can also suffer it. They are sensible of everything of this kind, but still meekness holds the reins. They are exceeding "zealous for the Lord of Hosts;" but their zeal is always guided by knowledge, and tempered, in every thought, and word, and work, with the love of man, as well as the love of God. They do not desire to extinguish any of the passions which God has for wise ends implanted in their nature; but they have the mastery of all: They hold them all in subjection, and employ them only in subservience to those ends. And thus even the harsher and more unpleasing passions are applicable to the noblest purposes; even hatred, and anger, and fear, when engaged against sin, and regulated by faith and love, are as walls and bulwarks to the soul, so that the wicked one cannot approach to hurt it (*Works*, V, 263).

This section opened with the statement, "The psychology of holiness simply means that grace is congenial to human nature." This means that *grace* is not, in the Scriptures at least, a theological word but a very personal word. God's grace is a way of saying, "All that God is in relation to man—His love, mercy, forgiveness, redemption—everything is revealed and made available to man. God acting in behalf of men alienated from Him by their own sin, God calling men to Him to share His fellowship, God crowding us with His presence and pleading for our response—this is grace. Then, when theology speaks of "states of grace," we must ask, What does this mean?

"STATES OF GRACE"

It will be noted that one major difficulty lies at the base of all questions and is expressed in such phrases as "work of grace" and "state of grace" and in the term "blessing." This difficulty arises from a failure to understand the meaning of *grace*. The dual aspect of the religious life is said to be structured by "states of grace," and that "works of grace" transfer one from state to state. If this pattern can be defended biblically, the answering of the specific questions about these states ought not to be too difficult. If not, the biblical teaching will have to be ascertained and distinguished from the deductions of theology, and the application of the biblical teaching related to experience.

A brief survey of the uses of the word *grace* quickly establishes the fact that neither "states" nor "works" of grace is a biblical phrase. "Blessing" when used to refer to them is also extra-biblical, though the original meaning may be proper enough when understood. It is observed also that neither "first" nor "second" can be defended *directly* by New Testament exegesis as adjectives numbering the stages of grace on the way. Of course, the Wesleyan knows this and he defends his usage on other grounds, believing that the personal appropriation of New Testament grace gives evidence of this dual aspect. However, in the attempt to remain strictly within the limitation of biblical exegesis, one can be embarrassed by these terms if they are insisted upon too dogmatically as an evidence of orthodoxy.

What is grace? Is it possible that grace could refer to a state or position? All that men receive from God is "by grace," from creation to final redemption. A careful study of the term reveals at least one clear fact, namely, that grace is never impersonal or *something* apart from God himself. It is, rather, precisely as a personal expression of God's nature (and as such spiritual and moral) that it has meaning. It is mercy and love and patience and long-suffering, never deserved by men, never compelled by any sort of divine necessity, but always freely given and always conditioned by moral considerations so far as its reception by men is concerned.

If it were possible to conceive of a "state of love" or a "state of mercy" (terms that are synonyms for "grace"), the validity of a "state of grace" could be defended. But these matters do not

198 / *A Theology of Love*

describe impersonal or static positions but relationships which are personal in the highest sense of that term. Wesleyanism, in its most responsible and perceptive moments, has always seen this. It has maintained that no man is to trust in any moment of experience, or in any psychological experience itself, or in any "state of grace," or in the results of any of these. He is to trust in *Christ alone,* not as an idea or a group of words—even biblical words—but in Christ himself as a Person.

This puts the whole of redemption on the highest possible plane and prevents the development of antinomian tendencies which are inherent in *any* system which fails to grasp this personal aspect of God's dealing with men. Wesley answered the question, "Does not talking of a justified or sanctified *state* tend to mislead men? Almost naturally leading them to trust in what was done at one moment?" by saying, "Whereas we are every hour and every moment pleasing or displeasing to God, *according to our works:* according to the whole of our inward tempers and our outward behavior."[6]

To the Wesleyan, grace is not properly called a state because it is never impersonal but is consistently conceived of as "God with men," loving them, but never forcing His will in matters concerning salvation. Grace is never merely power, or coercion. It is thought of in the most personal terms. This conviction lies back of its view of the *Imago Dei* and of primitive holiness, and consequently of the holiness which is said to be possible in this life. This means that all the commands of God in relation to man are consistent with God's moral order. God does not play with men, teasing them by impossible requirements. The Bible is a serious Book, trustworthy in all its moral teachings. No more is required of men than they are able to perform.

The requirements are related primarily to inner attitudes, not to achievements of prowess or perfections of which men are incapable, physically, mentally, or morally. But the demand is for *all* that man can be, and he is pressed to this utmost capacity as is consistent with personality growth. *God's grace stimulates moral experience, never substitutes for it.* Ethical considerations everywhere characterize God's dealings with man and man's response to God. This truth, allowed to penetrate Christian theology, cleanses it of nonmoral superficiality and incredibility.

The one important point in all this discussion is this, that God acts toward men in personal relationship. This means that He acts as whole Person to whole persons. This obviates the popular tendency to speak of God as giving a *part* of himself to a part of man, or God acting in mercy or justice or grace or wrath, each attribute apart from the others. Thinking of God in relation to only one aspect of man—such as his status, or in respect of his rational mind apart from his moral nature, or his will and not his emotions—arises from the failure to see the Person-to-person aspect of divine action. Grace represents the whole of God acting in respect of the whole man. When by grace we are saved, salvation is *potentially* complete. Grace cannot be divided off into layers, because God is a Person—not layers of anything. We cannot divide the Holy Spirit up so that we receive a part of Him at one time and more of Him at another time. The Holy Spirit is a Person and comes as a Person and He relates himself to persons. When one is saved, the Holy Spirit comes to him. This is a personal relationship, not a mathematical addition which can be divided by fractions.

But it is precisely at the point of the personal nature that this whole matter of "religious mathematics" lies, and how grace relates to it. But before the question of "first and second blessings" can be discussed, something must be said about human nature, and here the personal element is presented which brings the theological and religious into significance.

HUMAN PERSONALITY

If the experience of sanctification is a matter of spiritual and moral adjustment worked out at the juncture of human nature and God's grace, something needs to be known about human nature in order to be intelligent about the whole process. Biblical psychology is always contemporary and the theologian is never embarrassed by it.

1. *The person is essentially a unity.* A normal man is not at odds with himself though he may be contending with his best judgment over some matter. When he acts he acts as a unity. The whole man acts whenever he acts at all. Neither the Old nor the New Testament knows anything about a man whose spirit is good and whose flesh is evil. One's spirit—or body, for that matter— never acts without the real consent of the entire personality.

Responsible action, in fact, must engage the whole man. The Bible speaks of numbers of parts of the body as being the seat of responsible actions: heart, bowels, eyes, ears, mouth, feet, mind, spirit, flesh, and many other organs, internal and external. But never do the heart and the feet, for example, act out of harmony with each other in the same man at the same time. When the feet are "swift to shed blood," the heart is involved and to blame. When the feet are "beautiful" because they carry the message of grace, the spirit and flesh are included. Each designation is a figure of speech characterizing the action and attitudes of the whole man. It refers to a quality of character, taking its cue from the sort of symbol of action which the organ suggests. The trichotomous view of man as body, soul, and spirit is not biblical teaching. Some classical errors in Christology stem from this Gnostic idea, and some contemporary perfectionism is made possible only by this concept of personality. But the Christian view is that the clean heart is an undivided heart—a unified personality.

Any multiple view of personality makes the Christian life a source of conflict, not of peace. It makes salvation destructive of wholeness and integrity in that grace sets the soul against the body. It impugns the grace of God. A disturbed personality becomes the badge of Christianity, and death a savior.

The Wesleyan, and we believe the biblical, teaching insists that justification and the new birth integrate the whole personality. It is life which draws all elements into a dynamic whole. Life is unity. Death is disintegration, the falling apart of constituent elements. Salvation is the spirit of life in Christ Jesus that makes us free from the law of sin and death. The new birth means the beginning of growth of a whole person. It looks forward to maturity and service. It means one is wholly saved, wholly revitalized, remotivated, by the Holy Spirit. It means that by the ministry of the Holy Spirit the *person* has made Christ, Lord.

2. *Personality is dynamic, not static.* It is spiritual, not material. It is not a *substance* upon which from the outside may be imposed permanent "marks," as Catholic grace is said to do. There is a continuum of identity and self-consciousness, but in this there are flux and adjustment and enlargement and altered perspectives and relegation and movement that everlastingly constitute the "per-

son" a *vital* entity. Jesus' analysis is pertinent—not what goes into a man makes him, He said, but what proceeds from him. When *the person is operating as a responsible creature he distinguishes between simple stimuli and purpose, and responds rationally.*

This does not posit *absolute* freedom, but does assume *real* freedom. A person, so long as he is a person, is in movement, outgoing, expanding, reaching for completion, restless, seeking, driving. Spiritual "death" in a living person is not the death of immobility or quiescence but the direction of activity toward disintegration of the self.

Personality is dynamic as well as a unity. This means that man steps into a life of the fullest possible responsibility to God of which he is capable at conversion. This may be very small, but it is the first stage in the ongoing process. The personality is not passive, inert, but constantly meeting moments of decision which must be made in the spirit of the new life. The guarantee of grace is *not* that God will make these decisions for us but that we will be enabled by the Spirit to make them to please God.

Moral life is either progress or regression in a zigzag line, not usually by straight lines. New situations constantly confront us; new choices must be made. At every point a council meeting is held in which the prevailing attitude is determined by the whole man. He is now a Christian, but that does not make the right choices automatic or inevitable. The responsibility for right choices is not relegated but heightened in the Christian life. The essence of personality is moral freedom, and in the Christian life personality is ever more deeply spiritualized, never depersonalized. Everything involved in sanctification, then, applies precisely here. Sanctification is the bringing into total integration about the will of God every element of the personality. Sanctification is the "growing edge" of justification. What one contracts to do when he becomes a Christian, he must *in living situations* do. The new life needs what is termed, theologically, sanctification.

Grace and Human Freedom

To be a self means moral freedom. God acts in relation to man in harmony with his moral nature and psychological makeup. Freedom may not be great, but in order to maintain personal and moral integrity it must be real, not fictional. Persons cannot be real persons—spiritual entities—apart from this measure of self-transcendence and self-determination. Biblically, the whole appeal of the gospel is to the power of men to decide and initiate one course of action rather than another. Men are not free to choose the consequences of an act, but they are free to decide in which consequences they prefer to become enmeshed so far as a relationship to God is concerned.

But inevitably involved in personal freedom is personal responsibility. Freedom lies in a matrix of responsibility. To be free is to be responsible. Freedom is not amoral, with the matters of choice centered solely around the whims and interests of the individual. It is intensely and terribly moral. In other words, one does not begin and end his life of freedom as an unattached individual but only and always as a self-conscious entity standing in relation to God and to others. The self is a self only when it so stands. Self-consciousness is but another way of saying that one truly knows himself only as he is an entity distinguished from, but in relation to, others. In other words, moral freedom is the self sustaining a responsible relation to other selves. Freedom has no other meaning.

The Bible has much to say of this interrelatedness. The triune God is a community of Selves in love and communication. Men find their spiritual awareness only when they have been drawn into that divine life by mutual fellowship, and the resulting life is a community fellowship with other Christians. Somewhat parenthetically, but significant to this discussion, is a reference to the observation made earlier in the study, that the Holy Spirit is said to have fallen on, or filled, *groups* only, never individuals, though the individual's body is the temple of the Spirit, and such men as Stephen in the pursuance of their witnessing were characterized by this divine habitation. The body ("a living sacrifice") is related, by the Spirit, to all other persons in that fellowship. This interdependent life is absolutely crucial. Jesus' prayer in John 17 will not permit us to dismiss the obligation of the full implications of fellowship to salvation. The relationship we sustain to the Holy Spirit, of deepest necessity, makes us a part of a fellowship. Apart from that fellowship is spiritual death.

This leads us to observe that the ministry of the Holy Spirit under the terms of grace has a twofold thrust: (1) He compels persons to become sharply aware of themselves as responsible individuals, and the decisions to which they are driven are fully responsible decisions. (2) But the Holy Spirit also demands that such persons begin to sustain responsible relationships. This is highly significant. The Spirit assumes and respects our self-interest and other-interest and deals with us through this avenue of personality because it is essential to wholeness.

These two moments of the self, a self-interest and an other-interest, are both absolutely essential to mental health. The fulfilling of the whole law, or mental and spiritual health expressed in a religious way (the only adequate way), is to love God wholly and others as the self. Salvation must include both aspects or fail to do justice to the whole scope of biblical teaching. Self-consciousness is logically prior to the social dimension of the personality. One who has not become a true self will never be able to take his place in a society of selves. Self-love is not sinful in itself but only when it crowds out the "other" selves.

When theology speaks of denying self, it ought never to mean that the self is to be disparaged or destroyed. Paul drives for a proper self-estimate in all his letters.

No Christian "surrender" weakens the uniqueness and vitality of self-interest and personality. It is only the strong self that can give itself to Christ at all. The basis of spiritual living is the whole self in wholesome integration with all the uniqueness of personality intact, positive and strong, but under the domination of an all-controlling love for Christ—a cleansed self.

Too many people have never allowed the Holy Spirit to bring them face-to-face with their real selves—they never come to clear personal identification. They try to be someone else, follow some external code, mouth someone else's words, retreat behind the comfortable cover of convention. They give a fuzzy self to God, have a fuzzy testimony, and do a fuzzy service for God—dull, monotonous, uninspired, intolerant, unattractive, because of the fear resident in their uncertainty. Fear closes the mind and the heart and dries up the source of love.

This is not Christian, and not in keeping with holiness theology. God is limited by defective personality, psychologically speaking, and everything holiness requires of man tends to remove limitation. Holiness is wholeness and health, and everything God requires of the person from the first stirrings of conviction to the last act of life is in the interest of that wholesomeness.

When one becomes a Christian, or is born again, the ultimate in self-awareness and self-consciousness and personal identity is reached. God forgives the sin that has robbed the self of respect and security. The *fear* of God has changed to a sense of mutual love. In this experience every debilitating drag to self-identity is removed. The moment of release is an infinitely pleasant moment. We would like to preserve it, glory in it, live in it, retreat to it. But this is not spiritual health any more than arrested development is mental health. Personality is not static but dynamic. It cannot thrive in perpetual babyhood. It must commit itself.

The newborn person finds himself in a world of deepest responsibility. The inward look is no longer adequate. There must be the usually painful wrenching of self-interest from the self as center to the two-foci perspective of love to God and others also. Under the dominion of sin, the self lacks that element of true dignity which the child of God now enjoys. For the first time the *person* emerges as a true person and begins to function as a person. Self-interest—which is not of itself sin but which has functioned out of perspective and, because it has shut God out, has been sinful—must now of its own free choice transfer its authority to God, and the object of its interest to others. Without relinquishing self-identity it must identify itself with God and begin to live responsibly with others.

There is a tendency in all theological traditions to isolate the first step from the second and to think only in terms of being right with God—or self-interest. Perhaps Paul was speaking of this when writing to the Corinthians, whom he reproved for being "babes in Christ" when maturity was demanded. A characteristic of babyhood is an exaggerated interest in the self and the desires and outlook of the self. To end Christian experience in self-interest is to fail to complete normal moral experience. Paul said that when he became a man he put away childish things and he said this in the context of the discussion about love, the most spiritually maturing engagement possible to rational beings—and the cure for the Corinthian problem.

In Wesleyanism this same tendency to self-interest in salvation often robs those who professedly "go on to perfection" of the strength of the Spirit-filled life because the true nature of love has been missed. There remains a controlling interest in the self that can never permit soul health and Christian victory. There is an exaggerated engagement in introspection, a "feeling of the pulse," a "sore" conscience rather than a tender one, an overstress on emotional states and being "blessed." The self has never emerged out of its infantile state into wholesome maturity and moral vigor and responsibility.

A most interesting and significant suggestion is discovered in the Greek word used by Paul for "childish" in I Corinthians. It is not a word often used, and probably never in Paul for *son (uiós)* or *child (téknon)*. Paul chooses to use *népios*, which in the context always has the connotation of an adult who displays the irresponsible characteristics of a child. "Babyishness" would be a better word, more easily distinguished from "childlikeness," commended by Jesus. The term used here suggests a spiritual condition answering to the physical and mental state we now call arrested development. In Eph. 4:14, Paul exhorts those who are "tossed to and fro, and carried about with every wind of doctrine," to become men, growing up unto the perfect man, "edifying . . . itself in love" (meaning the whole "body of Christ"—the Church). The way to accomplish this is by "speaking the truth in love," growing up into Christ in all things (v. 15), walking from here on out, "not as other Gentiles walk, in the vanity of their mind" (v. 17). The author of Hebrews uses this same word in condemnation of those "dull of hearing," who ought to be teachers but who still need milk —they are "babes," babyish (Heb. 5:11-14).

The troublesome passage in I Cor. 3:1 uses this Greek word: You are "babes in Christ"; and then follows the catalog of feuding children's acts, tearing each other's hair out and pulling toys out of each other's arms. One does not just grow out of that. In I Cor. 13:11, Paul said he had been this kind of person, but he had *put away* childish ways and had become a man. Spiritual "babyishness" must be handled decisively. It does not simply "go away" by itself or by the passage of time. The problem in these cases, and others, was not simply immaturity, but a defect in love, and these two kinds of problems are not solved in the same way. It is instructive to note that *love*, the dynamic of Wesleyanism, the key to the meaning of sanctification, is the cure recommended for these cases.

When we say that the so-called "works of grace" represent, not God's arbitrary limitation of what He is willing to do at any one time, but man's psychological ability to appropriate the riches of God's grace, it is this two-fold aspect of personality that we have in mind. Men receive grace from God; but because men are persons, spiritual beings, they instantly step into a new world of responsibility in relation to God. The self begins to function in a new environment, and as a self it must behave in keeping with its own nature as a responsible person or forfeit its spiritual existence. And *love* is the law of this new life, not a "higher level" of grace.

These two things, freedom and responsibility, are in some ways separate things, but in a very true sense two sides to the same thing. When a person is "saved" he is wholly saved. God, by His grace (not "by grace" apart from the person of God), saves the whole man. Involving a personal act and a Person acting and a person reacting to God's personal action, salvation is complete and extends to the whole of the person's being. But a saved person is a responsible person, and the new birth instantly involves him in a life of responsibility commensurate with his spiritual life and liberty and personal development and psychological abberations and prejudices and disposition.

Now, psychologically, there are two kinds of human response in this single unit of experience in which God saves a person. There is the coming into fellowship. There is wholehearted yielding, and declaration of trust and love, and there is the whole lifetime of moral decisions regarding that new life. It is commitment that is more than a formal, signed contract. The biblical analogy of marriage probably cannot be improved on. Our relation to God is as real and life-changing and dynamic and as fulfilling and enabling and personal—really more so—as marriage where love binds the heart and enriches every facet of life.

It is our thought that this life responsibility involving a living obedience in specific instances of choice is an explanation of what a Wesleyan means by a second crisis. In no sense is one "work of grace" limited for the purpose of reserving a place for another "work of grace." God does not partially save and then fully save. Men do not respond with part of the personality and then later with the rest of it. Sin is not partially destroyed at one time and fully destroyed at another, nor is a second work of grace for the purpose of correcting the defects of the first. At least there is no biblical warrant for this kind of explanation. The *"second crisis" is different in kind, not different in degree, from the first.* The two represent two essential movements of the person as a person. They have respect for the double psychological aspect of selfhood in its freedom and responsibility.

Three strands of the analyzed elements of the subject under discussion come together at this point, and answer the question as to the relation of sanctification to human nature: life as dynamic, justification as the beginning of new spiritual life, and sanctification as the ordering of life about a proper center. But what, specifically, *is* the process of sanctification within the personality?

Justification (the new birth) is a "loaded" gift. Life is a "loaded" gift. In the spiritual realm as in the physical, the gift must be unpacked and put to use. In both cases immaturity must give way to maturity, scattered interests to one controlling passion, petulance to purpose. Discipline is needed to help a child brimming with life, pulling apart at the seams, to direct himself into a proper channel. A child must be under "tutors" and the learning comes hard. Maturity or manhood is reached, in a real measure, the day that the child, of himself, deep within his own being, uncoerced, commits himself to a worthy goal and realizes something of the cost of that dedication. The commitment is personal, voluntary. No one may share in it. Many legitimate desires must be forfeited in order to gain the cherished goal. In this formative decision the child becomes a man, the "servant" becomes the son. The analogy carries into the religious life almost unchanged.

It is hardly necessary, now, to add much more to the meaning of "entire" in relation to sanctification. "Entire" refers to the total moral integration of personality. It refers also to the aspect of total commitment to Christ. It must say something important about the mature, deliberate, personal decision of a thoughtful, deeply challenged person. Entire does not mean that all the process of character building and spiritual stabilizing is completed. The definition of personality as dynamic precludes that. It does mean that the whole man has united itself about Christ. It refers to a crisis moment when this full measure of commitment is realized. It refers also to a life of *continued* commitment. "Entire" is the whole man in spiritual decision. "Cleansing" has its real meaning at this point, as has been suggested.

Entire sanctification draws together the two major cords into one strong twist of rope.

1. God requires men to love Him wholly. Sanctification is the moral atmosphere of that love. It has two movements, a total renunciation of the self-centered life and a total commitment to God. Everything sanctification requires is in keeping with wholesome personality.

2. God accepts this living sacrifice and fills the "heart" with the Holy Spirit. *As religion,* this is loving God with the whole heart, soul, mind, and strength; *in psychology,* it is an integrated personality; *in theology,* it is cleansing.

Both crisis and process are recognized—crisis at crucial moments, process as a continuing life both before and after the more formative moments of decision.

CHAPTER XI

The Divine-Human Interaction

How much does God do toward our salvation? What does man do? These questions are raised in any Wesleyan, evangelistic presentation of the gospel. In some theological traditions it is a question of the priority of God's sovereign will over man's free will. The solution which makes God the sole Actor in the salvation drama is categorized as Augustinian, and any solution which posits freedom of response in man is termed Pelagian.

Wesleyanism, in principle, stands outside the Augustinianism-Pelagianism framework; but the questions with which this section began betray the subtle, though usually unconscious, influence of this tradition. It is the Augustinian/Pelagian controversy in Wesleyan dress. In emphasizing the moral dimension of man and the full responsibility of man in every step in salvation the startled question is often pressed in upon us in our teaching situations, "Doesn't man's freedom deny the supernatural?" Back of this question always lies the ancient Augustinian concept of man as wholly the recipient of grace, never its collaborator in any sense. Put in its baldest way, the questioner usually assumes that beyond the faith and obedience which are man's proper evangelical response to God, is a sub-rational, physical or psychological mutation which in some way creates a structural change in him. To question this is tantamount to denial of the "supernatural." Not only is this problem legitimate but it is one that cannot be ignored in a serious study of this nature.

In approaching this problem the assertion is ventured that any area relative to human life that lies outside the rational nature of man is not in the real sense moral. If that event cannot be described in understandable language but must be referred to only by some technical term devoid of existential meaning, it is not properly a moral or spiritual—or perhaps biblical—concept.

Coming into direct focus here is the basic truth that holiness is the element in Christian faith which prevents theology from becoming a mere intellectual exercise. Holiness is life. As the incarnation of Christ is God's answer to speculation about God, so holiness is the answer to theological abstraction relative to salvation.

The most direct and illuminating statement of our thesis is that sanctification is intimately related to moral responsibility and is itself an aspect—perhaps the central concern—of redemption. This conviction is grounded in a concept of nature and supernature which permits moral integrity to exist in the tension between them. It assumes that there is an "other than nature" and that in the commerce between them rational thought is "at home."

That there are both a natural world and a supernatural reality is a postulate of Christian thought. Man is not a part of God ontologically nor is God metaphysically a part of nature. God is self-existent, and man and the world exist in total dependence upon God. The Creator and the creation are in real ways distinct. But when this is said, the problem is only stated, not solved. What these two "reals" may be and how they are related constitute the broader area of problem. In this study, only the *relationship* of the "reals" is under consideration, not what they are in themselves.

THE ESSENTIAL VALUE OF MAN

Wesleyanism stoutly maintains the proper distinction between God and other-than-God. There is no merging of identity between them, nor does Wesleyanism posit a divine spark in man waiting to be fanned into flame. On the other hand, man is considered, under the grace of God, capable of fellowship with God. He is not simply a pawn to be used by God, nor is he a worthless clod deriving dignity only from character borrowed from another. In all his sin, which must not be underrated, he yet is, by virtue of his creation and the continuing grace of God, valuable and savable. In some way a position must be established and defended which does justice to the biblical revelation of God and to the value the Scriptures put upon man as created in the image of God. To disparage and discredit man beyond biblical warrant does not bring glory to the God who made him and redeemed him.

Wesley carefully charts the way between common errors in theological positions. In defending the savability of man he avoids dehumanizing him by an overstress on grace to the neglect of recognizing man's capacity as man. Nor can he accept the position that "every man living has a measure of natural free-will," as the Westminster confession asserts even of man in his fallen state before he receives the grace of God. Wesley's argument is worth recording.

[The contrary position]: I do not carry free-will so far: (I mean, not in moral things:) Natural free-will, in the present state of mankind, I do not understand: I only assert, that there is a measure of free-will supernaturally restored to every man, together with that supernatural light which "enlightens every man that cometh into the world." But whether this be natural or no, as to your objection it matters not . . . your assertion being thus, "If man has any free-will, *God cannot have the whole glory of his salvation*" [italics added] . . .

[Wesley's reply]: Is your meaning this: "If man has any power to 'work out his own salvation', then God cannot have the whole glory?" If it be, I must ask again, what do you mean by God's "having all the glory?" Do you mean, "He is doing the whole work, without any concurrence on man's part?" If so, your assertion is, "If man do at all 'work together with God,' in 'working out his own salvation,' then God does not do the whole work, without man's 'working together with Him.'" Most true, most sure: But cannot you see, how God nevertheless may have all the glory? Why, the very power to "work together with him" was from God. Therefore to Him is all the glory. . . .

If you say, "We ascribe to God alone the whole glory of our salvation;" I answer, So do we too. If you add, "Nay, but we affirm, that God alone does the whole work, without man's working at all;" in one sense, we allow this also. We allow, it is the work of God alone to justify, to sanctify, to glorify; which three comprehend the whole of salvation. Yet we cannot allow, that man can only resist, and not in any "work together with God;" or that God is so the whole worker of our salvation, as to exclude man's working at all. This I dare not say; for I cannot prove it by Scripture; nay it is flatly contrary thereto; for the Scripture is express, that (having received power from God) we are to "work out our own salvation;" and that (after the work of God is begun in our souls) we are "workers together with Him." . . .

How is it more for the glory of God to save man irresistibly, than to save him as a free agent, by such grace as he may concur with or resist? I fear you have a confused, unscriptural notion of "the glory of God" (*Works*, X, 229-31).

The speculative question about the relative priority of God's sovereignty and man's will has practical importance. It bears heavily upon the Wesleyan position on holiness. In fact, at the confluence of these contradictory streams of thought lies the real theological and practical issues of the Wesleyan position. In this encounter the deepest and most far-reaching elements of holiness doctrine become clear.

This discussion is important because the conclusion of it bears on such matters as biblical inspiration and interpretation; the Incarnation; revelation in general and miracle in particular; personality and the very inner meaning of moral responsibility, grace, faith, and works; sanctification; and the social and ethical implications of the gospel. Among the many other theological subjects affected by the problem, these are pointed up because of their relevance to this particular study. Perhaps the one most controversial point in a study of holiness theology will center around the concept of works and sanctification, because to misunderstand Wesleyanism here opens the door to the charge (false, we believe) that it teaches salvation by works, and it is difficult to clarify the issue on that level. We must push down to the level of presuppositions and establish definitions in order to engage in fruitful conversation on the level of theology and religion.

THE MEANING OF SUPERNATURAL

We have often noted the bald, flat statement made, "I believe in the supernatural." This assertion seems to successfully throw up the desired barrier to all other approaches to the Christian faith which are considered to be wrong. On the face of it this statement seems acceptable and true enough. But a more careful examination may reveal, below it, a disturbing context of thought. When to say, "I believe in a *supernatural* religion," is tantamount to saying, "The real elements of my religion lie beyond rational discussion," then the presuppositions of one's belief in supernaturalism need criticism.

The question asked in its most direct and practical way is, In relation to the Christian life, how much does God do for me and how much do I do for myself? or, How much and what kind of help does God give to a Christian by grace? In the specifically Wesleyan circles the question would be, What does entire sanctification *do* for a believer? What kind of change does it produce? The questions have been posed in this way because this is the way they are usually asked. Each of them reveals an underlying context of thought—a presupposition—which must be identified and criticized. The entire "Wesleyan movement" in America is divided over the answer to these questions—questions, incidentally, which were not inherent in Wesley's own thinking. Wesley was much more concerned about the basic relationship a Christian sustained to God than he was about a subjective *change* in the structure of human personality. The fact is, he did not entertain this concept.

Before we inquire more critically into the meaning of *supernatural*—and *natural*—it will be helpful to indicate the various possible relationships between the two that have been and are held and what each view does to theology. This is not an exhaustive review but an attempt to sufficiently open up the matter so that some conclusions may be warranted.

A. *The Supernatural Versus Nature*

A total discreteness between nature and the supernatural is emphasized by the concept of the *absolute transcendence* of God.

In this view, God and whatever realm He inhabits is totally other than the realm of created realities. The two worlds lie in two dissimilar dimensions. Nothing of what God is can be comprehended by or be contained in the created world. Knowledge of God is impossible; therefore revelation is impossible. God cuts down through the natural world in His activity, but this fact can only be deduced from what is observed, not recorded as a datum of revelation. The lack of capacity on the part of nature to record or measure anything of "supra-nature" on its apparatus makes any conversation about it irrational. Faith is irrational. Revelation is an "experience" but not knowledge. In this view, Christ can be a symbol only, not the divine-human Person of Christian faith, and Scripture is the record of human experience, not a part of divine communication.

B. *Mysticism and Supernaturalism*

On the opposite end of the scale is mysticism. *Philosophical mysticism* has a number of forms but basically it describes a direct, immediate contact with the supernatural which is always purchased at the expense of the integrity of human personality. Either human consciousness is lowered to the point of oblivion or the divine consciousness actually replaces the human will. In any case, the rational mind gives way to the divine mind, and is for the moment absorbed in it or is totally bypassed by it. In this concept, human personality is ravished and rationality is destroyed. Will is surrendered to that which is imagined to be God, and what the person does is identified as the activity of God.

The tendency in mystical religions is toward an unwholesome detachment from life, and a loss of ability to communicate with other selves. In fact there is often noticed a marked deterioration of personality integrity and a vague, unfocused semiconsciousness feathers off the sharp edges of the intellectual powers. It is difficult to penetrate into the rational reactions in the give-and-take of normal conversation. Social consciousness and responsibility evaporate in a fog of introspection and emotionalism and anti-intellectualism. Certainly not all so-called mystics conform to this pattern, but the history of the Church evidences the danger always associated potentially with an unguarded mysticism.

In the West, mysticism bows before the activistic Western mind. It is strange, then, that in the West theories of biblical inspiration should flourish which are based in this concept of the relationship of God to men. Nothing but a carry-over from old Hellenism could support the idea that the Holy Spirit "took over" the minds of men and, apart from their conscious rational cooperation, caused them to speak and write. One hears such statements as this: "When the prophet said, 'The Lord put His word in my mouth,' he meant that the word was put on the tongue and did not go through the prophet's mind." Back of a statement like that lies the belief that there is such a gulf between nature and supernature that God cannot get through to man except by bypassing his sinful mind and using the vacated facilities in this abnormal way.

That truth could result and be recognized as truth by the man whose consciousness was pushed aside is the real mystery. There is no allowance made for critical judgment, and we simply have another irrationalism. Since truth is imposed on the mind apart from its own cooperation and critical faculties, the subjective impulse is interpreted as truth. However objective or subjective truth and revelation may be said to be, the mind must take the responsibility for decisions regarding truth. If no objective criteria of truth can be accepted, the assumption regarding the amoral nature of man is implicit and inconsistent with the concept of the judgment of truth which man must and does make.

C. *Christian Conflict and the Supernatural*

Another extreme view of the difference between God and man, and between supernature and nature, is indicated by the teaching of a possible relationship of the two which is said to result in a lifelong conflict. In this view, the total incompatability between them does not necessitate the idea of a loss of human identity when in contact with God. Therein lies the area of conflict. In theology, the Holy Spirit is conceived as being added numerically and substantially to the human spirit in the "baptism of the Holy Spirit." So long as the human will invites the presence of the Holy Spirit, the divine nature is imposed on the evil human nature so as to control it. Suppression is a key word in such a position. It is used to guard against the idea of loss of human integrity, but at the same time it supposes that the human person is essentially incorrigible. Christian life, then, is a divine bondage in which all human powers must be curbed and the real self denied. One is moved to ask how an evil self can be induced to implore the Holy Spirit to restrain it. In this view, a divided personality is the necessary evidence of the spiritual life. Man may, and should, will to contest the will of the flesh, acknowledging an essential and ontological dualism. Sanctification consists in a "possession by" the Holy Spirit, who then subdues but does not—and cannot—"reform" the self. This view does not describe a truly moral relation between God and man. It is scarcely more than an armed truce.

D. *The Subconscious and the Supernatural*

A more difficult view to describe is somewhat related to the one above. In it, the spiritual nature of man, or the soul, is thought to be a sort of material out of which arises certain impulses which are in themselves right or wrong. The grace of God, regarded as an outside supernatural force which acts on the soul, acts sub-rationally, or by changing the wrong impulse to a right one below the level of consciousness. The passive, static nature of the soul is *acted on* by grace. It will be seen that in this view the radical disparity between nature and supernature is still characteristic of it in spite of the less pessimistic view of the savability of the person. But the nonrational element is there which also makes it nonmoral.

The theological problem here is that it is possible to conclude that, when properly received, the grace of sanctification eliminates all possibility of sin from the impulsive nature. It is based in the same view of human nature that gives rise to the conviction that human nature is itself essentially sinful and cannot be changed. The view under discussion simply affirms that the sinful nature *can* be changed. It is a "yes-no" argument that does not examine the structure of the thought it argues from.

According to this teaching, since sin lies in the basic impulse which is incapable of reformation, the character of the impulse must be altered by a sort of spiritual operation by the Holy Spirit if it is to be made good. Those who hold this view cannot account for the vicious and base temptations in the Christian which assails him, nor the need for the constant discipline and spiritual nourishment of the whole person which is demanded for good and faithful Christian living. There are many who feel it is a disloyalty to a theological commitment to ask forgiveness of God or man, because by doing so it seems to deny the power of the Holy Spirit to make sin virtually impossible—at least so long as one is "sanctified."

But those of other traditions are equally baffled by the realities of human life when the subjective "change" of the new birth is taken too materialistically. To a question posed by an inquirer about the repeatability of the new birth, Dr. Billy Graham gives an answer typical of this position:

> The Bible says: "If any man be in Christ, he is a new creature: old things are passed away; behold, all things are become new" (II Corinthians 5:17). When any person becomes tired of his narrow, selfish life, when he confesses his sins and asks the Father to forgive him, the Holy Spirit can enter his mind and heart and make him a new creature. Then he can make a fresh start. This should be necessary only once. The Bible says: "We know that whosoever is born of God sinneth not (I John 5:18). A person who has been born again will say "no" to temptation. When he has surrendered his life to Christ he will walk a new way, and no longer trip over the old stumbling blocks. If you once thought you were born again, and now have fallen back into the old sinful ways, you didn't experience a true rebirth. But our religion is one of the second-chance. Jesus didn't come to condemn, but to save. Completely surrender your life to Him and you will truly be born again. You will know when this happens for you'll experience the joy of new life in Christ.[1]

All of these views demand a radical, metaphysical discreteness between nature and supernature. They are essentially irrationalisms, because the relatedness of the two dimensions does not permit a true moral response on the part of man.

IDEALISMS

On the other end of the philosophical spectrum lies a cluster of concepts which relate man so closely to the divine as to virtually identify one with the other. In this view, man is a projection of Deity, or the finite experience of the Infinite, or a fragmentation of the Divine All. Man has no real, personal identity. Every man is a spark of the divine nature. He is a "lost" fragment of God whose "salvation" consists in merging again into God, or he is God coming into self-consciousness through man's experience.

Religiously, the problems in this view are no less great than those described above. If man is an element of God, he has no real moral integrity of his own. What he is and does is rigidly pre-determined. If God is limited by man's experience, something is said about God that puts an impossible limitation on Him if the Christian view is taken as a criterion. Revelation is any human thought or experience. Sin is not, and cannot be, personal rebellion against God. Christ is simply a better example of God-consciousness than the average—and other "Christs" are expected. Salvation, as biblically portrayed, is absurd, because sin is merely a figment of the imagination dissolved by reunion with the divine.

When the attempt is made to marry some philosophical concept of the nature of reality to the Christian faith in indissoluble union, logical and theological problems multiply. Many philosophies have accompanied and supported the Christian faith through history, but Christianity outgrows and casts aside all the human attempts to put it under philosophical bondage. No one needs to learn to understand and accept some specific theory of reality before he comes to Christ in saving faith. No more may it be said that one comes to Christ by the door of the theory of the nature of reality than that he comes to Him by way of the Church.

The metaphysical relationship of nature and God will probably always be a subject for lively debate. What *is* of importance, whatever outcome the debate may have, is the *moral relationship* of God and man. Moral relatedness is in a wholly different dimension than the metaphysical. *Depth* is an appropriate designation for it. It does not deal with the measurements appropriate to science nor in the abstract considerations of philosophy. It is equally at home in any theory of the nature of reality except that which rejects all possibility of human responsibility.

BIBLICAL SUPERNATURALISM

Hebrew concepts separated the being of God from the being of His creation, yet God was not a stranger to His world nor was He shut out of it by philosophical abstractions. The earth was the theater of His activity. In fact, the Hebrew mind knew nothing of laws of nature intervening between God and His world so as to restrict His freedom in it. All of nature was the direct expression of God's glory. This interaction was rational: Adam communed with God. It was moral: disobedience cut the communication. It was personal: God forgave sinners and opened His heart to them again. He desired the fellowship of men.

G. Campbell Morgan, in discussing the claims of Christ, said, "Supernatural is an awkward word; it will become obsolete when we have more light. If we could climb to the height where God dwells, things we call supernatural would be perfectly natural."[2] Christ, in His own person, linked the limitations and definable existence of men to the realm of existence indefinable by terms applicable to men—that of the "height where God dwells"—and by doing so brought the "supernatural" world into the intelligent grasp of humanity. Whatever "gulf" may have existed ended in the Incarnation. This is, indeed, the meaning of the Incarnation.

Miracle was not to be an intellectual hurdle to stand between God and men or a barrier to faith in Him. Whatever "miracle" was in the Bible, it was intended to be itself revelation and a rational aid to faith. Revelation is the communication of truth. Broken laws do not communicate truth but rather communicate confusion, because the mind reels in the presence of the absurd and irrational. Whatever Jesus was and did convinced the mind and the heart.

It is probably an error to present the gospel of Christ by way of those elements which are intellectually difficult. When one begins to try to explain how Christ could be truly God and truly man, two perfect natures in one substance, he is going far beyond biblical preaching. Rather, knowing Christ in personal encounter, these "miracles" help us to better understand the infinitely rich being of God. The Virgin Birth is a light thrown on an otherwise incomprehensible Person. The *doctrine* of the Trinity is a clue to the vastly complex and intriguing social nature of the one God. These doctrines are not themselves revelation but attempts to rationalize revelation. There is no better source of information about God and Christ than the Scriptures themselves, which are windows open toward, not shutters against, light. The *doctrines* of the Virgin Birth and the Trinity are intellectually incomprehensible, but the person of Christ is knowable and God is real in total experience. Doctrine is a guard against intellectual vagaries and error, not itself divine proclamation.

All this is to say that, though the relationship of nature to supernature may be clothed in mystery, it is not an irrationalism but the very core of the rational because by it the moral life of man is kept alert. Precisely at the juncture of nature and spirit, moral life begins because revelation or divine communication is established there. Jesus stood at the heart's door knocking. The judgment against the unbeliever was not that he *could not* understand but that he *would not*.

When God's grace begins to operate upon the person, it is at this point of moral responsibility. Grace awakens into sharp awareness everything that *moral* means. Both persons, God and man, confronting each other maintain personal integrity. Neither is merged into the other, nor is identity submerged in an irrational shadowland. The coming of the Spirit does not occasion an eclipse of human rationality and consciousness.

Any theology which countenances moral stupor and the dimout of full conscious awareness at the point of God's grace seriously impugns the natures of God and man. The will must operate uncoerced; the critical judgment must be heightened to its limit; love is not love when the attempt is made to coerce it; the whole person comes into the full focus of integrity. How then can it be said that the part of the person remains dormant, even hostile, to God while the mind assents to truth about Christ in the moment of new birth? The interaction of the whole being is absolutely required in the act of faith, else the immorality of a split loyalty is the badge of the Christian. If man is evil to the core of his being, how can it be said, as some do, that God blinds himself to that fact and attributes the holiness of Christ to him? To whatever one finds himself committed by way of a theory of the nature of reality, the interaction between God and man must be accounted for and must eventually mold one's basic philosophy.

Theories relative to the meaning of the supernatural and natural and the interaction between the two, i.e., one's philosophy, tend to dominate theology and determine orthodoxy. A limited concept of physics is projected into infinity and such ideas as "Natural law in the spiritual world," are developed. The concepts of revelation and miracle and human freedom, as well as the nature of faith and grace and sanctification, are determined by the basic presupposition, and Scripture is interpreted in the light of this. *Responsible thinking demands that this fact be recognized.* We may not be responsible for having presuppositions, or for having the ones we do have. But we are responsible for knowing that we *have* presuppositions and knowing what they are, and then putting them to the tests appropriate to adequate criticism. This study is not in the interest of substituting one theory of nature and supernature for another. It is critical in its aim and asks only that the questions be asked and answered: Why do I believe the way I do? and, Do my beliefs force an interpretation of the God/man relationship that contradicts the serious view Christian faith clearly proposes in Scripture?

The answer to the question, How much does God do for us and how much must we do for ourselves? is not, then, a question science or philosophy can answer but only the Scriptures, which speak to us in the realm of moral and spiritual matters.

The illogicalities and lack of practicality and realism and moral seriousness arise, not because men are not serious or devout or Christian, but because the Bible has been interpreted philosophically and not experimentally. *Moral,* when understood, relates all these soteriological truths to practical life. Holiness, when seen as a moral matter, is not something so unrelated to life that one must either be baffled and discouraged by it or reject it in the interest of honesty. Sin is not something that even God can do nothing about except pass judgment on it, or cancel it out *on the books,* or reinterpret it in Christ.

All of these things are related to human experience. They are to be worked out in the ordinary life of ordinary people. To make this impossible is to make a farce of Christian faith. If God says, in His Word, that those in fellowship with Him are cleansed from all sin, this fact must be accepted if one claims to be biblical, but only a biblical interpretation of sin can keep this sublime statement from absurdity, for the full moral fallibility of human nature and temporal probation must be kept within the concept.

CHAPTER XII

The Function of Faith

The subject of faith is introduced by this title to suggest two important things about it. Faith is a *living, dynamic exercise.* It serves an ongoing function in the Christian life. But, equally important, it *serves.* It is not an end in itself but a means to an end.

At this point Wesley was very clear, using very forceful rhetoric at times. In a sermon, "The Law Established Through Faith," he has some things to say of considerable interest to our study.

> Faith itself, even Christian faith, the faith of God's elect, the faith of the operation of God, is still only the handmaid of love. . . . Love is the end of all the commandments of God. Love is the end, the sole end, of every dispensation of God, from the beginning of the world to the consummation of all things (*Works,* V, 462).

Wesley continues:

> Let those who magnify faith beyond all proportion so as to swallow up all things else, and who so totally misapprehend the nature of it as to imagine it stands in the place of love, consider further that as love will exist after faith (referring to I Cor. 13), so it did exist long before it (*ibid.*, pp. 462-63).

The point Wesley was making as he discussed law and faith puts his whole theology into focus.

> Faith, then, was originally designed of God to reestablish the law of love. . . . It is the grand means of restoring that holy love where in man was originally created. It follows that altho faith is of no value in itself . . . yet as it leads to that end, the establishing anew the law unspeakable blessing to man, and of unspeakable value before God (*ibid.*, p 464).

At no point is Wesley's contribution to theology more obvious and specific than here. He stood squarely in the Reformation tradition in his declaration of salvation by faith alone as an antidote to the Roman Catholic emphasis on works. But he was equally emphatic about a vital correction to Reformation theology which he felt was biblical, that love was the antidote to faith as an end in itself without works. This is Wesley's significant footnote to the history of Christian doctrine.

If we are alert to nuances of thought, it becomes obvious that by Wesley's "footnote" to the Reformation emphasis on "faith alone" he has introduced a new dimension to faith, a new quality that is as far-reaching as the "faith versus works" emphasis of Luther and Calvin. Faith as an end and faith as a means are two vastly different concepts which not only reflect back on the meaning of faith in each case but say very different things about the salvation of which each speaks. In Reformation thought, saving faith —having been supernaturally given—encourages the Christian to trust the One who saves him, and in this confidence love is fostered, and developed. Love is a by-product of faith. In Wesley, faith is itself an element of love in that in life situations love and faith cannot be separated. Faith leads to love, which is the goal and essence of salvation.

Not only is the meaning of faith changed by its relation to love, as Wesley conceived it, but a transformation of the meaning of love is also involved. Care in understanding this, as we are attempting to show in this book, will nullify the suspicion that Wesley is borrowing the Catholic doctrine of love uncritically, although his understanding of love is closer to it than to the Reformation position.

Now, in devoting a chapter to faith, an inner ambiguity begins to show. Faith is so enormously vital to all biblical truth that it cannot be escaped, yet at the same time it is so overshadowed by its consequences that one cannot abstract it sharply enough to subject it to isolated scrutiny. Faith is not a *thing* which stands alone in human experience. It hides behind, or inside of, spiritual values. The searchlight of analysis sees merely the value, not the faith. Faith wears the clothing of the value it is important to. We are told that the most ultimate units of energy identifiable by the tools of nuclear science are unavailable to human sensitivity. To bring them into the dimension of sense experience is to destroy them. These "foundation stones" of reality are discovered by what they do— and they do plenty. This is dynamic with real meaning.

Faith is much like this. One need only to ask what one does to excercise faith to discover the problem. How does one believe? What is the procedure? In every case believing seems to become something else. The test of believing is not believing but involvement in a framework of opennesses to a new set of insights and a new direction of interests and values. One cannot subject the insights and values and interests to a fine enough scrutiny to locate whatever it is faith is. Even believing intellectual propositions or scientific theories partakes of the same curious phenomenon. Believing (and loving) has no independent psychological identity but structures other human activities.

Bibical faith is so entangled with love and obedience (to name two of the vast family of relatives) that it does not exist without them. Wesley well understood this: "There is one thing more that may be separately considered, though it cannot actually be separate from the preceding [love], which is implied, in the being *altogether a Christian;* and that is the ground of all, even faith" (*Works*, V, 22). Here Wesley points to the essential relationship of love to faith but also understands that, with this knowledge of that relationship, a discussion of faith is important. But it is interesting to note in attempting to determine Wesley's view of faith that it is impossible for him to cleanly separate it from love and holiness. Here is an example from one of his "conversations":

> In asserting salvation by faith, we mean this: (1.) That pardon (salvation begun) is received by faith producing works. (2.) That holiness (salvation continued) is faith working by love. (3.) That heaven (salvation finished) is the reward of this faith.
>
> If you who assert salvation by works, or by faith and works, mean the same thing (understanding by faith, the revelation of Christ in us,—by salvation, pardon, holiness, glory), we will not strive with you at all (*Works,* VIII, 290).

In another "conversation" the question is asked, "Is faith the condition, or the instrument of sanctification?" Wesley answers: "It is both the condition and the instrument of it. When we begin to believe, then sanctification begins. And as faith increases, holiness increases, till we are created anew" (*ibid.,* p. 279).

In like manner he speaks in another place: "What law do we establish by faith? Not the ritual law: Not the ceremonial law of Moses. In nowise; but the great, unchangeable law of love, the holy love of God and of our neighbour" (*ibid.,* p. 60).

If our observations thus far have been correct, we can feel increasing assurance that love *is* the dynamic of Wesleyanism. Love is the focal point of all its theology and its link with life. Love cannot exist apart from a moral being and it is, then, the key to the ethical concept of holiness. Some problems are solved, perhaps, by this approach; others are raised. But the question of immediate moment has to do with faith as it lies in the context of love and holiness. Three strands of our study throw some light on a deeper investigation.

1. The two-foci concept of *moral* saves it from a mere humanistic "self-realization" (Pelagianism) on the one hand, yet preserves true moral integrity in man on the other.

2. The concept of the whole-man psychology in which all aspects of personality are seen to work as a unit—faith and will, heart and mind, love and obedience—preserves the integrity of personality without losing the idea of dependence on God's grace.

3. The concept of faith as a changed direction of confidence and affection, rather than the initiation of a new power, preserves the theology of grace without loss of true human initiative and responsibility.

When these matters are held together and faith is seen as an element in it, faith is properly understood. The problems, as we shall see, arise as faith is abstracted from its proper context.

There are a number of elements inherent in the interrelation between God and man which are distinguished and arranged, in systematic theology, according to some principle such as logic or chronology or psychology. Some of these elements are: conviction, grace, faith, regeneration, repentance, obedience, sanctification, forgiveness, cleansing, love, justification, adoption, and others. Usually each treatment is determined by the underlying philosophy of the theologian. In fact, the distinctive character of a theological position can be quite accurately determined by noting the sequence in which these elements are placed and the relation each is said to sustain to the others. For instance, Reformation theology would usually place regeneration temporally prior to repentance, and Wesleyanism would reverse that order. The resultant theology in each case is quite different. Systematic theology is well aware of this fact but must defend its own position on other than biblical grounds.

If one approaches Scripture inductively, as we are attempting to do, it is not so clear that a chronological order can be detected. Rather there seems to be a spiritual "complex" of interrelated elements partaking so much of each other that it is difficult to isolate any one for examination apart from the others. However, the demands of rational thinking require an analysis of these elements.

THE PRIORITY OF FAITH

The prevailing logic in this study is controlled by the basic conviction which structures Wesleyan theology (though it is not always consistent with it) that truth is fundamentally moral and that redemption proceeds along the line of moral integrity. The particular relevance of this conviction to this chapter is that when the whole man acts in respect of God's will (as the concept "moral" indicates) every aspect of relatedness moves together. Hence, where obedience is, for instance, faith and love also operate. The task is to find, not the first element in chronological order, but the element most fundamental to the whole complex of truth. Faith seems to be the element upon which rest all the other aspects of redemptive truth. In it lies a concept that puts the whole into proper perspective.

FAITH AND MAN

In choosing the concept of faith as the common denominator in all other aspects of salvation, we are deliberately limiting this whole study to a consideration of the human side of redemption. Actually faith has no meaning apart from grace and love. Wesleyanism is a theology of grace, as is Calvinism, but it conceives of grace in a more personal way and in full keeping with moral responsibility. The opening paragraph of John Wesley's sermon "Salvation by Faith" states his view of grace:

> All the blessings which God hath bestowed upon man, are of his mere grace, bounty, or favor; his free, undeserved favor, favor altogether undeserved; man having no claim to the least of his mercies. It was free grace that "formed man of dust of the ground, and breathed into him a living soul", and stamped on that soul the image of God, and "put all things under his feet". The same free grace continues to us, at this day, life and breath, and all things. For there is nothing we are, or have, or do, which can deserve the least thing at God's hand. "All our works, thou, oh God, hast wrought in us." These, therefore, are so many more instances of free mercy; and, whatever righteousness may be found in man, this is also the gift of God. . . .
>
> If then sinful men find favor with God, it is "grace upon grace" . . . . Grace is the source, faith the condition, of salvation (*Works*, V, 7).

It is precisely faith as the condition of salvation in which we are interested. No word or idea in the New Testament carries so much significance to salvation as do faith and its cognates. No word better ties into the whole concept of *moral* as it is beginning to develop in this study. No word is more important to the whole of redemption than this one. Few theological words have been more abused and misunderstood.

FAITH'S RELATION TO GRACE

One is immediately confronted, in reading the New Testament particularly, with the fact that faith is a most vital aspect of human life in its relation to God. It seems to be an essential element in personality. It is a rational link between the tangible and intangible, between the divine and the human, between the objective and subjective aspects of atonement as well as between all events and meaning, fact and interpretation, in all of rational life.

A good synonym would be "appropriation." On one side of faith lies the objective atonement. Into that "mystic" realm where God has done so much for us we cannot penetrate with our finite intelligence. The full truth of what God has done must always escape our rational grasp. We have pictures and analogies which help to relate it to our world of understanding: the lawcourt, the Temple sacrifice, war techniques, vine and branches, family relationships, and many more—none of them the whole truth, all of them together helping us to know that God loves us and desires our redemption. All this is grace.

On the other side of faith lies a great world of sin and defeat and despair and fear and death. In this world live people whose capacity for good and evil is their unique *raison d'etre*. The capacity for nobility is itself the sharpest judgment for what men have become. Great evil in men is called sin because that same capacity could have been used for great good. Men are moral and this is their condemnation: They "loved darkness rather than light."

God's grace is on one side, "moral" man (in the sense already designated) on the other. Salvation is offered to sinners who are morally responsible. To keep the integrity of both of these truths is the heart of the gospel message and it is imbedded in the words "by faith."

The Church early saw the dangers in a failure to keep these two truths intact. God's forgiveness they saw could be too lightly regarded, and so the problem of how to handle sins committed after baptism had to be met. The question arose, How many times could one sin and be forgiven? How far does forgiveness reach—to past sins only? or to all sins reaching into the future? If God's forgiveness could be implored for sins after baptism, how would it be known that repentance had been sincere enough? In other words, the danger of a moral insensitivity creeping into the heart of those who could too easily presume on God's mercy was recognized. Whatever one may think of the whole penitential system, certainly the insight of our Church Fathers into the human peril immanent in the divine judicial acquittal unguarded from unprincipled human irresponsibility is to be sincerely respected. Easy, cheap, shoddy ideas of God's mercy were deeply deplored. But gradually there arose a well-organized and detailed system of penance that missed the proper moral point of the Early Church and stressed too much the ability and obligation of the penitent to demonstrate his sincerity and finally to earn merit—to pay an appropriate equivalent for sins. The commercialized aspect of this we believe is a distortion of the true intent of the original purpose of the Catholic church. The idea of faith was lost as it merged into works. The fine balance between God's initiative and human response was lost in favor of an overemphasis on human merit. The quality of moral life—the *personal* aspects—degenerated into quantity values, the nonpersonal.

Wesley was well aware of this truth and said in his sermon "Justification by Faith":

> Never was the maintaining of this doctrine more seasonable than it is today. . . . It is endless to attack, one by one, all the errors of that Church. But salvation by faith strikes at the root, and all [errors] fall at once where this is established. It was this doctrine, which our Church justly calls *the strong rock and foundation of the Christian religion* (*Works*, V, 15).

Faith's Relation to Works

The term "by faith" took on an extreme either/or antithesis to "works" in the Reformation period. In absolute contrast to the abuse of the Catholic system of human merit stood the Reformation doctrine of *sola fides*, "by faith alone," and no human effort could be granted as of having value in any sense. So great was the contrast between faith and works that all moral relevancy—all subjective desire, all human striving—was interpreted as itself sin. This characterizes some evangelical theology today.

Of course this reflected a definition of faith which emphasized the objective aspect of atonement but failed to do justice to the moral experience of men. It stressed only the forensic meaning of righteousness and justification and neglected the spiritual aspect. Unrighteousness as imputed guilt, and righteousness as the cancellation of that guilt, irrevocably and eternally by God's decree, tended to make justification abstract and lacking in human relevancy and life. In this view Christ's death on the Cross becomes somewhat incidental to divine decree, that death is "commercial-ized" to an exact value to cover so much sin—no more or less. It is difficult to conceive of a less personal and relevant way to think of salvation.

Faith then would be, and is often so conceived, as intellectual assent or the acceptance of an idea which, apart from all subjective consideration, permanently places the "believer" in a position of absolute safety from the wrath of God and judgment. Not only logically, but actually, this position forces one into the risk of anti-nomianism.

So long as faith is defined as an intellectual affirmation only which bridges the gap between grace and individual salvation, and works are thought to consist of all human activity even including "faithfulness," the problem of antinomianism must exist and per-sist. Certainly an "implanted" saving faith arising entirely apart from human participation misses completely the concept of moral integrity.

In a preliminary way it may be said at this point that the Bible makes it unmistakably clear that there is a "price" to be paid for Christian integrity. Dietrich Bonhoeffer gave contemporary expression to this in contrasting cheap grace with costly grace. It is shallow thinking to categorize that which the price involves as the same thing as the "works" which Paul so strongly denounced as the way to salvation. To make "works" cover all moral respon-sibility is to go far beyond biblical teaching. The ritual acts by which self-righteousness seeks favor with God are very different from the self-giving which is the dynamic of Christian integrity. In fact, such self-giving is one of the best definitions of faith that can be formulated. It is precisely the *end* of self-sufficiency that gives meaning to saving faith. Where moral beings are implicated in this kind of faith, "the cross" or self-giving is absolutely imperative.

A real saint, says Oswald Chambers, is never consciously a saint. A saint is conscious only of an increasing and profound de-pendence upon God. And this dependence includes obedience or it is not dependence. Any theology which encourages a satisfaction and comfort in anything less than this moment-by-moment de-pendence on God for "standing," for "state," for cleansing and power, apart from moral participation in God's will, is not biblical theology.

It is worth a moment's time to record some contemporary insights regarding this important point. Floyd Filson, in *One Lord, One Faith*, says:

> Accurate interpretation of the New Testament has been hindered by a tendency to let forgiveness stop at negative results. The guilt of sin is cared for. . . . But this does not leave man where the Gospel seeks to bring him. . . . Repentance and forgiveness involves the turning of the sinner from his evil ways, with sorrow and with deep desire to be forgiven, restored to fellowship with God and renewed in right purposes. A forgiveness that does not give a strong sense of moral obligation . . . lacks reality.[1]

James Stewart gives a powerful exposition of the involvement of life in faith in a chapter entitled "Mysticism and Morality" in *A Man in Christ*. From this chapter come the following words:

> To know oneself forgiven, and forgiven at so great a cost, is always a moral dynamic of the first order [importance]. It is a main spring of the dedicated life. It creates character. . . . It makes the forgiven sinner Christ's man, body and soul, forever.
>
> For to be united to Christ means to be *identified with Christ's attitude to sin*. It means seeing sin with Jesus' eyes, and opposing it with something of the same passion with which Jesus at Calvary opposed it. It means an assent of the whole man to the divine judgment proclaimed upon sin at the cross. . . . It means, as Paul put it tersely, death. In face of all this, to find antinomianism in Paul is simply to caricature his Gospel.[2]

WESLEYANISM'S INTERPRETATION OF FAITH

The emphasis John Wesley and John Fletcher gave to theology cannot be fully understood apart from their controversy with the contemporary antinomianism which prevailed. It was not to Calvinism as such that Wesley was opposed (as his relationship with Whitefield amply testifies) but with those aspects of it which were derived from its mere logic; namely, a limited atonement, unconditional election, and the disregard for law which seemed to arise from a confidence in unconditional eternal security.

Wesley was concerned with the problem of how to maintain the balance between grace and the moral nature of men. He saw that not only justification but sanctification as well was "by faith." This added the moral dimension to justification which Reformation theology had generally failed to maintain. "By faith" also saved theology from playing into the hands of the Pelagians, who would see no need for grace at all. Wesley rang that bell "loud and clear."

But "sanctification by faith" raises different kinds of problems than those raised by Luther's emphasis on justification by faith, and it is these problems which we want to examine in this chapter. The more formal concept of faith in Luther became dynamic when united with sanctification. This, in turn, for Wesley, reacted back on the meaning of faith itself. "When we say 'Believe and you will be saved,' we do not mean 'Believe and thou shalt step from sin to heaven, without any holiness coming in between.'"

"We acknowledge no faith but that which worketh by love. . . . Faith becomes the means of which love is the end" (*Works*, V, 462). "Being a Christian means having a faith active in love" (*ibid.*, p. 467). Wesley's works are so full of this teaching that it is futile to try to list all the passages.

FAITH AND THE MORAL LIFE

Christian righteousness is "by faith." The pseudo-righteousness to which this is the alternative is self-righteousness or salvation by works. To this basic affirmation evangelical Christians adhere and in it lies the basis for theological unity. But in respect of it there exist also differences of opinion that keep Reformation groups clearly distinguished theologically from those who follow "holiness doctrine." It is at this point, namely, the meaning of faith, that holiness theology begins to take its form.

New Testament teaching about holiness presupposes a vital relationship between faith and works. This does not mean that it teaches that any man can in any way merit salvation by what he does or thinks. It does hold that faith is an act which engages the whole of man, not simply his intellectual faculty alone or his emotions or will, but all the personality interacting as a unit. A passive idea of personality is rejected in favor of a dynamic one; that is, men are essentially men only as they are moral creatures. Hence faith, or lack of it, is a *moral* fact. The antithesis to saving faith is not no faith, or passivity, but active rejection.

The biblical emphasis on faith adds to the forensic meaning of justification an ethical dimension also. Such does not imply that we have it in our power by good works to reform and make ourselves righteous. Nor does it put righteousness *in* good works. Unrighteousness is more than imputed guilt. It is *a person rejecting God.* How he comes to this rejection is not here the question. That he does reject is both a biblical declaration and a fact of human experience. Righteousness or justification is most certainly the removal of guilt and is hence juridical, but it also has a subjective aspect, which is the concern of this chapter.

At this point it is well to be reminded that, if *moral* means any serious thing, we may expect to find that God's dealings with men will strengthen rather than weaken the concept of moral integrity. This fact will, in turn, have a bearing on justification and faith and the security of the believer. To account a man righteous who is a sinner and living in sin would be to deny everything that cost Christ so much. God does not change His definition of *sin* to make it go away. He does not make a moral universe and reveal to man the Spirit of Truth and then wink at man's sin and call it holiness.

Wesley could not have expressed a more thoroughgoing Reformation conviction about justification. His entire sermon on "Justification by Faith" (*Works*, Vol. V), should be carefully read. In it he spells out clearly the distinction between justification, the objective aspect of conversion, and the subjective, or sanctification. But he cuts an even finer edge to avoid the false concepts of Reformation teaching.

> What is it to be *justified?* . . . It is not the being made actually just and righteous. This is *sanctification* . . . the immediate fruit of justification. . . . The one implies what God does for us through his Son; the other, what he works in us by his Spirit. . . .
> Least of all does justification imply, that God is deceived in those whom he justifies; that he thinks them to be what, in fact, they are not; that he accounts them to be otherwise than they are. It does by no means imply, that God judges concerning us contrary to the real nature of things; that he esteems us better than we really are, or believes us righteous when we are unrighteous. . . . Neither can it ever consist with his unerring wisdom, to think that I am innocent . . . because another is so. He can no more, in this manner confound me with Christ, than with David or Abraham. . . .
> The plain scriptural notion of justification is pardon, the forgiveness of sins (*Works,* V, 56-57).

When the Wesleyan is consistent with his basic premise, he must hold to the unitary view of personality. He must not be tempted to settle for another kind of dualism by separating between his objective and subjective relationships. It is putting dishonesty in God to say that a man is objectively righteous and subjectively unrighteous even by virtue of Christ's atonement. The atonement, or Christ's obedience, does not change the quality of sin in any moral being so that actual sin in a sinner and in a believer are somehow different. If integrity means anything in the world of moral beings, including God, the Source of all Truth, something of that basic integrity must be a part of Christian experience.

It is to prevent the extreme to which human logic will go that the deceptively simple phrase so often appears, that is, "by faith." It stands as a ubiquitous guard against too easy answers. It is a guard against any idea that man can achieve righteousness by his own unaided efforts. But it is also, by implication, a reminder that the *whole man* is involved in his faith.

What Is Faith?

We are saved "by faith," but what does it mean to believe? And what is it that is believed? Is saving faith different in kind from the other experiences of faith which every person exercises? Is it faith itself that saves? Is faith a gift or is it a faculty over which a moral person has responsible control? These and other factors in the problem lie before us.

We have related faith to appropriation. At least it may be said that faith is the link between God's grace and man's need, and in the experience of appropriation from the first faint awakening of the person toward God to the end of rational life, that link is respected.

Now faith is a distinctly human response; that is, it is something that men do. It is significant that righteousness (or justification) is "by faith." This means that God's approval of us awaits in some way our appropriation of His approval. Apparently the objective (to us) act of God in Christ by which reconciliation was made a fact remains tentative and potential until faith actualizes it in experience.

Whether saving faith is different in kind or source ("the gift of God") than other expressions of believing is not at this point the question. The fact remains that, so far as men are concerned, salvation is not by divine decree nor even unconditionally by the work of Christ (though its possibility is only through Christ) so that whomever He died for would inevitably be saved (unconditional atonement). It is "by faith." This puts it in history where men live.

This effectively makes man a party to the transaction between himself and God. It is a "circulation from I to Thou, a sort of mutual 'flow' between God and man."[3]

Salvation, therefore, cannot be wholly objective, unrelated to human character or personal response. This means that in exercising faith for salvation something begins to happen to character. Salvation is not merited by any human excellence, but it is impossible to be its recipient apart from a consideration of moral integrity. "By faith" is the beginning of God-centeredness in contrast to self-centeredness. It is a *moral* commitment and has moral implications in life. One cannot believe in God in the intellectual area of personality without *all* parts of his being coming to a focus in the experience. "By faith" is the shift from one basic presupposition to another—from self as God, to God as total Lord. Life and thinking proceed out of the new presuppositions and are given character by it. In other words, "by faith" is dynamic, not formal and static. And it is of necessity traumatic, because it shifts the entire weight of life from self to God. It is *radical* (from the roots) revolution.

In his *Earnest Appeal*, Wesley presents the heart of his understanding of Christian faith. He says he sought for years for what he finally found by faith. But what is this faith? It is Wesley's purpose to shed light on this matter. He wished others to "profit by our loss, that they may go straightway to the religion of love, even by faith." But faith is dynamic. He adds: "Faith is the eye of the new born soul. . . . It is the ear of the soul. . . . It is the palate (if I may be allowed the expression) of the soul. . . . It is the feeling of the soul (feels the love of God)" (*Works*, VIII, 4).

GRACE ACTUALIZED BY FAITH

Faith *is* dynamic. Jesus often required the faith of the sick for their own healing; for instance, "Thy faith hath made thee whole."

Justification is by faith, and the just shall live by faith, not by the works of the law. The heart is purified by faith, not by cultic circumcision (Acts 15:9). Sanctification is by faith in Jesus (Acts 26:18). Propitiation is by faith in Christ's blood (Rom. 3:25). Our access into "this grace" in which we stand is by faith (Rom. 5:2). By faith we stand (II Cor. 1:24). We walk by faith (II Cor. 5:7). We receive the promise of the Spirit by faith (Gal. 3:14). We are children of God by faith in Christ Jesus (Gal. 3:26). Christ dwells in the heart by faith (Eph. 3:17). Faith shields us from the fiery darts of the enemy (Eph. 6:16). These are a few of the benefits of grace actualized by faith. It is exegetically impossible to interpret these and other passages eschatologically only, which would define faith in terms of hope and defer the benefits to another life. Faith and hope are related but never confused in Scripture. Faith is *not* a merely intellectual affirmation. It is a moral commitment with moral consequences. It is a this-life concern.

> This then is the salvation which is through faith, even in this present world: A salvation from sin, and the consequences of sin, both often expressed in the word, *justification;* which, taken in the largest sense, implies a deliverance from guilt and punishment, by the atonement of Christ actually applied to the soul of the sinner now believing on him, and a deliverance from the power of sin, through Christ *formed in his heart* (*Works*, V, 11-12).

THE FAITH-WORKS SYNDROME

Works and faith represent two ways—and opposite ways understood in Christian history—to achieve a legitimate (and necessary) acceptability by God (which is what justification or righteousness really is). If we keep in mind the central import back of all the various figures of speech in Scripture having to do with redemption, we can say that the intended goal is fellowship with God, the end of alienation, in which is realized, step by step in life, the cleansing by the blood of Christ (I John 1:7).

"Works" is one way to attempt to achieve this proper relationship with God. Faith is another way. The question arises as to whether either one, alone, is adequate, provided the two *can* be separated in fact. That is, is one without the other actually what it purports to be? Is it possible to exercise faith apart from the total involvement of the person and all he is and does?

FAITH OR WORKS?

The philosophy back of "works" salvation is built upon the presupposition that the estrangement between God and man is forensic and not moral. It cannot see that sin is a degeneration of moral integrity which destroys the possibility of spiritual affinity. Love for God as a personal relationship has been short-circuited in favor of a dependence on law and the impersonal and the superficial and casuistic approval of law to the conscience. It may be said that morality has become an end in itself—a god—rather than a means to the end, namely, of being right with God. This is a subtle difference but a very real one. In no case does Paul—or Jesus—intimate that moral law is wrong or that it can be dispensed with—ever. It is the form, structure, pattern of knowledge and truth (Rom. 2:20). It is never suggested that obedience to it is to be neglected or superseded. What is taught is that the keeping of law, alone, cannot achieve righteousness—or the personal approval of God and cleansing fellowship with Him.

WORKS—MORALISM

In a word, the philosophy of works proceeds on the assumption that legal impeccability can substitute for personal moral relationship. It is thoroughly objective. It discounts subjective, spiritual considerations and lives on a plane below the personal. It raises the nonpersonal to the status of duty. Law becomes "Lord." It is easy to "manage" law by human interpretation and hence human standards of approval. The ancient Jews did that; so do we. The Lord of the law, who alone can and must interpret the law in inner experience, is by our impertinence imprisoned in His law and hence reduced to servanthood. "Works" as deplored by Paul in Romans have made a god of law, and have made God the servant of law—often our law—or our interpretation of God's law.

> Our religion does not lie in doing what God has not enjoined, or abstaining from what he hath not forbidden. It does not lie in the form of our apparel, in the posture of our body, of the covering of our heads; nor yet in abstaining from marriage, or from meats and drinks, which are all good if received with thanksgiving. Therefore, neither will any man, who knows whereof he affirms, fix the mark of a Methodist here,—in any actions or customs purely indifferent, undetermined by the word of God.

238 / A Theology of Love

Nor, lastly, is he distinguished by laying the whole stress of religion on any single part of it. If you say, "Yes, he is; for he thinks 'we are saved by faith alone:'" I answer, You do not understand the terms. By salvation he means holiness of heart and life. And this he affirms to spring from true faith alone. Can even a nominal Christian deny it? Is this placing a part of religion for the whole? "Do we then make void the law through faith? God forbid! Yea, we establish the law." We do not place the whole of religion (as too many do, God knoweth) either in doing no harm, or in doing good, or in using the ordinances of God. No, not in all of them together; wherein we know by experience a man may labour many years, and at the end have no religion at all, no more than he had at the beginning. Much less in any one of these; or, it may be, in a scrap of one of them: Like her who fancies herself a virtuous woman, only because she is not a prostitute; or him who dreams he is an honest man, merely because he does not rob or steal. May the Lord God of my fathers preserve me from such a poor, starved religion as this! Were this the mark of a Methodist, I would sooner choose to be a sincere Jew, Turk or Pagan (*Works*, VIII, 341).

Faith—Moral

Faith, on the other hand, refers to an attitude toward God which the philosophy of works has neglected or rejected. It seeks the same approval of God, the same fellowship with Him; but it operates on the personal, not an impersonal, level. Faith is personal through and through. The philosophy of faith represents an entirely different approach to truth than that of works. It sees the lawgiver back of the law. Or if there be no objective law, it sees the Person and respects the integrity of that Person in terms of response to Him. Faith, interpreted as only a mental acceptance of some proposition or idea, falls far short of the biblical teaching regarding it.

Abraham, the "father of the faithful," had no proposition to accept. He had no revealed law to keep. He trusted God and the trust not only issued in but was expressed by obedience. Faith and obedience were to him inseparable. Faith which terminates in concepts and not in action is not the kind of faith Abraham had, which has become a pattern of righteousness for both Jew and Gentile for the Christian age. Abraham's example does not dismiss the intellectual in favor of action but adds the element of moral to the intellectual to make it truly rational.

FAITH AND WORKS

Biblical faith as a way to righteousness is classically illustrated by reference to Abraham. Hence a brief study of what constituted righteousness and faith in relation to him is in order. In Romans 2—4, the absolute contrast is drawn between ritual righteousness, which was wholly external and moralistic, and the spiritual nature of righteousness, which was of the spirit—or inner man—primarily. One was a dependence on an obedience to the letter of the law, with no regard for spiritual qualities; the other was a proper heart attitude toward God even in the absence of written law. One localized the possibility of acceptability by God to a chosen people on cultic grounds. The other opened that possibility to universal experience. The advantage of being a Jew was offset by the responsibility it entailed in knowledge and opportunity. The disadvantage of being a Gentile was offset by the basic law of righteousness, which, back of it all, was true for the Jew as well as the Gentile. By law, or without it, righteousness is possible only by faith in God. And Abraham, before there was a Jew or law, in believing God was considered righteous in God's sight. This effectively raises all people everywhere to the same standard of responsibility and the same possibility of redemption. This is the message of Paul's letter to the Romans (11:32).

It is a mistake to consider this section in Romans (2:5) primarily a *philosophy* of sin. It is, centrally, a presentation of the grace of God in Christ Jesus which is available to every man by faith. The fact that all have sinned is simply to show that atonement has been made for all sin by Christ and that the universal condition of receiving the benefits of grace is faith in God, not works. *None* are saved by works. All may be saved by faith.

Now it is also a mistake to identify all human effort and cooperation with "works" on the basis of this passage and contrast it to faith. The disparagement of works in this section is not a rejection of human activity and response as such, but a polemic against *dependence* on them without faith and all that faith means. It is not true to biblical fact to define faith, in contrast to works, as cessation of activity, or passive "acceptance." This is a false comparison. The writer to the Hebrews, with another purpose in mind for speaking of this same faith, gives us what Paul had no occasion to say in Romans, "By faith Abraham, when he was called . . . obeyed; and he went out, not knowing whither he went" (Heb. 11:8). Obedience defined his faith. James "confuses" the matter, too, until we look more deeply into the intention back of each of these three writers. Listen to James: "Was not Abraham our father justified by works, when he offered Isaac his son upon the altar? Seeth thou how faith wrought with his works, and by works was faith made perfect?" (2:21-22)

Wesley speaks to this point with his usual discrimination, and his answer is worth consideration.

> Q. 14. St. Paul says, Abraham was not justified by works; St. James, he was justified by works. Do they not contradict each other?
>
> A. No: (1) Because they do not speak of the same justification. St. Paul speaks of that justification which was when Abraham was seventy-five years old, above twenty years before Isaac was born; St. James, of that justification which was when he offered up Isaac on the Altar.
>
> (2) Because they do not speak of the same works; St. Paul speaking of works that precede faith; St. James, of works that spring from it (*Works*, VIII, 277).

It is equally untenable to isolate faith so decisively from its component parts that it becomes an end in itself. So great a reliance can be put on faith that it will seem to be faith in faith—our faith —upon which justification rests. If, then, there are discrepancies in our Christian lives we may conclude, "I do not have faith enough," or, "My faith is too weak to obtain salvation." Justification is not *faith in faith*, but *faith in God*—a vast difference. Faith is a quality, not an amount of something. It is all too easy to drift into "works," inadvertently, even when discussing faith.

LOVE, THE DYNAMIC OF FAITH

Wesley is careful to put faith in its proper relationship to the whole complex of the Christian dynamic and prevents distorting even faith into an object of worship.

> We so preach faith in Christ as not to supercede, but pro-
> duce, holiness. . . . In order to do this, we continually declare . . .
> that faith itself, even Christian faith, the faith of God's elect, the
> faith of the operation of God, still is only the handmaid of love.

As glorious and honorable as it is, it is not the end of the commandment. God hath given this honor to love alone. . . .

Faith . . . is the grand means of restoring that holy love wherein man was originally created. It follows, that although faith is of no value in itself, (as is neither any other means what so ever), yet as it leads to that end, the establishing anew the law of love in our hearts . . . it is on that account an unspeakable blessing to man, and of unspeakable value to God (*Works*, V, 462-64).

The dynamic of faith is, to Wesley, its task in establishing the law of love in our hearts and lives without which Christian faith is "as sounding brass" (I Cor. 13:1). As we walk by faith "we go swiftly on the way to holiness." And in its influence we cannot avoid growing in our love for God; "neither can we avoid loving our neighbor."

Interestingly enough, no New Testament passage gives the slightest hint that we are to "accept" Christ or "what He has done for us." We are exhorted *to believe in Him* with all that that means. Rather than a merely passive attitude, there is required an active participation in the reconciliation procedure, which is a two-way street. The tremendous exhortation of Rom. 12:1 is to the effect that we *present* ourselves "*holy and acceptable*" to God. In 14:18 it is said that he who in specified ways serveth Christ is *acceptable to God*. Peter says our task as lively stones in a spiritual house, or (to change the figure with Peter) as a holy priesthood, is to offer up spiritual sacrifices *acceptable to God* (I Pet. 2:5). The writer to the Hebrews exhorts (12:28), "Let us have grace, whereby we may serve God acceptably."

In none of the several places is a sinner ever asked to *accept* Christ in a merely intellectual way (II Cor. 5:10; Eph. 1:6; Phil. 4:18). It would be quite inaccurate to equate "accept" with "believing." By doing so, such problems are raised as: What does it mean to accept Christ? Is it to simply believe in the historical Christ and that He died for men? How can *our acceptance* of Him be a determinative factor in salvation? Is this not works? If our acceptance is of the verdict, "Acquitted," and the consequent man of faith is on the "heavenward side of the day of judgment," and "it is as though he had already entered heaven," and "when God looks down from above and sees the Lamb of God over me I am then righteous in His sight," why are the most morally demanding exhortations in the New Testament addressed to believers? Is not "acceptance theology" dangerously near perfectionism? At least without careful guards around the idea it could—and sometimes does—becomes so.

Parenthetically, it must be granted that there is a framework of thought in which "man's acceptance" is a proper word. It is that the extent of the atonement reaches every man. Forgiveness can only be offered by God, not demanded by man. Otherwise, it would put the responsibility for man's salvation squarely upon himself—not by earning it by what he does, but by exercising his moral responsibility in yielding his proud heart to God.

THE FAITH/OBEDIENCE/LOVE SYNDROME

The moral structure of faith is indicated by two key words, obedience and love. It is obvious that obedience alone is not itself a semantic or moral synonym for the faith which is requisite to justification. Obedience must have the ingredient of faith in it to appropriate righteousness. Conversely, faith must include obedience to make it saving faith. James's vivid and dramatic teaching that "faith without works is dead" is not antithetical to Paul's theology. To the Roman church Paul writes (6:16) that righteousness lies in the path of obedience, and he thanks God (6:17) that they had "obeyed from the heart." "Obedience of faith" is twice mentioned in the same letter, once of Paul himself (1:5) and once of the gospel message (16:26). Paul's deepest concern for the Corinthians was that every thought should be brought captive to the obedience of Christ (II Cor. 10:5). The writer to the Hebrews virtually identifies faith and obedience in 5:8-9; "Though he were a Son, yet he learned obedience by the things which he suffered; and being made perfect, he became the author of eternal salvation unto *all them that obey him*." To substitute "they who believe on him" would not be out of keeping with the whole of New Testament teaching, but it is highly significant that *obedience* should be the chosen word in this important passage.

That faith is morally oriented and not some magical, morally disjunctive method of assuring ourselves of salvation is further indicated by another consideration relative to human attitudes. We mean by "magic" any confidence in the power of word, thought, or act to effect supra-historical results, or any attempt to achieve effects without an adequate cause. When one says that "the future can hold no possible condemnation" for the man who has "received the work of Christ upon the cross and has exercised saving faith because for him *the future judgment has already taken place,*" he is interpreting faith as magic, in that moral men are thought to bypass moral responsibility.

Magic is always amoral and a-causal, whether it is religious or otherwise. Some critics of evangelicalism have called supernaturalism belief in magic. This charge cannot stand up under scholarly investigation, but a supernaturalism that supposes it can bypass the moral dimension of human experience *is* belief in magic. The Bible stands squarely opposed to just such perversions of truth. Its supernaturalism is preserved from the amorality of speculation precisely by the incarnation of Christ and the involvement of human experience in truth. Faith as taught in the Scripture is not credulity but is intellectually and morally relevant. Supernaturalism is not super-history but God's grace met by human faith.

THE HEART AND FAITH

The moral structure of faith is also indicated by its relation to the *heart* and to *love*. The heart is a common symbol for the moral center of the personality. The heart is never in the Bible distinguished from the seat of thinking by an emphasis on mere feeling. It is the "inner man" where moral considerations are tested and where the "atmosphere" of the whole person is determined. It is the seat of moral judgment and the arbiter of action. God makes all moral appeals to the heart. Jesus said it was out of the *heart* that evil proceeded and it was the *heart* which was to love God wholly. Paul speaks of the *heart* as being darkened and foolish and lustful and hard and impenitent (Romans 1—2), and the *heart* into which the Holy Spirit sheds love (Romans 5). To him it is the *heart* that obeys (6:16) and the *heart* that believes (10:9) unto righteousness. That Christ may dwell in the *hearts* of the Ephesians, by faith, was Paul's prayer (3:17), and this is related to a rooting and grounding "in love." To the Galatians, Paul said it was not the external things, whether circumcision or no circumcision, but faith working by love (5:6) that availed with God. Faith is put in the context of love in I Corinthians 13, not contrariwise. Love is the only permanent "virtue."

One of the most remarkable and significant teachings about the Christian life is that it is not faith that satisfies the law, but it is *love* that is the fulfillment of the whole law. This does not mean, obviously, that one could love without faith but that faith comes into its moral significance in love. It is remarkable the number of times these two words are conjoined. Paul had heard with delight about the Ephesians' faith in Christ and love to the saints (1:15), and his parting blessing is, "Peace . . . and love with faith, from God" (6:23). The Thessalonians were to put on "the breastplate of faith and love" (I Thess. 5:8). To Timothy, Paul wrote that the grace of Christ had been abundant to him in faith and love (I Tim. 1:14), and that Timothy was to pursue "righteousness, godliness, faith, love, patience, meekness" (I Tim. 6:11). Philemon was highly commended for his love and faith toward Christ and all the saints (5).

If faith is a moral act and its maintenance a moral concern, the righteousness which it brings is related most directly to the moral life. It is commonly said that righteousness, or justification, is a purely legal and eschatological matter. That is, (1) atonement is objective only and not in any sense connected with human renovation or actual sin or human will or actions. This viewpoint is expressed by Donald Barnhouse in *Eternity* (January, 1958): "God cannot improve human nature. . . . God will not improve the old sinful nature of man. God has never been interested in moral reform" (p. 26). And (2) the future judgment, for the one who "accepts Christ," is past, so that nothing can be charged against him no matter what he does, and that in the next life full redemption will be experienced. To put it in a modern metaphor, a believer enters a sort of premature heaven where temptation's force is lost by a reevaluation of sin. As another has said, "It is as though we had already entered heaven." This is the kind of perfectionism against which Wesley stood.

> *The nature of justification.* It sometimes means our acquittal at the last day. (Matt. xii. 37.) But this is altogether out of the present question; that justification whereof our articles and Homilies speak, meaning present forgiveness, pardon of sins, and consequently, acceptance with God; who therein "declares

this righteousness" (or mercy, by or) "for the remission of the sins that are past;" saying, "I will be merciful to thy unrighteousness, and thine iniquities I will remember no more." (Rom. iii. 25; Heb. viii. 12.)

I believe the condition of this faith; (Rom. iv. 5, &c.:) I mean, not only, that without faith we cannot be justified; but, also, that as soon as any one has true faith, in that moment he is justified.

Good works follow this faith, but cannot go before it: (Luke vi. 43:) Much less can sanctification, which implies a continued course of good works, springing from holiness of heart. But it is allowed that entire sanctification goes before our justification at the last day. (Heb. xii. 14.) (*Works*, VIII, 46-47).

MAINTAINING FAITH

The moral relevance is indicated in several ways, none more interesting than the biblical grammar and verb forms. The need for maintaining faith is indicated by the overwhelming preference for the present indicative or participle in referring to believing. This would indicate the dynamic character of faith in contrast to any static view. A few examples of this will suffice. John's Gospel is notable for its teaching about believing on Jesus. John 1:12 says that the power to become children of God is given to those who *continue to believe*. The third chapter has several such passages (for example, verses 15 and 36), with the familiar sixteenth verse a striking example. Whosoever *continues to believe* in him . . . not, "shall have eternal life," but (subjunctive), *may* have it. That is, eternal life is dependent upon the continuance of faith. The Greek makes dramatically clear what the English fails to quite fully express.

This contingency of effect to the continuing qualification of believing is expressed in a number of passages (e.g., John 6:35, 40; 20:31). In Acts we are told that *those believing persons* of the circumcised were amazed that the Holy Spirit was given to Cornelius (10:45); and Paul in preaching at Antioch in Pisidia (Acts 13:39) states clearly that *those who are believing are justified*. Paul says, in Rom. 1:16, that the gospel is the power of God to salvation *to those believing* (see also 3:20-26), and this same tense is used in Rom. 4:5 and 24. The tenth chapter is a commentary on the faith/works tension, making clear that it is a continually believing heart that is considered righteous. In this chapter no obedience is recognized as valid that does not have in it the "heart that believes" (continuing to do so).

FAITH AND THE WALK OF SANCTIFICATION

All New Testament teaching strengthens one's understanding of the necessity for a "walk" of faith and discourages any reliance on an amoral, intellectualized definition of faith. Whatever is involved in faith, it certainly makes a difference in life. It is this difference in which holiness theology is interested.

The contingency of faith determines the continuance of the Christian walk. This is clearly taught in the New Testament. John's "if" (15:6) cannot be lightly regarded. If a man does not abide in Christ, he is cut off from the Vine. No interpretation of Paul's "if" in Romans 8 and 11 which assumes it to be simply a rhetorical hypothesis quite does justice to the moral earnestness of these passages. "If ye live after the flesh, ye shall die: but if ye through the Spirit . . . [keep mortifying] the deeds of the body, ye shall live" (Romans 8). "If God spared not the natural branches, take heed lest he also spare not thee. Behold therefore the goodness and severity of God: on them which fell, severity; but toward thee, goodness, if thou continue in his goodness" (Rom. 11:21-22). Again, "You . . . hath he reconciled in the body of his flesh through death, to present you holy and unblameable and unreproveable in his sight: if ye continue in the faith" (Col. 1:21-23).

No biblical passage when taken in context gives the slightest ground for assuming that by a single act of faith (which has not gone deeper than an intellectual assent) eternal salvation is assured. Believing must be both a moral act and continuing moral commitment. That is, faith is a way of life, not merely an affirmation. It is hard to see how Barnhouse can say, "God's promises to a believer are unconditional" (*Eternity*, Jan., 1958). Obedience does not simply follow justification as a test of one's state of grace; it is itself an element in the faith by which justification is realized and the Christian life begun.

> If then you say, "We ascribe to God alone the whole glory of our salvation;" I answer, So do we too. If you add, "Nay but we affirm, that God alone does the whole work, without man's working at all," in one sense, we allow this also. We allow, it is the work of God alone to justify, to sanctify, and to glorify;

which three comprehend the whole of salvation. Yet we cannot allow, that man can only resist, and not in any wise "work together with God" or that God is so the whole worker of our salvation, as to exclude man's working at all. This I dare not say; for I cannot prove it by Scripture; nay, it is flatly contrary thereto for the Scripture is express, that (having received power from God) we are to "work out our own salvation" and that (after the work of God is begun in our souls) we are "workers together with Him" (*Works*, X, 230-31).

Summary Observations

Faith is not the cessation of all effort or the relaxing of all moral tensions, or the loss of any personal integrity. Faith is a reversal of all dependencies from other than God to God himself. It involves obedience, not primarily to law, but to God, whose Spirit interprets law spiritually to the inner heart. "By faith" is a new direction of all of life's activities and love. It initiates the lifelong, yea, eternity-long serving of God. Faith is not the surrender of moral responsibility but the beginning of real moral maturation. It is not *necessarily* a change in activity, but it is a change in moral atmosphere of the person—a change of the object of affection. It means that instead of living for the approval of others, or the self, or pride of personal integrity measured by the letter of the law, we now look beyond these things—not to despise them, for they are right in their places—to God, who has been made Lord of the whole life. There is a growing sensitivity to His approval or disapproval. We "take orders from God," without taking advantage of apparent freedom from external restraint.

Taking orders from God does not liberate us from social obligation and biblical teaching and common human responsibilities. It does not permit us to disentangle ourselves from the interlocking human relationships that constitute normal and proper humanhood. It does, in fact, put us at the crossroads of life. We cannot fly in the face of convention and push away the hands that cling to us for strength and help. "Taking orders from God" in the life of faith means that all our thoughts, words, and actions stand under the constant judgment of God as to the motivation, intention, and moral quality of our obedience. Paul described this life of faith in a clear and forceful way (I Cor. 4:1-5) when he said it is required of a steward that he be found faithful. The faithfulness was not a judgment which another could make, either favorably or otherwise. It was not even enough for the personal conscience to approve. The final word must be spoken by the Lord.

"By faith" is the moral link between the provision of Calvary and sinful men. It makes the juridical term "justification" a true ground of the redeemed life. It prevents moral complacency by defending moral relevancy. It undercuts all possibility of spiritual pride or the possibility of a religious aristocracy. It prohibits isolation from the world and forces full participation in it. It robs of any comfort from verbal symbols, or intellectualism, and compels a continuing, faithful, patient, prayerful, sensitive, growing awareness of God's Spirit and His directive for daily life. Some kind of idolatry is the only alternative to the lordship of Christ, and idolatry is the essence of sin. Justification is a falsehood if it is imputed to an idolatrous man. No idolatrous person can say, "I accept Christ as my Saviour and Lord." The saving Christ is not a proposition to be accepted but a Person to be loved and obeyed.

Faith is not the boundary around the Christian which sets him apart and defines him. It is the open-ended "growing edge" which keeps him from mere definition and makes him a flowing-out life, a dynamo of love.

Faith, then, is the continuing atmosphere in which all the benefits of grace and steps in salvation are made possible. We could say that the believer has everything provisionally, but nothing is actually his until by faith he appropriates it. And this appropriation is morally structured. It is of the essence of obedience and love. Faith gears into moral experience and "love, the dynamic of holiness," is ethical to the core.

CHAPTER XIII

The Clean Heart

> Almighty God, unto whom all hearts are open, all desires known, and from whom no secrets are hid; Cleanse the thoughts of our hearts by the inspiration of Thy Holy Spirit, that we may perfectly love Thee, and worthily magnify Thy Holy Name; Through Christ, Our Lord. Amen. *(Book of Common Prayer, 1695).*

Prayer for cleansing has been on the lips of the Church since it began. The particular wording above was that which Wesley used in the Holy Communion service as often as he partook of that means of grace. We are told that he partook of the Lord's Supper as many as four or five times a week when he was able to get to duly consecrated churches. The clean heart was a part of the spiritual quest which characterized his life. Wesley's spiritual children have made cleansing a cardinal element in the doctrine of holiness, as is proper for a "biblical" emphasis. The significance of this emphasis is important to this study.

"Cleansing" may be a technical, theological word communicating very little meaning to the layman or it can be a rich, warm, highly significant religious term.

As justification is the important word to the objective atonement, so cleansing and purity represent the central characteristic of the subjective aspects of man's relation to God. Cleansing (as the means) and purity (as the result) are good biblical terms and are recognized as proper theological concepts by all Christian traditions. But the meaning of *cleansing* is variously related to religious belief and practice.

To holiness theology, cleansing takes on a particular significance because it shares in the heavy emphasis on "experience" in this tradition. It is said to be related to sanctification in a way not universally considered essential to the meaning of that term. Holiness theology traditionally makes a point of stressing two aspects of sanctification as different things of equal importance, namely, *setting apart* or consecration, and *making pure*. When this dual emphasis is made, questions immediately arise as to the specific meaning of purity in distinction from consecration.

Cleansing or purity of heart is as difficult to lift out of its context as is faith or perfection or love or obedience because it partakes, like they, so intimately of them all that to abstract it robs it of the very thing it is.

It soon becomes obvious that the problem of what cleansing is reveals a deep-seated point of view regarding the nature of man that reacts back on one's interpretation of it. Basic interpretations are as follows:

One touches the whole matter of what happens in "the act" of cleansing. It is a problem in "spiritual ontology." Since it is understood to be subjective renovation and not simply a changed status before God, the question arises, In what does renovation or cleansing consist? The difficulties relative to expressing the concept of sin and its "removal" in terms of substance are involved here. Does God "do something" to the soul to make it pure? Do men make themselves clean? What is it that is not clean? How is it unclean? What is purity?

The second kind of problem follows from the first and arises

from it in the measure that subjective holiness is under consideration. It has to do with the nature of purity and the conditions upon
which it is maintained. It asks, Is purity a state? Is it something
which has "existence"? Is it a character implanted in the soul?
Something of the nature of the problem is suggested by the comment made by an eminent Wesleyan preacher to a Wesleyan theologian who said that I John 1:7 should read (and mean) the blood
of Christ *continues to cleanse* from sin. "If," asked the preacher,
"it *continues to cleanse,* is there not something left from which to
be cleansed? Do you mean that one gets cleaner and cleaner?"
This is a curious question in the light of the Greek reading, for it
clearly says, by its grammatical form, "continues to cleanse." Obviously the more correct rendering conflicted with a theological
concept. Perhaps the preacher supposed that sin was a sort of substance in the soul that could be *removed,* and after it has been removed the soul becomes and remains pure. In other words, purity,
to him, was an entity or rather a characteristic inherent in an entity
capable of self-existence. His comment is a significant commentary
on one of the prevailing views of what the soul is and how grace
acts in respect of it. At least the language, if unguarded, permits
the interpretation that the soul and sin are "things" which one has
or may get free from.

Underneath all these questions often lies the idea that in some
way uncleanness is concupiscence, that concupiscence is sex, and
that sex is unclean.

The Christian Church has interpreted purity in a number of
ways. Two opposite ideas outline the whole. On the one hand purity
is considered in terms of status only. It would be a legal pronounce-
ment of acquittal or consist in ritualistic practices or result from
them. Personal worthiness has no essential significance in this view.
On the other hand, status is subservient to personal purity in respect of moral life. The condition of purity may be brought about
by an act of God or by obedience to a moral code. Purity in this
latter position usually refers to some measure of rejection of human
desires and appetites and sometimes of all aesthetic pleasure.

It is moralistic in tone. One is a cultic purity; the other is a
moralism. One stresses the objective aspect of atonement; the other,
the subjective, performed either by supernatural means or by self-

252 / A Theology of Love

abnegation or obedience to law. Between these outside extremes lie many kinds of modifications of one or the other.

Here, as elsewhere, Wesley avoided the extremes and preached a most wholesome gospel where others fell into the many pitfalls along the way on either side of the path. He and his interpreters insisted on a very practical and biblical understanding of purity. In answer to the objection that purity, if it were an act of God, obviated the further need for the priestly office of Christ, Wesley replied:

> Far from it. None feel their need of Christ like these, even the most perfect; none so entirely depend upon him. For Christ does not give life to the soul separate from, but in and with himself. Hence, his words are equally true of all men, in whatsoever state of grace they are: "without (or separate from) me, ye can do nothing" (*Works*, XI, 395).

Thomas Cook, a later British holiness writer, spoke even more directly to this point: "We teach, not a *state of purity*, but a *maintained condition* of purity, a moment-by-moment obedience and trust. 'The blood of Jesus Christ cleanseth us from all sin' *all the time* by cleansing us every *Now*."[1]

Purity, to Wesley, was not something other than the "single heart" or integrity. He was greatly impressed by Bishop Taylor's *Rules for Holy Living and Dying*, particularly where he says, "Simplicity and purity are the two wings that lift the soul up to heaven: Simplicity, which is in the intention; and purity, which is in the affections" (*Works*, VII, 297). Purity is the single eye admitting the full light of God to the heart, and uncleanness is the consequence of the evil eye, or "the eye which is not single" (page 299) and which therefore maintains the darkness in the heart. Wesley said, "It is certain there can be no medium between a single eye and an evil one; for whenever we are not aiming at God, we are seeking happiness in some creature, which is no less than idolatry."

It is obvious that Wesley did not at all separate purity from the lowest level of Christian life and he associated it with the single-hearted "aim" at God. Its opposite, sin, was not concupiscence, as Augustine said, but perverted love—which in more biblical moments Augustine granted.

In one of Wesley's sermons on the Sermon on the Mount, he stresses this relation of cleanness to love. In fact, purity of heart in itself is the loving of God with the whole heart, mind, soul, and strength. It is not the suppression of human impulse but the centering of the entire heart and life and activity in God (*Works*, V, 298).

> Look at it again; survey it on every side, and that with the closest attention; in one view it is purity of intention; dedicating all the life to God. It is giving God all our hearts, it is one desire and design ruling all our tempers. It is the devoting, not a part, but all of our soul, body and substance to God. In another view, it is all the mind that was in Christ, enabling us to walk as Christ walked. It is the circumcision of the heart from all filthiness, all inward as well as outward pollution. It is the renewal of the heart in the whole image of God, the fullness of him that created it. In yet another, it is the loving of God with all our heart, and our neighbor as ourselves (*Works*, X, 444).

It will be instructive and necessary to look into the biblical meaning of the words *cleansing* and *purity* before considering their theological connotation. Whatever of relevant interest the etymological and cultural background of the words may contribute will be added, but the main concern is simply to find the obvious meaning of the author in each particular passage. The biblical study must be carefully distinguished from the observations and conclusions which will be drawn from the study and from the theological application made at the close of this chapter and elsewhere in this book.

In the New Testament, the English words pure, purity, purge, clean, cleansing, and suchlike, are used to translate a number of cognate Greek words. The New Testament borrowed from, and adapted to its specific needs, the classical Greek meaning of the term *clean*. The Greek word referred to physical cleanliness, to substances having nothing which did not belong, such as clean water, wind, sunshine; metals and foods which had been refined. This meaning entered into the analogy of proper human relationships, freedom from debt, honesty, sincerity. It meant, as well, genuineness, such as unmixed racial blood or an authentic statement which had been corrected as one now proofreads a galley sheet.

It also had a religious use. It referred to any thing or person properly qualified to come into the place of worship. Ceremonial preparation is implied. In the case of a worshipper, his hands and mind were to be clean in the sense of entertaining nothing contrary to the conscience or entertaining interests of daily life such as one's business problems or plans for a trip. These were to be put aside for the time.

There are two nouns, *katharós* and *hagnós* of particular interest to this study, and the verbs *katharídzo* and *ekkathaíro* used in the New Testament.

The noun *katharós* is translated either "purity" or "cleansing," or similar counterparts of these words. Standard translations of the New Testament vary in their choice of these words. Our analysis will follow the KJV use simply for the sake of familiarity and organization, not because it is more nearly or less correct than the others.

The passages translated "clean" refer: (1) To physical objects, such as a clean cup (Matt. 23:26), a clean shroud or sheet (Matt. 27:59), and clean or pure linen (metaphorical, Rev. 19:8 and 14). (2) To moral qualities, in which sense it is found three times (Acts 18:6; 20:26; and Luke 11:41). Each of these passages speaks of an obligation fully met or a declaration of innocence in relation to a crime. (3) To separation from the common, in which sense Jesus used the word twice. In John 13:10-11, He said the disciples were clean. He had just bathed their feet and the ritual signified the complete identification in fellowship between himself as Master and His disciples as fellow friends. The words "but not all" referred to one among them, Judas, who (though his feet had also presumably been washed) was not united in this fellowship because his heart was not with them. He remained unclean. Also, in the vine-and-branch analogy (John 15) cleanness refers to the vital unity of the believer with his Lord. On this passage Wesley commented:

> We have this grace not only from Christ, but in him. For our perfection is not like that of a tree, which flourishes by the sap from its own root, but, like that of a branch, which united to the vine, bears fruit, but, severed from it, is dried up and withered (*Works*, XI, 395-96).

Whatever, therefore, is involved in being "in the vine," and abiding there, is the atmosphere in which cleansing has meaning and reality.

Paul says (in Rom. 14:20) that "all things are pure," or "everything is indeed clean" *(RSV)*, *kathará*, but may become an occasion for sin when a brother whose intentions are selfish uses them in a way to cause others to stumble.

In Paul's letters to Timothy, he unites *katharós* with *heart* and *conscience* and associates purity with faith each time. (1) I Tim. 1:5 speaks of love "out of a pure heart, and of a good conscience," and sincere faith as being the fulfillment of the whole law. (2) The deacon should hold the faith in a "pure conscience" (I Tim. 3:9). (3) Paul's "pure conscience" commends him to Timothy (II Tim. 1:3); and (4) his exhortation to young Timothy is that he, too, "follow righteousness, faith, charity [love], peace, with them that call on the Lord out of a pure heart" (II Tim. 2:22). The meaning supplied by the context is clearly an open, sincere, honest motivation in God's sight.

The Roman reference, as well as those in the correspondence with Timothy, helps to shed light on the meaning in Titus 1:15. The "pure" man is a man living in truth. To him everything is clean. But, by contrast, to the man who is defiled and unbelieving and deceitful all things are evil. Both profess to know God. The pure man lives consistently with his profession; the impure man denies his affirmation by disobedience.

James says (1:27) that pure and undefiled religion (piety, worship) is practical in its outreach and involves integrity in the one professing it. He visits the fatherless and widow and keeps himself unspotted from the world.

Peter exhorts those who have purified their souls by obedience to truth through the Spirit to love each other "with a pure heart fervently" (I Pet. 1:22). Again purity is related to truth. The aid is of "the Spirit," but the act is a moral one—obedience—and must issue in love consciously given. That is, purity is experienced in obedience to truth; and out of the atmosphere of that obedience, love, fervent and sincere, is possible.

Perhaps the most significant example of the words is Jesus' use of the term in the beatitude, "Blessed are the pure in heart: for they shall see God" (Matt. 5:8). Theological concepts should not be imposed on this passage apart from the very practical and moral meaning so uniformly found in the New Testament. The moral rather than ritual or ceremonial meaning is indicated in this passage by the reference to "heart," which immediately puts it in the realm of the personal. Unmixed motives, sincere and single-hearted love, and personal integrity must surely be the meaning of *purity* here. Only such could come into and be blessed by the presence of God.

Ceremonial cleansing is indicated by *katharótes* and speaks of expiation or the benefits of Christ's atonement (Heb. 9:12-13). An analogy from the Old Testament lights up the parallel but more developed New Testament teaching. If the blood and ashes of sacrificial animals sanctified to the cleansing of unclean flesh, how much more shall the blood of Christ purge or sanctify your unclean conscience? This is a contrast between the old way of works and the new way of faith.

Katharismós is translated either purification or cleansing. Christ, after having "made purification for sins" (Heb. 1:3), sat down on the right hand of God—or in the place of authority and power. The purification was made once for all, and it was an expiation or an objective divine act cancelling out guilt. Peter refers to this purging from sin (II Pet. 1:9), saying that our God and Saviour has granted to us all things pertaining to life and godliness and the great promise that we should partake of the divine nature (vv. 3-4). To the new life we are to add faith, virtue, self-control, patience, godliness, love of brethren. And to be lacking in this is to forget the *cleansing from old sins*, which forgetting and consequent failure to "add" on our part may forfeit our "calling and election" (vv. 5-10).

Twice in the Gospels this word is used of the ceremonial cleansing which healed lepers were required to make in the Temple (Mark 1:44 and Luke 5:14).

The root word for "pure," "chaste" *(hagnós)* is found four times.

In Phil. 4:8, Paul exhorts the reader to be selective in his choice of thinking matter. Stability of character demands a disciplined thought life. Among the other things worthy of entertainment such as the true, the just, the lovely, the virtuous, stands "the pure," which is to be a consciously permitted and voluntarily chosen object of thought which conforms to the norm of holiness.

Paul's counsel to Timothy in a famous "charge" to him, was "Keep thyself pure" (I Tim. 5:22). This is obviously an exhortation to a morally disciplined life and indicates the need for a continuing maintenance of one's integrity.

James, by means of a strong contrast, (3:13-18) defines and explains purity. He says that wisdom "from above" is pure and peaceable in distinction from the alleged wisdom of those whose tongues betray their bitterness and devilishness and strife. In his characteristically vigorous manner, James presses some moral demands. The hands are to be made clean by *katharídzo,* and the heart made pure by *hagnísate,* which carries the meaning of deep inner sincerity in contrast to the "double mind" (4:8).

In discussing the matter of the pure heart in his sermon entitled "On a Single Eye," Wesley uses this illustration:

> Here is a father choosing an employment for his son. If his eye be not single; if he do not singly aim at the glory of God in the salvation of his soul; if it be not his one consideration, what calling is likely to secure him the highest place in heaven; not the largest share of earthly treasure, or the highest preferment in the Church;—the light which is in him is manifestly darkness. And O how great is that darkness! The mistake which he is in, is not a little one, but inexpressibly great. What! do you not prefer his being a cobbler on earth, and a glorious saint in heaven, before his being a lord on earth, and a damned spirit in hell? . . . What a fool, what a dolt, what a madman is he! (*Works,* VII, 302).

This is what James has in mind, undoubtedly. And the correction of the problem lies in the responsibility of those whose hands are unclean and whose hearts are double-motived.

St. John (I John 3:3) uses this word to indicate the progressive likeness to Christ which the living hope of seeing Christ inspires within the believer. Curiously, this aspect of purity, in keeping with the other three passages where the Greek word is used, emphasizes not only the responsibility of the Christian in the matter but also the progressive development in purification.

Hagnismós is found once (Acts 21:26) and is the "purification" which Paul performed by ceremonial acts by which he prepared himself as all good Jews did for certain Temple worship events.

The verb "to cleanse," or make clean or purge *(katharídzo)* is found about 20 times.

(1) The cleansing of lepers accounts for a number of the instances. It is a curious thing that this word should be used in con-

nection with recovery of the leper's health in contrast to healing or wholeness when other forms of sickness were reported. A blind or crippled person is healed, but the leper is cleansed.

(2) It was ceremonial cleanness to which the angel referred when Peter was reluctant to eat certain animals forbidden to the Jew: "Call that not unclean which God has cleansed," the voice said.

(3) Jesus told those who hid evil intentions behind external piety to clean the inside of the cup. This has a distinctly moral connotation and clearly states that men have an obligation to moral purity. Moral purity is defined by the purpose of one's heart. No *act* is better than the *intention* which gives it birth. Both must be in perfect harmony. Integrity is purity. Double motives testify to impurity.

(4) The last five passages are distinctly exhortations to moral decision.

(a) Paul exhorts the Corinthians (in II Cor. 7:1) to "cleanse" themselves (aorist subjunctive active) "from all filthiness of the flesh and spirit" and so be "perfecting [present participle] holiness in the fear of God." There is, here, the recognition of a personal responsibility to God's grace. The subjunctive indicates a possibility not yet realized and the risk that it may not be realized because of human failure. The aorist indicates the need for moral decisiveness in contrast to mere growth. The perfecting of or maturing in holiness is accomplished by this decisive rejection of that which is unclean. The whole exhortation stands in relation to the *process* aspect of holiness, as indicated by the present tense of the participle. Cleansing, in this passage has to do with a proper use of the body as it is regarded as a temple, or shrine, of the Holy Spirit and through which God is to be glorified (I Cor. 6:15-20).

Paul carries this analogy further in I Corinthians 12, where the establishment and maintenance of fellowship and unity of the Church are presented under the figure of the "body" of Christ. This corporate integrity is indicated in I Cor. 3:16. "Know ye not that ye [plural] are the temple of God?" Paul asks, and declares solemnly, "If any man defile the temple of God, him shall God destroy." The purity spoken of in this connection has to do with the integrity of the Christian witness in the world. The Corinthians were not to separate socially from their culture, else they would have to go out of the world. Instead they were to maintain such an atmosphere of purity of body and spirit and Christian fellowship that the spiritual cohesion would itself be a barrier to sin in their midst. Though the exhortation may be applied personally, the corporate meaning must not be lost, for that is Paul's prime concern in the Corinthian correspondence.

(b) In Eph. 5:26, Paul says that Christ came that He might sanctify the Church, having cleansed it. "Sanctify" here is aorist subjunctive, indicating that the goal of Christ's coming was the sanctification of the Church. The American Revised and Revised Standard versions probably translate this the most nearly true to the Greek meaning. Christ gave himself "that he might sanctify it [her], having cleansed it [her]."

In this Ephesian passage the objective aspect of the atonement is most clearly set forth. It describes in terms of Hebrew temple service what Christ came to do for His body, the Church. In this passage, the individual participation in subjective cleansing is not indicated. It has to do with status and the contingent relationship which the Church sustains to Christ in its days of probation. Individual responsibility can be deduced from this passage, and perhaps should be, but the specific teaching has to do with the great purpose of God for the Church. It looks past any *individual* aspect toward the outreach of the body of Christ as an organism.

(c) John's Epistle (I John 1:7) speaks of cleansing. In the relationship of fellowship the blood of Christ keeps cleansing (present indicative) from all sin. That is, cleansing is maintained so long as fellowship is maintained, and fellowship depends on walking in the light. It is clear in this passage that sin is a break in fellowship, which in turn is called darkness, and darkness is defined as hatred. Hatred, in turn, breaks the law of love, the keeping of which constitutes walking in the light, which maintains fellowship—and cleansing. Cleansing is thus defined in terms of fellowship.

Furthermore, cleansing is not a static, passive thing which exists apart from the dynamic of personal encounter. Nor is cleansing progressively achieved, that is, "getting cleaner and cleaner." It is not something impersonal, that is, a character impressed on the substance of the soul, a metaphysical real which has objective existence apart from moral relationship. It is akin to love if it is not itself love—an atmosphere in which mutual love interpenetrates and preserves integrity. This is the *principle* of cleansing, namely, a moment-by-moment reliance wholly on Christ. This Wesley taught. "The best of men . . . needs the atoning blood."

(d) Again, in I John 1:9 are the words, "If we confess our sins, he is faithful and just to forgive us our sins, and to cleanse us from all unrighteousness." Both "forgive" and "cleanse" in this verse are in the aorist subjunctive, agreeing in grammatical form with the contingency of the "if," but stressing the decisiveness of the moral change. It is God who forgives and cleanses when we confess our sins. Whether the forgiveness and cleansing are simultaneous or separated into two acts and times is not here the matter of John's concern and ought not to become a theological debate. Certainly the demands of grammar could not provide a dogmatic ground to make a case either way so far as this passage is concerned. The exegesis of the passage requires our understanding of the incipient Gnostic heresy to which this passage is an answer. Sin is real and atonement is necessary. Only Christ can provide this atonement. Its provisions can be appropriated only by an acknowledgement of sin, a confession of sin, and a continual maintenance of that attitude— walking in the light.

(e) James exhorts sinners to cleanse their hands and the double-minded to purify their hearts (4:8). Both terms obviously refer to acts and motives which were not honest and which needed to be brought into integrity. Again, this cleansing is decisive (aorist) and to be done by the person. The hands are made clean by *katharídzo,* but the heart is made pure by *hagnísate,* which signifies a more inner and spiritual concept—innocence, blamelessness, which has to do with sincerity. Here, again, is a tacit definition of and commentary on the term *cleansing.*

In Acts 15 there is a discussion in which purity of heart is mentioned, that is most important to a proper concept of the term. The question before the Jerusalem council which was in session had been raised by two events. "Certain men" coming from Judea were upsetting the Gentiles to whom Paul was preaching, saying that one could not be saved apart from circumcision according to Moses' law. Then, during the council meeting some believers among the Pharisees affirmed the same thing. The problem had to do with the grounds of men's acceptance by God: How is one saved? It was a most crucial matter to the expanding Church.

Salvation or purity was the goal of Jew and Christian Gentile. The Christian Jew, though he understood the more spiritual meaning of the Christian faith, had difficulty in freeing himself from reliance on the external ritualism of the Mosaic law. The council, however, was less concerned about the practical aspects of the problem than about the basic philosophy of salvation. Peter contributed to the discussion an observation which to him was convincing. He told the group that the Holy Spirit had been given to the Gentiles under his ministry when they had heard the gospel and had believed (vv. 7-8). The coming of the Spirit was, to him, a witness to the acceptability of their faith in God's sight.

Since both Gentile and Jew had received the Spirit, Peter was convinced that both had met God's conditions. The condition common to both was faith. Faith had resulted in the purity to which the Holy Spirit witnessed. Peter saw that purity was of the heart—and not of flesh: God, "who knows the *heart* . . . cleansed their *hearts* by faith" (RSV, italics mine). The Holy Spirit was pleased to acknowledge the validity of this heart preparation.

Now, Peter's final conclusion joined to the central question lifts the whole discussion into proper focus. The subject under consideration is laid open. An interpretation of the whole passage must organize itself around this. To the theological dictum, "Except ye be circumcised after the manner of Moses, ye cannot be saved," Peter answers on the basis of the given evidence. "But we believe that through the grace of the Lord Jesus Christ we [who are Jews] shall be saved, even as they [the Gentiles]." Something far deeper constituted salvation than they had previously imagined. Peter was saying that God's "chosen people" were subject to the same rules as the pagans. Wherein, then, did the Jew profit by being a Jew?

Peter's conclusion had less to do with what the Jew would require of the Gentile and more to do with the basis of his own salvation. The important thing was not that the Gentile did not need to meet the Mosaic ritual requirement, but that the Jew did not need to do it either. He must himself meet the same requirement exacted of Gentiles. All salvation was by grace, not ritual works. Faith was the door to purity because purity was of the heart, not the flesh. The seal of approval, then, on the Gentile apart from Mosaic law, and on the Jew at Pentecost *in* the law, was the coming of the Holy Spirit, who was himself the Witness to a pure heart.

This altered emphasis was a much greater shock to the Jew, who had then to acknowledge his own religious limitations, than the mere fact that the Gentiles were acceptable to God. Here was a standard which was permitting the Gentiles to find full acceptance with God *to which the Jew also must conform*. This truth was akin to the possible upset a Quaker would have were he to have to be willing to grant that the Baptist immersion was not only right for a Baptist but actually required of the Quaker; or contrariwise, the Baptist granting the Quaker view of spiritual communion would suffice for the Quaker and find, also, that he himself must commune spiritually and never again by the use of any symbol. Peter was saying, in this passage, "God is showing us Jews something about our own salvation through the Gentiles, whom we have despised."

Whatever teaching there may be in this passage about the relation of Pentecost to the Holy Spirit, and the Holy Spirit to cleansing, the central problem around which the Petrine discussion revolved must be kept in clear focus. It would not be exegetically proper to say, *on the basis of this passage alone*, that the coming of the Holy Spirit *produced* purity of heart. The tenses put purity prior to the coming of the Spirit. He is the Seal of the fact of the purity. Purity, according to the text, was from God on the condition of faith. Purity receives definition by the sense of the whole passage. The "faith" on which purity depends contradicts anything that human merit might achieve and points to the obedience of total capitulation to and dependence upon God—a single heart.

Titus 2:14 gives a further definition of cleanness. In the midst of a block of ethical teaching which Paul gave to Titus—"These things speak, and exhort, and rebuke with all authority" (v. 15), to the effect that "they may adorn the doctrine of God our Saviour in all things" (v. 10)—Paul introduces the saving Christ, as he so often does. He is the One "who gave himself for us, that he might redeem us . . . and purify [both aorist subjunctive] unto himself a . . . people, zealous of good works." The purity, here, stresses a separation from iniquity and a devotedness to good works which would, *if* we would deny "ungodliness" and "live soberly, righteously, and godly in this present world," make us *His* own possession. To be Christ's possession is purity, and that purity includes "good works." *Even purity is dynamic.*

To "cleanse out" *(ekkathaíro)* is another form of the verb. The Corinthian church had harbored an incestuous man within the fellowship (I Corinthians 5) and by so doing had defiled the temple of God (I Cor. 3:17). The failure to assume the responsibility of rebuking sin was a leaven that had to be removed in order that the witness to Christ be unsullied. "Purge out," or "clean away" from you, the leaven of malice and wickedness (or a bad attitude and evil disposition of mind), so that the Lord's Supper (for that is the background idea) can be eaten in sincerity and truth, Paul says. The exhortation certainly has to do with the sinner himself, but it is to miss the whole import of the passage to let this personal matter exhaust the meaning or even to eclipse the real thrust in this passage.

Paul is charging the church itself with insubordination. "To cleanse away" is much more, here, than to punish the erring man. It is rather to rectify the very heart of the church from evil irresponsibility to a mature and sanctified and responsible attitude toward truth itself. The purging is personal, most certainly, but a purging of individuals constituting the church—from self-interest to courageous sincerity before God—was needed. In like vein, Timothy is exhorted. to preach to his people that they must purge out "vain babblings" and profitless strivings, in order that they might be vessels "sanctified, and meet for the master's use" (II Timothy 2). The import of this word as it is used in these two passages is directed toward a personal, moral rectitude in which personal responsibility is assumed and the awareness of it sharpened. In these two cases, the active participation of the people in the church must be recognized as of vital importance.

In reviewing the use the New Testament makes of the word *cleansing*, several observations are in order.

1. It always has a positive, clear, and often pictorial and/or ceremonial meaning. It is never mystical or abstract. It refers, therefore, to some specific act or attitude which can be defined and identified. The question, "Is it pure?" or, "Have they been made

pure?" had a concrete answer: yes or no. Purity or uncleanness was less a condition than it was a response.

2. The references fall into two main categories, objective and subjective. There is a ceremonial cleansing with the Old Testament ritualism supplying the conceptual elements. Those passages which speak of the objective atonement made by Christ fall into this category. It suggests a change of relationship. Common things or unconsecrated things when properly prepared are then fit for Temple service and, by analogy, God's service.

Jesus' sacrifice was to effect cleansing from sin. This He did once for all. It is absolute and final, but provisional. It may help to recall other aspects of the purpose of Christ's death, for they are parts of a whole: "To save his people from their sins" (Matt. 1:21); to make reconciliation (II Corinthians 5; Ephesians 2); "to sanctify the people" (Heb. 13:12); he was delivered up for our trespasses and raised for our justification (Rom. 4:25); our "old man" was crucified with Christ that we might not have to serve sin (Rom. 6:6); to make purification for our sins (Heb. 1:3); to "redeem us from all iniquity, and purify unto himself a peculiar people" (Titus 2:14). There is an objective or judicial cleansing which means that our sinfulness no longer is a barrier to the presence of God.

There is a subjective aspect to cleansing. The leper, in the ceremonial cleansing, washed himself with literal water to symbolize this actual cleanness. When cleansing relates to persons in any way, it describes a real rather than fictional or imputational thing alone. In the case of redemption truth, the objective element was contingent upon individual, subjective appropriation. Hence a thing or person, physically or morally, to be called clean must participate in that which cleansing implied.

3. Both the objective and subjective aspects of cleansing indicate a *separation from* and *dedication to* something. The ceremonial cleansing becomes a pictorial symbol for spiritual cleansing. As has been noted, this spiritual cleansing is not mystical but is actualized in a real separation from evil in the flesh and in the mind and heart. The Old Testament concept, never wholly free from moral implications, becomes clearly a moral concept in the New Testament with thoroughgoing practical implications.

4. The ceremonial and moral meanings are fused in the re-

ligious aspect of cleansing. This is nowhere more evident than in First John, where the continuity of cleansing through Christ's blood is dependent upon walking in the light.

5. To this point we have focused a number of lights on the word "cleansing" to give it meaning. Now it in turn throws light back on some aspects of redemption which must be carefully distinguished from each other. These applications of the word do not change the meaning but relate to the subject in different ways. (1) The cleansing in which the disciples shared when Jesus washed their feet represents the separation from the world and dedication to God, which possibility is opened to sinful men by God on His initiative. This is not without the guards inherent in moral responsibility, as Judas' failure to be included in the "clean" ones indicates, but does point up the objective aspect. (2) Then sanctification and cleansing are used to express the same idea, as is the case in II Tim. 2:21, "If a man therefore purge himself . . . he shall be a vessel . . . sanctified, and meet for the master's use." (3) Finally, there are those references which speak of the need for men to make and keep themselves pure. There is a constant demand that men purify themselves, obviously meaning to maintain moral integrity, and this is the personal cost of being perfected in holiness. This cleansing is "by faith." That is, everything indicated by faith —namely, a new center of moral orientation, God and His will, in contrast to self-righteousness—is cleansing. This faith is the appropriation of the cleansing mentioned above and commits the person to Christ existentially.

6. The clean or pure heart is necessary. Sometimes this purification is men's task: "Purify your hearts, ye double-minded," meaning an act producing the condition of single-hearted love. The condition of purity of heart is often mentioned, usually indicating a "ground" of love. That is, only a pure heart can love properly. Love proceeds out of a pure heart. Love describes the character of a pure heart in contrast to an unclean heart.

7. The emphasis on a *heart* being pure is significant. Purity is a quality of "hearts." Briefly, it may be said to mean that the whole man is in moral integrity. Purity of the body or mind is a bringing into integration all parts of the personality, and each part derives purity from this central orientation. Obedience to

truth constitutes purity. A clean heart is one whose deepest purpose has been centered in Christ. It needs to be noted that never is the body as such considered unclean or evil. Purity, according to the New Testament, is not the prerogative of those who withdraw from secular work and sex. It is precisely the ground of a life lived to the hilt in service for Christ.

8. Purity or cleansing is a moral relationship to God and man, not a quality in the substance of the soul. In fellowship is cleansing and both are dependent on walking in the light. It is not an independent real which can maintain its character apart from this relationship. Cleansing is maintained, "moment by moment," as fellowship is maintained by obedience. It is not passive but dynamic. It is not abstract but in moral relatedness. It cannot be bestowed but only appropriated. At no point is cleansing conceived as a state apart from obedience and love. It would be improper to say, "I am cleansed," and suppose that this could be claimed apart from active obedience and continued fellowship with God. Rather one could say, "The blood of Jesus Christ keeps cleansing me," if this sort of testimony were ever in order.

9. Although nothing is directly said in the New Testament about the Holy Spirit cleansing the heart, it is not out of place to say that by the Holy Spirit's indwelling cleansing is maintained, because the Holy Spirit is the presence of God in the heart. To reiterate, a clean heart is a single heart, which is love, which is fellowship, which is guarded and nourished by the Holy Spirit. Impurity is a violation of moral integrity which grieves the Holy Spirit, and breaks fellowship, and changes love to lust, which is the essence of duplicity or double-mindedness or sin.

In the context of moral relevance and holiness, purity cannot be a sub-rational, impersonal "something" that happens to the substance of the soul. It must always be a right moral relationship which gives birth to love in which obedience is the joy of the heart and truth is the atmosphere. Cleansing is not a static thing but a continuing relationship. Cleansing then finds itself related to and in accord with all that has been posited about "moral." Nothing in the use of the term suggests anything other than a wholly moral relatedness. It describes moral integrity and is described by integrity. It is a quality of the person. Single-heartedness is its fundamental characteristic. Cleanness is violated only by duplicity and deceitfulness.

Furthermore, it is obvious that cleansing (or purity) is not an isolated or single-valued quality. It belongs to other elements of grace and the personality. It describes sanctification as well as justification and explains why Jesus died. It is equated with love and is dependent on walking in the light and confession of sin. In other words, what it involves is practically indistinguishable from these other matters. This point is of very great significance, as will be pointed out later.

CHAPTER XIV

Christian Perfection

One of the most distinctive Wesleyan terms is *perfection*. It is a word that has been variously interpreted and as a consequence widely misunderstood. Though *perfection* is a biblical word, the English words used to translate the several Greek words for the idea tend to obscure the rich connotation of the biblical usage. In Wesley's day, as in ours, the word "perfection" gave trouble. The implication of absolutism clings to the English word. Yet any theology attempting to be biblical (particularly a theology making reference to John Wesley) must come to some valid understanding of how to relate biblical perfection to theology. In this chapter the attempt is made, first, to examine Wesley's use of the term. A brief historical survey of the churches' understanding (and misunderstanding) of perfection will follow. A biblical survey of all the occasions of its use in the New Testament and some conclusions drawn on the basis of this study will close the chapter.

WESLEY AND CHRISTIAN PERFECTION

In the tension between theology/logic and life/experience lie the problems which cause considerable difference of opinion, as would be expected, and which caused Wesley the kind of problems which make it difficult to find in him "the answer" which is "Wesleyan." However, if we are willing to be actually Wesleyan we will not press absolute answers beyond the "given" in Scripture and life. If the foregoing principle outlined so far in this book is correct, and if the interpretation of Wesley and Scripture has been consistent, there should be a directive in this area also.

The principle by which to understand Wesley's doctrine is love to God and man, in the biblical sense of love. Love is the dynamic of theology and experience. Love, structured by holiness, links all that we know of man. Love is the end of the law. It is the goal of every step in grace and the norm of the Christian life in this world.

With this as a background we will attempt to suggest a path through the murky conflict area of the meaning of *perfection* and the significance of crisis and process in the Christian life. These two areas are integrally related. Perfection has been interpreted in terms of crisis or process according to the whole background of presuppositions brought to the subject. Some equate sanctification wholly with the crisis/perfection syndrome. Others, with a totally different concept of possibility, relate process and perfection, either distinguishing between sanctification and perfection so as to preserve crisis in relation to sanctification, or equating sanctification and perfection and dismissing crisis as a viable theological category, making all progress gradual and natural. There is here one of the points where a "magical" type of supernaturalism, a biblical supernaturalism, and some interpretations of naturalism cross swords.

We may say that Wesley gives little help in solving the problem absolutely because equally good cases could be, and are, made for any one of these, and other, options. But is Wesley so much a failure here as such a hasty judgment would indicate? Was he not true to the spirit of his whole approach, here as elsewhere? Where the Scriptures spoke unequivocally, so he spoke. Where they did not, Wesley sought answers that would relate to the way God's grace interacted with human experience as he carefully collated the records of cases under his administration and personal knowledge.

Wesley probably is somewhat to blame for the dilemma. Where Wesley identified full sanctification and Christian perfection he had the most difficulty. All the *practical* advice he gave weakens his own position at this point. That is, when he related perfection to the human situation, the "absolute" of sanctification was no longer "perfect." In this identification, the growth aspect of life hung loosely and ambiguously (however essentially and persistently) on the edge of Christian holiness, tagging along but unrelated to it. Yet his deepest conviction was that man could be saved from sin here on this earth in this life and live in the atmosphere of love to God and man. When the relatedness of grace to life was uppermost in his mind, however, a reinterpretation of perfection, logically at least, seemed to be called for, which also involved a redefinition of sanctification.

Well, here we are. We dare not be more dogmatic, theologically, than Wesley was, if we seek to stay on his basic ground. And we do. Both sanctification and perfection will require a biblical examination a little later in this study. This ought to be done, in any case. Too seldom do we go to the Scriptures as a child asking the Author to help us find the meaning. It is an exhilarating thing to do, however. Then the sticky problems of what the crisis of the full Christian life may be and achieve, and how process fits into the total scheme, will follow naturally.

The classic treatment of the subject is, of course, John Wesley's own summary of his developing views in *A Plain Account of Christian Perfection,* and it should be studied carefully. (This is currently available in paperback from Beacon Hill Press of Kansas City.) In it can be traced the source of his own understanding of Christian perfection gathered from his own experience and from others, such as Bishop Taylor's *Holy Living and Dying,* Thomas a Kempis' *Christians' Pattern,* and Mr. Law's *Christian Perfection* and *Serious Call*. Wesley concludes that renewal to the lost image of God, meaning "love to God and man" (as has been noted earlier), expressed as Christlikeness, sums up Wesley's definition of Christian perfection. But the following passages taken from his *Plain Account* reveal some of the problems he had in explaining his meaning.

Q. How shall we avoid setting perfection too high or too low?

A. By keeping to the Bible, and setting it just as high as the Scripture does. It is nothing higher and nothing lower than this, —the pure love of God and man; the loving God with all our heart and soul, and our neighbor as ourselves. It is love governing the heart and life, running through all our tempers, words, and actions.

Q. Suppose one had attained to this, would you advise him to speak of it?

A. At first perhaps he would scarce be able to refrain, the fire would be so hot within him; his desire to declare the loving-kindness of the Lord carrying him away like a torrent. But afterwards he might; and then it would be advisable, not to speak of it to them that know not God; (it is most likely, it would only provoke them to contradict and blaspheme;) nor to others, without some particular reason, without some good in view. And then he should have especial care to avoid all appearance of boasting; to speak with the deepest humility and reverence, giving all the glory to God (*Works*, XI, 397).

Q. But what does the perfect one do more than others? more than the common believers?

A. Perhaps nothing; so may the providence of God have hedged him in by outward circumstances. Perhaps not so much; though he desires and longs to spend and be spent for God; at least, not externally: He neither speaks so many words, nor does so many works. As neither did our Lord himself speak so many words, or do so many, no, nor so great works, as some of his Apostles. (John xiv. 12.) But what then? This is no proof that he has not more grace; and by this God measures the outward work. Hear ye Him: "Verily, I say unto you, this poor widow has cast in more than them all." Verily, this poor man, with his few broken words, hath spoken more than them all. Verily, this poor woman, that hath given a cup of cold water, hath done more than them all. O cease to "judge according to appearance," and learn to judge "righteous judgment" (*ibid.*, p. 400).

"But he does not come up to my idea of a perfect Christian." And perhaps no one ever did, or ever will. For your idea may go beyond, or at least beside, the scriptural account. It may include more than the Bible includes therein, or, however, something which that does not include. Scripture perfection is, pure love filling the heart, and governing all the words and actions. If your idea includes anything more or anything else, it is not Scriptural; and then no wonder, that a Scripturally perfect Christian does not come up to it.

I fear many stumble on this stumbling block. They include as many ingredients as they please, not according to Scripture, but their own imagination, in their idea of one that is perfect; and then readily deny anyone to be such, who does not answer that imaginary idea.

The more care should we take to keep the simple, Scriptural account continually in our eye. Pure love reigning alone in the heart and life—This is the whole of Scriptural perfection (*ibid.*, p. 401).

To those who wanted "proof" of a "perfect man" Wesley answered, "There are many reasons why there should be few, if any indisputable examples. What inconveniences would this bring on the person himself, set as a mark for all to shoot at!" (*Ibid.*, p. 391).

Christian Perfection and the Church

It must be kept in mind that sanctification and perfection are doctrines which belong to the whole Church. Wesley's contribution to Christian thought is not in the origination of these terms, or in the wide use of them. He, as a self-conscious and conscientious churchman, would have repudiated (and did) any suspicion of novelty in theology, and indeed *Christian perfection is no novelty*.

Wesley's contribution was in his ability to link the hands of doctrine and life—to close the gap between thought and act. In the aberrations regarding perfection in the experience of the Church in history it is to be noted that, in all of them, a compartmentalization of life is a characteristic of the faulty view. Wesley's position was that the more seriously perfection is held, the more compartmentalization is broken up and the life unified and strengthened.

Compartmentalization occurs when any part of the person— his social relationships, his business practices, his religious activities, his moral life—become autonomous segments of the personality, each dedicated to a different "god," each making its own rules and setting its own goals. Study conflicts with devotion. Sexual interests conflict with spiritual life. Cheating in business or in taking exams is justified on different grounds than would be permitted in home relationships. Every segment of man's complex life is run by a separate moral code, each judging its area of authority on its own private premise. It was this kind of Christian life that Wesley felt betrayed the biblical promise relative to love and wholeness and holiness. Holiness is one love unifying all the inner life and outer norms for activity. Christ must be Lord of all, or not claimed as Lord at all.

The Wesleyan revival was essentially a revival of subjective or experienced perfection. Wesley had sought perfection, seriously, as the evangelical Pietists had profoundly influenced him. When he found his "heart strangely warmed," he believed that he had recovered a lost or forgotten truth which was the rightful property of the Church Universal. Charismatic groups also seek perfection but in such a mystical and individualized way that all vital contact with Scripture and Christian history and life is lost. Wesley stands in the mystical tradition insofar as he stressed personal experience of grace. But that is as far as it can be said that he was a mystic. His feet were solidly planted in social relationships and he was an outspoken enemy of the erotic in life, in preaching, in testimony, in song, or in religious emotion. Perfection, to him, was to be defined rationally, biblically, ethically, socially.

CHRISTIAN PERFECTION VERSUS PERFECTIONISM

It is customary to class all theological positions which stress the subjective aspect of grace as "perfectionism." But there is a very real and important theological and practical difference between perfection which can be called Christian and that which we may term perfectionism. This difference may not be indicated in the dictionary definitions, but the inherent connotations can be utilized "by an arbitrary decree" to serve to distinguish two very different ways of approaching Christian teaching on the subject. The major problems arising out of any theological or religious use of the term perfection occur because this distinction is not recognized and taken into account.

Perfectionism will be used as a term describing a typically philosophical approach to thinking. Whenever perfection is understood in an absolute sense—a point beyond which there can be no further development—it can be called perfectionism. New Testament writers knew nothing of this kind of thinking. Biblical writers uniformly refer to man as well as nature in personal and dynamic terms. Even the perfection of God called "sovereignty" does not immobilize Him. He is not the victim of His own nature. His absoluteness does not rob Him of flexibility and the capacity to relate to men who have been endowed by Him with genuine, if limited, freedom.

To adequately understand this dynamic element in "biblical perfection" is essential to a sound hermeneutic and to a theology that has any justification for being called biblical.

As is true with the other key theological terms which characterize Wesleyan theology (or any other, for that matter), perfection considered alone fails to do justice to its evangelical meaning. It is not an abstract term which has an independent theological status. It is one facet of the larger truth which Christian theology seeks to rationalize systematically and must be considered in connection with the whole.

History of "Perfection"

Perfection as a religious goal has a long and noble history, particularly in the Judeo-Christian tradition, and has characterized both orthodox and heterodox segments of this religious persuasion.

The Jews believed in a perfect society yet to come. It would be created by the perfect God and would be ruled by a perfect Messiah. In it would be no "sinners," only righteous persons. The early Christian concept was more specific. Righteousness, or holiness, was Christlikeness. Holiness was a proper balance between faith and conduct—"the mind of Christ." The Spirit would fill each person and guide him. Hence the question, "Did you receive the Holy Spirit when you believed?" Love would be the law of the new society. Deliverance from sin and triumph over it and union with God in personal fellowship were expected. These possibilities are now realizable. This was the apostolic teaching.

Gnosticism (or incipient Gnostic thought) introduced a new element into the canonical teaching, and became the source of the major heresies in the Christian Church. The basic error arose out of Hellenistic philosophies which taught a cosmological dualism which conceived of reality as two contradictory kinds of being, matter (the shadow) and the real (or spirit), and these two things could not mix because matter was essentially evil and spirit was essentially good. Salvation, then, was not deliverance from sin but deliverance from matter. A corollary of dualism was the concept of *gnosis* in which knowledge was equated with goodness, and ignorance with evil. Hence, Socrates' dictum, "Knowledge is virtue," could be fitted into the Christian (sub-apostolic) quest for perfection. The result was that knowledge was prized more than virtue, and religion became a philosophy. Mankind was divided into three classes: the fleshly people *(sarx)* or unbelievers (those incapable of life above the animal level), soulish people *(psyche)* or believers (those who were not capable of true knowledge but who were credulous or capable of faith and who were superior to the lower class), and the spiritual people *(pneuma)* or those with perfect knowledge (the intellectual aristocrats who were "saved" by *gnosis*). The foreshadowing of this problem is seen in the background of some New Testament Epistles, Corinthians and Colossians especially. (Read I Cor. 2:3-4 with this in mind.)

Religion as a philosophy in general and Gnosticism as a philosophy in particular was consistently rejected by the Christian Church, but the shadow of Gnosticism was cast over the subsequent history of the Church in several ways. The insidious idea of a spiritual aristocracy inhering in the supposedly higher levels of spiritual attainment was prefigured in Gnosticism. It is not biblical.

But the most objective form of the heresy arose out of its dualistic view of the world. To subdue the body or even to destroy it in the interest of holiness was the idea underlying the ascetic practices which arose in the Post-Apostolic Church. Harnack has well said that the monastic movement was "the greatest organized quest for perfection in history." Since the body and its functions partook of sin, to escape from the body became the religious quest. The positive New Testament concept of perfection as outgoing love was reversed and a negative concept of a gradual destruction of the "body of sin," identified as the human body, prevailed. The idea of holiness changed from fellowship to self-centered individualism. The importance of this movement to an understanding of our own problems cannot be overestimated.

PERFECTIONISM AND SUBJECTIVISM

In this way, biblical holiness lapsed into perfectionism. Tatian preached renunciation as necessary to and the essence of holiness but his idea was to renounce literally *everything*, evil and good, wealth, home, friends, all. Groups of people gathered to strive for perfection by methodic practices of discipline—involving the most rigid self-control. In due time Montanus began to stress the separated and *Spirit-filled life* with major emphasis on mystical experience. Instead of discipline as the means to holiness, ecstatic experience became the means to and test of sanctity. Tatian advocated external conformity, Montanus nonconformity. Both stood in danger of the loss of true personal identity and spiritual and moral integrity.

Three concepts of holiness lay at the heart of three major heresies. If knowledge is virtue, philosophy is salvation, said one. If matter is evil, self-discipline, even emasculation, leads to perfection, said another. If the personal experience of Christ is the heart of New Testament religion, the ecstatic, Spirit-prompted mystical and emotional experience is holiness, declared the third. Knowledge, self-discipline, personal experience are all found in the New Testament in some form but in wholesome balance. But in the Church since, exaggerations of one or more of them have embarrassed good sense and created major problems in the Church.

The reaction between objective and subjective methods of reaching perfection, in the form of sacerdotalism and mysticism, accounts for much theological development in the Middle Ages. The Reformers' stress on grace and faith was a reaction to both, but they did not guard sufficiently the importance of inward righteousness and personal holiness and opened the way for extremes again, by way of reaction, in charismatic and mystical modes of religious experience.

Perhaps this background is sufficient to prepare for a meaningful discussion relative to "perfectionism." We are distinguishing between *perfection* and *perfectionism*. The popular understanding of these terms is good enough to begin the critique. A philosophical absolutism characterizes perfectionism; that is, it suggests a static perfection within which there can be no further development. When this is put into the context of religious life, the obvious imperfections and changeableness of human life give rise to difficult and sometimes unsavory problems. In every case where perfection is taken out of a solidly biblical context and yet made an imperative or a desirable quest for men, a distortion in some area results. Either human nature must be violated to conform to an impossible standard or moral integrity must be sacrificed, or both. Self-righteousness, pride, antinomianism, and loss of moral sensitivity lie in these aberrations.

CONTEMPORARY EVANGELICAL PERFECTION THEORIES

Evangelical perfection, defined as this biblical study has sought to do, stands in deepest contrast to perfectionism. Biblical perfection knows nothing of philosophical absolutism. It is fundamentally moral integrity and is consistent with human probationary status. It lies in the context of moral responsibility and proceeds in human life as moral capacity waxes or wanes. It never sacrifices moral and rational awareness to irrational emotional states. It has already been made clear that this is not ethical relativism or humanistic concession to sin. It is an emphasis on moral integrity defined by love.

Perfectionism, on the other hand, is some kind of intellectual, moralistic, or emotional truce with truth short of personal moral integrity. It may be found anywhere, even in theological circles ordinarily thought to be free from any taint of subjectivism. The classical errors show up in very different attire. Vehement denial of perfection may cover, inadvertently, a belief in perfectionism, as we shall see.

Perfectionism lies in any view of redemption which bypasses in any way the personal moral element. There are several forms and each is directly related to one of the theories already discussed of the relation of the supernatural to nature in human life.

1. The most obvious error is found in that religious practice which tends to surrender the clear distinction between the divine Spirit and the human spirit. To be filled with the Spirit, in this view, means that *the will of the Spirit merges with the human will.* Therefore, whatever the person desires is the right desire. Every

impulse is a Spirit-directed impulse. Perfectionism approves the surrender to blind impulse. One need not, yea, must not, question impressions but must, rather, hasten to obey them. There is a blind bondage to passing emotional compulsions and an irrational loyalty to them though they may lead to absurd actions and even immoral ones. It is considered a "quenching of the Spirit" to examine the validity of impulse. Great store is placed in antisocial and unconventional, erratic acts in the interest of religious "freedom." This way of thinking is supported by one of the concepts described in "divine-human interaction," which was rejected by Wesley.

2. A *materialistic concept* of spiritual values occasions another form of perfectionism. The perfect is defined in terms of *freedom from natural evils*. This is a subtle form of environmentalism. It downgrades moral issues by supposing that a sanctified environment can sanctify persons. If one is saved, it says, there can be no more sickness, poverty, or need of any kind. The presence of these things means that one is not saved. This view can be carried to such extremes that ordinary care of the human body, responsibility for families, and certainly the improvement of the human mind and moral disciplines are either neglected or repudiated. The logic concludes, If one is holy he ought not to need mundane human supports and should not be handicapped by concerns about them.

3. Perfectionism may manifest itself in *moralism. External conformity to law is of prior importance.* Every human act is regulated by law. The law becomes so complex and intricate that dress styles and colors for both men and women, recreational possibilities, and every minutia of personal and corporate life are carefully proscribed. Holiness is measured by this conformity. That a very unpleasant and harsh spirit may accompany this conformity is no argument against it. In fact, it is said, harshness is needed to maintain it and is finally considered to be a sign and assurance of perfection and sanctity. When human beings take over the task of the Holy Spirit in keeping one's neighbor pure, the job is too big and force supersedes persuasion, and becomes a virtue.

4. A wrong understanding of entire sanctification may lead to perfectionism, though we believe it does not inevitably, or in the nature of the case, do so. If the impression is left in the believer's mind that something is literally and bodily taken out of him which desires the things he ought not to desire, or if he comes to understand that he has no more personal responsibility for his own motives, perfectionism results. If his "experience" is not carefully related to every aspect of daily life and the *idea* of sanctity is not translated into a *practical life* of sanctity, perfectionism lies too near. If the standard of moral judgment for the personal conscience is less demanding after the religious experience than before, and one permits and excuses in himself acts and attitudes which he cannot allow in others or for which he cannot defend himself at the bar of good conscience, the charge of perfectionism is inevitable and just.

When there are no rational tests by which to judge one's own *motives*, it follows that conduct is determined solely on the basis of personal desire. The immoral excesses and self-righteous justifications for all kinds of unethical conduct that sometimes occur are not a pretty picture. It is the conviction of the holiness theologian, however, that these perfectionist aberrations are diametrically in opposition to the positive content of that which Christian or biblical perfection means, namely, love.

5. But there is another and less obvious form of perfectionism which must be pointed out. It partakes of a dualism just as surely as any of the above views. *It separates between the ideal perfection of legal standing and the practical possibility of human perfectibility*. It cannot relate spiritual realities to the capacities of human nature. It teaches that character can be transferred from one person to another—in this case Christ's character and our own. It redefines and then hides human sin behind the legal sentence of acquittal and supposes that men may continue in sin, yet profess Christ's own righteousness as their own. The dualism between fact and fiction is a serious concern to those who take moral integrity seriously.

This kind of perfectionism says that the soul is eternally secure regardless of its involvement in sin because man's legal status has changed in God's mind because of Christ. In effect, it abrogates law and moral obligation so far as soteriology is concerned. Though usually a good moral life is encouraged, it is not considered necessary to salvation.

In this way, salvation terminates probation. In the interest of a "serious view of sin" it includes all possible divergence from perfection in its concept of sin. In this view, the will is totally impotent. Salvation, consequently, is nonmoral in that the Holy Spirit activates the will of man and in the course of redemption "removes" the consequence of sin from man, so that his sinful acts no longer bear the judgment against sin.

The corollaries follow more or less logically. If God does anything at all, He does it perfectly. There is no place for development or progress in God's work, since He can do only perfect work. Since men are not perfect, they incur God's wrath. Christ's righteousness substitutes for that of man and therefore law is abrogated. This, of course, leads to antinomianism, logically, if not in practice. The relaxation of conscience relative to the consequences of personal sin tend to lower moral tone and ethical decision.

In this view, no human relevance can modify the thing God does for us. We may continue to sin (though we ought not to do so), but God's promise to save us cannot be altered; "God cannot deny himself." We are eternally safe. Therefore our sins are no longer culpable. Manning Pattillo, in *Christianity Today*, says,

> If we have faith in Jesus Christ, God accepts Christ's righteousness as if it were ours; or, to state it in another way, we participate in the righteousness of Christ by faith in him. If we believe in him, he shares his righteousness with us, and we can offer it to God in place of our own righteousness.[1]

Perfectionism cannot be more clearly stated than this.

We know that these men, and others, are too responsible to teach an unguarded antinomianism, but we do maintain that inherent in the position is an antinomianism which embarrasses it. Perfectionism lies at the heart of its logic in that what is lacking of moral character in men is said to be fully and absolutely made up in the moral character of another. Therefore, what the sinner does is, on the books, counted as perfect personal sanctity because it is the perfect sanctity of Christ.

Both subjectivist and objectivist fall into the perfectionist trap because neither group has balanced the two aspects carefully against the biblical standard. By neglecting one or the other the true moral dimension has been lost. Neither group actually needs the Bible for an objective Rule of Christian life and faith. The second group is secure and needs no law. The first has exchanged the "Holy Spirit's leading" for Scripture. The Bible in both cases is mainly read for eschatological information. Neither group, therefore, is amenable to moral law. Both find that the keeping of law, or whatever can substitute for it, is an automatic accompaniment of grace or a reinterpretation of conduct in the light of grace. Neither one has any real sense of personal obligation to God or men because redemption is conceived in terms of privilege and freedom and not moral responsibility.

6. There are erratic variations of perfectionism which need only to be mentioned. *Monasticism* with its ascetic emphasis, wherever it is found, follows the Gnostic dualism. As one is able to deny and eradicate human impulse, the spirit is made more free to pursue holiness, which is its natural condition. Any theology which conceives of the possibility of sinlessness in the spirit concomitant with sinfulness in the flesh partakes of Gnostic perfectionism.

Extreme emphasis on healing and freedom from economic need when "in grace" is perfectionism, as is also the tendency to withdraw from the world in order to keep pure. It is perfectionism that encourages a disregard for sensitivity to social situations and holds back the tongue from confessions of failure and wrong and humble asking for pardon.

Perfectionism substitutes external and amoral demonstration for inward grace. It may be fanatical philanthropy, or moralism, such as an undue concern about dress and adornment and austerity of life. It eagerly seeks persecution because of one's "standards." Or it may be an obsession with emotional displays and experience such as shouting, tongues, visions, and ecstatic trances which substitutes for the less spectacular quiet walk of love in daily life.

One may question anything proposed as "an evidence" of grace that can be duplicated by any human effort. *Everything "perfectionism" insists on can be duplicated by some other means. Nothing that "Christian perfection" is can be counterfeited.*

Perfectionism either acknowledges no sin in anything one

does, or it claims sin for everything one does and hides behind the substituting obedience of Christ. Either extreme discounts the moral seriousness of sin and is a practical perfectionism. Spiritual pride is the essence of perfectionism in each of the above classes. One glories in his sinlessness and his personal righteousness; the other glories in his humility and sin. Both are equally repulsive and repugnant to that which Christian perfection teaches.

In a word, perfectionism is nonmoral and conceives of redemption in nonhistorical terms. Christian perfection, on the other hand, is moral to the core and understands holiness to be thoroughly relevant to every area of life and not antithetical to the possibilities in Christ-centered human nature.

John Fletcher warns:

> Avoid all extremes. While on the one hand you keep clear of the Pharisaic delusion that slights Christ, and makes the pretended merit of an imperfect obedience the procuring cause of eternal life: see that on the other hand you do not lean to the Antinomian error, which, under the pretence of exalting Christ, speaks contemptuously of obedience, and "makes void the law through a faith that *does not* work by love." . . . Many smatterers in Christian experience talk of a *finished salvation in Christ*. . . . while they know little of themselves and less of Christ.[2]

Perhaps a characterization of evangelical perfection as distilled from many sources will be sufficient at this point, since a biblical study of the term is to follow. Christian perfection, or perfect love, stands for a full measure of personal obligation to the whole will of God, rather than an acceptance of Christian status without a commensurate responsibility attached. It stands for "obedience from the heart" rather than an abrogation of law. It requires the highest moral integrity and rational responsibility rather than a dulling of the conscience, a reinterpretation of sin, a surrender to blind impulse and irresponsible individualism.

Christian perfection is of the heart and was called by John Wesley perfect love. He preferred that term but was forced to use others many times because his enemies distorted his meaning. Instead of bypassing the moral, Christian perfection is moral to the core. Instead of abrogating law, it is thoroughgoing obedience to the law. Instead of reference to the excellence of the self, it rests wholly upon God and loves Him with the whole heart, mind, soul, and strength. It desires to please God in all things. This desire issues in a sincere compliance with God's understood will. It holds steady in doubt and ignorance and darkness, pressing relentlessly for more light and guidance. Acceptance of discipline and humble seeking for truth are its atmosphere.

Rather than Christian perfection standing in danger of perfectionism, it is the guard against it. Everything in Christian perfection stands in absolute contradistinction to perfectionism.

BIBLICAL SURVEY OF "PERFECTION"

Two considerations are necessary to clear thinking on the matter of perfection. The first one is to remember that the biblical teaching on perfection is not burdened with Hellenistic philosophy. Its relatedness to moral experience (as defined in the chapter "The Meaning of *Moral*") characterizes it and prevents the introduction of philosophical abstraction to a serious study of it. The second consideration is the observation that in a biblical study it soon becomes clear that the connotation of the English word "perfect" tends to obscure the several carefully distinguished meanings as delineated in the Greek by different words. Also, the translators' legitimate substitution of other more appropriate English words for the same Greek word tends to hinder the reader who is limited to the English language from catching the original nuance of meaning.

In this brief examination and analysis of all the relevant occasions of the use of the term perfection, the contextual implications will be considered as of crucial importance. Often the context throws light on the special and peculiar way a word is molded by the author to a specific need. Theological dogmatics must arise from, not predetermine, textual meanings.

There are several Greek words which are customarily translated "perfect" or "perfection."

Akribós is translated "perfectly" in the KJV and has the meaning of diligent, or accurate, and does not refer to redemptive truths. Apollos was instructed "more perfectly" in the way (Acts 18:26), and this usage is typical of all the examples (Luke 1:3; Acts 23:15; 23:20; I Thess. 5:2).

Artios, meaning "fitted" or "qualified," is the term Paul uses in II Tim. 3:17 to describe the goal toward which the "man of God" is to come and which is partially realized by a proper attitude toward and use of the Holy Scriptures. This obviously refers to personal fitness and educational training and not salvation. "Scripture is given . . . that the man of God may be perfect . . . furnished unto all good works."

Pleróo, "complete" or "made full," is found in Rev. 3:2 only. The works of the church of Sardis were not found *peplero-ména*, or "meeting the requirements" *(Amplified Bible)*, of God.

Katartízo means to be adjusted properly or to be fitted together comfortably. In I Cor. 1:10 and II Cor. 13:11 the word is used in an especially apt way, considering the peculiar problem of the church. Paul begins by exhorting the people to be "perfectly joined together" and closes with the same plea, "Be perfect," meaning that this interrelatedness in love was the one necessary, but lacking, virtue.

Peter uses the word in the same way (I Pet. 5:10) in a benediction, "But the God of all grace . . . after that ye have suffered a while, make you perfect, stablish, strengthen, settle you." Paul's concern regarding the Thessalonian church was that he might visit them again to bring into better focus those things concerning their faith that might be imperfect or out of balance (I Thess. 3:10-13). A benediction in the Hebrew Epistle (13:20-21) used the word: "The God of peace . . . make you perfect in every good work," with the same connotation. *Katartismón*, another form of the same word, is used in Eph. 4:11-12: "He gave some, apostles [etc.] . . . for the perfecting of the saints," with the idea of providing full equipment in a spiritual sense for the task of the Christian in the world in which his witness is to be given.

The rest of the New Testament words for *perfection* are those of the family of *téleios* (derived from *télos*). They are *teleióo*, *teleíos*, *teleíosis*, and *teleiotés*.

Télos means either "maturity" or "completion." It is usually translated "end" and means the maturity of time, circumstances, or character.

Téleios and its related forms carry the basic meaning of *télos* but with none of the philosophical idea which it is capable of bearing.

Téleios is that which has reached a completion consistent with an intended end. When used of persons it has to do with physical development, ethical maturation, and real goodness unrelated to maturity.

B. F. Westcott says of this word:

> In the books of the N.T. the adjective is used to describe that which has reached the highest perfection in the sphere which is contemplated as contrasted with that which is partial (I Cor. 13:19), or imperfect (James 1:4) or provisional (James 1:25) or incomplete (Rom. 12:2; James 1:17; I John 4:18) and especially of Christians who have reached full growth in contrast with those who are immature or undeveloped (Eph. 4:13; Col. 1:28; 4:12), either generally (Matt. 5:48; 19:21; I Cor. 2:6; Phil. 3:15; James 3:2) or in some particular aspect (I Cor. 14:20).[3]

Jesus used this word for "perfect" *(téleios)* in the Sermon on the Mount (Matt. 5:48). He said that the disciples were to be (future tense) perfect as the Heavenly Father is perfect. This strange verse has troubled serious readers because of its apparently impossible connotations. However, when the meaning of *perfect* is sought in relation to the immediate context, much of the problem disappears.

In the first place, it should be noted that the Greek future is often a command or exhortation and is so translated in some versions. (The ARV says, "Ye therefore shall be perfect"; but the RSV prefers, "You, therefore, must be perfect.") This puts a moral quality into the exhortation. The general tone of the whole passage emphasizes right attitudes as being acceptable to God rather than simply right conduct. It is a characteristic of quality, not a degree of accomplishment. God loves and cares for all men, good and bad. Our love should be as impartial as God shows himself to be.

In the immediate context an impartial goodwill is under discussion. Christian love is to be nonselective and all-inclusive in its spirit. The disposition to favor only those who can return favors and to ignore those who cannot contribute to our prestige is not the Christian way. It is that "your *Father* . . . in heaven," manifests paternal love toward all mankind—and thus provides the pattern of right motive and conduct for the Christian child—that is the point.

This verse cannot be divorced from the preceding section (vv. 43-47), in which the meaning of this perfection is spelled out, namely, extending our love and goodwill toward those who persecute us, "*That ye may be the children of your Father* which is in heaven." As a father loves the good and the bad *child,* so we are to extend our goodwill to all. The emphasis is on God as *Father* and men as *sons* of God. As His fatherhood is revealed to us, our sonship is to be patterned. And that pattern is love—a new dimension to human relations which Jesus came to reveal to us and make normative for Christians. Wesley's thinking was molded and vitalized by this concept of love as the norm for Christian life.

We are not free to carry the word "perfect" away to a philosophy book to define it after human judgment and then bring it back to cause havoc with biblical exegesis and theology. *The commentary is in the context.* It is not without point to recall that in Luke the parallel passage says: "Be ye therefore *merciful,* as your Father is also merciful," and the ethical implications are then clear. Perfection and mercy complement and give meaning to each other.

In Matt. 19:16-21, we are told of a young man who asked the way to eternal life. The answer did not bypass the Ten Commandments but went into and beyond them to the spirit of the law. "If thou wilt be perfect, go and sell what thou hast, and give to the poor . . . and come and follow me." Keeping the commandments is the way to life, Jesus said. Obedience was not wrong, nor was the new way to disregard the factor of obedience. But keeping the commandments meant a very practical life commitment which could change law-keeping into evangelical "perfection." In this passage perfection is defined as active obedience to Christ, a quality of moral life which had to be added to an already outwardly perfect obedience to law. It was personalized and livable goodness, a spirit behind the act.

The biblical context relieves the word *perfect* of abstraction.

Paul plays on the idea in the word and adds meaning to it in the Corinthian letter by contrasting it to *népios* (not *childlike* but *childish*). Of the vain Corinthians who claimed to be spiritual (by which they meant religiously mature, grown-up, "men come of age") Paul said, "I . . . could not speak unto you as unto spiritual, but as unto carnal, even as unto *babes* in Christ" (I Cor. 3:1). The thrust of this is apparent when this passage is held against I Cor. 2:6 where Paul said, "We speak wisdom among them that are perfect [or mature]," but "I . . . could not speak unto you as unto spiritual." Here *spiritual* is equated with maturation, and *carnal* with babyishness (in those beyond the years of childhood).

A further point, lost in English wording, was made by Paul in the use of *népios*. It is a word for "child," used by Paul, always referring to moral immaturity and deficiency. It had an *unpleasant connotation*. It carries the figure of a person who has come to a mature age but whose body and mind have failed to develop. Paul said, "Doesn't your quarrelling reveal your essential childishness?" The point went home with telling force.

In I Corinthians 13, Paul refers to this again. "When I was a *népios*, I spoke, understood, and reasoned like a spoiled baby. But when I became a man, I put away childish things." Normal growth does not cure this kind of arrested development.

Paul once more pushes the figure deep into the Corinthians' thinking in 14:20. The *KJV* is ambiguous in its translation: "Be not children in understanding: howbeit in malice be ye children, but in understanding be men." Paul is not teaching a dualism here. The contrast is between a child's *understanding* and a man's. The Greek verb translated "be children" could equally well be "you are being childish" *(nepiádzete)* and this in turn a contrast to the true childlikeness indicated by the use of *paidía* in the first contrast. Then the childlikeness, always associated with the spirit of teachableness, is contrasted to the childishness which in the Corinthians' case was a "passion for an over-evaluation of speaking with tongues, really a kind of childish ostentation. The product of the desire to show off like a precocious child."[4] In this way Paul is relentlessly pressing home the central point of the whole correspondence with the Corinthians, namely, that fellowship is the defining atmosphere of "the church of God," and divisiveness is a sign, not of the simple immaturity of youth, but of moral irresponsibility—and worse.

Paul uses the same contrast to make the same point in Eph. 4:13-14. In this passage, the "perfect man" *(téleion)*, which is "the measure of the stature of the fulness of Christ" to which we all come into "the unity of faith," is contrasted with "children *[népios]*, tossed to and fro, and carried about with every wind of doctrine."

Again, in the letter to the Hebrews (5:11-14) this telling contrast is found with the same deep reprimand: "Ye are dull of hearing. For when for the time ye ought to be teachers, ye have need that one teach you again . . . and are become such as have need of milk, and not of strong meat. For every one that useth milk is unskillful . . . for he is a babe *[népios]*. But strong meat belongeth to them that are of full age *[teleíon,* perfect], even those who by reason of use have their senses exercised to discern both good and evil."

In all these occasions the perfect man is responsible, dependable, poised, and generally behaving as a man of character. The contrast is not the child who is growing up normally, but one of arrested development, of "babyishness." It is a child who refuses to grow up, who hides behind his mother's skirts, who pulls on the milk bottle when he should be eating solid food. Modern psychology calls this arrested development infantilism, mother fixation, schizophrenia, *et al.* Put into a context of the moral capacity of humanhood it becomes a tremendously disturbing challenge to spiritual irresponsibility. This babyhood is not the kind that one outgrows. It is not the excusable immaturities of delightfully attractive, exuberant youth. The babyishness to which *perfect* is the antithesis is pathetic, reprehensible. It is to be "put away" and kept from returning by diligence and spiritual maturation.

But at the same time the perfection or maturity spoken of is not inconsistent with the immaturity of normal youth. In a word, it is moral integrity in whatever chronological age the possessor might find himself.

A further examination of Paul's use of the word *téleios,* or its cognates, adds instructive facets to the meaning of the word. Paul's exhortation in Rom. 12:1-2 is in the interest of proving "what is that good, and acceptable, and *perfect,* will of God." In this case it is the will of God which is perfect and clearly refers to the plan and purpose of God for the believer here in this life. Man is "to present" (aorist) himself and "be . . . transformed" (present tense, indicating long, faithful application to the task of renewing the mind) to prove, or test by experience, that God's will is utterly desirable—perfect. God's will is found to satisfy the most profound expectation of the human heart. The way to discover that will is to make God the center of our lives in affection and obedience.

In Eph. 4:12-13, Paul refers to the fully matured "body of Christ," or the Church. It is to this maturation as an end that Paul exhorts. Its content is unity and mutual helpfulness. God gives each man a measure of grace (4:7), and puts some men in places of leadership (4:11), "for the *perfecting* of the saints . . . for the edifying of the body of Christ: till we all come in the unity of the faith, and of the knowledge of the Son of God, unto a *perfect* man [not men], unto the measure of the stature of the fulness of Christ: *that we henceforth be no more* children *[népioi]*" (4:12-14).

"Perfecting" (v. 12) is *katartídzo,* and means "to knit together, to unite completely," and refers to the relationship of the "saints," or sanctified ones, to each other and all of them together as an adequate expression of Christ, whom they are representing in the world. The "perfect man" here is singular and does not refer to individuals as such, nor is the knitting together the work of a moment, but the goal toward which Paul sought to bring those in the Church in their responsibility as the Church.

Once more, the definition is clearly given us in the context by way of the contrast, "that we . . . be no more children," and indicates maturity that "grow[s] up into him in all things, which is the head, even Christ" (4:15). The personal application looks toward fellowship within the Church. *This is holiness in its interpersonal dimension.* The "perfect man" is made by "knitting" the saints together into a unity of fellowship (John 17).

Paul, in Philippians 3, gives us a helpful suggestion as to the meaning of perfection in spite of—or perhaps because of—the apparently ambiguous use of the word. In this chapter we have an excellent example of the lack of bondage to inflexible word meanings that characterized Paul's use of language. Twice words from *téleios* are used. He disclaims perfection in v. 12, and puts himself among those who are already perfect in v. 15. In the first case it is the resurrection body, or future redemption of all things, that he has in mind. In the second reference, personal spiritual maturity is meant. In neither case is Paul speaking of soteriological matters.

In this church, as in so many of the early churches influenced by the surrounding Greek philosophies, the Philippians were inclined to confuse immortality and resurrection. The Greeks taught that the soul was immortal; and the Philippians, being saved, assumed that they now lived in the assurance of eternal bliss. A false type of perfectionism prevailed in that they saw no more need for ethical responsibility or spiritual development. Paul refuted this with vigor. All mortal concerns were expendable. That we might gain Christ and know "the power of *his* resurrection" is "the prize of the high calling." It is not simply endless existence that is the Christian emphasis, but being conformed to Christ's death and so attain to resurrection through Him. Paul had not yet entered that resurrection perfection, nor could he in this life, but he pressed on toward the goal. And this is the *mind* of all who are mature.

Téleios, as a completed thing in some sense equal to the Philippian passage, is indicated in I Cor. 2:6. However, in the light of the whole discussion, to say, "We speak wisdom among them that are perfect," could mean, as the American revision puts it, "the full-grown" or mature person. This would help us to understand the Philippian passage and indicate that Paul understood maturation to be both a possession and a quest. One not only can become mature but he must continue in maturation. It is proper to say, "He is a mature person," but maturity evaporates into senility the moment it ceases to progress. There is no point at which maturity is reached as a sort of state. *Maturity is a dynamic relation to a changing environment.* It is acting responsibly in respect of changing and challenging circumstances. When changing ends, death begins.

Again, in Col. 1:25 and 4:12, Paul's use of the term gives good evidence of its meaning. It is to full realization of the will of God in each of the lives of those under his ministry that Paul and Epaphras labor, preaching, warning, teaching, and praying. One could not conclude that this maturity is anything less than spiritual and moral, but it seems quite clear in the light of the context and sense of the passage that it is not any one specific experience that Paul means but a Christian life guarded and disciplined successfully that is his concern. He is aiming at sturdy Christian character.

The writer to the Hebrews makes much use of the various forms of *téleios* with the general idea of consummation, or bringing to perfection—an idea which is central to the message of the whole Epistle. All the forms of this word used in the New Testament are found in the Hebrew letter. Of the various New Testament applications, one general meaning stands out: The one who is perfect has attained the goals set before him, such as maturity, development, privilege, knowledge. In the Epistle to the Hebrews the partial is made complete, the imperfect is made perfect, the undeveloped child is brought to maturity. Christ comes to perfection through suffering and obedience (Heb. 2:10; 5:8-9). The sacrifices for sin, transitory and provisional, are made perfect in Christ (c. 9). Men are warned to continue on to perfection (6:1), or "be borne on" (H. O. Wiley), and a magnificent list of those who did so are delineated in the eleventh chapter. It is Christ who brings men to perfection. Perfection is a quest unhampered by the limitations of the old covenant, the old sacrifices, the old priesthood. In Christ the way is opened to the perfection the Old Testament pointed toward.

The most striking use is in relationship to Christ, and in this use a large measure of allowable application is suggested as well as a hint as to a proper Christology. "It became him, for whom are all things, and by whom are all things, in bringing many sons unto glory, to make the captain of their salvation perfect through sufferings"(2:10). As a man he was brought to perfection by normal development. In absolutely sharing in the experience of humanity even to death and the fear of it, He conquered death and fear. As "God/man," He, through suffering and death, perfected salvation and makes His people "perfect." Then everything Christ had been and was through His participation in all our experience is a pledge of His ability to strengthen us in all our human needs.

James uses the word to refer to the end result of spiritual discipline. In 1:3-4, he says the development of patience is by the "trying of your faith," and that these together may (subjunctive) make you "perfect and entire, wanting nothing." The goal of perfection here is patience; and the means, the testing of faith.

In 1:17 and 25, it is the gift of God that is designated perfect, and appropriation of it on man's part is contingent on his faithfulness. A definition of a perfect man is given in 3:2 as one who does not offend by his words. And the whole chapter is a dissertation on the sins of the tongue. The perfect man is the truly wise man, who reveals that virtue in conduct which gives "practical proof of it, with the modesty that comes of wisdom" (3:13, *New English Bible*). Perfection, then, is related to ethical matters growing out of a right relationship to God.

John draws love into the orbit of perfection in I John 4:15-21. By dwelling in God and God in us, love has been perfected and those whose love has not been perfected have that fact revealed to them by the inner torment of fear of the judgment. In other words, perfection in this passage is related to a quality of love which in turn reflects a relationship to God. If there is no hindrance to love—no wrong spirit or hidden antagonism or pride—love is perfect and fear of God's judgment is completely ended. The practical element is love for "the brethren." Love for God is mirrored in love for others. Here is a good example of the relatedness of perfection to love, and love to God defined in terms of love to mankind.

Epiteléo, or "putting into practice," is used twice. Paul exhorts the Corinthians (II Cor. 7:1), to perfect "holiness in the fear of God," meaning to bring holiness into practicality—into daily living. *Perfect* here is not aorist as one might expect, but in the Greek present tense, that indicates a habitual attitude of life begun in the past and continuing into the present. To the Galatians, Paul poses the question, "Having begun in the Spirit, are ye now made perfect by the flesh?" (3:3) Here again, "perfect," as a verb, is in the present tense, indicating the working out of a principle, not the terminus of the action. Can the spiritual life, he asks in other words, be brought to maturity by unspiritual means?

We should note some of the same passages emphasizing the verb *teleióo,* "to make perfect," or "to complete," follows the same general pattern of meaning. Jesus told the Pharisees that after three days He would be perfected (Luke 13:32), meaning the completing of His earthly ministry. In John 17:23, Jesus prays that the disciples "may be made perfect in one," with the obvious meaning of a close-knit fellowship. Paul's strength, in his weakness, was made perfect, or brought to a peak of efficiency, by the power of Christ resting upon him (II Cor. 12:9). Heb. 2:10 tells us that Christ, as the Captain of our salvation, was made "perfect through sufferings." "Being made perfect" (5:9), He became the Author of salvation. This does not mean that suffering causes moral excellence but that in His suffering Jesus identified himself in the last respect with mankind.

A passage or two further in Hebrews shows the perfection of the new covenant over the old one. The yearly sacrifice could make no hopeful "comers" perfect (10:1); but by "the offering of the body of Jesus Christ" (10:10), God hath perfected once for all them that are being sanctified (10:14). "Perfected" is in the perfect tense or is an action completed in the past and continuing uninterrupted into the present; "for ever" (KJV), or perpetually, continuously; and "sanctified," being a present participle, actually make the phrase read, "Jesus' offering of himself, once [in contrast to the oft-repeated, ineffectual animal sacrifice], is always effective in bringing to perfection those who are being sanctified."

I John 2:5 says that the perfecting or maturing of the love of God within us is tested by our keeping God's word. (See also I John 4:12.) *Teleiótes*, used twice, lends aid in our quest for specific meanings. Paul, in Col. 3:14, among other practical instructions to believers, says, "And above all these things put on charity [love], which is the bond of perfectness." The verb "put on" is added as an extension of the main verb of the passage. The nature of this perfection is accurately defined by the cohesion at its heart, namely, love. And again, the interpersonal fellowship of believers as the body of Christ is emphasized and love is made to be the important ingredient of "perfectness."

"Leaving the [first] principles of . . . Christ, let us go on unto perfection" (Heb. 6:1). A wide reference to the context shows that the writer was pressing upon his readers the absolute need for the completing of that which had been begun in them by grace. The goal is perfection; the path to it, a plodding, faithful, determined, continuous "pressing on." *The Amplified Bible* has it, "Advancing steadily toward the completeness and perfection that belongs to spiritual maturity." The Hebrews were in danger of returning to the externalities of the Jewish religion. They needed to advance in the spiritual life which the Christian faith represents and to which it calls.

In this case, "press on" is not aorist, but subjunctive present, indicating, not one momentary step, but a "forward movement toward" the goal, conditioned by their own application to the task. Not to press on is so serious that apostasy is the result, and the obligation to press on is urgent. Fruit, says the writer, is expected by the one who planted and tilled the ground (6:7), and failure at this point precipitates the destruction by burning, which is the normal end for useless plants. Spiritual maturity, responsibility, service, "better things . . . that accompany salvation" (6:9), are some of the elements of the goal. This exhortation to press on to perfection or maturity, and warning against the danger of loss of God's redeeming grace, is one of the most solemn admonitions against spiritual complacency to be found in Scripture.

OBSERVATIONS RELATIVE TO PERFECTION

1. *Perfection is teleological.* The initial statement that evangelical perfection is very different from philosophical perfection is borne out. Never is perfection absolute in an abstract sense but always relative to an end appropriate to any particular case, that is, in respect of a particular standard. But it is equally true to say that the end as a goal is in harmony with the nature and possibility of that which is to be brought to perfection. Perfection is something that *ought to be the case*, in any particular situation, *and can become so* under grace. That which, in man, is to be considered under the term perfection was endowed with the capacity for perfection and must proceed to that goal if one is not to repudiate the grace given to this end. This simply means that evangelical perfection is not only consistent with the human probationary status, but is essential to it in that it marks out the goal of probation. Delbert Rose, in his analytical study of a recent holiness leader, Joseph H. Smith, had this to say of and by this thoughtful teacher.

> He labored to make clear his understanding of what was, and what was not, the *nature* of Christian holiness or Christian perfection promised in Scripture. . . . "It is a *perfect acceptance of and adaption to the probation that is involved in the imperfections of our lot. . . . It is 'strengthening with might by His Spirit in the inner man'* so that one may spiritually triumph over

all earthly or bodily handicaps." It is a perfection limited to *"that which Christianity contemplates for man while on earth and in the body."*[5]

It would be as proper to say that a Christian is obligated to come to perfection with the resources he has at hand as to say that a child is obligated to become an adult. Both obligations are inherent in life. This perfection is a dimension other than that of temporal duration. It is depth, relative to one's spiritual capacity at any one time. Whenever a Christian minister or teacher speaks of perfection, he will do well to make this matter clear, lest he be justifiably accused of illogicality by the question, "How can perfection be relative?" Wesley's words are wise:

> Walk in all the good works whereunto ye are created in Christ Jesus. And, "leaving the principles of the doctrine of Christ, and not laying again the foundation of repentance from dead works, and of faith toward God", go on to perfection. Yea, and when ye have attained a measure of perfect love, when God has circumcised your hearts, and enabled you to love him with all your heart and with all your soul, think not of resting there. That is impossible. You cannot stand still; you must either rise or fall; rise higher or fall lower. Therefore the voice of God to the Children of Israel, to the children of God, is "Go forward". "Forgetting the things that are behind, and reaching forward unto those that are before, press on to the mark, for the prize of your high calling of God in Christ Jesus" (*Works,* VII, 202).

2. Perfection, in the Bible, is an absolute requirement, in the sense that Christian status implicates one in the quest for it. It is to this end that redemption leads. The word is often at the end of Paul's pen. It cannot be ignored in any serious biblical emphasis on the Christian life. The goal of any serious enterprise is perfection. Goals are not adjusted to the failures of those who try to play the games or achieve some excellence.

3. Perfection has two aspects. As H. Orton Wiley points out in *The Epistle to the Hebrews,* (pp. 203 ff.), it has a legal as well as spiritual meaning. Spiritually, it has to do with maturing in experience. This is the quest. But spiritual maturity is not limited to mere programs. It has its legal aspects also. There is a point within the growing process where one becomes a legal adult with all the rights and responsibilities of citizenship. Christian perfec-

tion is the entering into a covenant with God, that is, the attainment of majority or spiritual adulthood. Wiley quotes Andrew
Murray from his *Holiest of All:*

> The full grown, mature perfect man, does not as in nature
> come with years, but consists in the whole-heartedness with which
> the believer yields himself to be all for God. It is the perfect
> heart that makes the perfect man . . . There is indeed a riper
> maturity and mellowness which comes with the experience of
> years. But even a young Christian can be of the perfect . . . with
> a heart all athirst for the deeper and more spiritual truth it is to
> teach, and a will that has finally broken with sin.[6]

4. This points up the more explicit observation that there is
an absolute and a relative meaning to evangelical perfection. This
means that the *quality* of integrity is capable of unalloyed sincerity of which the depth and the expression in life are *relative to
capacity. Absolutely,* it refers to a heart relationship to God which
is wholly satisfactory; that is, it has attained the condition which
is required of integrity relatively. It is an absolute moral quality
which must laboriously and faithfully be adapted to living situations. It is guarded from the destructive inroads of pride, complacency, and perfectionism by the living demand that the implications of this heart attitude be worked out in the daily grind
of life—both toward God and toward others. A perfect seed that
does not germinate and grow loses its claim to seedhood.

> What is then the perfection of which man is capable while
> he dwells in a corruptible body? It is the complying with that
> kind command, "My son, give me thy heart." It is the "loving
> the Lord his God with all his heart, and with all his soul, and
> with all his mind." This is the sum of Christian perfection: It is
> all comprised in that one word, Love. The first branch of it is
> the love of God. And as he that loves God loves his brother also,
> it is inseparably connected with the second: "Thou shalt love
> thy neighbour as thyself:" Thou shalt love every man as thy
> own soul, as Christ loved us. "On these two commandments
> hang all the Law and the Prophets:" These contain the whole
> of Christian perfection (*Works*, VI, 413).

5. Dr. Wiley, in the above-mentioned work, says that "Christian perfection does not supersede the need for atonement. . . . The
atoning blood sustains a state of cleanness in the soul of him who
walks in the light."[7] Further, Christian perfection does not pre-

clude further growth and is not to be interpreted as any particular degree of maturity. Wesley writes:

> There is no perfection of degrees, as it is termed; none which does not admit of a continual increase. So that how much soever any man has attained, or in how high a degree soever he is perfect, he hath still need to "grow in grace" and daily to advance in the knowledge and love of God his Saviour (*Works*, VI, 5-6).

6. This leads to the further observation that, according to the content of meaning supplied in the biblical passages, no abnormal, absurd, impossible, or dehumanized thing is ever indicated by perfection in Scripture. To be perfect does not mean stagnation, distorted physical appetite, unwholesome psychology, or any of the fantastic aberrations imagined by some careless critics of the Christian faith. A claim of sinless perfection, freedom from sickness and economic need, or a direct and infallible access to God either by way of supposed direct leadings or an amoral ignoring of means (such as the Church and the Scriptures) is not to be equated or associated with biblical perfection. Wesley has a word here:

> Is it not reasonable, then, that, as we have opportunity, we should do good unto all men; not only friends, but enemies; not only to the deserving, but likewise to the evil and unthankful? Is it not right that all our life should be one continued labour of love? . . .
>
> Well, this is the sum of our preaching, and of our lives, our enemies themselves being the judges. If therefore you allow, that it is reasonable to love God, to love mankind, and to do good to all men, you cannot but allow that religion which we preach and live to be agreeable to the highest reason (*Works*, VIII, 9).

7. Evangelical perfection has no meaning scripturally apart from an understanding of its "this-life" relevance. No exegesis can find textual warrant for deferring the biblical teaching of perfection to another life. Its terms, or the norms which determine it, have to do with the powers, relationships, and provisions of grace encountered in "this present world."

Wesley's position on this matter is so central to his whole message that any page of it evidences his "this-life" religion. This does not in the slightest degree indicate a lack of perspective relative to the next life. But it was precisely that Christianity tended in his day to disregard the implications of Christian living now that urged him on to delineate holiness as love—practical, real, here and now. "Many think of being happy with God in heaven," he says, "but being happy in God on earth never entered into their thoughts" (Works, VII, 267).

8. Perfection, as has been emphasized, has a moral connotation, hence no relation to a life which is exempt from the human in all its ramifications, weakness, ignorance, defective judgment, temptations, disciplines. It is meaningful, then, in relation to our communications with persons—both God and man—here. It is precisely in these relationships involving all the human powers and drives to which we are heir that perfection has meaning.

> In what sense, then, are Christians perfect? . . . It should be premised, that there are several stages in Christian life, as in natural;—some of the children of God being but new-born babes; others having attained to more maturity. And accordingly St. John, in his First Epistle, (ii. 12, etc.,) applies himself severally to those he terms little children, those he styles young men, and those whom he entitles fathers. "I write unto you, little children," said the Apostle, "because your sins are forgiven you:" Because thus far you have attained,—being "justified freely," you "have peace with God through Jesus Christ." "I write unto you, young men, because ye have overcome the wicked one;" or, (as he afterwards addeth,) "because ye are strong, and the word of God abideth in you."
> Ye have quenched the fiery darts of the wicked one, the doubts and fears wherewith he disturbed your first peace; and the witness of God, that your sins are forgiven, now abideth in your heart. "I write unto you, fathers, because ye have known Him that is from the beginning." Ye have known both the Father, and the Son, and the Spirit of Christ, in your inmost soul. Ye are "perfect men," being grown up to "the measure of the stature of the fulness of Christ."
> It is of these chiefly I speak in the latter part of this discourse: For these only are perfect Christians. But even babes in Christ are in such a sense perfect, or born of God, (an expression taken also in divers senses,) as, First, not to commit sin. If any doubt of this privilege of the sons of God, the question is not to be decided by abstract reasonings, which may be drawn out into an endless length, and leave the point just as it was before. Neither is it to be determined by the experience of this or that particular person. Many may suppose they do not commit sin, when they do; but this proves nothing either way (Works, VI, 6).

9. It is necessary to notice *explicitly* the clear distinction all these observations make—which is made *implicitly* in Scripture—between biblical perfection and perfectionism. For lack of careful scholarship and in some cases because of the absence of sheer honesty, those who take the biblical command relative to perfection seriously have been classed together with those who are perfectionists—a very different position. It fact, it is a position *contradictory at every point* to the biblical view of perfection.

10. The most important single characteristic of the biblical meaning of perfection is its positive nature. Perfection is not, principally, the absence of all that is less than perfect, but the presence of love with all the dynamic meaning of love. Biblical perfection does not isolate from the normal and intricate fellowship of human beings; it can only be "perfected" *in* them. In every case, the biblical content of perfection is defined in terms of communication and communion. Nothing destroys "perfection" any more quickly and decisively than a rupture of fellowship with God and/or man. But in this extremely human context, all the exquisite variety and possibility of growth and deepening within the individual and corporate fellowship becomes consistent with evangelical perfection.

> In the year 1764, upon a review of the whole subject, I wrote down the sum of what I had observed in the following short propositions:—
>
> "(1) There is such a thing as perfection; for it is again and again mentioned in Scripture.
>
> "(2) It is not so early as justification; for justified persons are to 'go on unto perfection.' (Heb. vi, 1.)
>
> "(3) It is not so late as death; for St. Paul speaks of living men that were perfect. (Phillip. iii. 15.)
>
> "(4) It is not absolute. Absolute perfection belongs not to man, nor to angels, but to God alone.
>
> "(5) It does not make a man infallible: None is infallible, while he remains in the body.
>
> "(6) Is it sinless? It is not worth while to contend for a term. It is 'salvation from sin.'
>
> "(7) It is 'perfect love.' (I John iv. 18.) This is the essence of it; its properties, or inseparable fruits, are, rejoicing evermore, praying without ceasing, and in everything giving thanks. (I Thess. v. 16, etc.)
>
> "(8) It is improvable. It is so far from lying in an indivisible point, from being incapable of increase, that one perfected in love may grow in grace far swifter than he did before.

"(9) It is amissible, capable of being lost; of which we have numerous instances. But we were not thoroughly convinced of this, till five or six years ago.

"(10) It is constantly both preceded and followed by a gradual work" (*Works*, XI, 441-42).

○   ○   ○   ○   ○

Q. Is love the fulfilling of this law [the law of Christ]?

A. Unquestionably it is. The whole law under which we now are, is fulfilled by love. (Rom. xiii. 9, 10) Faith working or animated by love is all that God now requires of man. He has substituted (not sincerity, but) love, in the room of angelic perfection.

Q. How is "love the end of the commandment?" (I Tim. i. 5).

A. It is the end of every commandment of God. It is the point aimed at by the whole and every part of the Christian institution. The foundation is faith, purifying the heart; the end love, preserving a good conscience.

Q. What love is this?

A. The loving the Lord our God with all our heart, soul, and strength; and the loving our neighbour, every man, as ourselves, as our own souls (*Ibid.*, pp. 415-16).

11. In noting the biblical use of the term perfection, and in dipping into Wesley's multiplicity of references to it, we could be justified in concluding that it is not quite accurate to equate the fullness of sanctification with Christian perfection. At least to do so raises the kind of question which could be resolved equally well in one of two opposite and inaccurate ways.

a. The definiteness of the "second crisis" could draw both sanctification and Christian perfection into an unchangeable state in which process would have no relevance or defense.

b. Or the process of perfection could rob sanctification of its crisis decisiveness.

Wesley would not surrender either the dynamic of perfection or the decisiveness of full sanctification. B. T. Roberts, an influential holiness writer in the nineteenth century, in studying this matter suggested, in *Holiness Teachings,* that the dynamic perfection as spoken of in the New Testament and Christian perfection as a theological term should be carefully distinguished. He said:

We never read in the Bible of any being made perfect by faith. We read of persons being "justified by faith" (Romans 5:1;

9:30; Gal. 3:24), of being "sanctified by faith" (Acts 15:9; 26:18), but never once of a person being made perfect by faith, quite another element enters into the making of the saints perfect. . . . The perfection which the gospel enjoins upon the saints can only be attained by fidelity in doing and patience in suffering all the will of God. A symmetrical, well-balanced, unanswering Christian character is not obtained all at once. We must not confound the perfection which the gospel requires with perfect love or entire sanctification. The scriptures do not use these terms as synonymous.[8]

To sum up, careful reading and interpretation of the New Testament will reveal a superb balance between the perfection of love which speaks of quality and may properly be related to full sanctification and the perfecting process which begins in the youngest Christian and continues, or should, to the end of life. To confuse these leads to unnecessary and serious problems.

Perfection is integrity at any point along the line of maturation. It is the process of ripening of Christian character. It begins in the genesis of Christian life and continues so long as integrity is essential to love.

CHAPTER XV

Sanctification--
the Substance

Christian Perfection does not imply (as some men seem to have imagined) an exemption either from ignorance, or mistake, or infirmities, or temptations. Indeed, it is only another term for holiness. They are two names for the same thing. Thus, every one that is holy is, in the Scripture sense, perfect. Yet we may observe, that neither in this respect is there any absolute perfection on earth. There is no perfection of degrees, as it is termed; none which does not admit of a continual increase. So that how much any man has attained, or in how high a degree soever he is perfect, he hath still need to "grow in grace," and daily to advance in the knowledge and love of God his Saviour (*Works*, VI, 5-6).

This quotation may well serve to link the chapter on sanctification into the chain of subjects under discussion. Sanctification in its religious sense bears so much relation to all the kindred terms that it is hard, if not impossible, to avoid slipping from one to the other, as Wesley did in the above passage. Wesley preferred other terms and it is like trying to escape the pull of gravity to abstract any theological or religious term from the central core of his thought—*love to God and to man*. When he discussed the subject of holiness he carefully distinguished between what he called the *substance* and the *circumstance* of the truth. Substance referred to the content of truth; circumstance, the means to that end. Substance must be biblical, circumstance related to the human appropriation of grace (which could not command the same authority as the substance).

To Wesley, sanctification in its definition did not unite equally these two aspects. One was God's Word; the other was "the way it happened to Methodists." When Wesley's followers virtually equate sanctification with some ordered methodology of human appropriation, they depart sharply from their mentor. We believe it is in the interest of clarity and scholarship to seek a sounder Wesleyan emphasis. It is true that Wesley used "sanctification" and "holiness" often, but only as *one term among many*. He was not "term-bound." He was far too conservative to feel free to coin terms simply to be different or flamboyant. But there was so much life in the transforming power of LOVE, and it radiated in so many glorious colors in so many areas of human existence, that no one term could possibly encompass all of it. Nor could it be pinned down in so much language. He adapted terms appropriate to each situation, as vibrant Christians have always done. This divine life infused a kaleidoscopic variety of new and creative wonder in lives otherwise drab and defeated. It simply demanded a flexible terminology then, as it always has.

REDUCTIONISM IN TERMINOLOGY

Perhaps something of the problem encountered in the use of the words under consideration should precede the Wesleyan and biblical studies to follow.

1. In the course of the years since Wesley, one pair of terms, "holiness" and "sanctification," has gone through a strange metamorphosis. It has changed from its rich connotation, in Scripture, and in Wesley, to a very limited meaning, and made to bear the full responsibility for most of the biblical and existential meaning

304 / *A Theology of Love*

of full salvation. In some circles, to fail to use "sanctification" in conversation, preaching, and witnessing in favor of other Wesleyan and biblical words is considered a compromise. In my own youth, it was our "cross," bearing merit, to testify with this word, whether understood or not. When all the rich nuances of a full, Spirit-filled life must be funneled through one or two words, it is inevitable that, first, the communication of life is strained, and, finally, the life itself weakened. The wonder of LOVE is severely limited by a poverty-stricken vocabulary. Words do have a bearing on meaning. Drop the colorful, poetical ways of expressing the inexpressible and communication suffers, to say the least.

2. Perhaps the more serious reductionism is to limit even that one pair of terms to one aspect of the total, biblical meaning, namely, to a second work of grace. It would be well to note Wesley's earlier experience in this respect. He and his preachers were identifying the second experience by "sanctification" in *distinction* from justification. Their hearers reminded them that all Christian believers were, in the New Testament, called saints, or sanctified. Wesley granted that this was true and so he and his preachers simply decided to add the term "entire" to distinguish between the two aspects of sanctification in the Christian life (*Works*, XI, 388, referring to a preachers' conference dated June 16, 1747). The term was not derived from the New Testament, but chosen for expedient reasons.

3. The most serious effect of this progressive narrowing of concept is that the anemic, "abstract" connotation of the once vibrant, dramatic, dynamic word reacted back onto itself and became the sole meaning of every occasion of the word in Scripture. There are those who hold that no scripture which does not use the word "sanctification" or "holiness" is considered to be a holiness passage. And worse, the voice of the Word is by this silenced.

4. The final step in the abstracting process is to lift sanctification completely away from justification, in *fact* as well as in thought, so that the great debate becomes, Who *is* a Christian—the sanctified only (meaning one who has received a second work of grace), or could one who is "justified only" be saved? All traces of the essential personal relationship so integral to the meaning of the

word is now gone and only the methodological husks remain to haunt and taunt the hungry man.

"Sanctification" cannot stand alone in theology. It cannot be lifted up out of the complex of theological doctrines to be separated from them. The interlocking relationships of all Christian doctrines are integral to the life and meaning of every other one. To lift faith, love, cleansing, justification, sanctification, crisis, or process *(et al.)* out of the complex is "abstracting" it, and the doctrine is then called abstract. It would be like taking the physical heart out of a man and expecting to find in that heart all that a man is. The heart is not the man, and the man does not survive long without that fantastically intriguing muscle connected to him so vitally. The man *has* a heart; the heart is not the man.

Much misunderstanding has beclouded sanctification in its path through history. We will venture the guess that the peculiar transvaluation which occurs when anything is taken away from its interrelation takes place in theology in connection with this word. Stripped of its natural environment, other supports foreign to its own nature and meaning are sutured on here and there and the original meaning is reversed. When "sanctification" is lifted out of biblical context and attached to other terms also lifted out of context, sometimes the contrived result has somewhat of an artificial look and a less than useful application to life. As an example, it is sometimes linked with certain emotional states, creedal expressions, dress styles, social mores, or personal idiosyncracies. This can happen when the construction of some biblical doctrine is made by collating a number of verses with some word in them which is the object of definition, and, apart from the context, are related in a quasi-logical construct. Almost anything can be "proved" by this method.

When the interrelatedness of justification and sanctification is severed and justification is slipped under sanctification as a sort of poor basement apartment under the luxurious upper-floor living quarters, or it is made to mark the difference between first- and second-class Christians, something essential is lost from the meaning of both of these terms.

May we suggest that in seeking the biblical meaning of the

306 / A Theology of Love

word sanctification we are not yet at the very heart of Wesleyan or biblical truth. The heart of it is, according to Wesley, love to God and man, with all of love's interrelatedness. But we *are* at the heart of the *problem* in the minds of serious men and women who try to impose the artificially limited meaning of the word onto the Bible and who then honestly seek to make life conform to a doctrine which limits Christian experience to the artificial moralism of a word taken out of context and then called scriptural.

The task before us in this chapter is to recapture the biblical meaning and to demonstrate its interrelatedness to the whole of theology and life. *This does not weaken the holiness message.* It rather puts love where it belongs—in the very center of theology and life. We must keep in mind also that which has already been pointed out, that the kind of love spoken of here cannot be divorced from holiness. Love and holiness are not two things which must balance each other with the heavy end really on the holiness side. Love and holiness are not merely related, or concomitant. They are two sides of one thing. The holiness message, then, vitalized by the Word of God, is clothed once more with the power of the Spirit. It is God's Word, not merely the words of men. It is love, fellowship, joy, peace, power, service, discipleship, life, and all the rest of what is involved in the grace of God.

SANCTIFICATION, THE SUBSTANCE

This chapter bears the title "Sanctification—the Substance." This recognizes a Wesleyan distinction between what is *essential theologically* in the use of this word and the circumstance (the next chapter), which refers to the varied human appropriation of God's grace. The "substance" must review Wesley's use of the term and a biblical study of its content.

Wesley's holiness theology is distinctive in one particular point—the moral relevance of sanctification for this life. This conviction colors every aspect of its theology and becomes the ground for its whole gamut of emphasis. This is actually not a departure basically from the mainstream of Christian teaching but a uniting of its various elements into a systematic whole. In Wesleyanism, sanctification is both an imputation and an impartation. It has in it elements of crisis and process. It is both a separation and a uniting, a cleansing and a discipleship. It is objective and subjective.

It is a theology and it is personal experience, theory and life. And yet it is a unit of experience and a unifying experience.

To unite these apparent contradictions into one rational system creates logical problems. While the contradictions are resolved in living situations because life is richer than logic, in the doctrinal expressions and theological dissertations it is inevitable that tension should arise between life and logic. Some people will prefer one approach over the other and apparent differences of theological position will occur.

There are two major reasons for the difference of viewpoint among Wesleyans. One arises out of the very nature of the Wesleyan emphasis. It is primarily a life rather than a formal doctrine, and hence has been and is expressed in the more unscientific and poetic language of religion and devotion. There is an enormous volume of literature written from this approach, and it must always seem to many persons that the more critical and objective approach is impious.

The other reason stems from the fact already noted that there are two distinct movements in Wesleyan doctrine within the total framework of this tradition. These are best expressed as Wesley himself did. In the opening paragraph of an early Beacon Hill Press edition of *A Plain Account of Christian Perfection,* he carefully distinguishes between the "substance" and "circumstance" of his teaching. One affirmation upon which "we are all agreed" is "salvation from all sin, properly so-called, by the love of God and man filling our heart."

> Some say, "This cannot be attained till we have been refined by the fire of purgatory." Others, "Nay, it will be attained as soon as the soul and body part." But others say, "It may be attained before we die: a moment after is too late." Is it so, or not? We all all agreed, *we may be saved from all sin before death; that is, from all sinful tempers and desires.* The substance, then, is settled (italics mine).[1]

The "circumstance" has to do with the way the change takes place. Is it gradual or instantaneous? He said it is "both the one and the other." In preaching, ought both aspects to be stressed? He answered,

> Certainly we should insist on the gradual change; and that earnestly and continuously. Are there not reasons why we should

insist on the instantaneous change? . . . Constant experience
shows the more earnestly they expect this the more swiftly and
steadily does the gradual work of God go on in their souls . . .
whereas just the contrary effects are observed whenever this
expectation ceases. They are saved by hope. . . . destroy this hope
and that salvation stands still, or rather decreases daily, therefore,
whoever would advance the gradual change in believers should
strongly insist on the instantaneous.[2]

The "substance," Wesley felt, was scriptural and he spared
no pains to show why he believed this was so. The "circumstance"
was another matter, and one which received a different sort of
treatment from his hands. Since it had to do with the subjective
appropriation of grace in experience, the only source of information about it was from experience. Concerning it Wesley was never
dogmatic. His appeal was to "constant experience." In fact, Wesley's meticulously kept case studies of hundreds of people whose
religious experience he examined through the years provided him
with a fund of information that gave him both a significant general
pattern and significant variations to the pattern. This enabled him
to give sound counsel to all who needed it. (A study of his letters
confirms this judgment.) He anticipated the methods of modern
scholarship, particularly in the field of psychological research.

Wesley, as a remarkably able "physician," coupled with his
ability as a psychologist, was able to "see through" the complex
of human data to locate the significant fact in any situation. He
antagonized local medical doctors often by pointing out the spe-
cious relationship between symptom and cause considered absolute
by them. He established wholesome theological principles because
he was able to distinguish between the important and the incidental
factors in religious experience as well as to see the difference between doctrine itself and an experience of that which doctrine
teaches.

His conclusion, "It happens this way to Methodists," was not
a theological dogmatism. Wesley never confused these two levels
of truth. Biblical doctrine was one thing; human appropriation of
the grace he preached was another. His deep concern was to relate
the one to the other in deep spiritual reality and inwardness, but
he knew the difference between eternal truth and the almost infinite variation in its reception by people subject to all the com-

plexities and weaknesses and ignorance to which men are heirs.

In the course of time, however, those who have followed Wesley's theology, while agreeing on the central issue, or the "substance," have tended to divide on the point just discussed. Many are Wesleyan in the same way Wesley was, that is, in emphasizing the deep moral obligation of believers to God and pressing toward full commitment to God which perfect love suggests. Others stress the psychological patterning of experience as representing the heart of the doctrine. The former will tend to use more biblical language and avoid stereotyped terms. The latter have standardized some of the psychological expressions and feel that the loss of them constitutes a denial of all that Wesleyan theology stands for. In this reversal, the psychological syndrome takes precedence over the deeply personal relation to Christ which issues in Christlikeness. "Experience" is the pretender to the throne which should be occupied by Christ himself.

WESLEY AND SANCTIFICATION

A brief trip through some of Wesley's works will serve to characterize his position.

> By justification we are saved from the guilt of sin, and restored to the favor of God; by sanctification we are saved from the power and root of sin, and restored to the image of God. All experience, as well as Scripture, show this salvation to be both instantaneous and gradual. It begins the moment we are justified, in the holy, humble, gentle, patient love of God and man. It gradually increases from that moment, as a grain of mustard-seed, which, at first, is the least of all seed, but afterwards puts forth large branches, and becomes a great tree; till, in another instant, the heart is cleansed from all sin, and filled with pure love to God and man. But even that love increases more and more, till we "grow up in all things into Him that is our Head;" till we attain "the measure of the stature of the fulness of Christ" (*Works*, VII, 507).

> When we are born again, then our sanctification, our inward and outward holiness, begins; and thenceforward we are gradually to "grow up in Him who is our Head." This expression of the Apostle admirably illustrates . . . the analogy between natural and spiritual things. A child is born of a woman in a moment, or at least in a very short time: Afterward he gradually and slowly grows, till he attains to the stature of a man. In like manner, a child is born of God in a short time, if not in a moment. But it

is by slow degrees that he afterwards grows up to the measure of the full stature of Christ. The same relation, therefore, which there is between our natural birth and our growth, there is also between our new birth and our sanctification (*Works*, VI, 74-75).

The thrust of Wesley's religion was in the personal relationship established between God and man. Justification is the open door of God's heart receiving sinful men into His fellowship. Faith and repentance and glad obedience were man's response to that invitation from God to him. In evangelical circles the biblical expression "in Christ" describes it theologically. Sanctification is related to this but refers to another phase of Christian experience. Wesley was more than usually careful to distinguish clearly and pointedly between justification and sanctification. This study does not permit more than a passing reference to justification, but to fail to note that such a relationship to sanctification and distinction from it were in Wesley's mind, as well as in Protestant theology, could undercut and distort if not destroy the full significance of sanctification.

Wesley was very conscious of the fact that there was a danger of making such a point of the difference between justification and sanctification that the very deeply spiritual relatedness was lost. Justification, in this way, tends to be downgraded to make room for sanctification. The fact is that an emasculated justification cannot lead to full sanctification at all.

> Q. "Do we ordinarily represent a justified state so great and happy as it is?"
> A. "Perhaps not. A believer, walking in the light, is inexpressibly great and happy."
> Q. "Should we not have a care of depreciating justification, in order to exalt the state of full sanctification?"
> A. "Undoubtedly we should beware of this; for one may insensibly slide into it."
> Q. "How shall we effectually avoid it?"
> A. "When we are going to speak of entire sanctification, let us first describe the blessings of a justified state, as strongly as possible" (*Works*, VIII, 298).

Wesley's concept of justification is a challenge to Calvinist and Arminian alike and "strikes a blow" (as he says so often) at the weaknesses in each. His high concept of justification makes it imperative for any Christian to consider sanctification as important.

Now the Word of God plainly declares, that even those who are justified, who are born again in the lowest sense, "do not continue in sin;" that they cannot "live any longer therein;" (Romans vi, 1, 2;) that they are "planted together in the likeness of the death" of Christ; (verse 5;) that their "old man is crucified with him," the body of sin being destroyed, so that henceforth they do not serve sin; that, being dead with Christ, they are free from sin; (verses 6, 7;) that they are "dead unto sin, and alive unto God;" (verse 11;) that "sin hath no more dominion over them," who are "not under the law, but under grace;" but that these, "being free from sin, are become the servants of righteousness" (verses 14, 18.) (*Works*, VI, 6-7).

Q. 22. Is not the teaching believers to be continually poring upon their inbred sin, the ready way to make them forget that they were purged from their former sins?

A. We find by experience it is; or to make them undervalue and account it a little thing: whereas, indeed, (though there are still greater gifts behind,) this is inexpressibly great and glorious (*Works*, VIII, 298).

Wesley's concept of justification is very high—so high indeed that it may seem to some that he is confusing it with sanctification. BUT THIS IS JUST THE POINT. Wesley insisted that sanctification began in justification,—not only is Christ *for* us, but He is *in* us. This lifts the whole redemption enterprise to a new level of meaning. Something begins in justification that has no ceiling. It ushers the new Christian into a relationship to Christ that entails a way of life. It opens up new depths and new vistas of meaning and new levels of personal relatedness to our Lord. The newest Christian is not a second-class citizen of heaven but a real member of Christ. Justification and sanctification are not two *kinds* of grace, but two *dimensions* of the experience of God's love and grace.

You in Christ and Christ in You

The absolute distinction between those who are "in Christ" and those who are not is the Christian's distinctive characteristic that he is indwelt by the Holy Spirit—sometimes expressed as Christ dwelling in the heart. This is not a distinction between the "believer" and the "sanctified." No such difference is intended in biblical expressions, such as, "You are not in the flesh, you are in the Spirit, *if the Spirit of God really dwells in you. Any one who does not have the Spirit of Christ does not belong to him"* (Rom. 8:9-11, RSV). The test of being in Christ is *Christ in you.* "If the Spirit of him who raised Jesus from the dead dwells in you, he who raised Christ Jesus from the dead will give life to your mortal bodies also through his Spirit which dwells in you" (Rom. 8:11, RSV). (See also Gal. 2:20; Eph. 3:14-19; I John 3:23-24; 4:4, 12-13, 15-16, and many more.)

In this brief survey, and much more so in any extended study, the glorious fact begins to come through that justification is simply the door into a personal fellowship with God through Christ that cannot be "abstracted" in real life from the whole complex of a living relationship with God. Listen to Wesley's explication of this matter, which adds a living dimension to a study of sanctification. Notice his careful distinctions.

> [Justification] is not being made actually just and righteous. This is sanctification; which is, indeed, in some degree, the immediate fruit of different nature. The one implies what God does for us through his Son; the other, what he works in us by his Spirit. So that, although some rare instances may be found, wherein the term *justified* or *justification* is used in so wide a sense as to include *sanctification* also; yet, in general use, they are sufficiently distinguished from each other, both by St. Paul and other inspired writers (*Works,* V, 56).

> Q. 7. "Is every man, as soon as he believes, a new creature, sanctified, pure in heart? Has he then a new heart? Does Christ dwell therein? And is he a temple of the Holy Ghost?"
> A. "All these things may be affirmed of every believer, in a true sense. Let us not therefore contradict those who maintain it. Why should we contend about words?" (*Works,* VIII, 291).

> As soon as his pardon or justification is witnessed to him by the Holy Ghost, he is saved. He loves God and all mankind. He has the mind that was in Christ, and power to walk as he also walked. From that time (unless he make shipwreck of the faith) salvation gradually increases in his soul. For "so is the kingdom of God, as if a man should cast seed into the ground; and it springeth up, first the blade, then the ear, after that the full corn in the ear" (*Works,* VIII, 48).

> (See also Wesley's sermon "The End of Christ's Coming," *Works,* VI, 275.)

> Q. When does inward sanctification begin?
> A. In the moment a man is justified. (Yet sin remains in him, yea, the seed of sin, till he is sanctified throughout). From

that time a believer gradually dies to sin, and grows in grace (*Works*, XI, 387).

I believe it [the new birth] to be an inward thing; a change from inward wickedness to inward goodness; an entire change of our inmost nature from the image of the devil (wherein we were born) to the image of God, a change from the love of the creature to the love of the Creator; from earthly and sensual, to heavenly and holy affections;—in a word, a change from the tempers of the spirit of darkness to those of the angels of God in heaven (*Works*, I, 225).

In "The First Fruits of the Spirit" (*Works*, V, 87-97), Wesley speaks clearly about the radical nature of the Christian life change. (1) They dwell in Christ and Christ in them. (2) They are joined unto the Lord in one Spirit. (3) They are ingrafted into Him. (4) They are united, as members to their Head. (5) In regard to Gal. 5: 16-19, where Paul says, "Walk in the Spirit, and ye shall not fulfill the lusts of the flesh," he immediately adds, "For the flesh lusteth against the Spirit, and the Spirit against the flesh: and these are contrary the one to the other: so that ye . . . [may not] do the things that ye would," Wesley adds,

> So the words are literally translated, not, "So that you *cannot* do the things that ye would;" as if the flesh overcame the Spirit: a translation which hath not only nothing to do with the original text of the Apostle, but likewise makes his whole argument of nothing worth; yea, asserts just the reverse of what he is proving (*Works*, V, 88).

Wesley continues:

> (6) "Those in Christ have crucified the flesh with its affections and lusts". (7) Although the root of bitterness is felt in themselves, they are given the "power from on high to trample it continually under foot." (8) They "walk in the Spirit" in heart and life. (9) They love God and neighbor. (10) The genuine fruits of the Spirit show forth in their lives because "they are filled with the Holy Ghost." (11) Further, those in Christ, *(a)* are not under condemnation for past sins; *(b)* for present sins; *(c)* for inward sin (even though it now remains and they are increasingly conscious of it, but do not yield to it); *(d)* for sins of infirmities; or *(e)* for anything which it is not in their power to help (cf. *Works*, V, 88-93).

These are but samplings of Wesley's thinking, mostly chosen from works that he designated especially as expressing the most essential Christian truths. We have made a point of this in order

1. To indicate the high standard Wesley held of justification.

2. To show the essential and close relationship of justification and sanctification, and both of these to love and Christian perfection.

3. To demonstrate the extreme, almost tedious, care with which he handled easily confused issues.

4. To reveal the positive approach to full sanctification. (Wesley never drove men but always led them. He did not condemn men for "inbred sin" but encouraged them in their inner struggles to trust in God and to move in closer to Him who loved them.)

5. To emphasize the Wesleyan hermeneutic—Love. The appeal of God to man is not fear but love—to be God's servant in the world.

6. To point the way to the framework of thought in which crisis and process have meaning, and ultimately lay the foundation for the meaning of "second blessing."

This summarizes Wesley's understanding of the terms holiness and sanctification. If one is seeking sharp, clear, dogmatic definitions and assertions from Wesley, he may be disappointed. But if he listens well to Wesley, he will hear in him the strong beat of love's dynamic in the words for the Christian life and sense the urgency of God's invitation to personal encounter with Him.

°   °   °

We turn now to a review of the biblical teaching regarding the use of the terms sanctification and holiness. Particular and complete reference is made to the New Testament usage. The examination of every occasion where these terms are found is necessary to the conclusions which are vital to this study. Wesley could never be accused of arbitrarily selecting or rejecting any grouping of scriptures or lifting any of the passages out of the context in order to make a theological point.

Sanctification in the Old Testament

Very briefly, in the Old Testament, sanctification was the means by which certain objects, individuals, and a nation were made holy. Sin had separated men from God. God was holy, separate, shining, unapproachable, fearsome. He stood in awful judgment against men's sins. The estrangement between God and man was complete. Men were alienated from the life of God. But God provided a way to restore mutual fellowship. It took centuries of divine education to build concepts into words which could and would be used to convey the moral meaning of the redemption which was to make communication possible between God and men.

At first, physical separation from the common, accomplished by rigid regulations, was the way things and days and men and a nation became holy. Certain ritual acts permitted men to come into the presence of God and to be accepted by Him. The ritual, however, was never completely separate from moral and ethical considerations.

Under the law, obedience was emphasized. Perfection was defined in terms of physical and ethical behavior. Cleanness consisted in a total separation from forbidden things and total dedication to God and His service. This was sanctification. This is not to say that the moral meaning was missing, for it always lay in the background, but ceremonial observance was the most prominent and important emphasis.

The prophets stressed a proper attitude, which was considered of more importance than acts of ritual without the right spirit. "Obedience," said the prophet Samuel, "is better than sacrifice." Perfection was of motive, intention. Job was "perfect" because his integrity before God remained intact. He dared to trust God in the darkest hour of God's apparent anger at him. A proper fast is not to do without food only, said Isaiah, but to give this food and clothing to the hungry. Sanctification came to include personal obedience and social obligation, which were important ethical considerations.

George A. Turner summarized Old Testament teaching by saying that in essence it was a religious concept, the central idea being separation from the unclean and devotion to God. Holiness was the Godlikeness required of God's people. It was a derived and not a natural virtue. It was conditioned upon obedience, hence could be forfeited. Turner adds, "Holiness is equivalent to godliness; godliness is akin to goodness; man may become like God;

hence, the holiness required of man is essentially godliness or goodness."[3]

NEW TESTAMENT USE OF SANCTIFICATION

A general contextual study will precede a more critical analysis and conclusion. The wide use of the terms indicates the rich content of meaning.

1. *Ceremonial and largely impersonal meanings* are to be found in such passages as Matthew 23, where Jesus speaks of the Temple and altar sanctifying the things in and on them; I Corinthians 7, where marriage is made holy and the children legitimate by the faithfulness of the believing partner; and I Timothy 4, where meats eaten with thanksgiving are made holy.

2. *The central purpose of Jesus' ministry and death was for the sanctification of the Church.* All other elements in redemption are incidental to this in that they are supporting parts of this one thing. For instance, forgiveness is to make sanctification possible and is not to be considered an end in itself. Paul said, in Eph. 5: 25-26 that Christ gave himself for the Church in order to "sanctify and cleanse it with the washing of water by the word." The Greek forms are not fully expressed in the English. However awkward it may sound, the Greek reads something like this: "Christ loved [aorist] the assembly and gave up himself [aorist] for it, in order that he might sanctify it [the subjunctive indicates purpose and possibility], having already [or first] cleansed it by the washing of water by the word [aorist participle]." To whatever particular custom the figure of speech referred, the preparing of the Church as a bride is the general and fundamental idea, and perfect fitness as a bride is the goal. To be without "spot, or wrinkle" parallels "holy and without blemish [blameless]" in the negative-positive relation and shows the moral connotation intended by Paul.

Two major emphases stand out: (1) It was a corporate body, a fellowship, which was Christ's concern. This idea of the unity of the Church is the central idea in the Ephesian letter. (2) It was for the sanctification of this body that Christ gave himself. He looked past the individual to the total body of believers. This does not minimize the importance of the individual but it does show in what context an individual experiences that which Christ died to provide.

In Heb. 13:12 the same idea is expressed as a climax to the whole letter. As the Old Testament yearly Temple offerings were to sanctify the people in prospect of Messiah's coming, so now once for all "Jesus, that he might sanctify the people with his own blood, suffered without the gate." The central purpose of the Cross was to sanctify the *people,* the emphasis being on the whole, not the individual apart from the group. These two passages draw into the meaning of sanctification much more than is often included. In fact the whole scope of redemption benefits belong to the term sanctification either as accompanying features of it or as specific details in the whole.

These passages throw light on Jesus' prayer in John 17. The prayer in general is for the nucleus of believers, and *all others who would believe on Him through their word,* that they might be so fitted together in union with Christ and to each other and together with God that their witness would glorify Christ on earth. Thoroughgoing oneness is the fitness and is reiterated several times in the prayer. Spiritual unity is its characteristic. Effective witnessing is the goal: "that the world may believe." Jesus had no complaint to register in regard to those for whom He prayed. They had not failed or disappointed Him. Rather the opposite was true. His commendation of them was unqualified. It was not to correct anything that was wrong with them that He prayed, *so far as the passage reads,* but it was in respect of the tremendous responsibility which He left with them that He was concerned.

The sanctification of himself, in v. 19, was a personal ratification of the sanctification received by Him of the Father in preparation for His redemptive ministry. "Say ye of him," Jesus asked, "whom *the Father hath sanctified,* and sent into the world, Thou blasphemest?" (John 10:36) In John 17:18, Jesus says, "As thou hast sent me into the world, so have I also sent them into the world"; and this comment, standing between vv. 17 and 19, relates sanctification to the divine commission mentioned. His part of the task is finished. He commissions His disciples to carry out their own part. *The Father who sanctified Him for this task is asked to sanctify them for theirs or to make them His own and set them apart and anoint them for their task.* Jesus rebuked the Jews in one of the most serious passages in the New Testament for saying that He, *sanctified by God,* was a blasphemer. His works should have convinced them. Now, in the seventeenth chapter, the work of convincing the world was laid upon those whom Jesus left. The sacrifice of himself on the Cross was the summation of His prepa- ration in their behalf. Prepared men were to become spiritual engineers for Christ: "The works that I do shall he do also; and greater works than these shall he do" (John 14:12). It is totally impossible to gather from this passage the idea that the world could be convinced of God's love by believers whose only claim to Chris- tian uniqueness is a secret standing in God's sight. It is precisely this claim unaccompanied by concrete evidence of moral fitness that hinders the world's faith. The fellowship into which sanctifica- tion brought them was morally and spiritually structured.

There seems to be no exegetical demand that the meaning of sanctification change from verse to verse, that is, from one meaning in relation to Jesus and another meaning in relation to the disciples. It is precisely the analogy carried from one to the other that gives point to the passage. Rather than imposing a formal meaning on the word and requiring the passage to conform to it, biblical exe- gesis ought to be informed by the meaning and emphasis in the text. There is rich significance to the word here if this approach is allowed. Notice the parallels:

a. That they may be one . . . as we are one (v. 11). This is repeated in vv. 21 and 22.

b. As Thou *art in me, and I in thee. . . .* so they may be in Us (21).

c. They are not of the world . . . as I am not of the world. Twice this is mentioned, vv. 14 and 16.

d. As thou hast sent me into the world . . . I have *sent them into the world* (18).

e. I sanctify myself . . . that they may be sanctified (19).

f. The glory which thou gavest me . . . I have given them (22).

g. I in them . . . and thou in me (23).

h. As thou hast loved me . . . so Thou *hast loved them* (23).

i. Thy love for Me *. . . may be in them, and I in them* (26).

In no case is there a contrast expressed or implied between what they were and what they should be, morally, or between himself and them in respect of moral integrity. In every case the comparison is positive and dynamic.

All of this gives concrete meaning to the word sanctification as Jesus intended it in this passage. That it is more than ceremonial is obvious. They already belonged to a "holy" nation. Nothing could be added to this qualification. They already had separated themselves from the world to God. The prayer was not for their removal from the world but for their being kept from evil in the world. The prayer was not for the disciples alone, but for all who would believe on Christ through their word. And that it was not merely for supra-earthly experience is indicated by the purpose, "that the world might believe."

Some of the meaning of sanctification, then, can be derived from this analysis of this passage.

a. What sanctification meant to Jesus, it is to mean to us.

b. It included a God-ordained commission—God's choice of prepared persons for a specific purpose. God sanctifies. It is objective.

c. It involved, also, a response of personal dedication to God and His will on the part of those who are sanctified. There is a subjective aspect.

d. This dedication is a very strong word—not the cheap, popular meaning which it has acquired. It includes a very real commitment of the self to God so that there is no contrary purpose in the heart. It is moral union. The passage is particularly strong at this point.

e. As Christ was one with God in moral rapport and singleness of love and purpose, so our oneness with Christ, and with each other, constitutes the moral integrity which structures sanctification.

f. As with Christ so with us, sanctification was more than an ordination by God, or the internal felicity of fellowship. It was also an outward expression which must always round out the meaning of love. To exist, love must be expressed in obedience to God. Its essential nature absolutely demands this. Sanctification means life flowing outward, never a mere pool of satisfaction. The Spirit's coming would be like an outward flow of living water, Jesus said (John 7:38).

In fine, the meaning of the word sanctification derives from the *parallel* elements in this chapter, not from any difference between Christ's experience and ours which theology imports from the outside into the interpretation. If it be insisted that "to make pure"—an added theological phrase—be included in the meaning of *sanctification,* here, and that this element be deleted from the meaning in relation to Christ and added in relation to men, it must be said that this idea betrays a concept of purity not supported by the context.

This passage is a definition of purity. Cleansing is given existential and concrete meaning by the text. What purity meant to Christ it must mean to us, namely, a single heart, and that is precisely what sanctification means as a subjective experience. The objective and subjective aspects of sanctification are not two things but one thing looked at from different sides. The ceremonial, prefigured in the Old Testament, was personalized in Christ, in whom we are sanctified. If we are "in Christ," subjective, moral renovation is as necessary as moral rightness is in Christ.

Sanctification is *in truth,* not in falsehood. In the atmosphere of truth every idol is cast down, every area of personality is made to center in Christ. This moral fellowship *is* purity. In this fellowship *is* cleansing from sin. John 17 does not permit by grammar or sense a formal imputation of sanctification as "standing" only. No impersonal, amoral interpretation can do justice to Jesus' intention in His prayer. Moral relevancy is stamped on every phrase. Sanctification is not abstract and impossible but existential and ethically relevant. It is not a striving after purity but a relationship in which purity is experienced. It is a relationship made by Jesus' mediatorial work but contingent on human response (as indicated by the tenses of the Greek verbs).

John 17 parallels the Ephesian passage remarkably. (1) Jesus had in mind a spiritually unified body of believers, (2) that would bring glory to himself. (3) He died to sanctify *them.* All other elements of redemption were included but incidental to this. (4) Sanctification was *in the word* and *truth.* This "word" obviously was not the Scripture primarily, but was found in an intimate fellowship with the living Word, who is himself Truth. (5) The commission was accompanied by a moral fitness—for the unity of spirit indicated in both passages is moral clear through.

In the interest of clarity it is well to note that Jesus, in John 17, did not indicate the manner in which sanctification would take place. He did not equate it with the coming of the Holy Spirit; in fact the Holy Spirit is not mentioned in the prayer. Though theology is inclined to relate them, it is of interest to note that *so far as any specific scripture* is concerned, the Pentecostal experience is not said to be an answer to Jesus' prayer in John 17. John does, however, equate Jesus' breathing on them (20:22) with the coming of the Holy Spirit. In fact never is sanctification, as such, directly identified with the coming of the Spirit on that day. This does not mean that these three things are *not* related, but it does mean that *on the strength of the passages cited* the identification cannot be made. The great overwhelming and overarching truth seems to be that sanctification as presented in John 17 is inclusive of everything Jesus was and did for us, and that a Church perfected for its commissioned task is the purpose. These central truths must be kept sharply in focus, however we may add them to other truths in a systematic theology.

Paul further shows the source of sanctification as being *in Christ,* in the Corinthian letters. The ideals which both Greek and Hebrew vainly tried to achieve were found in Christ—wisdom, righteousness, sanctification, redemption (I Cor. 1:30). This does not suggest that the elements of atonement are only these four things and in that chronological order, but is a summary of the virtues men seek in philosophy and religion and cannot find of themselves and which are provided in and by Christ. In 6:11, Paul contrasts the Corinthian Christians as they were against what they had been in heathendom to show how inexcusable were their divisive spirit and their actions. He reminded them, "But you were washed, you were sanctified, you were justified in the name of the Lord Jesus Christ and in the Spirit of our God" (RSV). All they enjoyed by way of spiritual life they had received from Christ and in Christ. It further complicates the already difficult theological problem in Corinthians, namely, calling them both sanctified and carnal, if one limits the meaning of sanctification here only to a "second work of grace" (I Cor. 1:2 and 3:1-4).

3. *God's pre-creative plan* for man's redemption was in *sanctification of the Spirit* and belief of the truth" in stark contrast to the progress of sin (unrighteousness) because of rejection of truth (II Thess. 2:13). Peter makes use of this same unusual expression (I Pet. 1:2), "Elect . . . [in] *sanctification of the Spirit,* unto obedience and sprinkling of the blood of Jesus." In both cases the reference is to the divine plan of redemption, which was sanctification by the Spirit's ministry on the one hand and the ethical response of the people in obedience and right relationship to truth on the other.

"Sanctification of the Spirit" included and *led to* obedience and "sprinkled blood." It was not, according to this passage, conditioned by them. It is also permissible and probably more correct to translate "the spirit" so as to mean the believer's spirit, since the context supports such an interpretation (W. R. Nicoll, *The Expositor's Greek Testament*). This puts the divine method of salvation, namely, belief in and love of the truth, in absolute contrast to all that stands opposed to truth. Sanctification is here directly related to truth in either case, and *this is the point* and the larger meaning of sanctification. That which includes the whole redemptive process is the proper interpretation of these passages.

4. *All believers are in the New Testament called holy,* or sanctified, or saints, irrespective of spiritual maturity or any other qualification. Examples are found in I Cor. 1:2, II Cor. 1:1 and 13:13; Eph. 1:1; and many others. No reference is ever made to unsanctified believers in distinction from sanctified believers so far as the express statement of Scripture goes. All believers are in some way sanctified. This Wesley taught.

5. *The Gentiles were to be included,* by divine prearrangement, *among the sanctified,* as indicated in Acts 20:32; 26:18; and Rom. 15:16. This is the subject under discussion in each case. The inheritance of the sanctified was universalized to include those outside the Jewish nation. This refers to the promise given to Israel as the holy nation, but make both Israel and its sanctification to be a spiritual matter which other than Jews could share. In all these passages this universalizing of God's redemption of mankind is the central thrust. In two passages Paul's personal, divine commission to the Gentiles is stressed. He delivers the message of God's

mercy and love. One passage speaks of the inheritance among those who are sanctified as a gift of God's grace. Another speaks of this inheritance received by faith in God. The third says that in the Holy Spirit this sanctification takes place. In all of them, being included in God's favor and fellowship and being the recipient of His redemptive grace are central.

This is not something the Gentiles seek, but something they receive. Sanctification is received only by the ministry of the Holy Spirit. Yet a proper attitude on the part of the recipient is necessary to its personal appropriation. None of these particular passages speak specifically of the subjective aspect of sanctification. Sanctification in these particular passages "should be taken in its widest sense as applying to all 'saints' (holy ones) as set apart to God."[4]

6. *Of the two prayers for sanctification* recorded in the New Testament, both were petitions in behalf of others and not for the one who did the praying (John 17:17 ff. and I Thess. 5:23). Both were prayers in behalf of a corporate body. Both asked that *God* sanctify that body of persons and both were prayers for groups which were first highly commended in spiritual matters and unblameable in these spiritual things. In connection with the Thessalonian church, it seems unlikely that the reference to incomplete faith could mean anything other than immaturity.

a. Jesus' prayer in John 17 has already been discussed with the contextual meaning of sanctification indicated.

b. Paul's prayer in I Thess. 5:23 is the passage from which the term "entire sanctification" is drawn and the only passage where even the English language gives any idea of *partial* or *complete* as modifications in degrees of sanctification. The following textual analysis is not a rejection of the theological use of the phrase "entire sanctification" (which is an *idea* deeply grounded in the Scriptures when it is properly understood) but an examination of the passage itself to see what it contributes to the meaning of the word sanctification.

The word "entire" when attributed to sanctification, as holiness theology uses it, has given some trouble. Some have seemed to say that it is sanctification that is completed, giving the idea that the end is reached and all that sanctification means (in its

324 / A Theology of Love

general sense) is accomplished. By implication there is in life no
process aspect at all beyond this. This would controvert the earlier
prayer in the letter (3:12-13) that a continual increase of and
abounding in love was to "stablish your hearts unblameable in
holiness." It is this for which Paul prays as if it were the *establishment* in holiness that the Thessalonians needed.

It would also be difficult to make the finished nature of sanctification accord with the Corinthian exhortation (II Cor. 7:1),
"Cleanse [y]ourselves . . . [continually] perfecting holiness [present
tense]," which, as we have seen, speaks of maturation. It is that the
person changes in relation to holiness rather than that varying degrees or amounts of sanctification are received or bestowed. Sanctification, or holiness, as such does not ever seem to be a matter
which can be described in terms of degrees. Never does one have a
little sanctification, more of it, or all of it. At least this passage
does not seem to permit this kind of interpretation.

I Thess. 5:23 can hardly be understood apart from the fourth
chapter, which is a twofold exhortation. Both follow from the third
chapter, that holiness may be established by increase in love.
First, they were to "abound more and more" in a "walk" that
would "please God." Holiness is not static. Then they were to
"increase more and more" (4:9-10) in love for one another.
But since Paul said he did not need to write about this last matter
because they excelled in it (v. 10) and were taught of God regarding it (v. 9), the elaboration of the "walk" of holiness, to which
point Paul spoke in vv. 3-8, will be of interest to us. It is the biblical
philosophy of holiness.

There are a number of elements in this philosophy mentioned
and implied.

(1) *Holiness has to do with the practical affairs of life.* The
"walk" is the daily quality of behavior. The Thessalonians were
not asked to improve in their understanding of the doctrine.
Their wholehearted acceptance of *that* is mentioned several
times. However, there *were* some points in their *lives* that needed
attention.

(2) *Holiness and moral uncleanness were antithetical.* In
fact, moral cleanness is defined by holiness, and uncleanness is
absence of moral integrity, or holiness. Coming out of Greek cul-

ture, some Thessalonian Christians carried into the Christian religion the idea that either physical sins were necessary to a full life and therefore not sin, or that the body did not and could not partake of spiritual sanctity. The conclusion of such reasoning was that physical sins were no hindrance to grace. This Gnostic (or pre-Gnostic) heresy was the bane of the early Christian leaders. Holiness as a bestowal of grace was not necessary to prevent sex sins according to this passage (or any passage) but these sins were shown to be absolutely antagonistic to the Christian walk. They had to be put away by any and all Christians. A consistent Christian life included in it the participation of the whole man. Greek dualism was rejected.

(3) *Holiness is God's will.* To it men are called. The gospel call is not merely to forgiveness but to holiness. The Holy Spirit is given to Christians to make holiness a possibility. To refuse to walk consistently is to despise God, who has given us the Holy Spirit. There is no acceptable alternative to God's call to holiness. Uncleanness is moral revolt against God. Now Paul is both adamant at this point and patient at the same time. Some of them *were* sanctified but ignorant and engaging in uncleanness. Paul was giving instruction at this point and, for him, to *know* the truth was to constitute them absolutely liable for further sin. He could excuse ignorance but not rejection. To reject him, he said, was to reject God with all the serious consequences. The call, in this letter, is not abstract, but to practical consistency in holiness—namely, cleanness. And cleanness means bringing every power of the body into harmony with God's will and purpose for men.

Now when we come to I Thess. 5:23, in which Paul prays again, something of this background of understanding is needful. The prayer is twofold. One petition asks for sanctification, the other for preservation in moral integrity. He prays that every one of them will be sanctified and that the whole personality of everyone will be held inviolate in this sacred relation.

7. *There is a human obligation to this relationship.* We are to sanctify in our "hearts . . . Christ as Lord" (I Pet. 3:15, RSV). This emphasizes the demand that a Christian not only become a

believer but that he very consciously make Christ Lord indeed. The *Saviour* must become *Lord* to him, and that is possible only when He is made to be by conscious ratification of Christ's lordship. Effective service, "good works," are possible only as one "purges himself" from the unworthy and entangling things which Paul itemizes in II Timothy 2. As in the analogy of honorable vessels in a great house, he will be set apart as an honorable vessel, "sanctified, and meet for the master's use." In this figure of speech, "master" is contrasted to the kitchen help or any of the menial slaves. It is for God's special use that we are to devote ourselves in contrast to any other devotion. Only one who has purged himself, that is, eliminated all other loyalties, is qualified to be sanctified, or (as with Jesus) commissioned for God's service. In this case, again, the ceremonial figure becomes useful to us as we see the spiritual significance emerge and the deep moral relevance stand out.

The Corinthians (II Cor. 7:1) were exhorted to "perfect," or bring to maturity, "holiness in the fear of God" by cleansing themselves "from all filthiness of the flesh and spirit." In the light of the promises itemized in I Corinthians 6, cleansing (aorist) the self was the moral minimum required in the lives of believers to bring to completion (present tense, continuing action) "holiness in the fear of God." The Thessalonians were pressed to abound more and more in love in order that the Lord would establish their hearts "unblameable in holiness" (I Thess. 3:12-13). In Romans 6, Paul indicates that a self yielded to God in obedience leads to righteousness and has fruit unto holiness. In no sense is holiness achieved by personal striving but by a continuing attitude of reckoning oneself dead to sin and alive to God and by the settled attitude of yielding to God by a life of obedience from the heart. The fruit of this is holiness and everlasting life.

8. *Holiness is a quality of life—the teleology, or purpose, of holiness.* Something of a *further definition of holiness* is given in Eph. 1:4, where Paul gives us the *pattern of God's purpose* for the creation of men, to be "holy and without blame before him [God] in love." The abstract austerity of "holy" is personalized in the blamelessness of love. These modify each other. The philosophical abstraction which often clouds the evangelical meaning

is dissolved in the words "before him." This takes all definition and judgment out of our hands and puts it in God's hands. "Blameless" is an existential word, too. "Faultless" would be the language of perfectionism, but "blameless" is a moral word and thoroughly Christian. This is no impossible and supra-historical standard. It has relevance *only* for this life of probation. *Blameless,* when joined with *love,* is not a certain code of conduct or quantitative excellence; it is a spirit, a *quality* of devotion that is "perfect" at every stage of its development. Holiness and love proceed together. Holiness is deepened by love. Love is the very essence of holiness. Neither is static or simply positional but as obligated to expand as the personality in which it inheres.

That the Church should be holy and blameless (Eph. 5:27) is Christ's redemptive purpose. The same words are given in Col. 1:22, "to present you holy and blameless . . . before him" (RSV). It is to be "preserved blameless" that Paul prays for the Thessalonians (I Thess. 5:23). This is an oft-repeated thought in Scripture. Peter in his first letter (1:15-16), in the midst of various and sundry exhortations to proper Christian conduct, cries, "But as he who called you is holy, be holy yourselves in all your conduct" (RSV). This is not an abstract, mystical idea of holiness. Peter is not given to speculation. It is a contrast to their former evil life. Obedience and Christian sobriety must characterize their conduct in keeping with their faith and hope. It is a mistake to theologize "holy," in Peter's discussion, apart from the very specific area of human experience which qualifies the meaning. The context makes *love* the test of holiness.

This has been a study of the words against the context with no attempt to analyze the words more critically. However, a study of words themselves would confirm the judgments made.

An interesting fact begins to come clear as these words are studied in the immediate context, namely, that they do not raise any questions relative to the numbers of works of grace, "levels" of grace, temporal succession of "blessings," relative measure of permissible sin in any stage of the way, classification of Christian status by examination of psychological reactions, or any other like matter. The moral, personal, practical obligation to God crowds all these peripheral concerns into the background. *The moral imperative stands out clearly at every point.*

The whole sweep of biblical teaching relative to sanctification centers in one major concern—man's practical relationships to God and his fellowmen. Sanctification presupposes God's initiative in salvation and His provision for it. Nothing man could possibly do of himself could commend him to God. Sanctification has to do with every aspect of man's responsibility to God in the light of God's initiative, provision, and invitation. Sanctification is God's answer to abstraction and antinomianism in regard to salvation. In the fullest sense, it circumscribes the whole measure of human responsibility. It is the one word that has in it everything for which a man is responsible to God, to himself, and to others. Religion is not a compartmentalized thing, theoretical and abstract. It invades all of life and confronts every moment of responsibility.

The word sanctification, then, is richer in meaning than any limited theological term permits. It is not an academic word, or philosophical in the sense of being abstract and "schoolish." It is intensely practical and religious. *Basically it means separation from sin to total devotedness to God. Its atmosphere is love. Its life is service or an expression of love.*

Note the complex usages in the New Testament. Sanctification sometimes is the epitome of the whole plan of salvation; sometimes it is a part of it. It is for the Church as a corporate body: Christ died to sanctify the Church. Sometimes sanctification is considered the only end of redemption—a holy people. Sometimes it is the method of making them morally fit. It is often one facet in the method, but when thus itemized, there is no uniformity of classification. It is sometimes a status which is conferred; it is sometimes a life to be developed and perfected. Men never *achieve* sanctification. It is always given by God but must be appropriated by men and lived out painstakingly. It takes moral integrity to maintain it—"Cleanse yourselves," and a growth and deepening of love for progress *in* it. It is objective and subjective. It is a status and a life. It is a given and a process. It is the antithesis of sin and yet it fits the human frame with all its fallibility and imperfection.

By a careful analysis of the use of this one word against its context we are made aware that few if any of the rational problems which have been mentioned are raised by the biblical use of "sanctification." In every case, except where it has obviously a non-theological meaning (such as a holy marriage), the original word is given a specific moral meaning—a meaning which makes a difference to one's practical life. It is, in other words, a spiritual relationship. It goes *inward* and presses against the conscience and requires a moral response. The exhortations in relation to the use of sanctification have to do with the moral obligations one sustains to God. Never are the exhortations impersonal, that is, in relation to a psychological experience as such or a formal theological belief. They are personal to the core. The obligations one sustains to God in sanctification are moral obligations and hence require decisive and inclusive moral response.

In general, then, sanctification is a right relationship between persons, that is, between God and man. Within the relationship are significant events on God's side and on man's side which initiate and preserve the relationship. It relates God's provision of salvation to man's human personality. It is the whole process by which the abstract and theoretical is made actual and vital. In particular, sanctification includes every step taken toward God and His will on our part and the approval and inner renewal on God's part. Sanctification is needed to safeguard against antinomianism, which inevitably arises where human responsibility is discounted or where grace is in any way restricted to *God's* act only. It is needed also to maintain the structure of moral integrity in God's world. Salvation is not a different way of looking at sin on God's part, but a different attitude toward sin on the part of men. Moral distinctions are retained and strengthened rather than weakened. Sanctification is not only a present possession but a quest, and these two things must be kept related, distinguished, and in perfect balance.

OBSERVATIONS REGARDING SANCTIFICATION

1. Sanctification is the one word that by contrast most adequately explains the "awfulness" of the death of Christ. Only in it can a proper perspective be maintained concerning God's redemptive purpose. It cannot be merely said that Christ died to provide forgiveness for sin or for our justification only. Nothing less than our sanctification is sufficient to comprehend the mystery of the death of Christ on the Cross. "Jesus . . . suffered without the gate" "that he might sanctify the people with his own blood."

"Christ . . . loved the church, and gave himself for it; that he might sanctify and cleanse it." To misunderstand sanctification or to consider it lightly or unbiblically is to set ourselves adrift from the central affirmation of the Christian faith. Justification does not exhaust the meaning of the atonement.

2. Jesus' interest in our sanctification is further evidenced by the words given us in John 17 as He prayed. It is not trite to say that in this prayer the most urgent and profound insights to Jesus' purpose are revealed. It is sacred ground. The whole purpose of Jesus' sacrifice is that the world might believe on Him, but more— that the world might believe that God loved it. Back of every phrase of that prayer shines through the ultimate purpose— bringing God and man together into cleansing fellowship. The world's confidence in us (inspired by our unity with each other) must lead to Christ's love, which in turn terminates in God. There is theology enough here to stagger the mind. Here is the progress of thought. Jesus was to sanctify himself in order that the disciples might be sanctified, so that the resulting oneness with God and man would convince the world of God's love in Christ. The majesty and scope of this purpose plunge us into the deepest humility and require of us the most profound obedience. There is no room in the face of John 17 for a shallow, trivial view of the Christian life or for any excuse for less than God's full possession of and mastery of our lives. Individuals are brought into sanctification, but sanctification is not individualism or aristocratic isolationism. Sanctification is never a virtue which may be worn like a halo or garment of distinction. It never terminates in oneself. Sanctification is a fellowship in which the individual conscience becomes acutely aware of its responsibility to glorify Christ, the One in whose fellowship sanctification is.

3. The third observation follows from these two. There is a twofold dimension to sanctification. (1) It is related to God and the provision of grace which He extends to us via the atonement. It seems clearly to represent the reversal of the situation in which men find themselves because of sin. It is, in Christ, all that the Old Testament sacrifices typified by way of atonement for sin. It is God's restoration of His presence and fellowship with man. (2) But in sanctification there is also, of moral necessity, a require-

ment that fellowship be moral—that the oneness be real, not fictional. In redemption God offers all men salvation, but all must be appropriated by the fullest measure of moral response on the part of man. The deeply personal nature of sanctification signifies the deeply spiritual nature of the relationship. Fellowship is impossible apart from a self-giving on the part of each person. This giving cannot be forced; it must be freely and gladly offered. God's gift cannot be received until men submit to the terms of fellowship. All the benefits of grace are appropriated *by faith* in God and appropriated only so far as faith appropriates.

4. There is nothing about the relationship to God to which sanctification refers that is earned, worked for, or achieved by our actions. It would appear to be more true to say that the steps to it include a clearing away of moral hindrances; and the steps within it, a progressive carrying out of the implications of it in all of life's relationships. Sanctification itself seems to be a relationship to God open to us into which we are received when God takes us into His family. *It is not properly a state but a living, vital relationship to God.* The crisis and process refer to our own side of this covenant. It is a crisis in life when we make our commitment and are accepted of God. Within this sacred fellowship we develop and grow according to the laws of spiritual life. The full, personal commitment to Christ, crucifixion with Christ, and the Holy Spirit's indwelling are by their very nature climactic and abrupt. It may take time to align our central self to God's will, but when it is done a crisis, not necessarily a clock-time point, has properly occurred. It is a crucial and formative act and has repercussions in all of life. But it is not sanctification which is again, or in a deeper way, experienced. It is rather ourselves conforming to the moral obligations native to the divine fellowship.

5. If we are properly observing the implications of sanctification, an even more specific statement ought to be made. In all of God's dealings with us, in all of His requirements of us, He acts in the interest of moral integrity. In other words, we must respond to the new moral environment as Christians. There is no neutral "no-man's-land" in moral experience. We are not free not to be committed, for commitment is the necessary act of moral persons. To stand in the sanctified relationship to God, as the New Testament uses the word "holy," is to stand obligated to actively commit

ourselves to Christ as *our* Lord. Christ *is* Lord, constituted so by God independent of our acknowledgment of the fact. We do not make Him Lord; we enter the Kingdom where He is Lord. This basically is the "law of the land." There is no Christian alternative to a personal ratification of this lordship, and this lordship means that we capitulate to it in deed and truth. It seems proper to interpret Rom. 12:1-2 in this light. This commitment is *reasonable*. And *reasonable* meant to Paul, not simply an acceptable idea, but the conclusion to which all right thinking drives one. Another way to say it would be that in the Christian community Christ is Lord, and since we are persons and not automatons, our active, personal acceptance of this fact is called for. To fail to do so is in some real sense a defiance of that lordship. This lordship is not dependent on our acceptance; it is a fact which must motivate our relationship to Christ or exlude us from the Kingdom.

Paul's exhortation in Rom. 12:1-2, to the effect that "the brethren" present their bodies as living sacrifices to God, is not then an added "upper story" to justification, nor a Christian alternative to higher or lower levels of grace, nor a luxury enjoyed by the excessively devoted and almost fanatical fringe enthusiast. It is, rather, the theological point of his whole argument. *The whole-body presentation is not the maximum Christian attainment but the minimal Christian commitment.* As the Roman letter proceeds, it is seen that all of Christian living, with all its problems and vicissitudes, lies beyond this particular point.

Sanctification begins in justification and proceeds throughout Christian experience. Every stage in the way is related to every other stage. Wesleyanism teaches, because it thinks it is more biblically defensible, that *grace is a unit of divine self-giving.* The Calvinist speaks of two kinds of grace, common and saving grace (or comparable terms). Common grace does not and cannot lead into saving grace. The two are discrete. Wesleyanism sees no evidence of this disjunction in biblical teaching. God's grace leads to repentance and faith and salvation when properly received. *But Wesleyanism tends to forget its basic premise when it distinguishes too sharply between "saving" and "sanctifying" grace as if these were two kinds of grace.* Such a view raises impossible logical problems. It cannot escape the question, When, then, is one saved? Can one be justified and not be saved? Also, if sanctification begins with justification and one is saved in this relationship, how can it be said that it requires another kind of sanctification to *really* save the soul? Actually Paul never permitted himself to fall into this logical trap. Paul did not recognize legitimate levels of grace. He *did* recognize the fact that not all Christians had appropriated the grace available to them, nor had they responded in obedience as Christians should. He knew that deep spiritual antagonisms in the heart threaten Christian status and until the full, deep commitment is made, and kept intact, the danger of desertion is imminent. *There is a continuity of grace* and moral obligation of men in grace which sanctification preserves and does not violate.

6. It is not clear from New Testament study that sanctification is a different *kind* of grace from the other redemptive provisions. We should think that all the benefits of the atonement provided by Christ's blood are appropriated by us according to our psychological abilities rather than that there are any essential limitations of the application to stages of experience on God's part.

Every offer of grace on God's part to man must be met by the fullest possible measure of moral readjustment on man's part. The ultimate meaning of redemption is the restoration of fellowship with God which can consist only in holiness. In fellowship is cleansing, says John, and both depend on walking in the light. The provision of grace in salvation is a unit, not levels of grace. But the appropriation of this grace required of man conforms to the ability he has of making moral commitments. From the first stirring of conviction for sin to the last breath on earth, the moral obligation is operative in human personality. There may be justly two crucial moments identified, not because God has structured salvation that way, but because He has structured man as a moral creature.

The first truly moral act is an acknowledgement of sin and a plea for pardon—a turning of the whole self toward God. The whole of God's grace is available at that moment because God is giving *himself* to ourselves. Nothing is withheld on God's part, but it may fairly be said that the appropriation of grace at that time may be variously experienced by each person. Some are weak, left in the bondage of habits, needing a very great deal of divine help. Others seem to come into a far richer measure of spiritual life. Both must accept the responsibility of probation.

It must always be held possible that the spiritual insight of some individuals is great enough, at that moment, to make the total human commitment which moral experience requires and the second distinctive kind of act performed. Wesley thought so, though he knew no cases to exemplify it. In any case, the deeply personal nature of the total commitment is usually more slowly and painfully realized. In other words, the benefits of grace and our own place in the Kingdom as effective commissioned ambassadors do not automatically follow from justification. Grace and faith are personal matters, and hence intensely moral, and require the fullest measure of response of which we are capable at any one time.

7. The preaching approach to this grace must be in keeping with the New Testament approach. The central truth seems to lie in the need for a deep moral adjustment to God which brings into integration the whole man. The New Testament does not distinguish legitimate levels of spiritual living. Only one way is right and that is walking in the light. We are not left in comfort "in Christ" or "in the Spirit" but only in *walking* in the Spirit, with all the deep adjustments involved in maintaining this "walk."

There will be no question in anyone's mind as to the "state of grace" in which he may be if this goal is pressed home. There will be no break in fellowship over counting "blessings"; there will be no unbiblical barriers raised about methodology when the full measure of responsibility to God and to ourselves is presented. The hidden stronghold of self-righteousness needs to be uncovered in the most theologically fortified person. To press "sanctification" as such on men is too often too abstract. It may obscure the concrete moral issue which the New Testament always lifts high.

To speak of states of grace and particularly of sanctification as a state of grace in which one relies, distinguishable from justification, is not biblical. It seems wisest not to use the term except under some special condition. The danger is that one comes to limit sanctification to a possession and to forget that it is also a quest. What was done in a moment needs continuing dependence on God's mercy. Wesley used this term with care lest a static view of sanctification be implied. Regarding it he said, "We are every hour and moment pleasing or displeasing to God, *according to our works*, according to the whole of our present inward tempers and outward behavior" (*Works*, VIII, 338). John Fletcher spoke warmly to the point. He said,

> Mr. Wesley has many persons in his societies who profess they were justified or sanctified in a moment; but instead of trusting in the living God, so trust to what was done in that moment, as to give over "taking up their cross daily, and watching unto prayer with all perseverance". The consequences are deplorable.[5]

"Perhaps you object to the word 'every moment,'" he said of Wesley's statement, but "if it be not *every moment*, it is *never*."

In another context he said,

> He [Wesley] to keep his followers from antinomianism directs them not to talk of a justified or sanctified state so unguardedly as some, even Arminians do; which tends to mislead men, and relax their watchful attention to their internal and external works, that is, to the whole of their inward tempers and outward behavior.[6]

A later holiness teacher, preacher, and writer, whose interpretation of Wesleyanism was widely accepted, spoke to this point:

> We are not preaching a *state*, but a *walk*. The highway of holiness is not a *place*, but a *way*. Sanctification is not a thing to be picked up at a certain stage of our experience, and forever after possessed, but it is a life to be lived day by day, and hour by hour.[7]

A modern-day holiness writer, in analyzing Wesley's position, thinks that the word eradication when used in this connection is weak because it permits a view of holiness as "a state instead of a quest." He said, "The emphasis on spiritual crisis and victories often made religion a state of grace rather than a quality of graciousness."[8]

In the New Testament, then, the distinction between crisis and process and the balance between them is properly held so that the logical problems arising from an improper relatedness are never raised. Preaching must never violate this fine balance.

8. This leaves the problem of time. When ought one to come into this cleansing fellowship with God? Rather remarkably, this

336 / A Theology of Love

matter is not directly handled in the New Testament, except by implication. It is significant that this question is not raised nor answered. The significance is understood when the absolutely moral nature of the requirement is recalled. In the New Testament no comfort is ever provided for any conformity to God's will less than the ultimate at any moment. There is no place to hide behind anything such as method, time sequence, levels of grace, etc. There is no trace of a double standard for Christians—or for *any* kind of person for that matter. No less is permitted a young Christian by way of moral responsibility than the mature and more perfect Christian. He does not have the same ability or insight or understanding, but he *must* use all he has. It is not maturity that brings the fellowship, but responsibile decision. Time is not the question. Moral rectitude does not know anything about time. Decision is always now.

CHAPTER XVI

Sanctification-- the Circumstance

Every line of investigation has led to the point now under consideration. The *substance* of doctrine meeting the crucible of life must adjust its abstractions to the flowing dynamic of life. Wesleyan theology asserts: (1) that sanctification is a "this-life" experience, (2) that it is a relationship to God logically distinct from and morally of quite a different dimension than "justification," (3) that it follows regeneration, (4) that it is crisis-oriented as well as life-oriented, and (5) that in a proper sense it can be called a "second crisis."

Doctrine in life may look like a straight rod in a container of water—bent and wavering in the restless liquid and changing perspectives. Wesley knew that the logical simplicity of theology always undergoes an alteration when it meets the complexity of human life. He could not be as dogmatic about the reactions of the human psyche to grace as he was about grace itself. Wesleyanism has been convinced that it is proper in some way to speak of a second crisis in relation to sanctification. Is there a justifiable rationale for this "circumstance" of sanctification? Six elements already discussed will be briefly summarized and related to the attempted answer.

1. *Moral*

The analysis of the word *moral,* a word which structures "holiness," shows that (1) "moral" relates to this life and must do so; (2) moral life proceeds on the basis of crisis/decision points; (3) moral experience is not static but is as vital and dynamic as life itself; (4) moral responsibility is respected and assumed by all steps in redemption, and (5) everything the Holy Spirit is and does undergirds the life and theology of Christian faith.

2. *The Holy Spirit's Ministry*

The Holy Spirit's ministry is made possible by and works in the interest of moral integrity with all that is implied by the moral awareness of persons. By His ministry such terms as faith, cleansing, perfection, and sanctification are related in dynamic spiritual reality. *Faith* is a moral experience and relates grace to life. Biblical truth is couched in the language of moral experience and its appeal is to the conscience in terms of moral responsibility. *Cleansing* refers to the process of bringing the entire man—the whole self— into a unity about the lordship of Christ. *He* is made the actual Center. It is moral integrity with Christ as the integrating factor.

3. *Purity*

It is a single-hearted, unalloyed love for God. *Sin,* on the other hand, is the absence of this integrity, or disintegration because of a morally destructive center of one's love. Sin is antagonism toward God and inordinate love of self. *Perfection* is akin to cleansing in that it is the positive side to which cleansing is the negative. It is the description of life lived out of an integrated heart. It is not finished and static but growth to and in moral maturity. *Sanctification* is the whole complex of redemption procedure structured by decisive steps under the guidance of the Holy Spirit and in His immediate presence.

4. *Psychology*

Human personality, as understood in biblical psychology and verified by personal experience, is moral to the core. It is a unity, not an unresolved dualism of flesh and spirit, and it acts as a single unity. Grace does not destroy that unity but creates it and strengthens it, not to be a self-sufficient, autonomous entity but as a true moral integration which includes God primarily and other persons necessarily. But personality is not static. It grows, relegates, comes into new perspectives, expands, matures, discards, and deepens. Life needs discipline; immaturity needs to come into adulthood; childishness must change to responsibility; ignorance must be overcome, and smallness stretched out into a great heart. Narrowness cannot remain content with itself but must give place to increasing vision and expanding understanding, love, and empathy. Spiritual and cultural provincialism needs the enlarging therapy of love. And the molding effect of a great love and self-interest must expand into a concern for others without losing its own identity and integrity. Only a strong self is capable of the demands of a great love.

5. *Biblical Exhortations*

Biblical teaching emphasizes the moral demands of God on man. The sinner is to repent and believe, and the believer is to obey and cleanse himself, take up his cross, and walk in the Spirit. He must put off the old man, and put on the new man, increase in love, and mature in holiness. He must present himself to God a living sacrifice, and not think more highly of himself than he ought. He is to pray without ceasing, to be transformed by the mind's renewing, and to be renewed in the spirit of his mind. He must put away the lie, and a host of other things too numerous to list here.

6. *Christian Experience*

Not only are the above moral elements to be considered, but practical human experience adds its voice to the questions before us.

Christian experience gives ample evidence of an experience after conversion that, by whatever name it is called—or by no name—has opened the door to a new realm of spiritual vitality.

Inadequacy occasioned by a morbid self-interest and "proneness to wander" has given way to a fresh and vital life because of the conscious presence of the Holy Spirit. Waning spiritual tone has recovered to become a vibrant, undying, and passionate zeal. Duty has turned to the dynamic of love, moral inability to a victory for which no personal willpower could account, and childish vacillation to holy steadfastness. Dragging feet acquire winged heels, and lack-luster eyes begin to glow.

No theological tradition is lacking in testimony to this truth. It is a universally recognized phenomenon in Christian life. Rather than increasing spiritual pride, this new vitality is its antithesis and a Christlike spirit and tenderness and strength prevail. Drab ministries begin to sparkle and an awakening of spiritual interests often results.

When asked to account for the change, the person concerned will almost invariably recall a period of mounting spiritual tension because of failure in the things in life that matter most and often in relation to one's Christian service and witness. He remembers an aroused consciousness of an inner reluctance relative to some service which he knew was, for him, the will of God. Then came a "moment" of deepest personal obedience to God involving a painful blow to pride and selfish independence and a new and inexhaustibly deep self-yielding to God.

Sometimes this experience is associated with a call to the public ministry, sometimes a clarification of the daily responsibilities of common life which are seen to be themselves a ministry; sometimes it is a deliberate choice of the less personally desired of alternative ways of life. Always this spiritual encounter strengthens and confirms faith in God—"the rest of faith." Abstract ideals are translated into action of a specific sort under the impulse and compelling guidance of the Holy Spirit. Always it is a crisis in obedience, not in respect of some external law, but in respect of one's deepest commitment. Very small issues touch the central nerve of the heart, issues which of themselves seem trivial.

The result is not always great outward success, but is usually an end of enervating inner conflict, resulting in the strength of a unified purpose. It is a "clean heart" without the contrary drives that spoil service. It is the beginning of an unspeakable love for God and people that lifts life to a new level. It brings stability, vision, purpose, drive, humility, and a devotion to Christ never before known, even in the milieu of unusually difficult circumstances.

All of these lines converge on one point and present a problem. How can all of this be rationalized without distorting the vitality of it into a rigid formalism or without losing its truth by an inadequate guarding of its basic truths? Five elements at least must be preserved: (1) The personal and moral relationship; (2) the crisis which is implicit in moral; (3) the distinction between the *pre* and *post* kinds of spiritual experience which is the affirmation of testimony; (4) the infinite capacity for change in the human psyche —its fallibility, imperfection, and weakness which must always remain less than a philosophical perfection; and (5) the part played by the Holy Spirit in every moment of the soul's contact with grace.

ANTITHETICAL VIEWS OF SANCTIFICATION

Protestantism has offered two major theories of sanctification, extreme and totally antithetical. One has neglected the essential moral character of redemption. This solution says that either effective deliverance from sin must await death's deliverance of the soul from the body (making death the real savior from sin) or the "body of sin" is gradually replaced during this life by the "new man" of holiness. Evil is pushed out and replaced by good. The person grows into sanctification. Protestantism is embarrassed by the logical problem of locating the time when sanctification thus conceived can be considered complete, since death ends all change and has no power to redeem.

The other extreme position tends also to overlook the important moral dimension of redemption and emphasizes the crisis element of experience almost to the exclusion of any recognition of the fallibility of the human psyche. In a crisis experience it is said that man is liberated from all liability to temptation to evil and that perfect holiness and finished character are instantly bestowed. The first stresses process without moral crisis. The other puts perfection *in* the human person, in the sense that capacity for sin is virtually ended. This view puts an overemphasis on crisis without an adequate rationale for process in spiritual life. Neither one is wholly realistic but tends to oversimplify a most complex and deep-seated problem. Both are varieties of perfectionism.

Wesleyanism attempts to do justice to whatever truth may be in both of the above systems of theological thought, speaking of both crisis and process without overemphasis on either, yet relating both meaningfully. In this mediating position the terms "second" and "crisis" have not always been satisfactorily explained and related to the process element. Such an explanation will now be attempted.

The major cause for problem in this area is that the theological and psychological aspects of holiness have not been distinguished, and consequently families of terms appropriate only to one or the other have been used uncritically and confusedly.

QUALITY VERSUS QUANTITY VALUES

The fundamental distinction between moral and all other elements must be made. *Moral* is not a time-space concept but a quality concept. Terms suitable for use in measuring quantitative values are inadequate for moral values. Moral and spiritual qualities do not have linear dimensions nor do they have the sort of reality that can be measured by the rules of corporeal things. There is no past or future or mathematical sequence in *moral* so far as its essence is concerned. It transcends space and time just as *person* transcends them.

Moral, spiritual, and *person* lie in a different dimension than material things. They have to do with quality and not quantity. If persons were bound absolutely to the time-space matrix, they could not even speak of *moral*, let alone understand it. Only that which is rationally free from absolute determinism can attribute qualitative values to anything. The behavior of planets and stars cannot be judged right or wrong. The automobile and television are neither good nor evil. Only intelligent creatures are subject to qualitative value judgments—and they cannot escape them.

Now this does not mean that *moral* has no relation to the time-space continuum or that its nature cannot be known by persons who are conscious of time and think rationally in seriatim patterns. The truth is they must do so. The relevancy of *moral* consists precisely in its affinity for persons and all the relationships of persons.

It gives meaning to life through persons. It does mean, however, that measurements apropos of "things" are not adequate to measure moral values. Holiness cannot be weighed or counted. In this sense the mathematics of the doctrine of holiness, namely, first and second, causes confusion when not guarded in meaning. Since we think (more or less) logically, it is necessary to structure events by before, now, and after. We enter into moral experience *now*. There was a *before* in regard to it, and there is a future ahead of it. But the counting is in relation to us. It does not describe the character of moral truth, no part of which may be changed or deleted.

Obedience to law, as such, is linear or temporal, chronological, even mathematical. "I have done that, and that. Now I am doing this, and will do the other when the time comes." The rich, young ruler said as much, "All these things [Decalogue] have I kept from my youth up: what lack I yet?" Religious life was for him still in the realm where time-space measurement could tabulate its values. It had never entered the moral dimension, where quality transforms quantity into spiritual values. The basic questions raised by the holiness affirmation of first and second lie in a false understanding of the use of these terms. If *second* stands only in temporal relation to *first* and the seriatim relationship is unduly emphasized, the moral truth is "defused" and powerless.

Moral truth is always relevant because it is always structured by truth. No moral truth is to be accepted now and discarded or replaced by a higher truth later so that one steps from less permanent to more permanent elements and hence into an ultimate perfection after a while which is qualitatively different. This idea has kinship with the early Gnostic stratification of believers into somatic, soulish, and spiritual people. A spiritual aristocracy very easily develops in this view and can issue in a gradual independence from the common means of grace and even of Scripture when this philosophy is permitted to take root in the life of the Christian. Some look for so-called "higher truths" beyond the Bible and find emancipation from the common "herd" in emotional states— mysticism, or "experiences" beyond all the confines of the physical into pseudo-mental sciences masquerading as religion.

What we are trying to say is that all the demands of moral life are always *true* everywhere because they deal with truth. Even the first feeble steps in the moral realm are permanent matters and must be well taken because they will bear all the weight of whatever spiritual growth develops. No truth appropriate for past crisis can be discarded for subsequent truth. No first moral steps are ever outdated. This means that all the Bible is always relevant to all people in any situation. We do not live through one moral stage and then graduate to another stage, considering past stages as finally having no more application for us in favor of other and higher (or deeper) truths. The principles of moral integrity structure *all* "stages" of human development in grace.

Significantly, the Bible never mechanizes truth. We are not able to stratify religious experience by mathematical designations, at least on the authority of biblical exegesis. No first work of grace is retired in favor of a second. This does not mean that the appropriation of the benefits of the atonement has no psychological structuring or that biblical writers are unaware of this need; but it does mean that the Bible does not permit us to miss the central, moral issue, which could be lost in an undue emphasis on methodology. This is precisely the difference between letter and spirit, a distinction which does not let us discard the "first" from the "second" but puts them in permanent moral relation.

In other words, Romans 7 is not *superseded* by Romans 8, nor is sanctification superior to justification, nor is repentance relegated by faith, or faith outdated by the witness of the Spirit. John 3:16 is not exclusively for sinners, to be discarded as irrelevant by the mature, sanctified Christian. The "believing" which initiates the beginning of eternal life (a *quality* of life, not its length) in Christ must continue as a settled life attitude. The truth of "whatsoever a man soweth, that shall he also reap" is not limited to sinners but remains a truth for the holiest person on earth.

Nor does this mean that the "concurrent theory" of Romans 7 and 8 as interpreted by some is true. This is the theory that the conflict in 7 and the peace in 8 is always true for all Christians at the same time and in the same way, that the warfare between human flesh and God's Spirit is normative for all Christians. Sin, according to this view, is inherent in flesh and therefore must always offer a protest to the ministry of the Spirit, and the fact of conflict is the assurance of Christian status. But what does seem to be true is that the self-righteousness described in Romans 7 is always condemnable wherever it is found, no matter how many "experiences" one may have gone through, and that righteousness is always by a vital faith in Christ and walking in the Spirit as in Romans 8. The seventh chapter stands as a guard and warning to those who have shared in the victory of chapter 8.

In other words, a passive and complacent attitude does not seem to square with biblical teaching. One does not come up out of Romans 7 and into 8 so that the door can be closed and the matter forgotten, *except as one continues to walk* in the Spirit, in the "newness" of the Spirit of life in Christ Jesus. The truth of Romans 7 reaches into Romans 8 and serves to warn against lethargy and carelessness and in this warning structures, negatively, moral experience. Sanctified people have not outgrown the need for the penetrating spiritual truth of Romans 7. It is needful "devotional" reading for all Christians everywhere.

What does all this have to do with holiness theology and its two works of grace? Basically, it means that true moral experience is not exhausted by or completed in the experience of the grace of justification. Sanctification is not simply a mathematical addition that is needed but the rounding out of what constitutes true spiritual life. There are three continuing elements in moral experience:

1. *Repentance*

Repentance must be a settled life attitude toward sin, not a momentary emotional upheaval. In repentance we take God's point of view on sin—our sin. This isn't just past sin, but sin always, everywhere. Hatred of sin is to be a permanent element of our Christian lives. We do not graduate from this. *The whole weight of moral life rests on this.* When and if this is relaxed, the whole personal moral structure collapses from within. No work of grace subsequent in time can have meaning apart from the integrity of a repentant attitude that never ends. This increases moral sensitivity and humility and awareness of one's moment-by-moment reliance on Christ, our Saviour.

2. *Faith*

Faith is also a permanent life attitude. Repentance is negative; faith is positive. Faith is a new direction of love and is as stable as the repentance that guards against a wrong center of affection.

These two elements of moral life are not simply the first steps in a series. They are foundation stones which support everything one builds into life. In fact this repentance-faith complex is the atmosphere in which all other elements of grace are unfolded. These are the elements essential to moral integrity always, everywhere in time and possibly in eternity. To call their inception a first work of grace is a concession to logic and human experience and must not be pressed beyond the immediate semantic need.

3. *Responsibility*

But repentance and faith are not all there is to moral experience. There is immediately involved *responsibility as persons.* The New Testament never teaches a time lapse between believing and obedience. This does not mean that in the absence of a recognition of this temporal sequence the two movements of moral experience are confused or thought to be automatically included one in the other. It is precisely this that is *not* the case. Justification involves the individual in responsibility. Faith is not quite faith until it is also obedience. The forensic has an existential dimension which is the personalizing of any abstract element in redemption. Sanctification is this personal dimension and it, of necessity, begins in justification. In it is the moral power which is implicit in the new life in Christ. Jesus did not die to justify us, and then die to sanctify us. When He came to "save us from our sins" and "to sanctify the people," these were not different things He died to procure but two aspects of the same thing. Justification opened the door to the moral rectitude which sanctification means. Forgiveness is actually incidental to the real purpose of redemption, namely, the sanctification of the Church, and its mission in the world.

Sanctification, then, is begun in repentance and believing, but is given moral meaning and brought into moral experience by the deeply personal commitment of the justified person to God. All the potential of sanctification lies in the justified relationship.

Why Two Moments?

There is a profound significance in the structuring of the Christian life into more than one "moment." The *definite* number, rather than the indefinite "many blessings," is also highly significant in the Wesleyan way of thinking. It must be granted that the number—two—is not directly derived from Scripture. But this is the point: The meaning of "second" is not in the mathematical sequence of blessings. What is called "second" points to a different *kind* of step in the process of redemption, a "depth" relationship for want of a better term. Perhaps God could have devised another way to recover men from the bondage of sin. That He did not testifies to the fact that God is interested in engaging the whole man in responsible interaction with himself. What man *must* do in his response to grace, and to enter into the deeply personal relationship into which God invites him, God will *not* do—yea, *cannot* do and at the same time maintain man in responsible moral integrity. What God *requires* is a startling commentary on what man *is* by God's grace.

"Two" simply points up the moral/spiritual dimension of grace. Salvation is not merely one act of God "for us," releasing us from any further obligation. Nor is it, on the other hand, a building up of merit on our part by adding to our fund of virtuous acts. Salvation takes place in the rendezvous of God and man in which all of man's responsible nature is brought to bear upon the task of total orientation to God's person and His will. Forgiveness is the launch into a new orbit. The second "moment" is a crucial, midpoint correction which "locks" the compass to the Morning Star. This analogy cannot be carried much farther, but it may indicate the fundamental relatedness of the "stages in the way."

"One" and "two" simply as a mathematical sequence misses the biblical emphasis of salvation. When viewed as two related kinds of human response in moral experience—privilege and responsibility—the errors of regarding grace non-historically, that is, non-relatedly to actual human experience, are avoided. One/two is a guide to the kinds of personal adjustment to God which Scripture teaches and the human psyche experiences and understands. In these two kinds of response to God lie all the crisis moments, major and minor, and the processes in grace which characterize responsible Christian experience.

ENTIRE SANCTIFICATION AND "THE CIRCUMSTANCE"

Now the term "entire sanctification" can have proper moral meaning in this context, provided it is understood. The question,

"What is it that is entire?" must be carefully answered. It is not sanctification that is entire if by that is meant that all the implications of sanctification are fully realized and completed. To speak in this manner is to miss the point of what sanctification is (see Chapter XV).

If sanctification is basically purity of heart, and purity of heart is single-hearted love for God, or an undivided heart, we speak of a dynamic relationship—not a static, impersonal state. The substance of the soul is capable of neither holiness nor unholiness, but the person is holy or otherwise in respect of his moral relationship to God. If he loves God with his whole being, he is holy; if he does not, he is unholy. This love with the whole heart is not a quantity measure or a perfect expression of love but the quality or wholeness of love.

"Entire" in relation to sanctification is mentioned only once in the Bible (I Thess. 5:23). But here it is not sanctification that is qualified but that to which sanctification refers, namely, the Thessalonian church. The entire person needs to be drawn into the orbit of this kind of moral response to God. Paul clearly says, in I Thessalonians 4, that no physical immorality is consistent with holiness, that one cannot be holy or devoted to God in single-hearted love so long as he has failed to bring his whole person—spirit, soul, and body—into the holy moral union of himself and God. This is just another way of saying that holiness is for *this* life with all of its relationships and that he who refuses to bring himself wholly into the orb of grace despises and rejects the Holy Spirit, who cannot tolerate duplicity.

In a very real sense, this marshalling of the whole man into the realm of grace is a thoroughly moral act. It is deliberate, voluntary, decisive, often difficult. No responsible Christian is satisfied until it is done. He will certainly need divine guidance as to how to do it. But it cannot be truly said to be higher truth than the conversion experience, simply a more inclusive one—a wholly inclusive one, anticipated in conversion.

In relation to the designations "first and second," the truth seems to be that the significance of two experiences is not a quantitative value or addition. It is not a higher level which gives the lower level an inferior status.

It cannot be simply an emotional or psychological state which is passed through. The second is not a correction of the first nor a completion of a partially realized work of grace. It is most certainly not a stratification of the spiritually elite, elevating them from the common crowd—a sort of "heavenly 400." The question, "How do you know which of the many religious experiences is second?" is not idle or facetious. It is a morally relevant question. It requires a norm of judgment which is rational and "testable." It is properly criticizable. *One* and *two* are parallel and interpenetrating moral experiences in relation to a human response to God. They are usually separated in time but by their basic nature are not necessarily so. They are really two halves of a sphere or two elements in a substance (such as H2O). Together they constitute true moral experience which is impossible without both. *Second* is implicit in *first* and completed by it. The Bible does not know anything about a place between *first* and *second* which can be considered "normal." It speaks only about the danger to the person of failing to put into life the commitments which saving faith made to grace. Privilege and responsibility are two sides of the same coin. Justification and sanctification are parallel truths, both very personal, each describing an aspect of the relationship of God and man but separable only theologically, not in life.

That there is a time lapse between the two elements simply testifies to the moral weakness and psychological makeup of mankind. That moral experience is a this-world possibility is everywhere assumed in Scripture. The human heart may be and must be integrated in this life. Spiritual schizophrenia is healed by the ministry of the Holy Spirit bringing fulfillment and wholeness to the broken person. It is this moral integration that is holiness or perfection in love. It is a quality, not quantity, and the whole of life's unfolding must be prayerfully and patiently and painfully and humbly and deliberately and joyfully worked out in this moral atmosphere.

It must be recalled that moral integrity is not merely self-realization as such but the self integrated with God, and in this way a realization of one's true self. This is a restoration of the sanctifying fellowship of the Holy Spirit. No one sanctifies himself but is *sanctified by the Holy Spirit,* who in this moral atmosphere is enabled to lead men into the heights and depths and lengths and breadths of the love of God which growth in grace implies.

The emphasis on the second crisis experience, then, is not on the temporal succession implied by *one* and *two*. It is not on the limitation of life's religious experiences to two. It is not any crisis as a terminal point. It is not an experience as an emotional or psychological state. It does not leave the answer to the question as to whether one has had one or two crisis experiences to irrational or nonmoral tests. There must always be an objective and practical test of the validity of experience. This test is inherent in moral experience itself.

The Wesleyan emphasis on experience is one of its distinctives and must be understood in this discussion relative to crisis points in religious experience. In the most general way it means that God's grace operates in the living fabric of men's lives. We are not simply saved "on the books," but also, "in our hearts," and not only in the "heart," but in the whole of life to which "heart" refers.

EXPERIENCE

At the risk of being repetitious, the terms *experience* and *crisis* need to be fitted into the subject under discussion.

When the Wesleyan speaks of *experience*, there are those who assume that he is grounding religious authority in personal experience or that he means to limit his religious faith to some psychological state, some feeling, or some specific moments in time. To the critic this is intolerable because it appears wholly subjective and undependable and negates the objective aspects of the grace of God. This criticism misses the real point of the intent of Wesleyan theology. Wesleyanism always presupposes the priority and objectivity of Christ's atonement. It is a theology of grace but grace as a personal, moral quality in God, not merely causal and amoral. God's grace does not compel; it enables. And enablement places the locus of redemption squarely in the center of all man is.

By *experience* the Wesleyan means that the *whole man* is caught up in the involvement of saving faith. The atonement not only does something for man but also makes demands on his entire responsible nature. It is an inner transformation by the "renewing of the mind." The Scriptures force this concept of life involvement upon us. Eternal life is contingent upon the continued activity of believing. Faith is never simply an intellectual act only but a revolution of inner commitments which changes the whole life pattern.

Christian status is contingent upon obedience from the heart. In a word, the biblical call is not that one *initiate* acts of faith, love, and obedience in respect of God—or that these things be added to personality apart from human will—but that the direction of life's whole love and motivation already active in the wrong direction be reversed from serving and loving self to serving and loving God. The very act of becoming Christian involves men to the core of their beings. The same faculties and capacities once engaged in serving sin are now engaged in serving God. This is *experience* in the Wesleyan sense and, we believe in the biblical sense also.

CRISIS AND SECOND CRISIS

Experience raises the problem of two other theological terms: *crisis* experience and *second crisis,* both of which are important to Wesleyan theology. *Experience,* as defined above, would seem to limit Christian life to growth or process. Precisely to avoid this very limitation, the Wesleyan stresses *crisis,* which puts the decisiveness into life necessary to moral quality. Men do not *grow into* Christian status, nor is the progress *in* Christian grace realized apart from points of moral decision.

The second crisis already discussed comes more clearly into the picture here. Although it is not a biblical term, *second* is used to emphasize a point in Christian life particularly stressed in Scripture where the entire personality is united in total love to God, where the divided heart is made one under the lordship of Christ and double motives are cleansed. *Cleansing* (the means) and *purity* (the end) find definition here. This point of moral integration is reached under the prodding and guidance of the Holy Spirit. No man can know himself as he is apart from the ministry of the Holy Spirit. The Spirit uncovers hidden areas of self-will and pride and duplicity. He drives the Christian to the place of moral decision regarding himself and Christ. Although all Christians "have" the Holy Spirit, there is a unique and proper sense in which one may be said to be "filled" with the Spirit only when the total commitment has been reached. In statements like this, any corporeal concept of the self or Spirit must be resolutely avoided. These are personal relationships only—not personality "invasions."

First and *second* crisis are far more than numerical distinctions. In no sense is *first* limited in order to make room for *second*. Properly, *first* is the entrance of the person into the whole provision of the grace of God. Provisionally everything God can do *for us* is done. Nothing is reserved arbitrarily. But a response is required of men and in this human response *second* has definition. The beginning of it must occur in relation to forgiveness because every interaction with God is a *moral* event. The least requirement of God for man at any one point in redemption is the highest possible measure of obedience of which he is capable. But *second* has unique significance at the point where human commitment is so intelligently complete that the Holy Spirit is not thwarted at any conscious level. The abiding Holy Spirit maintains cleansing (or the unified heart) so long as one walks in the light of His moral demands.

In order to clarify this discussion, one more word needs to be said regarding *crisis*. As has been previously stated, *crisis* is a moral word, not a "clock time" word. This means that it is not the time value of the word in experience that is of ultimate importance but the changed direction in life which is stressed. Both John Wesley and John Fletcher, as well as subsequent holiness writers, recognized that "spiritual anniversaries" or definite psychological time points in experience were often unstressed or completely missing or at least quite indefinite in certain persons. Certainly no experiential pattern can be imposed on everyone in regard to this. Though it is desirable to have such an "anniversary," the more important matter and the one giving the only real assurance is the changed direction of life which is itself crisis and the consequence of crisis.

Summary

What then is "entire"? It is the entire man in moral decision and spiritual oneness with God. Sanctification is not subject to the descriptive terms *initial* or *entire*. These qualifications are human ways to distinguish man's spiritual progress and they are legitimate expressions only when so understood.

What is the "second experience"? It is the completion or authenticating of moral experience—privilege met by responsible commitment to Christ. It is not something that terminates anything but it is what makes continuing possible. It is not the goal, the ceiling, but the beginning of life. The emphasis on *second* is not on an arbitrary number, but means that nothing less than what it represents is acceptable in a moral context.

What is freedom from sin? It is moral union with God. It is the fellowship which cancels out the essence of sin which is alienation from God. It is not "some*thing*" but a moment-by-moment trusting in the merits of Christ met by a continuing *walk* of faith.

What is perfection? It is loving God with the *whole heart* regardless of the relative level of ability or capacity of the person at any one time. Perfection has a dynamic element when related thus to love. It must continue and grow or it ceases to be. Its very nature is growth and maturation.

Is Christian perfection a state? Not in any nonpersonal or merely legal sense. It is personal relationship which must be nourished and deepened. This leads into the final question.

What is process? It is a *life* of love to God. It must presuppose all that has been said to this point. Sanctification is the life of holiness beginning in the new birth and never ending. Within it are the crucial crisis moments which moral experience demands. Holiness is not static. It is not a goal but a highway. It is not the end of problems but the beginning of them. It is not the termination of probation but the atmosphere in which probation has meaning.

Dr. Ralph Earle, in a guest editorial in the August 6, 1958, issue of the *Herald of Holiness* says:

> Too many who have "crossed over Jordan" and enjoyed a rapid conquest of Jericho—their previous "besetting sin"—have failed to follow through in the occupation of Canaan. The first flush of victory has given way to defeat.
>
> The fault lies partly in the way holiness is too often presented. The impression is given that if one consecrates himself completely to Christ all his problems are settled forever. People are prone to treat entire sanctification as a goal, rather than as a *very significant milestone on one's way to heaven* [italics mine].
>
> The truth is that holiness must be a lifelong quest as well as a present possession. . . . If we would pursue holiness of heart and life as persistently and perseveringly as a hound dog pursues a fox, we would never lose out [referring to Heb. 12:14]. . . . The use of the present tense in Heb. 6:1 suggests that there is to be a constant and increasing sanctifying of our lives which should go on until death.

This process of sanctification was taught by Wesley. "Our perfection," he says, "is not like that of a tree, which flourishes by the sap derived from its own root, but . . . like that of a branch which, united to the vine, bears fruit; but severed from it, is dried up and withered" (*Works*, XI, 380).

Wesley said again that it is only by the power of Christ resting every moment upon us that "we are enabled to continue in Spiritual life, and without which, not withstanding all our present holiness, we should be devils the next moment" (*Standard Sermons*, II, 393).

To Mrs. Pawson, Wesley wrote from London, November 16, 1789, regarding Christian perfection:

> You do well strongly to insist that those who do already enjoy it cannot possibly stand still. Unless they continue to watch and pray and *aspire after higher degrees of holiness* [italics mine]. I cannot conceive not only how they can go forward but how they can keep what they have already received (*Letters*, VIII, 184).

We have already quoted Thomas Cook to this effect. We do not teach a *state of purity*, he said, but a *maintained condition* of *purity*—a moment-by-moment salvation. "The blood of Jesus Christ cleanseth us from all sin, *all the time*, by cleansing us every *Now*."

If holiness is wholehearted love to God, it *must* be morally structured and as dynamic as life and as relevant to our changing personalities as the constantly renewed blood in our physical bloodstream. Holiness is wholesome life in God.

What's in a Name?

The need to give a name to things and feelings and beliefs and all those matters about which accurate communication is important is no less important in religious experience and theology. The problem in regard to moral realities which corporeal realities do not share is that tendency to transfer the real from the experience to the word symbol which points to it. This process has been called "holiness scholasticism."

This kind of rigidity of expression is particularly to be deplored in a spiritual and dynamic interpretation of a biblical faith. By using vital terms to define, and thereby limit, theological concepts and then attempting to force life back into these narrow categories is little less than tragic.

Wesley apparently met the same problem and left us some instruction at this point. When asked about the use of the word *sanctification,* he said that "the term *sanctified* is continually applied by St. Paul to all that were justified. That by this term alone, he rarely, if ever, means 'saved from all sin.'"[1]

Following Wesley, the preferable term among holiness theologians for the critical experience which is of most concern to them is perfect love or Christian perfection. Wesley was aware of the danger even in these terms of thinking of *perfect* in a philosophical way, so he stressed the wholeness of one's love for God—the undivided heart—as describing what he meant. The other terms used by holiness theologians must be understood in the light of this preference. J. A. Wood, in his book *Perfect Love; or Plain Things for Those Who Need Them Concerning the Doctrine, Experience, Profession and Practice of Christian Perfection,* said, "Sanctified souls are inclined to name the blessing after their principle [sic] *sensations* [italics his], harmonizing with their emotional experience."[2] Some of these terms he gives with the reasons for each: the rest of faith, resting in God, the fullness of God, holiness, perfect love, the baptism of the Holy Ghost, entire sanctification, and Christian perfection.

Daniel Steele, who was a spokesman for the American holiness movement, said this in regard to terminology:

> Wesley studied a great variety of terms and phrases expressive of this experience, a good example for all its teachers. I have counted up twenty-six, but "the baptism of (or with) the Spirit," and "the fulness of the Spirit," are phrases not used by him, probably because there is an emotional fullness of a temporary nature, not going down to the very roots of the moral nature. Nor did he use "receiving the Holy Spirit," because in a sense of entire sanctification the phrase is not Scriptural and not quite proper; for they all received the Holy Ghost when they were justified.[3]

Probably the reason it is so difficult to pinpoint Wesley's "second experience" in his writings is that he so studiously avoided all stereotyped expressions.

Actually, love to God out of the whole heart, mind, soul, and strength and love to one's neighbor as to oneself are the key to understanding the Wesleyan or holiness position. This definition must always take precedence in any discussion. To the objection

356 / A Theology of Love

that such love is impossible, Wesley answered in *Plain Account*, and in the answer helps us to understand his terminology.

> Q. What is Christian Perfection?
> A. The loving God with all our heart, mind, soul and strength. This implies that no wrong temper, none contrary to love, remains in the soul; and that all the thoughts, words and actions are governed by pure love. . . .
> Q. Can any mistake flow from pure love?
> A. I answer, 1. Many mistakes may consist with pure love. 2. Some may accidentally flow from it. I mean love itself may incline us to mistake. . . .
> Q. How then shall we avoid setting Christian Perfection too high or too low?
> A. By keeping to the Bible and setting it just as high as the Scripture does. It is nothing higher and nothing lower than this . . . love governing the heart and life, running through all our tempers, words and actions. . . .
> Christian perfection is purity of intention, dedicating all the life to God. It is giving God all our hearts, it is one desire and design ruling all our tempers. It is devoting, not a part, but all of our soul, body, and substance to God.[4]

Hannah Whitall Smith avoided with studied deliberateness the formal theological terms. She preferred "the life hid with Christ in God." Upham called it "the interior life"; and A. B. Earle, the Baptist evangelist, "the rest of faith." "The deeper life" is a common term today, and many find "full salvation" more expressive of what they mean.

George Allen Turner well says:

> Much opposition comes from the lack of a satisfactory nomenclature. There is no phrase or term, Biblical or otherwise that expresses the whole doctrine, without partiality or ambiguity. Wesley's own central emphasis on love to God and man has never been improved upon. Even Perfect Love is but a partial expression of its content since it ignores the category of holiness. . . . The basic danger in the Wesleyan pattern is not a fundamental error within itself but is that danger inherent in any pattern—that of substituting the letter for the spirit. . . . Inevitably the forms which the new spirit assumed again became stereotyped and dogmatic.[5]

Daniel Steele, in his book *Half Hours with St. Paul*, defends his thesis that we ought to testify to this grace but in the careful, modest, various, and judicious ways which Jesus and Paul demonstrated. The book then is systematized according to a wide and rich variety of Pauline expressions.

A decision regarding the use of terms must be made in the light of the foregoing evidence and, more particularly, in the light of the biblical meaning of the word as revealed in each context. It will be seen that sanctification begins with, and parallels, justification. There are crisis points within it but it does not end at any moment in this life or probably in the life to come. Whatever the significance of the crisis moments (and they *are* significant), the process aspect must be taken into consideration also. Very few holiness teachers would contest this.

If one could allow a rather general expression for the sake of putting up a signpost, "an experience beyond conversion" would be a useful designation. In fact, the author is borrowing this term from a contemporary leading holiness preacher. The term indicates that believers are involved. It says by implication that some kind of crisis point was reached. It is intended to carry the idea that in the progress of the Christian life a notable point was passed that is worthy of mention and which intensified the reality of Christian faith. It was both a part of, and an advance in, the Christian life. If we could identify this point as the New Testament does, in terms of actual moral content, how much more meaning would be conveyed by preaching!

Jesus spoke of loving God with the whole heart, mind, soul, and strength. He called His disciples, and us, to responsible stewardship. He urged men to deny themselves, take up their cross, and follow Him. No one could deny that to attempt this is not easy. It takes a thoroughgoing revolution in human personality. Nor is this sort of thing to be relegated to another life. If it doesn't fit this life with its demands and opportunities and responsibilities, what life does it fit? Neither can one who takes the Bible seriously escape the personal demands this makes on the Christian believer. Most specifically, this kind of Christian life is not entered apart from a radical commitment to it. Furthermore, to comply, however inadequately, is impossible apart from God's grace. But every Christian knows that grace is available to one who goes through the very narrow gate into a deeply committed life. And, yet, all these things are the *content* of what the holiness people have come to call sanctification.

Paul's terminology is also flexible. Righteousness "by faith" is the epitome of God's requirement for man, and faith is the key word here, in contrast to any other attempt at personal rightness with God. Love, to Paul, was the fulfilling of the whole law and expressed the deep inwardness of the Christian life (Rom. 13:8-10). "Reckon ye also yourselves to be dead indeed unto sin, but alive unto God," was spoken to the Roman believers; and the obedience "from the heart" spoken of in Romans 6 is the path to righteousness, holiness, and eternal life. "The Spirit of life in Christ Jesus hath made me free from the law of sin and death" (Rom. 8:1), is hardly less than what sanctification has been theologically made to mean.

Paul's testimony, "I live; yet not I, but Christ liveth in me; and the life which I now live in the flesh I live by the faith of the Son of God," is an existential and effective way to say what is so prosaically and ineffectively said by, "I am sanctified." It is interesting to note, at this point, that no New Testament writer gave a personal testimony to his relationship with God by reference to this word. Paul, who often testifies, and whose works most particularly structure holiness doctrine, never claimed sanctification *by the word itself*. The nearest he came to it was a reminder to the Thessalonian church of his walk before them ("how holily . . . we behaved ourselves"), but even here the original Greek word is not the one from which *sanctification* comes.

It must be repeated that there is no exhortation to seek sanctification, as such, in the New Testament. Rather there are calls to "put off the old man," and "put on the new man," "cleanse ourselves from all filthiness of the flesh and spirit," "let this mind be in you, which was also in Christ Jesus." Paul exhorted the Corinthians that "every thought" should be brought captive "to the obedience of Christ." And the writer to the Hebrews urged, "Let us lay aside every weight, and the sin which doth so easily beset us." Paul's most earnest appeal is that believers present their bodies "a living sacrifice, holy, acceptable unto God." There is positive exhortation enough.

These are but a few of the very many synonyms for the crisis and continuing life of holiness, and they shed necessary light on the matter. None of them may be neglected nor none isolated from the others so that any one is made to include the whole truth. Any stereotyped or monotonous approach is avoided by the freshness and relevancy of the scope of biblical presentation.

The objection is made to the effect that sanctification is the key word and must be required. To this we concur provided the entire meaning of sanctification is retained. To limit it to a single crisis experience is to betray the genius of New Testament teaching. Its meaning covers every aspect of redemptive experience.

To the insistence that, according to the dictionary, two meanings—no more, no fewer—lie in sanctification and that both *must* be respected, and experienced, again we concur. It is said to be both dedication, or separation, and a making pure. But, as we have seen, these are not two things but two aspects of one thing. Separation, in the New Testament, *is* purity or moral rightness. Love is defined by purity, and love purifies. But neither of these is static and self-sustaining. *Love flows away from itself endlessly.*

Holiness in God is not one attribute among others. He does not *have* holiness. Holiness is not a quality which stands against justice or love. God *is* holy. Holiness is the nature of God in which all elements of His being exist in perfect balance and relation. It is the white light which is the sum of all the colors of the spectrum. It is self-sustaining because it is not a secondary matter or a-personal. Holiness is personal in that only that which is personal is subject to this appelation. Being personal, it is not truly a status but a vitality—a life. Health is a status of a person whose body is functioning properly, but in this case the status is simply a judgment about a relationship. It has no existence otherwise. So with God's character. Holiness, in God, is much more than freedom from sin. There is something fundamentally erroneous about such a concept. It implies a standard to which God must conform in order to qualify as holy. Rather, holiness is a positive quality. It is radiant moral health—*perfect integrity*. It is the very life of God expressing itself in all its relationships.

Holiness in men is analogous. It is not *something* imparted from without, such as the superadded grace of Catholic theology. It is not simply the added presence of the Holy Spirit which creates a moral dualism in the human personality. It is not a change in the substance of the soul—an irrational, nonmoral concept. It is very much more than an imputed judicial standing. It is moral health in the same way that a physical body is healthy, in that health is not a quantity which can be measured or counted, or added, but is a proper relationship of all parts. But holiness in man cannot be self-existent, as is God's holiness, because moral experience is not completed within the resident resources of the human personality.

One of the focal points of moral integration is God himself, so that spiritual health is absolutely dependent on a proper relationship to God. And since this is personal, it must be mutual. If God is unwilling to accept us, our advances are fruitless; but just as truly, if God finds us unresponsive or willful, the situation cannot exist wherein "holiness" would be an appropriate word. But a mutual agreeableness constitutes holiness. In essence it is a quality of relationship. Quantity is always a by-product of this and is wholly dependent on secondary and temporal matters worked out from the center.

Holiness is *moral integration,* which in man requires God as the true Center of moral life. Sin is basically the decentralization of this integration. Death is simply the absence of the cohesive power of life. The elements fall apart. Spiritual death is moral decentralization. Alienation and estrangement are proper words. Moral life cannot exist truly while God is separated from us. Redemption restores the possibility of the reestablishment of moral union. But it *cannot* be a one-sided affair. God cannot impute moral integrity externally to those who are not in spiritual union. Imputed righteousness is a limited concept and cannot bear the weight so often put upon it.

Reconciliation is the healing of moral estrangement and requires that the union be morally mutual. Holiness must be initiated by God, but it cannot be a completed experience until a suitable response comes from men. Holiness is not a bestowed but a moral-mutual relationship and a living involvement in that relationship. Therefore every requirement of grace is in the interest of moral integrity. Nothing is done for us that moral integrity demands that we must do. Holiness is moral soundness, the precise antithesis of perfectionism. It is of deepest necessity Christ-centered and the very negation of self-centeredness. It speaks of the whole-man relationship to God and men, not merely a juridical or intellectual or emotional or moralistic relationship. It is dynamic—a "way," not a state; a life, not a static goodness.

In this sense, then, sanctification is primarily the *process* of redemption. It is process precisely because it is moral and personal and not simply legal. But in the process lie crisis points without which *moral* degenerates into a nonmoral naturalism.

My Controversy with Christ

The "last word" is an intensely personal word. It has actually been said in this book time and again, in many ways. But the author needs to point it up sharply again.

I have a deep rebellion—a "beef"—against the critics of the Christian religion. It is said that to be a Christian requires an inhibition of life and vitality and creativeness. But Christian faith is not a negation of life. Rather, everything we find in the Bible suggests that God is trying to liberate us from sin and failure and false ideals and low ceilings and smallness and individualism. God wants us, *in this life,* to live fully, creatively. Being good is not simply *not doing things,* but living out the dynamic of God's purpose for men.

That is why a pure heart is so essential. Without it, Christian life is a smothering of life's impulses, and grace would be an enemy of normal personality. There is a basic urge to self-expression without which wholesome personality is impossible. An impure urge is death. God does not suppress the urge but cleanses the heart of double motives.

There *is* a cross in the Christian life, but the cross is not an end of the self but an end of the sin that shackles the self and blocks the way to goodness. The cross is always at the *beginning of life.* The whole of real life lies beyond it.

Rather than Christ curbing our personal development, He requires that we put the whole personality to work. This puts a new light on our Christian faith. It is not a retreat but a moral obligation to advance.

I have a controversy with Christ. He will not let me rest. In His presence I cannot relax and rest on my "faith" in Him in a lazy way which dulls moral sensitivity. He will not let me settle for less than my best—not yesterday's best, but *today's* best. When I have done a job, He confronts me with a bigger task—one always too big for me. When I am selfish, He rebukes me until it smarts. When I am insensitive, He has a way of prodding my conscience into activity. When I cry and pray for a little heaven in which to go to heaven in, He shows me the hell in which other people live. It isn't time for heaven, yet.

Purity is not an end in itself. Purity permits the personality to live in full expression of love to God and man. It is the power of a single-hearted devotion and must be kept intact by a daily fellowship with God.

Reference Notes

CHAPTER III:

1. W. E. Sangster, *Why Jesus Never Wrote a Book* (London: Epworth Press, 1952), p. 12.
2. *Ibid.*, p. 16.
3. Paul S. Rees, *Don't Sleep Through the Revolution* (Waco, Tex.: Word Books, 1969), p. 21.
4. Gerhard Ebeling, *The Problem of Historicity* (Philadelphia: Fortress Press, 1967), p. 21.
5. *Ibid.*, pp. 26, 28.

CHAPTER IV:

1. Quoted by William Luther White, *The Image of Man in C. S. Lewis* (Nashville: Abingdon Press, 1969), p. 75.
2. John Wesley, *A Collection of Hymns for the Use of People Called Methodists* (London: Thomas Cordeux, 1821), pp. iii-iv.
3. *Ibid.*, p. v.
4. Wesley Hill, *John Wesley Among the Physicians* (London: Epworth Press, n.d.), pp. 1, 8.
5. Alfred North Whitehead, *Adventures of Ideas* (New York: The Macmillan Co., 1933), p. 114.

CHAPTER V:

1. G. Osborn, ed., *The Poetical Works of John and Charles Wesley* (London: Wesleyan Methodist Conference Office, 1868), I, xxii.
2. John Deschner, *Wesley's Christology* (Dallas, Tex.: Southern Methodist University Press, 1969), p. 197.

CHAPTER VI:

1. Sydney Cave, *The Christian Estimate of Man* (London: Gerald Duckworth and Co., Ltd., 1949), p. 9.

2. Nels F. S. Ferré, *Evil and the Christian Faith* (New York: Harper and Brothers, Publishers, 1947), p. 33.

3. Alan Richardson, *A Theological Word Book of the Bible* (New York: The Macmillan Co., 1951), p. 70.

4. Claude Tresmontant, *A Study of Hebrew Thought* (New York: Desclee Company, 1960), p. 6.

5. *Ibid.*, p. 7.

6. Jacques Sareno, *The Meaning of the Body* (Philadelphia: The Westminster Press, 1966), p. 119.

7. *Ibid.*, p. 121.

8. *Ibid.*, p. 122.

9. George A. F. Knight, *A Christian Theology of the Old Testament* (London: SCM Press, 1959), p. 27.

10. *Ibid.*, p. 31.

11. Gesenius, *A Hebrew and English Lexicon of the Old Testament* (Boston: Houghton Mifflin and Co., 1893).

12. Joseph Henry Thayer, *A Greek-English Lexicon of the New Testament* (New York: American Book Co., 1886), p. 578.

13. B. Davidson, *The Analytical Hebrew and Chaldee Lexicon* (London: Samuel Bagster and Sons, n.d.), *loc. cit.*

14. Gesenius, *op. cit.*, p. 105.

15. *Ibid.*, p. 440.

16. James Hope Moulton and George Milligan, *The Vocabulary of the Greek New Testament* (Grand Rapids, Mich.: William B. Eerdmans Publishing Co. 1949), p. 183.

17. Thayer, *op. cit.*, p. 445.

18. Moulton and Milligan, *op. cit.*, pp. 448-49.

19. Roger J. Williams, *You Are Extraordinary* (New York: Random House, Inc., 1967).

20. Carl E. Braaten, *History and Hermeneutics, New Directions in Theology Today* (Philadelphia: Westminster Press, 1966), II, 35.

21. Sydney J. Harris, "Strictly Personal, Psychiatric Flaw," *Nashville Banner,* July 30, 1968. Copyright, 1968, by Prentice Hall Syndicate.

22. J. Philip Hyatt, "The Old Testament View of Man," *Religion in Life,* Autumn, 1945, p. 528.

CHAPTER VII:

1. G. Campbell Morgan, *The Teaching of Christ* (New York: Fleming H. Revell Co., 1913), p. 113.

2. *Ibid.*, p. 114.

3. *Ibid.*, p. 121.

4. Thayer, *op. cit.*, p. 393.

5. *Ibid.*, p. 54.

6. *Ibid.*, p. 429.

7. *Ibid.*, p. 140.

8. *Ibid.*, p. 658.

9. Moulton and Milligan, *op. cit.*, p. 676.

10. *Ibid.*

11. W. Robertson Nicoll, *The Expositor's Greek Testament* (Grand Rapids, Mich.: Wm. B. Eerdmans Publishing Co., n.d.), p. 627.

12. Albert Barnes, *Notes, Explanatory and Practical, on the Acts of the Apostles and the Epistle to the Romans* (London: George Routledge and Sons, 1866), p. 125.

13. G. Campbell Morgan, *The Epistle of Paul the Apostle to the Romans* (London: Hodder and Stoughton, 1909), pp. 72-73.

14. Richardson, *op. cit.*, p. 60.

15. John Fletcher, *The Works of John Fletcher* (London: New Chapel City Road, 1802), III, 282.

16. *Ibid.*, p. 283.

CHAPTER VIII:

1. Edmund Jacob, *Theology of the Old Testament* (New York: Harper and Row, 1958), p. 154.

2. *Ibid.*, p. 155.

3. James R. Dolby, *I, Too, Am a Man* (Waco, Tex.: Word Books, 1969), pp. 3, 6.

4. *Ibid.*, p. 8.

5. *Ibid.*

CHAPTER X:

1. Daniel Steele, *Steele's Answers* (Chicago: Christian Witness Co., 1912), pp. 130-31.

2. H. Orton Wiley, *Christian Theology* (Kansas City: Beacon Hill Press of Kansas City, 1952), II, 356.

3. *Ibid.*, p. 402.

4. *Ibid.*, p. 423.

5. *Ibid.*, p. 95.

6. Quoted in John Fletcher, *The Works of the Reverend John Fletcher* (New York: Methodist Episcopal Conference Office, 1836), Vol. I, Preface, p. 9.

CHAPTER XI:

1. Billy Graham, syndicated column, "My Answer." From the *Nashville Banner,* July 24, 1968.
2. Morgan, *The Teaching of Christ,* p. 42.

CHAPTER XII:

1. Floyd Filson, *One Lord, One Faith* (Philadelphia: The Westminster Press, 1943), p. 198.
2. James Stewart, *A Man in Christ* (London: Hodder and Stoughton, 1954), p. 196.
3. Tresmontant, *op. cit.,* p. 125.

CHAPTER XIII:

1. Thomas Cook, *New Testament Holiness* (London: The Epworth Press, 14th ed., 1950), p. 43.

CHAPTER XIV:

1. Manning Pattillo, "Good News to a Harassed World," *Christianity Today,* Nov. 10, 1958.
2. John Fletcher, *Checks to Antinomianism* (Kansas City: Beacon Hill Press, abridged, 1948), p. 22.
3. B. F. Westcott, *The Epistle to the Hebrews* (Grand Rapids, Mich.: Wm. B. Eerdmans Publishing Co., n.d.), p. 64.
4. William Barclay, *Letters to the Corinthians* (Philadelphia: Westminster Press, 1956), p. 146.
5. Delbert Rose, "The Theology of Experience." Unpublished manuscript.
6. H. Orton Wiley, *The Epistle to the Hebrews* (Kansas City: Beacon Hill Press, 1959), p. 205.
7. *Ibid.,* p. 209.
8. B. T. Roberts, *Holiness Teachings* (North Chili, N.Y.: "Earnest Christian" Publishing House, 1893), pp. 211-12.

CHAPTER XV:

1. John Wesley, *A Plain Account of Christian Perfection* (Kansas City: Beacon Hill Press, 1950), p. 3.
2. *Ibid.*
3. George Allen Turner, *The More Excellent Way* (Winona Lake, Ind.: Light and Life Press, 1952), p. 31.
4. Charles W. Carter and Ralph Earle, *The Acts of the Apostles,*

"Evangelical Commentary on the Bible" (Grand Rapids, Mich.: Zondervan Publishing House, 1959), p. 312.

    5. Fletcher, *Checks,* p. 61.

    6. *Ibid.,* p. 26.

    7. Hannah Whitall Smith, *The Christian's Secret of a Happy Life* (Westwood, N.J.: Fleming H. Revell Co., reprint, 1968), p. 130.

    8. Turner, *op. cit.,* pp. 249, 256.

Chapter XVI:

    1. Wesley, *Plain Account,* p. 11.

    2. J. A. Wood, *Perfect Love* (Chicago: The Christian Witness Co., 1904), p. 125.

    3. Daniel Steele, *Steele's Answers* (Chicago: Christian Witness Co., 1912).

    4. Wesley, *Plain Account,* pp. 15, 18.

    5. Turner, *op. cit.,* p. 261.

Alphabetical Index

Index of Names

Bibliography

A. Works of John and Charles Wesley

Collection of Hymns for the Use of People Called Methodists, A. London: Thomas Cordeux, 1821.

Earnest Appeal to Men of Reason and Religion, An, and, A Farther Appeal. 14th edition. London: Wesleyan Conference Office, n.d.

Explanatory Notes upon the New Testament. New York: Eaton and Mains, n.d.

Letters of the Rev. John Wesley, The. Edited by John Telford. London: The Epworth Press, 1931. 8 vols.

Plain Account of Christian Perfection, A. Kansas City: Beacon Hill Press, 1950.

Poetical Works of John and Charles Wesley, The. Edited by G. Osborn. London: Wesleyan Methodist Conference Office, 1868. 14 vols.

Wesley's Standard Sermons. Edited by Edward H. Sugden. London: Epworth Press, 1921. 2 vols.

Works of John Wesley, The. Kansas City, Mo.: Nazarene Publishing House, n.d.; and Grand Rapids, Mich.: Zondervan Publishing House, 1958, concurrent editions.

B. General Works

Barclay, William, *Letters to the Corinthians.* Philadelphia: Westminster Press, 1956.

———. *More New Testament Words.* Philadelphia: Westminster Press, 1958.

Barnes, Albert. *Notes, Explanatory and Practical, on the Acts of the Apostles and the Epistle to the Romans*. London: George Routledge and Sons, 1866.

Bonhoeffer, Dietrich. *The Cost of Discipleship*. New York: The Macmillan Co., 1963.

————. *Letters and Papers from Prison*. London: SCM Press, 1967.

Brataan, Carl. *History and Hermeneutics, New Directions in Theology Today*. Philadelphia: Westminster Press, 1966.

Buber, Martin. *I and Thou*. Edinburgh: T. and T. Clark, 1937.

Calvin, John. *Institutes of the Christian Religion*. Philadelphia: Presbyterian Board of Christian Education, 1936, 2 vols.

Carter, Charles W., and Earle, Ralph. *The Acts of the Apostles, Evangelical Commentary on the Bible*. Grand Rapids, Mich.: Zondervan Publishing House, 1959.

Cave, Sydney. *The Christian Estimate of Man*. London: Gerald Duckworth and Co., Ltd., 1949.

Cook, Thomas. *New Testament Holiness*. 14th ed. London: The Epworth Press, 1950.

Deschner, John. *Wesley's Christology*. Dallas, Tex.: Southern Methodist University Press, 1969.

Dolbey, James R. *I, Too, Am Man*. Waco, Tex.: Word Books, 1969.

Ebeling, Gerhard. *The Problem of Historicity*. Philadelphia: Fortress Press, 1967.

Ferré, Nels F. S., *Evil and the Christian Faith*. New York: Harper and Brothers, Publishers, 1947.

Filson, Floyd. *One Lord, One Faith*. Philadelphia: The Westminster Press, 1943.

Fletcher, John. *Checks to Antinomianism*. Kansas City: Beacon Hill Press, Abridged, 1948.

————. *The Works of the Reverend John Fletcher*. New York: Methodist Episcopal Conference Office, 1836. 4 vols.

————. *The Works of John Fletcher*. London: New Chapel, City Road, 1802.

Hill, Wesley. *John Wesley Among the Physicians.* London: Epworth Press, n.d.

Jacob, Edmond. *Theology of the Old Testament*. New York: Harper and Row, 1958.

Kierkegaarde, Soren. *Purity of Heart Is to Will One Thing*. New York and London: Harper and Brothers, 1938.

Knight, George A. F. *A Christian Theology of the Old Testament*. London: SCM Press, 1959.

Kuhn, William. *Environmental Man*. New York: Harper and Row, 1969.

Morgan, G. Campbell. *The Epistle of Paul the Apostle to the Romans*. London: Hodder and Stoughton, 1909.

————. *The Teaching of Christ*. New York: Fleming H. Revell Co., 1913.

Murray, Andrew. *Holiest of All*. New York: Fleming H. Revell Co., 1894.

Nygren, Anders. *Agape and Eros*. Philadelphia: Westminster Press, 1953.

Ramsey, Paul. *Fabricated Man*. New Haven, Conn.: Yale University Press, 1970.

Rees, Paul. *Don't Sleep Through the Revolution*. Waco, Tex.: Word Books, 1969.

Roberts, B. T. *Holiness Teachings*. North Chili, N.Y.: "Earnest Christian" Publishing House, 1893.

Sangster, W. E. *Why Jesus Never Wrote a Book*. London: Epworth Press, 1952.

Sareno, Jacques. *The Meaning of the Body*. Philadelphia: The Westminster Press, 1966.

Smith, Hannah Whitall. *The Christian's Secret of a Happy Life*. Reprint. Westwood, N.J.: Fleming H. Revell Co., 1968.

Steele, Daniel. *Steele's Answers*. Chicago: Christian Witness Co., 1912.

Stewart, James. *A Man in Christ*. London: Hodder and Stoughton, 1954.

Taylor, Jeremy. *The Rule and Exercises of Holy Living*, and, *The Rule and Exercises of Holy Dying*. Cleveland: World Publishing Co., 1956 and 1952.

Tresmontant, Claude. *A Study of Hebrew Thought*. New York: Desclee Co., 1960.

Turner, George Allen. *The More Excellent Way*. Winona Lake, Ind., Light and Life Press, 1952.

Westcott, B. F. *The Epistle to the Hebrews*. Grand Rapids, Mich.: Wm. B. Eerdmans Publishing Co., n.d.

White, William Luther. *The Image of Man in C. S. Lewis*. Nashville: Abingdon Press, 1969.

Whitehead, Alfred North. *Adventures of Ideas*. New York: The Macmillan Co., 1933.

Wiley, H. Orton. *The Epistle to the Hebrews*. Kansas City: Beacon Hill Press, 1959.

————. *Christian Theology*. Kansas City: Beacon Hill Press, 1952. 3 vols.

Williams, Daniel Day. *The Spirit and the Forms of Love*. New York: Harper and Row, 1968.

Williams, Roger J. *You Are Extraordinary*. New York: Random House, Inc., 1967.

Wood, J. A. *Perfect Love*. Chicago: The Christian Witness Co., 1904.

C. Articles

Culbertson, Paul. "The Dynamics of Sanctification." An unpublished paper read at the Nazarene Theology Conference, Dec., 1969.

Earle, Ralph. A guest editorial, *Herald of Holiness*, Aug. 6, 1958.

Graham, Billy. "My Answer." *Nashville, Tenn., Banner*, July 24, 1968.

Harris, Sydney. "Strictly Personal—Psychiatric Flaw." *Nashville Banner*, July 30, 1968. Copyright, 1968, by Prentice Hall Syndicate.

Hyatt, J. Phillip. "The Old Testament View of Man." *Religion in Life*, autumn, 1945.

Ingles, Wesley J. "Hollow Words." *Christianity Today*, Oct. 27, 1958.

Pattillo, Manning. "Good News to a Harassed World." *Christianity Today*, Nov. 10, 1958.

Rose, Delbert E. "The Theology of Experience." Unpublished manuscript.

Squire, Cyril J. "Lythograph of Wesley." Bristol, England, New Room, New Chapel.

Stewart, James. "A First Century Heresy." *Scottish Journal of Theology*, Nov., 1971.

Wiley, H. Orton. "Psychology." Unpublished lecture notes, n.d.

D. LEXICONS

Davidson, B. *The Analytical Hebrew and Chaldee Lexicon.* London: Samuel Bagster and Sons, n.d.

Gesenius. *A Hebrew and English Lexicon of the Old Testament.* Boston: Houghton Mifflin and Co., 1893.

Moulton, James Hope, and Milligan, George. *The Vocabulary of the Greek New Testament.* Grand Rapids, Mich.: William B. Eerdmans Publishing Co., 1949.

Nicoll, W. Robertson. *The Expositor's Greek Testament.* Grand Rapids, Mich.: Wm. B. Eerdmans Publishing Co., n.d.

Richardson, Alan. *A Theological Word Book of the Bible.* New York: The Macmillan Co., 1951.

Thayer, Joseph Henry. *A Greek-English Lexicon of the New Testament.* New York: American Book Co., 1886.